MILTON
AND
FORBIDDEN KNOWLEDGE

by
Howard Schultz

NEW YORK
Modern Language Association of America
1955

Approved for publication in the Revolving Fund Series.

PR
3548
.S42

AD FILIAM EVÆ

PREFACE

AT the time Mr. Douglas Bush first pointed out to me the kind of caution that Christian humanism walked with, a study like this one would have been a lonely waif. To that time, nobody had methodically tried to get at the late Renaissance through its negations. By now we have been shown that the approach is possible and that it can be rewarding, for the years have brought with them illuminating books to chart the counter currents in the Renaissance, to speak of Christian humanism wasted by the wars of truth, or to ravel the subtle knots of skepticism.

Not unlike these works in every particular, my own gathers together some formulas of piety by which, unwittingly for the most part, preachers and moralists undermined rational science, religious zeal, and historical Christianity. Some of the thought that I have drawn toward Milton's may advance a bit the history of ideas; some may assist the reading of Milton. I do not suppose that all will serve both ends.

To students and associates whose ideas I have unintentionally pilfered, and to the staffs of the Huntington, Newberry, Harvard College, and British Museum libraries, who have shown me so many courtesies, I acknowledge my great debt. And I remember with special gratitude the many occasions when Mr. Bush has come to my rescue.

A comment on the critical apparatus is prefaced to the notes.

CONTENTS

Chapter I

TRADITIONS OF SOBRIETY

Some Ancient Wisdom and Newer Folly

In a certain moral allegory written probably about the year Milton was born we meet Curiosity, a lady who deserves our attention, since it is her extraordinary range of powers that we are about to explore. In masquerade, she calls herself Admiration, the "mid-way between knowledge and ignorance." To her ingenuity all the vices are indebted for the respectable disguises they wear. "Can any question trouble me?" demands Curiosity, having confessed herself devoted to Pride. She knows all about purgatory and the two limbos of hell, the nine orders of angels and "those late sciences of equivocation," to say nothing of the philosophers' stone and all the arts of witchcraft. But no sooner does she mention the motion of the earth and the element of fire, lately extinguished, than Justice rips off her mask and condemns her for crimes rather more political than intellectual—for treasonous libels and satires Marprelatical, "itching crotchets" troubling the land and poisoning the church. Some of these details mark the author a conservative Anglican, but we can find this lady Curiosity and nearly the same association of ideas in an allegory of self-deception written by a Puritan. While Milton and modern England were growing up together within a period conveniently to be bounded by the dates 1600 and 1660, it is safe to say that intellectual sin came in for a scolding somewhere in every influential kind of writing. An exposition of the Ten Commandments would list curiosity as a form of pride, violating the First, or of blasphemy, setting at naught the Third. A commentary on the Creed would open with a sermon on the inviolable secret of God's nature. Notes on the Third Petition of the Lord's Prayer would commend the wisdom of doing, not searching, God's will. A manual of self-denial or a "marrow" of divinity had somewhere to reprove pride in intellectual gifts. Charactery exposed the mere scholar, the speculative or scholastic divine, the sorcerer, and the virtuoso, whom Butler knew as the Curious Man. Satire whipped these and other offenders, with some extra lashes for the pedant. Didactic versifiers borrowed tone and even phrase from Bernard to admonish those sinners who forgot that the Incarnation had been revealed to shepherds first, or who tried to plumb the depth of mysteries with wisdom's short line. A composer set for singing a few of Greville's sonnets on this theme. In emblem books, archers levelled at remote herons, stargazing Thales tumbled into a well, Amor lectured the wise and pointed children the plain highway to heaven. Men of adventurous and timid intellect alike did honor to the Apostle's rule that Wither rendered thus:

> Above thy knowledge do not rise,
> But, with sobriety, be wise.

As scholars knew, there lurked in the Latin *sapere ad sobrietatem* a pun linking St. Paul's caveat to Adam's diet.

The pages that follow will revive some controversies in education, philosophy, theology, and politics to the end that we may hear divinity preaching this kind of sobriety wherever we find it most profitable to listen—that is to say, where grave occasion warranted the sermon, where its effects now seem reasonably clear, and especially where it helped to shape Milton's thought. Thus we shall not be obliged to examine all the merely conventional piety guarding mysteries—warnings that God's bright essence will blind the eye that stares, or that pills and mysteries must be swallowed without chewing. We shall not hear every curiosity sermon by which a preacher made his peace with prudence before breaking his own rule in some woolly speculation, or listen to any private squabble only because somebody in it cried out against curiosity.

No sane man can embrace every learning or speculation that he meets, and in a day when conservative and reformer spoke the language of piety, each knew how to show that God disapproved what the writer disapproved. Could any man doubt that he might somehow sin with his mind when he saw everywhere that his neighbor did so? Historians of thought in the period have remarked how incessantly the pulpit reminded men of their intellectual depravity. Adam's fall had corrupted the rational soul of man in both its faculties, in intellect as well as in will. Almost nobody cried *mea culpa,* naturally. In the each-against-all warfare of ideas, every man stood accused and accusing; on every hand, thinking was condemned as useless or erroneous, and texts were hunted to make it somehow impious. The actual sins thus denounced fused, but only in a nebulous, general notion, an abstraction that any man could fill out as his conscience required. At our later station in history we enjoy an unearned advantage in that we can point out some consequences that apparently flowed from this abundant preaching of sobriety. When rival dogmas fighting to cancel each other abated some measure of zeal after the mid-century, they found in their own crusade against curiosity and its concomitants a religious warrant for tepidity and for a divinity reduced largely to ethics. Perhaps the crusade may have been a reason as well as an excuse for latitude and skepticism. Assuredly it abetted every motion toward nominalism, or toward pragmatic, utilitarian, positive philosophy and education. We are better able than Cromwell's generation to see how subtly Mammon appropriated a shield forged in the service of God.

Our theme, then, is to be the bifurcated sin of dubious speculation (curiosity) on the one hand and corrupted learning (vain philosophy) on the other, or broadly, allowing for important exceptions, the radical and reactionary tendencies bounding any given thinker's Christian sobriety. Conservatives normally branded uncomfortably new notions as curious; advanced thought, looking backward, often looked upon intellectual vanity. But it often found curiosity in the past, too—cautioning us thereby to beware of oversimplifying. We shall do particularly well not to identify the virtue of intellectual sobriety narrowly with skepticism. The authoritarian dogmatists who praised modest thinking outnumbered the skeptics who, to be sure, did the same. Whoever, out of unusual distrust of our cognitive apparatus, challenged its conclusions (and so I shall use the vexed word skeptic) had the support of St. Paul and the Preacher, and could appeal to religion as readily as the dogmatist. Antiquity, reason, nature, or private revelation—whatever men alleged for their warrant they hedged with much the same pious language. The language added up, out of context, to a potent measure of skeptical caution or even anti-intellectualism, and it was a language that could make men look nervously at themselves and their neighbors. It was a most real and honestly felt skepticism, beside which the Pyrrhonism talked by certain wits appeared the feeble chitchat of idle paradox. But few of the men who spread it were consciously or unconsciously skeptics.

The form of words used to clothe this concept made religious humility a kind of ellipse with two foci—self-knowledge and correct belief. The classics emphasized the one, the scriptures the other, and traditional theology both. Without entering into the whole history of an idea as ancient as the human race, expressed in formulas sometimes older than Christian homiletics, let us be reminded by the seventeenth century's marginal credits that expressions of the idea had descended to the Renaissance from pagan as well as Christian sources. We cannot, therefore, make the curiosity sermon out to be a legacy from the Reformation, or medievalism's bridle for imposing thought-control, or Christianity in conflict with paganism. Pyrrho and the Academy could teach practicality and, in their own fashions, the primacy of self-knowledge. Every Renaissance humanist knew that Aeschylus or even Homer could teach the inviolability of mysteries. Hesiod left a useful Adam and Eve in Prometheus and Pandora. Pentheus, the Babrius fable in Æsop, Pliny overwhelmed by Vesuvius, Icarus (a ubiquitous *exemplum*) could adorn sermons that had nothing to do with classical skepticism. Seneca, especially revered by preachers and moralists, found the high-strained paradoxes of Zeno and the quibbling of dialecticians to be a science falsely so called. He made a few more of Bacon's points against merely curious studies than perhaps Macaulay realized. "This desire to know more than is sufficient

is a sort of intemperance," Seneca wrote, but wrote in defense of self-knowledge, not of Pyrrho and non-knowledge,
not of Posidonius and natural knowledge. Seneca directed
his much-cited Epistle 88 against the illiberal pursuit of
mathematics, literary scholarship (Perseus helped later
satirists here), and some other windy sciences. Socrates,
the inventor of the ethical science of self-knowledge, out-
stripped all the ancients in allusive popularity. After ages
so respected the Socratic ideal that, far as they might
stray from it, they dutifully dignified their own cherished
studies as self-knowledge. The term could commend any
branch of learning for which an ethical defense could be
made out, not pure ethics alone. To know what a given
writer meant by self-knowledge, then, we may need to determine what studies he valued. Before the modern breach
between natural science and humanistic studies, natural
knowledge violated no rules so long as it could be proved
useful, even philosophically useful. In contrast to self-
knowledge, astronomy became a favorite symbol of idle
curiosity, the stars being the objects most obviously remote
from man. We shall presently find that we need not read
every Socratic tribute to self-knowledge (contrasted with
star-knowledge) as a calculated sneer at astronomy. The
stars would probably have been associated with curiosity
without the help of Socrates, but when we read *Paradise
Lost* we need to remember that schoolboys grew up with
Xenophon's story of his great renunciation. The sage who
set the course for Western culture allowed the stars some
value for traders and farmers, who could teach all the astronomy needful to be known. Beyond, "to search out
what the gods have not chosen to reveal must be displeas-
ing to them." Like Augustine, who delighted in the study
of astronomy, hundreds praised Socrates in Cicero's language for having first called philosophy from heaven to
earth and compelled her "to ask questions about life and
morality and things good and evil."

These were the popular resorts in the classics. It would
be easy out of Montaigne alone to pile up other passages
from Horace, Propertius, Juvenal, Anaximenes to demonstrate that the Greek tradition could subdue Renaissance

intellects. The Hebrew naturally pronounced the determinate sentence. A thousand years and more of text-cul-
ling had taught God's spokesmen how to reach quickly
for appropriate scripture. St. Paul's solemn warning they
translated thus to the disadvantage of any dubious learning: "Take heed lest any man spoil you through philosophy and vain deceit." It paired well with Christ's choice
of ignorant fishermen or the Preacher's lament for the
making of many books. If the books happened to be occult, there was the Ephesian book-burning in the Acts—
περίεργα the Greek called the fuel, but the Syriac version
could be translated *magices artes*. Against speculative curiosity, too, the Apostle had written powerfully to disparage
the "oppositions of science falsely so called." *Sapere ad sobrietatem* implied, in religion, "The natural man receiveth
not the things of the spirit," and in the human sciences,
"Knowledge puffeth up, but charity edifieth." Bacon
found this last text most comfortable. Controversial divines could be entreated to "receive him that is weak, but
not to doubtful disputations." In the Old Testament, the
story of Adam and the tree stood with some minor texts:
"Go not up into the Mount." "Secret things belong unto
the Lord our God." From the Psalmist, "Such things are
too wonderful for me." And finally, for meddling Puritans
and other simple busybodies, the sudden death of Uzzah,
who dared to touch the Ark.

The Fathers left quotable texts as useful in Milton's day
as in the Middle Ages to chasten classical learning and
check human wit. Divines, including good humanists, borrowed from this source dozens of summary school-by-school
confutations of the pagan moralists like the one that
Milton wrote in *Paradise Regained*. From the illiberal Tertullian to the cultivated Clement of Alexandria the patriarchs of Christianity had hacked away in dead earnest
against the paganism and assaults of Ammonius Saccas,
Porphyry, Celsus, and Hierocles with weapons that the
Academic Cicero had already tested against the schools.
It was apparently the skeptic Varro, for example, who
taught Augustine that by mere philosophy 288 definitions
of the *summum bonum* would be mathematically possible.

One might readily gather from the late preachers that philosophy had produced all 288, but even so, the godly rhetoricians intended more of a compliment to religion than a serious slander of philosophy. Paganism easily survived it, as it survived more than a millennium of Tertullian's "Quid Athenis et Hierosolymis?" The stern precisian's observation that philosophers are the patriarchs of heretics sounded foolish by 1650 to university divines; England swarmed with heretics who disowned Athens and had little to do with philosophy. The established clergy, in their own way modest, preferred the medieval axiom *Philosophia ancilla theologiæ*, which called to their minds Philo's allegory of the seemly handmaid Hagar (learning), whom Queen Sarah (divinity) had tolerated as long as Hagar served obediently. In Justin Martyr the doctors found additional sanction for their university learning in proper subordination to divinity. Or they found it in Origen's allegory of Moses permitting the Israelites (divinity) to marry captive Midianite women (learning) when duly shorn. After the patristic age of the church the theologians kept some kind of rein on intellectualism, but added little to what the Fathers had said. Tainted as they were with Popery, they seldom appeared marginally in Puritan England. Aquinas found an advanced point at which he had to curtail his logic, and, since Anglicans continued to study him, was occasionally called to witness against curiosity.

But on this theme, English divines by long odds favored, before all authority except scripture itself, the testimony of Augustine and Bernard. Augustine had transmitted to an unbroken line of medieval disciples, to Christian skeptics of the Renaissance, and to all Protestantism, a volume of precept that hardly fitted his own practice; for it was he who originated or popularized most of the speculations that Renaissance critics like to saddle upon Scholasticism. Like his admirer John Donne, the bishop had run through skepticism, neoplatonism, and heresy to come to uneasy rest in an intellectual Christianity. He played with bizarre analogies in his defense of the Trinity, with theories of the soul's origin in his work on free will and foreknowledge, with natural science in his comment on the letter of

Genesis; and whether answers came to him or escaped him, like John Donne he littered his pages with lectures to admonish the curious. His commentary on Genesis had raised too many unanswered questions, he owned in his retractations (ii, 1). No theory of the soul's origin seriously mattered, he once remarked while wading through all the theories. At any rate, it mattered more where a soul was going than where it came from. Late preachers dutifully copied out such saws, along with samples of foolish questions that would not always have troubled or seriously interested their own generation. From Augustine they borrowed hallowed examples of curiosity: only fools asked for the local habitation of Abraham's bosom, the flames of hell, or the rich man's tongue. After Augustine they rehearsed our need to know in mysteries that a thing is, but not how it is—a better single text than any in scripture against transubstantiation. Milton and a legion of others ridiculed, like Augustine, those who asked what God was doing before Creation, a question that Manichæans would have been likely to ask by way of establishing a plurality of worlds. Inhabited planets or successive creations, the pluralist theory in any form counted as curious with the Fathers, as with any later writer who needed an easy and unchallenged illustration of curiosity. Many of the Fathers rebutted, too, and Augustine most influentially, the claims of magic and astrology with arguments drawn from both science and religion. Their teaching stayed fresh in Puritan England while the memory of the early Fausts of edifying legend—Simon Magus of the pseudo-Clementines, Cyprian of Antioch, Theophilus of Adana—grew dim. Augustine delighted in legitimate natural science. Yet he glorified self-knowledge as the only knowledge not curious, and when he did so, he had, perforce, to choose his illustrations of unprofitable speculation from natural science. By his light, self-knowledge might include contemplation of the Holy Trinity. The unclassical stretch was to become the rule in devout humanism, or what Gilson has called the Christian Socratism of the Middle Ages.

From the twelfth century the Protestants salvaged their most honored divine after Augustine—Bernard of Clairvaux. Luther heard him gladly. English devotional writers found no taint of the Papal heresy in him. In spite of his late date they numbered him with the primitive Fathers. If their numerous allusions and quotations mean that they read him at first hand, they knew his extended chapters "De Curiositate" and "De Vitanda Curiositate," and a hundred other passages in which the thoughtful mystic humbled Abelard's reason and his own, for he placed intellectual humility at the very center of his divinity. He found this humility only in self-knowledge. Actually, self-surrender interested Bernard probably more than any knowledge, but the Socratic ideal could be variously understood. Calvin, though no Bernard, could have found nothing wrong with the saint's Socratism: man achieved the highest wisdom, knowledge of himself, by discovering his own impotence, learning humility, and thus knowing God. Calvinist, Arminian, and Quaker agreed with Bernard that man fell into curiosity, the first degree of pride, because he had been blinded by his ignorance of original sin. Man could never understand regeneration until he thoroughly understood himself to be a divine image disfigured. Milton preached this catholic orthodoxy in his reflections on the pagan moralists:

> Alas what can they teach, and not mislead;
> Ignorant of themselves, of God much more,
> And how the world began, and how man fell
> Degraded by himself, on grace depending?

So the Middle Ages had delighted to honor the antique "Know thyself," but always in the theological frame of original sin and redemption. The road to self-knowledge lay through knowledge of God. In this scheme natural science could be comprehended, at least when familiar and approved, for science led to God. William of Saint-Thierry, for example, thus included much science in humanism when he compiled in his *De Natura Corporis et Animæ* the utterances of the Fathers and the ancient philosophers and medical men who had commanded, "Know thyself."

Bernard opened his theology, his earliest treatise, warring against curiosity. To the first degree of pride he devoted the space that he gave to the other eleven together, illustrating his long meditation with the stories of Dinah, Eve, and Satan. No serious reader of *Paradise Lost* ought to ignore the passage, for Milton, shaping the doctrine of his epic, would have been likely to review it—if it was ever out of his mind. Addressing our universal mother rhetorically, Bernard reminded her of some sins comprehended in her great folly. First, she transgressed, with the fruit of ill savor, the Apostle's rule *sapere ad sobrietatem.* Milton underscored this word-play (ix.1019) as soon as his Adam, newly fallen, turned punster. Again, she violated God's rule that bade her attend to her own condition. And she fell easy victim to curiosity of the eye. While she stood gazing at the tree, coveting, rationalizing, explaining away God's commandment, deceiving herself that God had forbidden no fruit, the serpent found her pliant. Bernard next turned to Satan, the serpent, who had peered too inquisitively at the heights above him. When he pictured himself in the seat of the Most High did he presume upon secrecy and God's ignorance? Or did he count on God's weakness and his gullible goodness? Whatever his calculation, when he rationalized the treason he planned, he fell from the truth because idle speculations led him to unlawful desire and thence into presumptuous aspiration. "Curiosity therefore rightly claims first place among the degrees of pride, and is thus revealed as the beginning of all sin."

In religious essays, especially in that form known technically as the meditation, and in didactic writing generally, Milton would have seen often enough the doctrine of humility credited to the saint, or he would have seen phrases known to be Bernard's. Hall wrote them into his quietistic meditations whenever they turned upon curiosity and its wages in Eden. Among other moralists, the Earl of Manchester, meditating upon death, remembered that curiosity brought death into the world, with a world of woe. Bernard's wish to be a *pius pulsator* instead of a *temerarius scrutator* made a popular line for devotional writers. But nothing he wrote was borrowed with more affection than a passage with which he had opened his beautiful threnody on Gerard. In these lines he reckoned up a list of sinners, beginning with the *curiosus* who knows only that he may know. John Robinson, the scholarly pastor of the Pilgrim Fathers, wove the passage into his excellent essays. Quarles thought it worthy of the pious courtesy book that he wrote for the Prince of Wales. Since we shall meet it again, here may suffice an economical translation by the lawyer Robert Aylett:

> Some only seek to know that they may know,
> And this is foolish curiosity,
> And some of learning make a goodly show,
> And this is base and idle vanity;
> Some knowledge seek for their utility
> Or their preferment, which is filthy gain.

The regimen of devout sobriety by which the Renaissance guarded its ideal of self-knowledge needs always to be understood in context, for this "medieval" humanism, isolated, may savor more of pious anti-intellectualism than authors intended. For illustration, La Primaudaye countered Paduan atheism with a superficial encyclopedia of knowledge. He borrowed Bernard's sentiments whenever his rational apologetics came within scent of God-forgetful science, sorcery and judicial astrology, pagan wisdom without grace, imprudent divinity, or subtle theology tracing the angelic orders and the origin of the soul. We must not, for these echoes, associate him with the mystics or skeptics. Subtlety and bold curiosity gave rise to uncertainties, and La Primaudaye had a dogmatist's horror of uncertainty. In the third part of his digest of learning, a summary of natural science, we find high on his index the "curious inquisitors of the causes of natural things." Wit applied to self-knowledge would be so profitably busy that it would never alter the familiar picture of nature; and its best textbook of self-knowledge, as we might expect, would be the author's own *speculum* or something like it. "Let us learn not to know more than we ought, but unto sobriety," he pleaded in his own interest, "that we may embrace a simple, popular, and academical kind of knowledge, which will teach us to know ourselves and our duty." Du Bartas versified such learning in a storehouse of orthodox science even more popular in English than La Primaudaye's.

Guided by Moses, the conservative naturalist fumed at the "rage of human arrogance" or ignorance that squared theology by pagan philosophy, fretted about God's occupation before the world began, or searched for the site of Paradise. But none of these trite sins angered him so often as unaccustomed natural science. His own he carefully subordinated to scripture and the demands of self-knowledge. He concluded that a good Christian would study, not nature—a child could observe enough nature to find God— but the amendment of his life.

For portions of La Primaudaye's doctrine, including cautious humanism, Englishmen could read either John Davies of Hereford or Sir John Davies. The latter followed chiefly the Frenchman when he wrote of the immaterial soul and opened his poem bewailing man's intellectual depravity. Prefaces ordinarily dignify subjects, pleading their importance. Knowledge of the soul—Davies had written of the soul—meant knowledge of self, of original sin. The lawyer's brief Part I has been once or twice isolated from its obvious purpose in context and read as an essay in skepticism, which it is by a broad enough definition. But Davies nowhere dabbled in knowledge-criticism. He wrote consistently, if hyperbolically, in the tradition of Bernardine Socratism. He discovered the root of our weakness in our grandparents' foolish desire to know evil, and in that weakness we descendants pursue knowledge in "fond fruitless curiosity," seeking to know the motion of the spheres or the ebbs and floods of Nile, heedless of the counsel whereby the devil mocked us in his oracle—"Know thyself." If life is short and art long, surely we are no wiser than the heir who hopes to regain his lost patrimony by earning a groat a day. We should do better to study ourselves. The author, of course, expected one to begin by reading Davies on the soul.

His antithesis between self-knowledge and study of the Nile (a topic that the ancients had, in the words of Sir Thomas Browne, "drawn to a proverbial obscurity") reminds us that he owed his language to convention, however personal his conviction. One might argue by a plausible guess that the stars as a cliché antonym for "self" had taken fresh significance from the new astronomy, that the symbol, though a commonplace, held new and somewhat sinister implications. One could hardly say as much for the river Nile, and yet Davies used the Nile exactly as he used the stars. If there were others who could write thus without taking a serious stand for or against astronomy, it might be cautiously inquired whether John Donne made one of their number when, in his poem *Of the Progress of the Soul* (189–194), he caused the soul to fly heavenward without stopping to ask about moon-dwellers or the sphere of sublunary fire. In the companion poem, *An Anatomie of the World* (205–212), he wrote with the same standard sarcasm of astronomy (new and old in the same poem), the plurality of worlds, and the deletion of fire from the list of elements. To praise self-knowledge in this fashion sorted with either rational humanism or Bernardine pietism, but the pietism pleased Donne in the Anniversaries. Both in their form and in their medieval Socratism his meditations on the soul's ascent to beatific vision forcibly recall Bernard. Having determined, for whatever reason, to cast his elegies in this mystical mould, the poet found a measure of pessimistic gloom and a notice of curiosity to be obligatory. And a sermon on curiosity must be illustrated or sag. His choice of illustrations that were rapidly becoming stereotyped impugns neither his piety nor his gloom; it only cautions us not hastily to hold astronomy accountable for either. In this satirical vein, Montaigne picked the stars, or the sources of the Nile, or the cause of tides. As a good Pyrrhonist he bore Copernicus and planet-dwellers no grudge, but when in need of a stock metaphor for curious men, he turned all into astronomers, new or old, in strong language. Charron followed him in this mixture of tolerance for particular astronomies and formulated indignation against curiosity, illustrated by astronomy. La Primaudaye disliked plural worlds and Cardan's meddling with elemental fire. In morality and divinity, he explained, so many profitable analogies had been worked out for a square of four elements that three would be inconvenient—precisely the argument for four that Bacon ridiculed. Du Bartas thought as little of the

presumptuous wits who dared to suggest that the earth
turned daily; and while Sylvester applauded in the margin
he denounced the kind of curiosity that would tear away
the world's "best" element, the lovely fire. Donne, too,
took the conservative side of these arguments, but ordinarily without much heat, even in the Anniversaries. There,
we shall not be guilty of reading his Socratic commonplace as a mere flower of rhetoric if we doubt that the new
philosophy literally filled him with dismay. His language
suggests that his depression, if real and if the consequence
of a real insecurity (two bold assumptions), came first. For
the gloom of the *Anatomie* a number of reasons come
to mind more likely than, say, Copernicus: Donne's personal problems; the blight on man and nature demanded
by the rules of the form he chose; the current fashion of
melancholy in letters; or the poet's occasion. Funeral elegies are not usually merry. If our object is only to read the
Anniversaries, we may perhaps examine their "astronomy"
as well in the accepted patterns of satirical wit as in the
works of Cardan, Bruno, and Kepler.

The recurrent triad—heliocentrism, plural worlds, and
the elimination of fire as an element—now and again
adorned satires and essays "On Presumption," some of
them acknowledging by that very title their descent from
Montaigne. Their distinguishing feature was not their
title but a nexus: man's indignity coupled with his intellectual arrogance. What we have found in Donne's Anniversaries clothed in Bernardine piety we may conveniently
digress to pursue, briefly, in these satires. The few skeptics
who thus made fun of cosmological speculation added to
what many dogmatists had written on a theme from Socrates and so helped to prepare an audience for Milton.
The poet rejected their low opinion of human dignity;
he profited only by the symbols of presumption that their
laughter had prepared for him. Montaigne and his disciple
Charron ("Of Presumption") told alike how man, the
earth-creeping wretch, lodged at the foot of the world's
ladder where the lees and dregs of nature settle, presumed
to think himself the center and final cause of the universe.
Charron, whom Milton may have looked into at one time,

would not absolutely forbid a modest conjecture that God had not wasted his planets on man alone. William Drummond appropriated for his *Cypress Grove* much that Montaigne had taught about human presumption. It was from Donne's *Anatomie* that he borrowed, to illustrate curiosity, the three standard speculations in cosmology. To them he added a fourth, the new magnetic studies that had already set Vanini praising Cornelius Agrippa's wise ignorance. George Wither as satirist in "Of Presumption" began faithfully with doubt that the world was made for man and moved on to illustrate intellectual pride with astrology searching the future, idle wit searching God's history before creation, will-worship adding to scripture, and dogmatism in general "prying though . . . forbidden Into those secrets, God meant should be hidden." In Burton, debtor to Montaigne for observations on the indignity of man, we find the proper triad of cosmological speculations. Much later, Thomas Bancroft, writing satire in the Roman tradition, used them "Against Presumption." He ridiculed the wretched prisoner confined amid the excretions of nature at "the stair foot of the world," yet fancying himself to be the final cause of all. Man's pride obtruded dogma; high-flown wits imposed their opinions as settled laws. One dogma by Bancroft's time had won a new convert; for to the company of Democritus, Leucippus, and Bruno had been added John Wilkins, doubtless

> He that upon the Moon had spent his wit,
> And found both sea and land enough in it
> To furnish a new world.

One of his fellows teaching magisterially—in these satires only the innovators dogmatized—"to the earth gave motion, and Would have the sun as the world's center stand"; another "would try whether the elemental fire Have the same heat with ours," and "be acquainted with the Selenites."

Selenites in *Paradise Lost,* or speculations about them, as a crowning illustration of Adam's curiosity, surpassing in futility even the stellar motions of Raphael's doubtful reply, made themselves useful to Milton by this triteness.

Only a few readers could have allowed them any grave philosophical importance for good or bad. The poet's own innocent interest in multiple worlds, a theory to which he alluded seven times in his long epic and to which he contributed a speculation of his own (III.460) should assure us that he did not consider the pluralist theory vicious enough to warrant the heavy artillery that he called out to demolish it. A too solemn study of the interest in it that the new astronomy is supposed to have quickened, or of the dangerous questions that it might have posed in philosophy and religion, in soteriology especially, may obscure the fact that only a handful of thinkers seemed at all in earnest about the doctrine. Henry More, John Wilkins, the few professional astronomers who wrote of it with some seriousness—these roused almost nobody besides Alexander Ross to protest, so indifferent seemed the public to the ancient guess. The notion that the planets might be inhabited drew no fresh evidence from the new astronomy; writers who offered an airy kind of "proof" were more likely to argue, like Charron, from the analogy of the new geography, from Columbus and his once incredible new world. Spenser's banter in the Prologue to his second Book is as typical as familiar: if a Columbus, why not plural worlds; and if either, why not Fairyland? Excellent students of seventeenth-century cosmology have not overlooked such pleasantry and light sarcasm. I would only suggest that the laughter went further to commend the pluralist theory to Milton as an illustration of curiosity than any danger that he scented in the doctrine. Readers of *Paradise Lost* had been taught to smile, especially at moon-dwellers, by Ariosto's lunar paradise or Donne's in *Ignatius,* the supplement to the *Satyre Ménippé,* Ben Jonson's masques, Francis Godwin's fantasy, and even the masthead of a Royalist newspaper, until "world in the moon" had become in everyday speech almost slang for nonsense. Perhaps enough anti-curiosity sermons cut to a constant pattern have been collected already in these pages from classical and Christian morality and from skepticism to enshrine self-knowledge. Astronomy, new or old, and stellar worlds could be counted on as foils to set off the virtue when mentioned in the proper tone of voice. For his grand commonplace, the kind of ground upon which the epic poet must always weave his flowers, Milton wanted a symbol whose meaning had been fixed, not one that required a polemic.

To this point we have considered the anti-curiosity sermon as the protective shield of humanism, variously conceived. Because the Reformation drew heavily upon the Fathers, especially Augustine and Bernard, its language often smacked of humanism or Socratism in its medieval sense, not that the language invariably fitted the intent. The same kind of preaching guarded, of course, the *données* of traditional theology. Before we leave this sin of curiosity at the threshold of Milton's period and go back to the matter of vain philosophy, let us call back a former witness, now Dr. John Donne, Anglican, whom we left, as poet, in an unwonted mood of mystical pietism. The Fathers taught him better than any other preacher in James's England how to be curious in small things and cautious *in extenso*. His sermons, unlike his Anniversaries, afford a context of normal Anglicanism in which we can read, without Genevan commentary, the teachings of Bernard, cited about a hundred times, and of Augustine, cited about three hundred. Donne's youthful Pyrrhonism and the escapes of neoplatonism had helped him to make submission to his adopted religion complete, faultless, and probably more honest than some have thought. His Scholastic education would have carried him to the stream of medieval Augustinianism, and his studies for the pulpit to its fountain. There he would have learned that if the mysteries of Christianity were *credenda ut intelligantur,* they were also *intelligenda ut credantur.*

When Donne subscribed the Articles, he engaged himself to quarrel as his church quarreled; he took upon himself her normal aversions to mystical exaltation, Brownists and sects, and authoritarian Rome, manufacturing mysteries and new fundamentals at will. Against these forms of what would have seemed to him anti-intellectualism, he cheerfully put on the armor of reason and learning, even as he preached against curiosity. Bishop John King liked

to remind the established clergy of their duty to the prerogatives of learning, assailed on opposite sides by Popish
and Brownist obscurantism; and his protégé in orders
lost no occasion to ring changes on *philosophia ancilla
theologiæ*. The maxim set a mild yoke on the pagans (the
first breath of the Lord's indignation "disorders thy Seneca, thy Plutarch"); and Donne listed the diverse and defective theories of the *summum bonum* by which the philosophers unwittingly exalted Christ. But he whipped the
bigots who scorned pagan philosophy, along with the incurious dullard who made his stupid passage through the
world and the monastic orders vying to outdo each other
in swinishness. The Fathers extracted learning from the
heathen as the Israelites carried gold out of Egypt; the
university was a paradise; in the creatures alone could man
apprehend God sensibly and without tabu—the premise of
natural scientists. The mind's infirmities that had troubled
Donne in the Anniversaries sobered him now and then in
his pulpit, but one who therefore took license to sin against
learning either by wilful ignorance or by curiosity sinned
against the Second Person. A great light struck Saul blind,
not the darkness of retirement to the country or to a mon-
astery. Thus ran Donne's eloquent defense of intellectual
divinity. Like Hooker, Donne honored reason partly because it justified the outward acts of religion and his
church.

One may guess that he preferred reason to Calvin's idea
of God, but the point is difficult to clear up in the absence
of a formal statement. Donne wrote of human reason in
language that would have made Calvin uneasy; he quoted
with approval what he took to be the consensus of the
Fathers that holy pagans may be saved—a dangerous doctrine. He repeatedly held (like Milton) that where scripture spoke of predestination, the places were to be understood of election only. But none of this flatly contradicted
the prevailing Protestant theology. What is more importantly orthodox, Donne frequently praised his beloved Augustine for having first exposed the error of predestination
for merit foreseen. God predestined by his mere grace.
We may add, for what it is worth, that whenever Donne

in the pulpit mentioned Calvin he did so with respect, just possibly because the Protestant patriarch's name never came up in connection with his distinctive doctrine. The easiest resolution of the difficulty is probably that, though Donne did not like Augustine in Calvin's straitjacket, and possibly would have questioned the predestination of particular men, he saw no reason to raise a genuinely controversial question inside the church of his adoption. He crowned a bright, intelligible rationalism like Hooker's with a more voluble profession of faith, for which he borrowed more mysticism than he practiced. At the same time, he peered more often into the psychology of religious experience than into dogma and pried less curiously into mysteries than into himself. In the humility of devout self-knowledge he sought the ignorance that he expected would lead him to the highest wisdom. One form of *nescientia,* "a not knowing of things not pertaining to us, we should have had though Adam had not fallen."

This hydroptic thirster after knowledge who, as poet, had once set out to trace the soul of Eve's apple through the bodies of the great heretics had, as theologian, much to say of intellectual bounds. A probable cause has been sought in his fondness for what the age identified with scholasticism—the small, peripheral conjectures that eked out facts revealed in scripture. His religion could never quite persuade him to stop with the revealed word. The schools, he owned, had their subtlety; but they had their wisdom, too. An editor has remarked the connection between Donne's preoccupation with the sin of curiosity and his own interest in strange, scholastic questions. If Donne had defended himself on this score, he might have pointed out that the Fathers had classified indiscreet questions under three heads: questions of What? How? and Why? His exuberant fancy broached many unimportant questions of What?- but his agile wit liked better to ask them than seriously to hunt the answers. He often refused to answer what he needlessly asked, and in refusing, wrote at length against curiosity. Privacy, like modesty, could take the sin out of some inquiry. In a letter to Sir Thomas Lucy, Donne broached the traducianists' question *de modo*—how is each of us supplied with a soul?—a matter that occupied many good minds, and Milton's among them. He admitted the danger in the question, but cleared himself of curiosity on the ground that it had been seriously asked of a learned man in a private letter. Elsewhere he proved out of Luther that questions of How?—of God's unrevealed means—demanded a greater measure of diffidence. Protestantism agreed to know only a little about the manner of Christ's presence in the sacrament and descent into hell: "These are *arcana imperii,* secrets of state, for the manner is secret, though the thing be evident in the scriptures." In this kind of inquiry tone meant much, and many reasonable questions might be asked if asked reverently. Milton's Adam made his first mistake when he asked in a critical spirit; he made his second when he called upon God to account for his intentions. This kind of question reminded Donne and many others of the old story of the astronomer Alfonso, who regretted that God had not sought his advice while creating, since he could have saved God from some mistakes. Alfonso fell into this blasphemy by the unpardonable sin of asking Why?—Donne's third and gravest curiosity. Final causes, the poison of experimental science and good meat for scholastic Aristotelians, died hard; but the new learning found them easier to remove eventually from philosophy because theologians, writing like Donne, were removing them from divinity. Questions of What? and even How? might sometimes be justified, but "God's unrevealed and bosom purposes are *arcana domus.*" When the time grew ripe to banish design from God's universe, this kind of piety gave its blessing to the "atheistic" philosophers.

The questions that Donne forbade were all doctrinal; he exonerated secular learning entirely except for the routine condemnation of sorcery and necromancy—and he was not unread in the occultists who sometimes counted as magicians. Nothing in his sermons can be taken as restricting natural learning; he repeated, like naturalists from Bacon to Boyle, the stock biblical defense of science —that Adam in innocence had mastered physical sciences, for he named the animals. (In giving himself no name, Adam betrayed his lack of self-knowledge.) He acknowl-

edged the wisdom of the ancients, particularly Seneca. He
ranked the philosophers only little below the apocryphal
authors. All human learning he encouraged to the point
of fanaticism with only the proviso that it serve God's
glory; else it was but "a giddy, a vertiginous circle." In all
this we perceive that for Donne curiosity was no quantita-
tive sin. In what, then, did it consist? Not in the kind or
amount of knowledge, but in the motives and the manner
and the relevance:

What is curiosity? "Qui scire vult ut sciat." He that desires
knowledge only that he may know, or be known of others to
know; he who makes not the end of his knowledge the glory
of God, he offends in curiosity. . . . That is only in the end.
But in the way of knowledge there is curiosity too; in seeking
such things as man hath no faculty to compass, unrevealed
mysteries; in seeking things, which if they may be compassed,
yet it is done by indirect means, by invocation of spirits, by
sorcery; in seeking things which may be found, and by good
means, but appertain not to our profession; all these ways men
offend in curiosity.

Where curiosity embraced knowledge devilish, proud, useless, invalid, or unorthodox, what knowledge could wholly
escape its taint? Almost any Englishman except Bacon
might have replied, "Self-knowledge," leaving us only a
little wiser by his answer.

Some New Wisdom and Older Vanity

An outcry against vain wisdom and false philosophy,
unlike the curiosity sermons heard everywhere, rose a
little more often than not from the ranks of the mystics
and the skeptics. But here again we may remember that
Thomas Hobbes quoted St. Paul and desist from oversimplifying. In the Renaissance, the Apostle's warning or
an equivalent sermon so often chastised clerics and their
rationalizing that to collect all the instances would be to
write a history of crumbling Thomism. Long before Erasmus, John of Salisbury had rebuked the subtle divines. Between Aquinas and Milton, overwise divinity changed
shape under pounding by Scotus, Occam, Richard Rolle,

John Tauler and the Friends of God, Reuchlin, Pico, Pomponazzi, Telesio, Luther, Ramus, Hobbes, and at last everybody, including Protestant scholastics. The vanity of learning as a topic in the Renaissance before 1600 has already been explored in some detail. Its miscellaneous teachers quarreled first and most violently with the dotards of Paris and Salamanca, though by no means solely with these. Bernardine and Victorine mysticism, grown scholastic and tolerable, early dropped out of this combat. It consisted so well with respectability that Aquinas built a corner for it in his commodious structure, with the result that, in Gerson, for example, mysticism ossified and nearly expired while the more rash and perfervid religiosity sought the upper Rhine. The intellectual Platonic strain of the Dionysian *Theologia Mystica* meanwhile blended with cabalism and various other Platonisms or Plotinisms to emerge in theosophy. Nothing in divinity could be less "ignorant" than Cusa's *Docta Ignorantia,* though in some of his works Cusa reached the point of contemplative prayer in which all mystics must lay aside the ordinary faculties.

So far as the occult sciences loosely linked with this theosophy breathed revolution, they produced a literature of the strongest protest against tradition. Since they drew from scripture as well as from nature, they made themselves the scourge of godless natural science, old or new. Paracelsus allowed no difference between medieval Aristotelians, Galenists, or newer enemies of both when he found reason to hurl his pungent terms of abuse. In particular, he damned every paganism, religiously sure of his ground in scripture, nature, and the peculiar cabala that he manufactured to join the two. Some of his exclusive piety descended upon English physicians, the utopian Rosicrucians, and John Amos Comenius, confirming them all in at least their religious disdain of paganism and carnal reasoning. The vagabond spirit of Giordano Bruno, sheltered in England, dedicated to Sidney the disordered, Rabelaisian laughter of the *Spaccio della Bestia Triunfante* (the Beast being stagnation and reaction) and its even wittier sequel, the *Cabala del Cavallo Pegaseo.* With a nod to the old gowned ignorance and to the new pedantry, he gave the eminent place in his tribute to asininity to the Peripatetics. Whatever his affinities with the skeptics, he would have none of the Pyrrhonists; they were Buridan's ass. By long odds he preferred submissive Christians, the ass of the Gospels. A generation or two later a more devout theosophy taught sacred antirationalism in England when the works of Valentin Wiegel began to be "much cried up," and John Sparrow with others undertook, some time before the Restoration, to translate the works of Jacob Boehme.

By the time the "sect of Behmenists," as Baxter called them, had risen to attention, England had produced plenty of indigenous enthusiasm writing for piety and ignorance, but it was usually, as we shall see, a by-product of the church-government controversy. Seeking genuine quietism for its own sake, a handful of translators turned to foreign sources—to Germany or, more decorously and less frequently, to early Christianity and to Spain. Nicholas Ferrar, notable contemplative, Englished some mild pages of Juan Valdés; Samuel Rutherford, speaking correctly for the established Presbyterian clergy, damned the heresy. John Everard, the thorn in the side of King James, quickly passed from mere Puritanism into Seekerism or like sectarian aberration. He translated the *Theologia Germanica,* Sebastian Franck's *Forbidden Fruit; or . . . The Tree of Knowledge of Good and Evil,* together with bits from Hermes, Dionysius, Denck, and Tauler. He and the antinomian Giles Randall published some minor rhapsodies of Cusa. These names remind us of an anti-intellectual tradition stretching from the Germany of Dante's time to Quakerism and beyond, trickling into England in the first and every subsequent generation. Strictly speaking, the fourteenth-century Rhenish mysticism repudiated, as Inge has written in kindred context, "intellectualism, not intellect, moralism, not morality." Even so, in holding personal inspiration to be the source of religion, it lived uneasily beside a largely superfluous priesthood, ethics by reasoned precept, and theology in forensic system. Luther thought highly enough of the *Theologia Germanica* to publish it. There he found comfort for his solifidian religion and his low opinion of the "wild beast" of reason, famous in his comment on Galatians iii:6. But then Luther, unlike Calvin, wrote enough passages in contempt of human learning for a collection of them to reassure Cromwell's sectaries. The earnest antiphilosophical pages of the *Theologia* squared with the opinions of a still more radical editor, Hans Denck. They instructed restive Anabaptists as well as the quieter Spirituals whose historical connection with the English Quakers has been traced through the Seeker movement. It was fitting and prophetic that Calvin, to whom contemplative mysticism meant nothing and his own authority everything, should call the *Theologia* a "hidden and mortal venom that has poisoned the church."

Cornelius Agrippa's work of great fame and many editions, *De Vanitate et Incertitudine Scientiarum Declamatio* (1530—Englished 1569), pretended a connection with this kind of German piety; and indeed the eminent occultist needed to sweeten his reputation for black magic with a work of Paracelsian devotion. But Agrippa's was no work of devotion except perhaps in a few opening and closing pages. It is barely possible that the exposé of vanity in an even hundred professions owed some popularity to the gratifying detail in which the author was dismayed by one of the oldest. It would be easy to make out a case for Agrippa as a serious educational reformer, a forerunner of Bacon and Comenius. In clearing away the rubble of corrupt tradition, he paused to speak in defense of natural, or white, magic if purged of charlatanry. Like some other arts, for example, logic and school divinity, it suffered by abuse at the hands of its professors, not by the essential *vanitas* of common alchemy, necromancy, and astrology. The last suggested to Agrippa the nonsense of multiple worlds. For all its popularity, his work was sometimes mentioned with less than profound respect, doubtless because as a writer the author preferred overstatement and paradox to precision. Because much of his book still reads, therefore, like a *jeu d'esprit* undertaken in a spirit of peevishness, his religious pose seems somehow theatrical. With the Preacher's lament for book-making and other appropriate texts the nominally Catholic author everywhere turned error into impiety to support his heretical conclusion that the Bible teaches all things.

The better part of a century after Agrippa's work was first translated, a selection from the matured mysticism of Sebastian Franck, written after the popular chronicler had turned Spiritual, exasperated the Presbyterian clergy in England. It may serve as our final illustration of imported quietist doctrine. Franck declared his allegiance to Eckhart, Tauler, and Staupitz; we know that he had translated the *Theologia Germanica*, Erasmus' *Praise of Folly*, and Agrippa's *Vanity*. His title page discovered learning to be the Beast, or the tree of Genesis, deadly alike to Adam and his sons. With something suspiciously like logic he premised that whatever was not of God was against God; but learning was of neither the word without nor the spirit within; ergo. Its errors and uncertainties had brought man only misery and would bring eternal damnation. Every man knew that St. Paul had warned of it, but every man supposed that the Apostle spoke of some neighbor's learning: "No man remembers to renounce and give farewell to his own." If arts had been in any way necessary, God would have created them in the beginning. (As Milton and many took pains to say, God did so.) Since human knowledge came, then, from Antichrist, sin, death, and the devil, a wise man would unlearn it, though at great pains, and be like Socrates, knowing only his own ignorance. "Behave thyself to God quietly, like a liveless trunk, as thou didst in thy creation. Suffer God to do," the Quietist admonished, "and do thou nothing at all, lest it happen that thou be taken with a desire of the forbidden tree."

The bare fact that Erasmus could be translated in the interest of religious obscurantism compels us to remember that in the Revival the educators' gospel of learning was no uncritical exuberance. Humanists needed some of Bernard's sobriety and more of the ancient moralists', if only to discredit scholasticism. When Petrarch applauded his own ignorance, he appealed for support to Ecclesiastes,

and the Preacher came seconded by a host of diffident
pagans like Homer, Cicero, and even Aristotle—more modest than his commentators. Whenever a humanist went
flailing into combat, like Rabelais against Sorbonnists, he
might rain by-blows upon all pedantry or pretentiousness.
Though not precisely a humanist in the narrow sense, Petrarch will serve to remind us that learning, when revived
from the antique source, fell foul of some antagonists besides the theological Aristotle. He damned not the prevailing divinity alone, but the English Occamists in the
schools, the atheistic Arabs, and any other philosophers
who exalted themselves. His devout self-knowledge would
never propose a doctrine of eternal matter or infinite
worlds when it "had not explored the thousandth part of
this one." Lorenzo Valla, writing of free will, spoke the
Apostolic language, *scientia inflat,* for a man could believe
God's promises without resolving all the difficulties. The
schoolmen and Valla stood often at odds, but not distinctly
here. The same schoolmen, raising such monstrous questions that Vives wondered how they could sleep nights,
made one, but only one, of learning's hazards as the Span-
iard listed them in his most celebrated book of pedagogy.
He had a more modern class of sinners in mind when he
built a religious fence around his own respectably experimental science.

Philosophy and literature had been similarly fenced by
Gian Francesco Pico's *Examen Vanitatis Doctrinæ Gen-
tium* and by Wimpina's *De Erroribus Philosophorum.*
By the time England's intellectual traffic with Italy had
become routine, in that country a chastened mood of skeptical sobriety had already replaced the first enthusiasm of
the Revival. Ascham followed no exclusively northern
fashion when, in words now grown familiar, he checked
paganizing readers of human letters. Erasmus in the *Ci-
ceronianus* had meanwhile drubbed the trivial pedants
among the grammarians. We might multiply texts from
eminent grammarians and educators who had more to conquer than a too rational theology. In other kinds of philosophy and philology a student might imitate the Giants of
old, or follow the bad example of Aristotle, who, by a pa-

tristic legend in Nazianzen, drowned himself in an inlet because he could not understand the tides. According to the hardiest of the commonplaces, all study not reducible to morality (action) remained curiosity (mere contemplation). To such a secular level Petrarch had brought a debate that in earlier centuries had belonged to religion. After Petrarch, the argument between action and contemplation kept its mundane level, as a rule, and seldom allowed contemplation (study) for its own sake any merit beyond sweetness.

Setting action above contemplation can be one way to commend mere ignorance. Ascham saw the danger when he replied, as it were by anticipation, to Montaigne and exalted learning above experience. Besides the Popish conspiracy against learning that all Protestants deplored, Ascham singled out two dangerous secular fashions: the Erasmian satire that threatened to sweep away learning along with the abuse, and the habit of certain Frenchmen of paying homage to ignorance. Humanism had indeed revived the classical exercise of praising the abhorrent. Ortensio Lando's collection of paradoxes (Lyons, 1543) contained a defense of ignorance on practical and religious grounds. Translated by Anthony Mundy from Estienne's French, these paradoxes appeared in England (1593) with a title page proposing them as suitable for debate topics in the schools. Notable humanists could be found writing something like Lando's form of satire. In this tradition Giraldi wrote his *Progymnasma adversus Literas et Literatos,* taking for his text Seneca's eighty-eighth Epistle. Sextian Pyrrhonism, a revival fostered but hardly inaugurated by Estienne's publication of the *Hypotyposes,* furnished grist for the paradox-mongers. Their flippancy blurred the line between serious skepticism and mere wit until Frenchmen were prepared to take Agrippa lightly. Today it is not easy to read Francisco Sánchez' *Quod Nihil Scitur* as more than cleverness, though the physician sometimes invoked religion and Richard Baxter prescribed him for the godly. Equally paradoxical and classical, the theme of man's inferiority to the animals brought with it a measure of anti-intellectualism, designed to wound pride and

not to be taken too literally. But in these paradoxes we
see the humanists' everyday cautions magnified abnor-
mally and threatening to undercut serious values. Such
would have been the danger that Ascham feared in Erasmus' *Praise of Folly,* the grandest of the paradoxes. When
the manifold and involuted ironies of the book had been
planed out to level assertion, there remained a generous
measure of wistful primitivism and religious humility to
restrain the intellect in good earnest. We remember easily
the parade of fools: the grammarians and humanists in the
van, followed by the lawyers. Next, the scientists with their
multiple worlds and stellar dimensions, as if they had been
with God at creation. Last, the divines, arguing the mysteries of original sin, the consecrated wafer, and whatever
else the Apostle meant by vain philosophy. We may not so
readily recall that in the face of this "scholasticism" Erasmus could argue with more than half seriousness that sciences are harmful, that children and fools enjoy advantages, that in the blessed golden age men had been too
simple to need grammar, too wise to dispute with logic, too
good to need law. With so much serious intent he wrote
the devout close of his work, exhorting to simplicity. The
beasts are happy; man alone attempts the preposterous.

This small stone in the structure of Erasmus' thought—
the felicity of the animals—became in some of Montaigne's
latter meditations the head of the corner. As we accordingly pass beyond the elastic limits of the humanistic tradition we find the familiar formulas of modesty employed
with lower aim. Whatever the essayist's sins against the
humanistic creed as, say, Pico might have recited it, he
professed through two changes of philosophy his faith in
the virtues of self-study and knowing for the sake of doing.
And indeed as we read his plan for educating boys, we find
some narrowness but no serious break with humanistic
orthodoxy. Complete education taught the uses of wealth,
distributive justice, duties to friends and country, and the
purposes of life. All the liberal arts served these ends in
some measure. Montaigne required only that education
begin with what professedly served them—simple morality.
It might proceed thence to the more remote, provided

only that it postpone indefinitely the disciplines of "grammar," baralipton, and astronomy—or pedantic humanism, scholastic logic, and the curiosity of useless fact. These vanities corresponded in some sort with Bacon's three—delicate, contentious, and fantastic learning—but they corresponded as well with vanities satirized in the *Praise of Folly*. The details that filled out Montaigne's principles helped to mould aristocratic academies in France and to guide essayists and courtesy writers in England for half a century.

Writing to train young gentlemen in his own image, Montaigne seemed to differ so little from Castiglione on the one hand and Milton on the other that we must read the primitivism of his essays on pedantry and on cannibals to realize how much of the humanistic tradition he would have discarded. And unless forewarned that no humility, as Bernard measured humility, inspired the consummate egoist, we should find his praise of self-knowledge disarming. His succession of tutors—Seneca, Plutarch, Pyrrho, and Epicurus (if we may call his naturalistic phase Epicurean)—agreed, he thought, in teaching him modesty's first lesson. Scripture supported them, and he adorned the ceiling of his library with the familiar texts in the spirit of *Que scay-je?* Christians had better reason than even Pyrrho of Elis to know that curiosity had been the original sin and the source of lies. But he turned most easily to the pagans to find his skepticism approved as sober wisdom. Had not the sirens sought to gull Ulysses with the gift of knowledge, and Plato and Cicero objurgated subtle theology, and the wisest of men known only his own ignorance? Yet between ABC ignorance preceding knowledge, as he called it in a line that became popular, and doctoral ignorance following, lay a legitimate knowledge proscribed by neither reason nor religion. Once away from Pyrrho, Montaigne forgot to swim in perpetual doubt.

As a moralist teaching the modesty of naturalism, he continued to wreck some important assumptions, and cries of protest echoed for a hundred years. The self-sufficient Stoics seemed to him, when he no longer needed them, the philosophers who most arrogantly sat in God's chair. Erasmus had agreed. But Erasmus had not gone so far as

to consider learning to die a superfluous discipline because
nature would take care of the matter. At least once he had
agreed with Montaigne about the happiness of the innocent beasts, and probably would have let pass Montaigne's
half-hearted identification of man's indignity with the
Christian dogma of man's depravity. Where Montaigne
broke completely with Bernard, however, not even Erasmus' Pelagianism would have ventured. The saint had defined self-knowledge as a conviction of original sin and of
the need for repentance. Montaigne the naturalist declared flatly that man could not be honestly penitent for
being man. Bernard would have shuddered at the arrogance in the strange new doctrine, but to Montaigne it
seemed that the arrogance lay on the other side, with a philosophy and religion smugly anthropocentric. "Lodged in
the mud and filth of the world" and "the lowest story of
the house," man set himself "above the circle of the moon."
He added stellar worlds to his demesne and supposed that
his awesome setting endured "for his service and convenience." Dimly conscious of his own decay, he had devised
the fiction that nature's decay kept pace, a pure invention
to salve his vanity. For man's claim on God's exclusive
concern Montaigne demanded to see his patent, for the
noble crane seemed to have a better right. The crane, we
may be sure, would not have been among those who went
aloft to scribble over the sphere, cycle and epicycle, or
straddled the epicycle of Mercury to peek into heaven.

The reformed religion strengthened its claim to the
human center remote from astronomical curiosity by repudiating the contemplative life. As its prejudice spread from
things heavenly to earthly, Protestantism sanctified, as
sober humanity, more and more outward and visible activity. At the threshold of Milton's era Fulke Greville, with
his *Treatie of Humane Learning,* took his place beside
Ascham, Daniel, and Bacon as an apostle of action and a
reformer of learning. This latter character has been somewhat obscured by much special attention to his poem's
gloomier stanzas, the first sixty-one. Like Vives or Bacon
or many another constructive critic, Greville began by

sweeping a dour glance over the state of knowledge, but only to propose, in his last ninety stanzas, a set of abstract counsels for fruitful learning that his friend Sidney would have welcomed. For his faith in learning we may read the fifth Chorus in *Mustapha* against the Turkish, or the *Treatie* itself against the Popish doctrine "Ignorance is the mother of devotion." For overwisdom he forged gyves not only in the *Treatie,* but in his *Cælica* sonnets. There is no contradiction or even ambivalence if one agrees that learning and curiosity are different things. We shall probably never know whether Greville wrote the posthumously published *Treatie* in his youth as an "exercise for Sidney" or in his maturity as a directory for young public servants. A late date has been suggested chiefly on the strength of its Stanza 73, assumed—unnecessarily, I think—to refer to Bacon. Early or late, the poem is a neat summation, distinct from Baconianism, of neo-humanistic practicality tinged with secular skepticism. The kind of religion that it appealed to was the same that advantaged Bacon, faith in the sanctity of usefulness. Essayists and courtesy writers often taught that kind of piety in the early sixteen hundreds, before, or independently of, the *Novum Organum.*

If arts failed of their purpose to repair the damage that Adam had done to the human intellect, Greville more sincerely than Montaigne found sin at fault, darkening the understanding. He half agreed with those who argued (like Lando, to supply one authority) that learning multiplied care and perverted innocence. Spartans, Romans, and Turks had banished arts, and scripture had called them vain. Yet sprung up among thorns, a true learning could still be discovered by resolute purgation and "bloodletting" of "all curious science" if educators would only hold fast to a principle:

> The active, necessary arts
> Ought to be brief in books, in practice long.

"While Contemplation doth the world distract With vain ideas which it cannot act," one is obliged to choose and read with care. Let induction, Greville urged by way of offering some positive precepts, having drawn its princi-

ples, turn them again to solving particular problems (St.
73). Let sciences be drawn from "nature" and arts from
practice, not from books—a doctrine that Paracelsus, for
one, had spread earlier than Bacon. Let authorities be reduced and standardized. Let divinity give up school questions. Let law be framed by the Decalogue, the general
safety, and the service of the Crown. Let medicine forego
its dogmatism and its bookishness—Paracelsus again perhaps. Let logic forget its sleights and rhetoric its dis-
honesty. Let poetry serve morality and religion, Greville
and Sidney recited alike, and not possess the heart for itself alone. Let the quadrivial studies, including astronomy, Greville continued, serve "for practice in material
things"—buildings, camps, fortifications, traffic, and accounts. Above all, let there be no unlawful arts and no
borrowing from them for good ends. If all arts served
God's glory and man's welfare, they had latitude enough,
as Solomon proved. But only by regeneration could Adam's
posterity learn to know itself and, understanding the depth
of the Fall—it was Greville's last word—"judge ALL
OTHER KNOWLEDGE VAIN." Thus the service of
man's welfare in, for example, traffic and accounts could
be styled an acceptable branch of self-knowledge. Preaching the active life, Greville saw no incongruity in urging
the contemplative Bernard's rule:

> Yet some seek knowledge, merely but to know,
> And idle curiosity that is;
> Some but to sell, not freely to bestow,
> These gain and spend both time, and wealth amiss;
> Embasing arts, by basely deeming so:
> Some to be known, and vanity is this:
>> Some to build others, which is charity;
>> But these to build themselves, who wise men be.

When Francis Bacon, the lawyer, arose to defend the
study of nature, he correctly assessed the temper of his
audience and framed his plea by its received principles.
In some respects, such a plea did scant justice to the scope
of his thought; but his philosophy itself we must leave to
other commentators. His defense of it reveals more about
his generation.

The advocate found it expedient to parade one of Greville's doctrines, the humble charity of works, in demeanor so religious that the jury would not object to the absence of another—the utility and dignity of self-knowledge. In a lonely passage he conceded this knowledge to be the "end and term" of moral wisdom, but by no means that of all wisdom. That place he reserved for his First Philosophy, which embraced the studies of both self and nature. He dared to find fault with Socrates for defining the practical as the moral. In view of such declarations of principle it seems gratuitous to suppose that Bacon's extant work is heavily weighted toward the study of nature only because it is incomplete. If we grant that he advanced learning where it had been most neglected, we are not therefore bound to think that he sacrificed a great private enthusiasm for ethical philosophy, or to censure him even if he had none. When he surveyed all learning in his several "Advancements," he gave generous space to ethics, including politics; but the only advancement he desiderated for this rational science amounted, in all, to little more than a *Georgica animi, sive de cultura morum*. Efforts to minimize his neglect of ethics by collecting all his advice bearing on conduct or by proposing his essays as tentative notes toward a textbook of ethics hardly explain how, without cultivating a nonscientific logic, he could ever have done more for ethical *science* than to go on with his unphilosophical and generally empirical maxims of prudence. We have his own word that he wished no more. He rejoiced that revealed religion, in prescribing charity, had obviated further inquiry into the matter of a *summum bonum*. The thought-consuming part of ethical study he surrendered to faith and escorted upstairs, out of the way of natural philosophy.

Much moral philosophy thus went by the board because it belonged to the rational sciences that Bacon called curious contemplation. He would leave man in his accustomed place in the center of the universe—its final cause—but shorn of his idolatrous respect for the human mind. That particular form of self-worship had only diverted study from nature. Mind studying mind had produced the aridities of scholastic philosophy as the spider spun from its own entrails. In sweeping out such cobwebs, Bacon swept out mathematics, though some better advised naturalists before him had perceived that they would have to preserve a science of number from the wreck of speculative thought. In metaphysics properly so called, he projected a "summary philosophy" beyond any particular science, even beyond nature; but he took no further interest in it. The study that he designated "metaphysics" turned out to be a pure form of natural science, operative in "magic." His psychology quickly became his inductive dialectic for the study of nature. His essays in mythography wrung natural science out of the stories of Proteus, Cupid, Proserpina, and the Sphinx, and gave the ancients credit for having anticipated in their fable of Pan much of the *Novum Organum*. To keep his forward-moving intellect thus bound to nature's book he made use of some skepticism, but no more than any other crusader with a special interest to plead. By means of the senses, man could discover the long road out of doubt. In this fashion Bacon could be importantly anti-intellectual but not unusually skeptical: the doubting philosophies of the past had chiefly erred in blaming the senses for a weakness that belonged properly to the understanding. He taught philosophers to observe moderation even in doubt, to suspend judgment, but not foolishly or indefinitely. We have degrees of probability; we shall in time have certainty, provided that we correct and aid the senses and learn to circumvent the idols. Thus Bacon countered the Pyrrhonists. The empirics of any sort he called ants (as opposed to the too rational spiders) for the way they grubbed unrelated facts. The bee, the true philosopher, eschewed neither mind nor matter altogether. Bacon respected reason walking humbly with fact, not reason for its own sake.

By virtually removing the rational sciences from the hierarchy of studies, he left a safe gap between science and religion. The gap is important. Pomponazzi, Paracelsus, every eminent naturalist, and many practicing physicians before Bacon could distinguish sharply enough between philosophy and divinity, even when they mixed the two.

They failed to declare the short way to prevent the mingling. There is no doctrine of the double truth in Bacon. A proposition cannot be true in divinity and false in philosophy when the same proposition cannot exist in both. Bacon lived too soon to be seriously troubled by "unscientific" facts in scripture. The study of the rational soul's immortality—the battleground invaded by Pomponazzi and Davies—he cheerfully surrendered to divines. His sobriety in removing the rational soul (as substance) from among the objects fit for scientific study descended, as Sprat recorded, to the Royal Society. Except for some timid suggestions in the *Advancement* for purifying theology and some unexciting peacemaking, all outside his science and all scrupulously orthodox, he gave theology a wide berth. For failing to do likewise he denounced the mystically religious scientists, whose break with Aristotle was sharper than his own. The Paracelsians, torturing a whole system of physical science out of Holy Writ (while traducing all other science as heathenish) had degraded the sacred writings, filled religion with heresies, and stuffed science with nonsense. Sense-experience could not disturb religion if it would. There Bacon found "the true and legitimate humiliation of the human spirit." He entered the kingdom of nature like a little child. He dwelt, he said, among facts, rising only high enough above them to draw elementary inductions. Secure in the belief that he had legitimately united sense and reason, he left the rest to faith. "Da fidei," he could honestly exhort, "quæ fidei sunt."

Though religion never stooped to inform science in details, in general it expressly commended the pursuit of natural truth. True religion held to a mean between atheism and superstition. Natural philosophy, foreign to both extremes, served religion as handmaid by displaying God's regular providence. Whoever understood the laws of nature would be neither superstitious nor an atheist. As we read Bacon the philosopher and then Bacon the popularizer we perceive a kind of confusion that was to persist as long as science had to be justified in the name of religion. Without regarding teleology and final causes, sci-

ence makes a feeble advocate for God. Yet devoted to
guessing at God's purposes and intentions, at final causes,
science becomes a speculative philosophy at best. Like
Da Vinci and others before him, Bacon discouraged the
natural philosopher from seeking final causes, but only
because the philosopher should have more important work
to do. They were a practical point of moral philosophy;
they had real validity only with respect to human conduct,
as Hobbes was to agree. Descartes was to go further: we
must not examine the final causes of created things lest we
"presume so far as to think that we are sharers in the counsels of Deity," a point that preachers like Donne were making. Yet however eager the naturalists might be to shear
away some of the vain speculations of Aristotelian science
with an anti-curiosity preachment, they could ill afford
to give up their claim to being the most acute observers
of God's providence, better schooled than other Christians
in countless wonderful executions of his purposes. Bacon
used this defense of science in his well known essay "Of
Atheism" and elsewhere. The pages of Sir Thomas Browne
and Robert Boyle repeatedly assure us that the natural
philosophers were no more ready than other men to live
in a world without teleology. Henry More liked to be
philosophical by endlessly guessing at God's intentions, as
earlier preachers had done with no help from the Royal
Society. This kind of foolishness, perpetuated into the
eighteenth century, earned the lash of *Candide*. Ralph
Cudworth and John Wilkins more soberly tried to defer
to Descartes in principle and yet persuade science not to
bow direction and meaning out of the world with a pious
formula of modesty: it was the philosopher's business, they
said, to know that God had a purpose, not what purpose
exactly, in every one of his appointments. Perhaps if Bacon
had formulated the matter carefully, he might have said
something of the sort. He was far from deleting final
causes from ethical science, or from any other science
where they were a "true and worthy concern." Thinking
in the Aristotelian pattern of the schools that he abominated, he set up as the goal of inquiry the "form" or definition. Four causes—efficient, material, formal, and final—

normally yielded a definition, or essence; and Bacon retained all four, assigning the first two to "physic" and the
latter two to "metaphysic." This division had the effect
of checking premature concern with purposes in nature,
but left them on the periphery of natural science. What
place Bacon would have left them in his ultimate scheme of
the sciences is a question neither easy nor, here, pertinent.
It has sometimes been too flatly said that Bacon threw out
final causes. He tried to keep experimenters away from
them during working hours, so to speak; but his plan for
harnessing nature, presumably by imitating her structures,
permitted him to keep the causes where they could make
physical science a mighty ally of religion. With them, science could prove God's wisdom as well as his existence.
Bacon's own natural theology came to the end of its tether
sooner than that of Abelard or Herbert of Cherbury. Science invited the mind to turn to God; it said nothing of
a God in three persons, of the origin of sin, or of the means
of salvation. All truth could not be read in the book of
nature, and those who would rise to religious mysteries
on the wings of natural reason might profit by the misfortune of Pentheus.

Much of his religious mandate for natural science had
grown familiar in the defense of learning that Eusebius and
many others had already collected out of scripture. Bacon
wrote it into the opening sections of his *Advancement* and
De Augmentis partly to confute the "simple divines" who,
he thought, might oppose his program. As it happened,
many of the divines were mining the same scriptural vein
for texts to excuse their own learning and dignities, and
some of them even cited Bacon. In a spirit unlike theirs
Milton went to some of Bacon's sources when he too wrote
for the advancement of learning in *Areopagitica*. Milton
and literally hundreds—a few, mostly scientists, are listed
in the note—found scriptural warrant for learning in the
example of Adam, who in a state of innocence had philosophy enough to name the creatures according to their natures. Bacon harped on it repeatedly, interpreting it as
made for the naturalists: it was no desire to know nature
that brought about the Fall, but a desire for moral omnis-

cience, overwisdom in ethics. When the Psalmist directed us to consider God's works and magnify them, he meant more than gazing at their outsides. The scriptures revealed the will of God, but only the creatures showed his glory. It was the will of God that we should study the creatures, else why the stories of the early creation of light, of the exalted cherubim, perfect in knowledge, or of Tubal Cain, Solomon, Job, and St. Paul? Why the learning of the Fathers? If the captious should ask why God had hidden so much from us, Bacon replied with something like Milton's elaboration on Proverbs xxv:2—it was "as if according to the innocent play of children the divine Majesty took delight to hide his works, to the end to have them found out." Regarding truth, religion spoke thus to the intellect. To the practical will it spoke more imperatively of charity.

Knowledge for action—Bacon took up the old cry. It belonged to only God and the angels to be spectators at the scene. If Adam had been mindful of the true end of knowledge, the charity of works, he would have run no risk in desiring to be like God. The adroit propagandist liked to turn his opponents' weapons on themselves in this fashion, quoting their own best texts to bless natural science. By what we now call transfer devices he appropriated the piety that inhered in any useful education and associated it with his own project. A critic of the Royal Society laughed at the pious *non sequitur* by which Bacon, Gassendi, and Descartes, from the premise that notions must produce actions, had conferred on man the benefit of air pumps, lenses, and anatomies of insects. He put their folly another way: a good philosopher is a good man because his study of nature induces him to extol its Author, so that "out of a physical knowledge a moral one starts, and we see science and virtue have the same basis." We are not called upon to arbitrate this dispute, but rather to distill from Bacon's apology those principles that he knew to be public convictions—here, in particular, the righteousness of secular works. What man, what Englishman especially, ever loved useless knowledge, admitting its uselessness? When old Skelton gave Parrot leave to prate of μόνον καλὸν ἀγαθόν only if Greek could order a bundle of

hay or frame a syllogism, he spoke for the ages, even if he
lost for the moment a trifling point or two in the argument. Bacon phrased the constant rule thus: "All knowledge is to be limited by religion, and to be referred to use
and action."

Squaring his own teaching by the first half of the rule
presented, as we have seen, no great difficulty, in spite of
his nervousness that some parsons might be "weakly afraid
lest deeper search into nature should transgress the permitted limits of sober-mindedness." No accredited teacher
or preacher in Bacon's generation found anything actually
wicked in natural science merely because it took nature
for its object. If Paracelsus and Agrippa had been sorcerers,
there was still a legitimate science, the preachers conceded;
if one Copernicus had been "troubled with the vertigo,"
he had not tainted his profession. For Calvin as for Aquinas, science was the handmaid of divinity, not of commod-
ity; yet even so, the natural proofs of God's wisdom included "that secreter sort of things, for the nearer marking
whereof . . . all natural philosophy serveth." For Juan
Luis Vives, who wrote sometimes like Bacon and generally
like Ascham, it was the handmaid of humanity, but it
served to increase reverence, too, so long as teachers kept
it from charges weak in religion and expunged its impious
passages.

Without noticeable help from Bacon, a "medieval"
Christianity carried into the seventeenth-century pulpit,
Puritan and Anglican alike, this qualified allowance; and
the satirists who ridiculed eccentric virtuosi hardly re-
scinded what divinity sanctioned, for they ridiculed no
physical studies in the abstract. The preachers needed sermon-illustrations of God's power and wisdom; and the
Physiologus left them the ancient habit of moralizing on
the creatures—the habit that the noble Robert Boyle kept
to Swift's infinite boredom. In his popular exposition of
the Creed, Nicholas Bifield worked down from the phrase
"maker of heaven and earth" to more than fifty pages of
lessons drawn from every class of creatures. The modest
science needed for a meditation on charitable pelicans and
saintly eagles could carry the standard apology: science is

legitimate because Adam named the animals. "It is good
to be a natural philosopher," the preachers repeated, and
Thomas Adams at ardent length, "but better to be a supernatural"—a point that Bacon would never have disputed.
The theme found its way into Calvinists' commentaries
on scripture. On Romans i:20 ("The creation . . . that
they should be without excuse") a commentator cheerfully
confessed and copiously proved that true science made for
sound divinity, and the Apostle therefore required it of
men. The parson reproved only those naturalists who
stood "poring upon the creatures, and searching out their
natures, without even casting an eye unto the maker." The
advancers of science leaned heavily on the dogma of the
pulpit that the Fall had darkened man's spirit most, his
reason less, and his senses least. In its place at the bottom
of the scale of nobility lay the hope and the safety in nature. To John Wilkins, who earlier than most understood
Bacon's drift and disapproved some of it, the many questions that the Holy Ghost left unanswered on the lowest
plane proved that God wanted man to answer them, leaving higher matters alone. God left the world to our disputations to keep us out of mischief. In such fashion the
preachers worked at building for the naturalists a cellar
excellently lighted, below the level of curiosity, secure
from the storms of controversy. Bacon and his disciples
were humbly content to do nothing more than enlarge it.

On the second half of his rule—knowledge must be referred to use and action—Bacon debated by principles that
humanists and divines laid down in their reading of St.
Paul: "Knowledge puffeth up, but charity edifieth." Bernard had reproved learning idle and selfish as well as impious. Educators and preachers echoed the saints. Mere
knowledge is as wind, Milton quoted. "If learning be
taken without the true corrective thereof," an Anglican
divine wrote of St. Paul's corrective, charity, "it hath in
it some nature of poison, and some effects of that malig-
nity, which is a swelling." Of curiosity in this form, even
more importantly than of impiety, science had to be
cleared. It is not for this place to settle an academic question whether Bacon personally preferred *Nutzen* to *Wahr-*

heit. He usually preached utility, and it is likely that the Macaulays will therefore forever praise him as the Hegels will damn him. But his private dedication to truth becomes at least more plausible, despite some contradictory expressions, if we bear constantly in mind the apologist's need to respect the prejudices of his audience. Though legitimate science violated no religious tabu, it became curious when overemphasized in that most men counted it a study of limited charity and virtue. Bacon knew what he did when he accepted their principle and applied it his way: let men seek Truth before all else, but seek her in the realm of fact, not in the wishful fictions of man's reason. Thus, and only thus, could they have what religion demanded—works. Without works, he too quoted, *scientia inflat.* Unless used for the relief of man's state, all knowledge was a poison that made "the mind of man to swell." This kind of piety his contemporaries could understand. Sometimes they quoted it without perceiving that Bacon did not mean exactly what they said.

The Advancer has been considered here in part as an echo instead of a voice because his constructive teaching bore no fruit until after the early decades of the seventeenth century. Ben Jonson remarked that the *Novum Organum* was "a book," one that opened "all defects of learning whatsoever," but that few men read it or could understand it. Such praise will not alone prove that Jonson read and understood it, but it is informative to know that he liked it for its destructive criticism. By skeptical attacks on reaction Bacon drew his earliest audience. Like most good propaganda, his succeeded because his audience was already half persuaded; it read with relish of the three Vanities in studies, or fantastic, contentious, and delicate learning. These forms of curiosity in matter or words, excesses in the competing disciplines—traditional science, scholastic logic, and literary humanism—had been laughed at by Montaigne, as we have noticed, and by dozens of educators, Erasmus among them. The logomachy of the schools and the pedantry of prevailing fashions in rhetoric, though still nuisances, had long since become tired jests. When we look narrowly at one of the Vanities, Bacon's

"fantastic" learning—the old wives' tales of history as well
as the fictions of Aristotelian science, much astrology and
alchemy—we may find lurking in his doctrine some newer
seeds of cultural revolution. The "vain imaginations" that
men preferred before truth remind us of the Idols of the
Theatre, those received systems constructed like stage
plays and imposed upon the uncritical as fact. Aristotelians mixed science and logic in a structure too broad and
too symmetrical. Empirics reared science on a base too
narrow. The "superstitious" wrested it out of Genesis or
Job. Scripture, properly scanned, had warned of such impostures. Bacon's own philosophy was in some sort a system and much beholden to the encyclopedists, but it allowed for disorderly expansion and change. It could never
prevail until men were willing to give up their static
analogies and rational stage-plays. The spirit of man, undisciplined by fact, would forever construct perfect circles
in the heavens to satisfy its own passion for regularity.
Busy with their works of art, those late fantastics the philosophers could never bring themselves to add bit by bit
to an unfinished structure. Each thinker had twisted and
misinterpreted to make his preconceptions prevail; each
in his arrogance wished his foregone conclusions to account for all truth. Systematic philosophy in this purely
rational sense became, then, for Bacon vain philosophy,
because it transgressed the sober bounds of fact and use.

His admirers in the early part of the century, as distinguished from his disciples, missed much of this; but where-
ever their revolutionist spoke familiar language, they honored him for having so well expressed what they had often
thought. If they did not perfectly understand his *Novum
Organum* they liked his praise of learning; readers with
no intention of studying nature minutely agreed with his
gospel of utility; scholars learned in the humanities overlooked his slight to ethical philosophy and prized his summation against scholasticism. For all sorts of reforms, some
of which would have interested him little, they made him
a kind of spokesman, less by his inductive logic than by his
eloquence on the vanities of tradition.

Chapter II

SCIENCE FALSELY SO CALLED

Curiosity and Pseudo-Science

When penitent Adam owned in full confession (XII.279) that he had sought "Forbidden knowledge by forbidden means," he dyed his crime in the horrible black of witchcraft, and with some reason, Eve's traffic with Satan considered. Yet Milton nowhere actually preached against curiosity in this flamboyant shape. He mentioned black magic at least twice; like Donne and some others, when he wrote a studied definition of curiosity he remembered to include it. But we shall not reconstruct the *curiosus* as Milton or his generation ordinarily conceived him if we conjure up a Faust. Men literate enough to be printed had little to say of a body of *knowledge* prohibited by a sacred tabu or of learning to be bought from Satan, and what they actually wrote of these matters they confined largely to their tracts against astrologers and kindred prophets. It was such writing that usually condemned Nostradamus or Tritheim, teachers of Agrippa and Paracelsus. These four magi, easily the most glamorous, were all, significantly, figures in the past. Occult practitioners and weapon-salve doctors who continued the tradition of Paracelsus usually enjoyed the mere disdain of pedestrian scientists. Clad in Aristotelian virtue, Père Marin Mersenne aimed occasional shots in the dark toward Dr. Fludd, hinting at unlawful arts. In unrecorded folklore much naïve religious suspicion of strange and unusual knowledge doubtless persisted. Slanderous whispers of black art, or what Cudworth called the higher sorcery, followed pioneers in science and mathematics as they had followed Northumberland, the Wizard Earl, and his three magi, Harriot, Warner, and Hughes. Francis Osborn recalled, for whatever his memoir is worth, that when the Savilian chairs were endowed at Oxford in 1619 some of the gentry refused to send their sons there to be smutted with the black art. Such survivals of prejudice notwithstanding, it appears that by Milton's time sorcery, like heresy, had relaxed its ancient grip on learning. It seldom aspired higher than vulgar witchcraft and thus associated itself with ignorance and malice. In a compendious exposure of sorcery designed to frighten clients away from white witches, we may read of petty tricks by the dozen, but of no science.

The witchcraft that Perkins and James I described, though curiosity in the worst sense of the word, was an illicit activity, not a forbidden knowledge. Not even prophecy properly belonged to it. Whoever would pursue this unintellectual bypath will find an abundant literature to occupy him. In the courtroom it was fear that punished English witches, and punished them for their mischief, not for membership in the covens of a pagan nature-cult, or for Manichæan devil-worship, and least of all for their meager learning. Corporal punishment seems to have been meted out to wizards as to witches in almost inverse proportion to their wisdom. After working hard to be a necromancer, the learned Dr. Dee lived quietly in his old age, safe except for having earlier lost a library to the mob. Still earlier he had been briefly held in durance, as much for suspicion of treason as for witchcraft. Simon Reade and Simon Forman, possibly Jonson's Subtle, owed their arrests to medical quackery, William Lilly to political bias. Cromwell's Triers had so little sympathy with theosophy or "Familism" that they ejected Dr. John Pordage from a pulpit. The ignorant Dr. John Lambe indeed died at the hands of a mob, but not so much for the crime of being a devil as for being Buckingham's devil. Gossip seldom accused anybody of the old-fashioned compact that had once dignified the learned necromancer. The skepticism of Reginald Scot, who had demanded to meet just one witness to the signing of a visible paper, had so far infected the godly that even the simple witches legally convicted were seldom accused of anything more substantial than an implicit contract. Astrologers were only warned that their art might in time lead them to invoke Satan.

The naïveté in Marlowe's pact scene we dare not attribute to the playwright's simple faith, nor yet do we need to make a great point of the spectator's simple mind. The *curiosus* as Ascham and Donne knew him would have bored any theatre-going crowd. In a sober treatise, a pact-signing wizard would probably have amused Marlowe. But by casting the *curiosus* as such a wizard, by using an easy symbol fit for the stage, he could make his didactic point lively enough to satisfy scholars, politicians, preachers, and citizens. The fact that everybody conceded the possibility of impious knowledge makes it easier for us to fit *Doctor Faustus* into the Renaissance than into some counter-revolution against it. Let us think of the uneven morality play only as it dealt with a purely intellectual curiosity, the kind of speculation and irreligion that Ascham described when he preached to Italianate intellectuals. We find nothing of this in the wonder-working career of the magician after his astronomical conversation with Satan, and next to nothing after his signing of the pact. When new in bondage, Faustus casually asked a curious question or two—in astronomy, inevitably. But when Satan, who gave no magician an honest measure of the knowledge he sold, replied evasively with some devilish, un-Ptolemaic information, Faustus never protested the cheat. As sorcerer, he never thereafter showed an interest in knowledge, but settled easily, like any witch, for power. Who, then, was that victim of an insatiable thirst for knowledge whom Marlowe described in both the prologue and the epilogue of his play? It would appear that the *curiosus* whom he held up to gaze was the Faustus of the opening scene. There Marlowe made it so abundantly plain that, before the bargain, Satan had been at work in his victim's mind that the author might have forgiven his private friends for reading the pact scene symbolically and thus saving his own intellectual integrity. As redundant as a love potion to Wagner's already enamored Tristan was a diabolical contract to a student already resolved to "be a divine in show" and "live and die in Aristotle's works." Marlowe could detest such hypocrisy with his intellect as well as his imagination. As for the magical curiosity, "atheism" in any degree surely implied Sadducism in some degree. Men of no remarkable piety—Montaigne, Selden, Hobbes, Osborn, Wagstaffe—who flatly disbelieved all witchcraft and dared to say so in the face of a Bible full of texts invite us to think that Marlowe, however grossly or mildly heterodox, could not have believed his elaborately orthodox fiction.

Milton's private opinion of diabolical curiosity in his own day must remain largely a topic of conjecture. He did not, to say the least, ignore the Bible, though by rescinding the letter of Moses' law he left persecutors with as little scriptural excuse for hanging a witch (Ex. xxii:18) as a blasphemer. His materialism damaged the kind of spirit-world that the witchmongers needed. His mortalism was of a piece with that Sadducism which More and Glanvill used witch lore to disprove. The interpretation of the Sons of God story in Genesis vi:4 that gave witch-hunters their sacred evidence for the intercourse of devils with women seemed to him not the only possible interpretation. Yet the *Christian Doctrine,* overlooked by those who have studied Milton's opinion of witchcraft, briefly but seriously listed sorcery and, by unmistakable implication, judicial astrology as sins. In this passage Milton wrote evidence for his belief that some kind of devilish craft was possible. His purely artistic drafts upon witch lore and its demonology prove little—the suggestion of a sabat in *Comus,* the devilish tempests in *Lycidas* and *Paradise Regained,* the Lapland witches of Olaus Magnus in *Paradise Lost,* the knowledge and power of his fallen angels, the toad-familiar and other details of Eve's demonic dream. By the "witchery" that he tucked obscurely into a long list of feminine offenses, he probably meant nothing supernatural. If he had had no doubt whatever that Satan made extraordinary tools of some women, the Divorcer would surely have elaborated an argument that jurists had already advanced for stretching the canon law. It is not conclusive, but not irrelevant, that witch-hunters multiplied with the Presbyterian inquisition and often looked for witches among the religious sects that had Milton's sympathy. Quakers became peculiarly liable to suspicion. John

Gaule, an Independent supporter of Cromwell, by opposing ended the Witch-Finder General, Matthew Hopkins,
who had the backing of Edmund Calamy and the Presbyterians. We know Milton's political allegiance after the
middle forties; what we cannot dogmatically assert is that
witchcraft formed a real issue in the party strife between
Presbyterians and sectaries. Of Milton we can say with assurance that, because he wrote of a supernatural diabolic
art, he believed it to be, or to have been, theoretically possible; and further, that the matter interested him little.
The rest is guesswork, but because he dealt briefly and
perfunctorily the one time when he dealt directly with the
subject, we may guess with some confidence that he
doubted the prevalence and just possibly the existence of
sorcery in his own age.

Unless the occult sciences, considered as a body of learning, dabbled in prophecy, the devil took no unusual interest in them. The alchemists who abounded from the
time that Elizabeth encouraged them remained for the
unsympathetic satirists what they had been for Chaucer
and Ben Jonson—cozeners. They were not *ab essentia* wizards by anybody's estimate. Paracelsus happened to be remembered by nearly everybody except Paracelsians as a
witch, probably because in the first place he had gone
about selling prophecies and horoscopes; as a vulgar alchemist he was so far from condemnation that one of his
enemies supposed that he had used alchemy as the very
front of virtue to hide sinister magic. Humanism had a
quarrel with the alchemical multipliers over and above
its censure of their gulling, but it objected to their art as
too low, not too high. Patrick Scot wrestled to persuade
the "philosophers" that they should become philosophers,
transmute Raimond, Albertus Magnus, and Friar Bacon
into Solon, Pythagoras, Aristotle, and wherever the moralists racked supreme truth "with tenterhooks of curiosity,"
substitute sacred writ for the lot. In the alchemists he discovered a metaphor for man's depravity: the understanding, the sun of the soul, left its true objects for falsehood
and greed. The alchemists, of course, had a stock reply, that
the greedy artist would never succeed; Jonson had Subtle

explain the point to Mammon. Scot took for granted the
artists' greed and laziness as he taught them a philosophy
that refined in virtue, extracted benefit from injury, and
transmuted want into wealth by honest work. Adam in
blessedness, laboring in his garden, had no more. At one
moment it seemed to Scot that the "curious or metaphysical spirits" whom he addressed reached toward forbidden
fruit. At another, they seemed more like moles burrowing
in the earth. The date was too late for the argument.
Paracelsus had already taught "philosophy" to glory in
dirty hands and in its humble, safe abode with nature.
Robert Boyle and the rest of the alchemists in the Royal
Society had not fought free of a science based upon untenable moral analogies, but they knew as well as Bacon
the modest answer to Scot's plea for divinely exalted self-
knowledge.

The spiritual alchemy that Reuchlin had dignified as
worthy of the Cabala refined the heart. It could escape—
and redouble—the kind of criticism leveled against the
simple puffers. At the same time, by pretending to religious mysticism it invited another kind, mild enough on
the whole. By the seventeenth century cabalistic studies
encountered no important enmity unless misused for
prophecy. Hermes too remained a tower of more or less
legitimate loftiness when Milton commended him in *Il
Penseroso* as an escape from more pedestrian science; in
1614 Isaac Casaubon brought down to something like
accuracy the date of the Hermetic books, but left the
Divine Pymander still a repository of the best Egyptian
learning, published in the purest Christian age. In Rosicrucianism, if we may use a portmanteau word for the
vague mélange of theosophy and natural magic that apologists expected would reform the world in a twinkling,
scoffers found visionary folly more easily than impiety.
It would have been hard to find any of the latter in
Dr. Fludd's Rosicrucian *Tractatus Apologeticus*. Saturated
with sanctity, the new alchemy must disarm any critic not
himself desperately impious, it seemed to John Heydon.
Ben Jonson nevertheless wrote for common sense a pair
of masques ridiculing in turn the Hermetists and the Rosi-

crucians for their silliness, and John Hales joined in the railery. Samuel Butler, who denied in almost so many words that an art could be black, yet sneered at the Hermetist and the Rosicrucian for laboring the same point. In the opinion of sober divines, reformed occultists might be unnecessarily and unprofitably obscure, but unless their mysticism led to religious heterodoxy, like Pordage's, they committed no mortal crime.

The Ancients knew no adversaries so bitter as these Moderns. The occultists could cudgel the scholastic philosophers "unmercifully, without giving quarter," Butler observed as he added a buffet of his own for the schools and their Aristotle. Milton at Cambridge probably came under the influence of an eminent occultist in Joseph Mede, and when the poet fled from the scholastics his refuge, we know, was to be for a time not the new philosophy but the speculations of Hermetic Platonism. Besides Plato and Hermes he may have looked into Fludd and Boehme, though the evidence is not overwhelming. The third Book of *Paradise Lost* shows us that he read analogical scientists with attention. His Christian classicism everywhere declares that he took their indiscriminate antipaganism with a grain of salt. He could never have been temperamentally at ease with the men who pleased Everard and Pordage, but he would have approved as readily as Bacon or Hobbes some of their criticism of learning. If he indeed read Dr. Fludd, he found in the fourth section of *Philosophia Sacra,* in the second Book of the *Mosaicall Philosophy,* and often elsewhere St. Paul demolishing Aristotle and the rest of ethnic philosophy. The Rosicrucian wrote like Vives, Bacon, or any other reformer the section of his *Tractatus Apologeticus* that he called "De Scientiarum hodierno die in Scolis vigentium impedimentis." We may hear the occultist John Webster reforming schools in accents that have sounded to many like Bacon's. Not even Thomas Hobbes chafed oftener under the dead hand of the scholastics than did Thomas Vaughan the mystic, or lamented so plausibly "our salvation translated from the cross to the rack, and dismembered in the Inquisition-house of Aristotle."

Among the blows rained upon the Stagirite from the occultists' quarter we may consider for a moment a rhymed treatise probably in largest part attributable to John Pordage, though published as the work of his eldest son Samuel. Like Cornelius Agrippa or Bacon, Pordage too ran through the abuses in professions, arts, and sciences. Yet what had been poison to man in innocency, the fruit of earthly knowledge, had become a thing indifferent except where Satan still substituted poison. The formidable tree of death that Satan kept in hell yielded apples ordinary and extraordinary. The former bred linguists, sophisters, "mechanics," mathematicians. The latter—the choice of Jannes and Jambres, Simon Magus, and Faustus—conferred necromantic powers. Wise men sought, across the gulf in heaven, a banquet of knowledge that included divine magic. More men might have resorted to it except that Satan infected them with Aristotle's vain philosophy and taught them thereby to regard divine magic as diabolical. If the alchemists of their number "lay groveling" upon Aristotle, they could hope at best to work through Geber and his kind to vulgar alchemy. At worst, they might pick up Tritheim or Agrippa, invoke the devil, and achieve some success, but at a horrible price.

Orthodoxy turned Pordage's kind of fuzzy speculation into sin of deeper dye the moment it presumed to know the future. There lay the strictly forbidden knowledge. In the sermons of Elizabeth's time, when the drum of Doomsday sounded at least as often as in the decades following, the same preachers who warned their flocks that the end drew near might warn them also that no man dared to say how near. More or less legitimate biblical scholars, cabalists, and pretenders to revelation sometimes sinned, nevertheless, by calculating the date of the Judgment. Seventeenth-century preachers added their voices against the prophets, and even the new millenaries joined the chorus. These students of the Apocalypse had, ordinarily, no idea how many years beyond a thousand mankind would wait for the General Judgment, though a few of them, reproved by most, had strong opinions about when Christ would return. Scripture had not told them the day or the hour, of course; only the year. One scholarly millenarian pondered an orthodox objection to futurism: since most men were convinced that the end of the world was at hand, would not the millennial expectation, a thousand-year respite, breed confidence and sin? He thought not. And indeed the orthodox preterists could think of stronger objections. Many who had grown up with the medieval idea of a Millennium past or passing associated the futurist's innocent optimism with the outrages of the Anabaptists' Fifth Monarchism at Münster. They raised the voice of sobriety, therefore, not only against those who too mathematically prophesied the end of the world, but against those who expected only the Second Coming. Millenarian dreams were supposed to fill men with a "fierce, unnatural zeal" that caused them to look upon the rich and great as earmarked for destruction. To the Fifth Monarchist and to him alone, Butler sneered, all prophecies spoke. In his own manner Tom Fuller took a turn at predicting the Advent. It would come, he prophesied, in the precise year and day—in the very moment—when providence thought best "for God's glory and for thy good. Thou canst not wisely wish it to be any whit before that time, and I do confidently assure thee, it shall not be any whit after it." The aged satirist Joseph Hall was never wittier than when poking fun at the "changed saints." They all knew infallible ways to calculate the time until the Second Coming, but no two of them could get the same answer. Poor experience with prophets in all ages had placed the date of the Last Things high on the list of matters hid; and many who felt the nearness of the end knew the discredit that exact prophesies, failing, could bring upon religion.

Political wisdom also bade them keep the future dark. As early as the fourteenth century the old political prophecy as Geoffrey of Monmouth had written it became a tool for shaping opinion, later potent enough to call for repressive legislation. William Lilly, prophet and propagandist for Parliament and forthwith for Cromwell, studied Merlin as well as the stars, and filled the Presbyterians with apprehension. Times of change breed prophets, who may in turn promote turmoil; it behooves the party in power, which has everything to lose, to silence them. Shakespeare had perceived the threat in a Glendower divining of lion, dragon, and wolf. Even while protecting prophets who had befriended him, Cromwell learned the troublesome use that Vavasour Powell could make of the Apocalypse; and it is politically significant that a spate of prophecies preceded Venner's rising against the Restoration government. Lady Eleanor Davies, eccentric relict of Sir John, pursued her sybilline career in peace until she began to see trouble ahead for monarchy. On the very title page of his standard work against all forms of prophecy— rational, enthusiastic, cabalistic, astrological, and others "not worth naming"—Northampton gave as his motive for writing not the glory of God, but the safety of the throne. The Earl found (Ch. 5) "Curiosity of Deep Knowledge" at the root of all divination, and painted astrology as wickedly curious quite apart from witchcraft, which he treated in a separate section altogether.

By the time Jaggard reissued Northampton's much earlier *Defensative* in 1620 the stalls were filling with the regurgitated arguments of astrologers and their critics, and the storm thickened with the pestiferous increase in the number of figure-casters. One reason why there was a Society of Astrologers before there was a Royal Society in London was doubtless the coincidence of prophecy with political unrest, though some of the silly Eves who patronized the artists could have had no political motives. As one of their innumerable satirists wrote,

> Lilly's by these approv'd, and lik'd so well,
> To know their husbands they'll consult with hell.

Another reason would have been the growing popularity of natural studies, even among the misguided. Some of the encouragement that the radical, sectarian wing of Independency is supposed to have lent to science may be more exactly transferred to pseudo-science. The more studious astrologers like Ashmole and Booker, or like Robert Gell, who taught Henry More occultism at Cambridge, joined the spiritual alchemists in embracing a cabalistic, Hermetic, or Rosicrucian theosophy that counted as religious heresy in the Presbyterian inquisition. They accordingly made common cause with the Independents and prospered as Independency prospered. Their leader, William Lilly, recorded the political issue. In 1633, when he began to practice, astrologers in London were "very rare." Until 1646 he was abused on all sides by "many lewd Mercuries," by the Cavaliers and especially by the Presbyterians. Though he and Booker easily persuaded Fairfax that their art was godly, Lilly quarreled with powerful Presbyterians and conservative Assembly Independents, especially Gataker, Nye, and Dean Owen of Christchurch; and in 1651 he was imprisoned over the protests of Cromwell and Peters, for predicting the end of the tottering Presbyterian Parliament, whose fall soon insured the success of his whole fraternity.

The technical arguments from physics and common sense by which the godly rationalized their annoyance—the prophets' continual failures, the difficulty of horoscopy in multiple births, the inaccuracy of clocks—had been anticipated by Petrarch, Pico, and the whole Renaissance. For that matter, except for the added doubtfulness thrown upon the science by the new astronomy, most of the technical argument was as old as Cicero and the Fathers. The religious argument sometimes contrived heresies by the doctrinal interests of the moment. Predestinarians objected to adding stellar responsibility to their account of God's providence, for any sin that came from the stars seemed to be subtracted at once from God's gracious will and from man's answerable account. And in physics, government of the universe by means of the stars and planetary angels amounted to idolatrous denial of God's particular government. A Calvinist who doubtless knew the proper shifts to absolve God from authorship of sin refused to absolve the astrologers: whatever the stars foretold they caused. Whatever they caused, God caused. Therefore astrology made God the author of sin and exonerated man. The artists retorted that only presumptuous itching after Pelagian free will repined against the overmastering stars, and that to deny God's special government by stellar means could only give him a deistic or Epicurean holiday in perpetuity.

The critics needed desperately whatever homilies they could strain from religion, for the Bible explicitly declared that the stars in their courses fought against Sisera; and in the earlier decades of the century if any man was bold enough to say in so many words that the stars influenced no destines, either he was not bold enough to say so publicly or my reading is deficient. The astrologers' premise conceded, it still did not follow, of course, that any living man possessed enough true science to predict, by that influence, particular events. From a dozen passages we know that Milton accepted in some general fashion the power of the stars, but in one place he sneered at contemporary astrologers and in another damned their art with the best texts of scripture. He probably despised the figure-flingers for reasons not entirely doctrinal, for he wrote not a line betraying confidence in their accuracy. Satan's pretense to astrology in *Paradise Regained* (IV.382) stamped the art as devilish but nothing else. By the subterfuge Satan concealed the true source of his knowledge and hence his ill will; he could, by all good demonology, predict ill that he himself had devised—he needed no stars. Confidently the serious critics, and loudly the satirists, avouched that astrology had been invented by the devil, that eminent practitioners of the past had been magicians like Cornelius Agrippa, that magic (to which astrologers cheerfully admitted their art to belong) was never natural or white, for all Porta's distinctions. Its chief aim, prophecy, was intolerably curious, for the future belonged to God, and astrologers proved as much by their errors. The ancient maxim *Sapiens dominabitur astris* appeared in elaborate variations to overthrow the pretenders to accurate prognosticating. "Though the stars have great influence," William Bridge began with the damaging concession, "yet if a man shall undertake by the stars to foretell future events, which are accidental, depending upon the will and actions of men, he doth plainly step into the chair of God."

However erroneous, the art was allowed by all serious

controversialists to be a learned sorcery, the kind of craft that invited devils. They might, it was thought, intrude help even without the wizard's knowledge. The hostile critics were not foolish enough to contend that every almanac-maker had bound himself to Satan by deliberate contract, explicit or implicit. But on the other side of the argument, Robert Gell, himself an "artist" in holy orders, preached to the Society of Astrologers of their peril from that great Searcher who had tempted Adam with knowledge. The devil lay still in wait to seize the unwary astrologer and drag him outside the pale of his lawful art. On this theme King James I, probably borrowing, wrote lines popular enough to be sometimes filched in their turn. He explained how the study of astrology could lure weak Christians onward, so that mounting from rung to rung the slippery ladder of curiosity they might come to a point where lawful arts would fail to satisfy. Whoever should reach that point and invoke Satan would find himself cheated like Adam, his knowledge "nothing increased." A convert who wrote of himself in Bunyan's confessional style as a brand snatched from the burning (he parroted some of the King's good phrases) left a particularly sensational memoir of his early diabolical ways, yet kept it plausible by mentioning no contract and no conversation of any kind with Satan unless we count some merely wicked thoughts.

To the scientific and religious objections raised against the astrologers' curiosity it was possible, not popular, to add a third kind, this time from humanity. Theirs was, in its way, a natural science. Groping for every available argument, critics sometimes used against the prophets a language that nobody would as yet have been willing to use against an inoffensive science. Milton turned from his own sermon against astrology to exonerate legitimate astronomy in a passage that might make a profitable note to the eighth Book of *Paradise Lost*. The very astrology-baiters punctiliously cleared astronomy, though preachers deprecated their own curiosity if, to the glory of God, they happened to mention Tycho's measurement of interstellar space. The Socratic formula that set star-knowledge in op-

position to self-knowledge lay so pat to the hand of every
critic of astrology that one may wonder why few of them
used it. The few who did so were obliged to decide whether
astrology was too high for man because it was astronomy,
or too low because it was a study of nature. One of them
might argue that God had put the stars far from Adam,
the gardener, because he would have us let them alone
and work; another, that it was shameful for man to place
his affection on a mere art. John Gaule, who, though not
himself a perfect Sadducee, protected helpless old women
from the witch-hunting ferocity of Matthew Hopkins, left
from his younger days some undistinguished humanism—
meditations on Adam's curiosity and our own, the impedi-
ment in our path to blessed self-knowledge. He put his
doctrine to work with a vengeance when he attacked astrologers on rationally humanistic grounds in a work that
he dedicated to Cromwell in 1652. His words could have
damned any experimental science; astrology only happened to be the earlier nuisance. Gaule could see no merit
in "supervacaneous" investigations of nature. Astrologers
boasted their highest learning in the meanest matters,
sought only to know for the sake of knowing, neglected
"life, state, calling, manners," and either elevated nature
as a deity or tortured her as a servile slave. Gaule's was
the language of the Ancients, but it was not to be heard
in full chorus against legitimate science until foes as disparate as Henry Stubbe and Richard Graham, Viscount
Preston, should rise against the Royal Society.

To their critics, the artists often replied with the kind
of religious humility that Bacon taught, or the astronomers
before him. Knowledge was incurious that consisted with
revealed truth, charity, positive fact, and use. A few wizards admittedly diabolical could not taint the whole art
of astrology, and nobody admitted knowing any wizards
personally. Like Apuleius (*Apology*) and Naudé, Ashmole
exculpated his profession by listing the great men of the
past accused of black magic. The artists admitted that it
would be bold to give the stars undue influence, so as to
limit God or restrict man's free will in worldly affairs, and
denied that they did so. Their art, like any good learning,

was Hagar, the very handmaid of divinity. Astrology had
its practical uses, too; indeed, it was but applied astronomy. And knowledge of the future could not be curious
if it charitably helped an unfortunate to fortify himself
against calamity. The elder Heydon antedated at any rate
Bacon's scientific work when he so segregated the natural
and the supernatural that scriptural texts against curiosity
would not apply to natural science. By another of Bacon's
rules he taught religion to commend the study of nature
as a form of worship that skirted presumptuous dabbling
in religious mysteries. Natural study boasted a peculiar
virtue in that there could be no excess of it, as Elias
Ashmole proved by the scientists' application of Adam's
story: our grand parent before the Fall was "so absolute a
philosopher" that he could instantly know the nature of
every creature and name it appropriately. By Ashmole's
exegesis therefore, and Bacon's, Adam transgressed not in
natural but in moral philosophy, "proud inquiry into the
knowledge of good and evil," and proud reliance upon
his own free will. Ashmole wrote late enough to fill his
margins with references to Bacon, on whose great authority he threw out scholasticism and correctly substituted
natural magic.

   The ill success of critics in dropping Sir Thomas Browne
into a neat category warns us that before we pontifically
set him beside Ashmole, our celerity should be contem-
pered with cunctation. One of his readers, who makes more
of his Hermetic occultism than do some others, seems convinced of his rational infidelity—thus making him a kind
of mystical Deist. One would extend his mystical science
almost to religious ecstasy; another finds his occultism restricted by experiment; a third wonders how his humor
(even this has been denied) could abide with mysticism.
Some perceive his patient study of fact and, embracing one
leg of the elephant, declare him a true scientist, in experiment rivaling the best. His obedience to Bacon's behest
in writing *Vulgar Errors* and his debt to the Idols for its
skepticism have been repeatedly affirmed and as often denied. The affirmative has the latest word. Here a student
would have him earnest in nature-study and rhetorically

perfunctory in religion; there, some have perhaps thought his *Hydrotaphia* nobly rhetorical in humanity, as most have found his *Garden of Cyrus* poetically vagabond in nature. Still others prefer to set him scientifically among the dabbling virtuosi, with his science limited by his lyrical gift or by his occultism, drawn to medicine by its burden of pseudo-science and its humane charity. Thus the critics have wrangled about what to call a country doctor who, while gathering facts, often contemplated the divinity immanent in nature. New studies of his pantheistic leanings have portrayed an experimenter devoted not to induction but to symbols to be deciphered in God's public manuscript. These inquiries have at least done justice to the intuitive bent of a mind that kindled at the occultists' promise of some great theosophic revelation.

Intellectual humility is our theme, not Browne's philosophy, but we shall hardly find either intelligible in his writings if we reckon by his modicum of Bacon's lore. If we start with Browne the scientist, we quickly run afoul of extraneous or contradictory characters—Browne the pseudo-scientist, the "Platonic" theosophist, the paradoxical wit, the curious exegete, the metaphysical poet in prose. If we start with Browne the pseudo-scientist, the amateur of Hermetic philosophy, the Platonic sort of naturalist, the friend of William Lilly and young Dee, his other characters become credible, some of them even predictable. In all his characters he turned away from system, and from neat, orderly coherence. He hunted correspondences, but he hunted the anomalous as well, and relished the incongruous with no inner compulsion to hammer all into grey and level theory. The occult philosophies limited his science, in our sense of that word, but suited his brand of piety and learning. Those studies, too, he curbed safely short of arrogance, and like Donne admired more mysticism than he practiced. There is no harm in calling the humorist a mystic if one means only that he apprehended God without help from forensic divinity, that he set his face against the vain philosophy of the schools and the hard theology of the embattled preachers. He professed no contemplative ecstasy. His unambitious writing in religion served him chiefly to sustain a mood of piety while he remonstrated gently with the presumptions of doctoral ignorance.

As a gatherer of facts he shared Bacon's and Thomas Vaughan's contempt for tradition that perpetuated mere ignorance and for a simplicity that swallowed tradition when the truth was easier to "go see." But it was not Browne's way to blast Aristotelians with the frenzy of Paracelsus or dismiss tradition with Bacon's scorn. He conceded it nothing in mathematics, much in ethics, law, and history. In science, authority had weight if reason supported it, and so he appealed to it repeatedly in *Vulgar Errors* when tradition served his turn. The contemporary reader who thought that Browne took Montaigne for a model probably meant that he exploited himself, and not that the doctor wrote more than a dash of Pyrrhonism. *Hoc scio quod nihil scio*, Browne supposed like most men, was never intended to be anything but legitimate hyperbole. Valid knowledge from well grounded reason and especially from sense-experience he took for granted. Satan used Pyrrhonism as one means to sow the world with vulgar errors, but in spreading the falsehood he had not exposed a race destitute of the power, by education, "to repair our primary ruins." Somewhere a forbidden knowledge lay "within command of the flaming swords," but the vulgar many came nowhere near the appointed limits. The laggards delighted more in a vain philosophy that the Preacher had found a weariness to the flesh—not all tradition, but its accumulated rubbish. Bacon would have agreed that two of Germany's three great inventions had their incommodities, and that a general synod to reduce learning to a few solid authors could grieve nobody except typographers. Fulke Greville had entertained some scheme of reducing and standardizing authorities. Progressives and conservatives alike said something of the sort; Browne was safe to call it no "melancholy utinam" of his own, if only the paradox-loving doctor could have left the subject without adding a touch of Cornelius Agrippa. In a world that had too many books already, he would not, given the missing pages of Solomon and Cicero, weep over the ashes

of the Alexandrian library or even the Vatican. The rhetorical flourish set Sir Kenelm Digby off on the glories of
learning. Alexander Ross grew violent. The Calvinistic
schoolmaster, learned in the older fashion and guarding
it like a watchdog, was adjudged the arch-obscurantist by
Wilkins and Osborn; yet he saw Browne as the enemy and
himself as the champion of learning when he put the doctor on one of his title pages in the illustrious company of
Bacon and Comenius. It was the correct attitude for scholastic orthodoxy to take, and Ross counted the physician
as one of the near-Popish heretics. Among his other errors
listed by the score, the doctor would turn the undoubted
virtue of a modest ignorance into the foolish proposition
of Popery: ignorance is the mother of devotion.

To Browne, as to Bacon and Ashmole, it seemed that
true natural science could find no way to sin. The "noble
eluctation of truth" going on about him—indebted to
Paracelsus, to Helmont, and to Aristotle as well—broke no
rule of sobriety, for "philosophy" knew no *sanctum sanctorum*. But the Paracelsian philosophy of micro- and mac-
rocosmic correspondences that he clung to in spite of the
"severe schools" encouraged him to include within his
own physical science a form of dubious speculation—final
causes, and guessing at God's purposes. For one who liked
to flee to St. Paul's "sanctuary," an *O altitudo!*, he showed
a questionable eagerness to explain why God had the sun
move as it does or the chameleon feed on air. He declared
searching for the ends of providence to be the diviner
point of "philosophy," questionable only where the inquiry implied discontent. Perhaps it was the white magic
of Porta's *Phytognomy* that encouraged him to value the
final causes of natural things and seek cryptograms in nature, outward signs of plants, for example, by which the
adept might know their inward forms and their reasons
for being. In the *Garden of Cyrus* he showed his affection
for a disappearing rational universe in which, by analogies
pregnant with important meaning, the natural world of
"nobler" and "baser" existed to serve man by answering to
his value-judgments. But with a newer scientific modesty
he put away the medieval notion that nature existed pri-

marily to teach man facile lessons in morality and divinity. The Physiologus in its late survivals he patronized as misguided piety; that is, the practice of using natural facts for divinity lessons. In 1637 Samuel Ward, the father of Seth, wrote *Magnetis Reductorium Theologicum Tropologicum,* and thought it worthy of reissue in English (1640) as *The Wonders of the Load-Stone.* Probably thinking of Ward's moralizing, Browne yielded that "honest minds" might draw "precarious inferences" from the lodestone—"moral, mystical, theological"—and "entreating a courteous assent," glorify God thereby; yet he added that "they do most powerfully magnify him" who, by experiments, "demonstratively set forth its magnalities."

Perhaps the bare demonstration of magnetic facts best glorified God, but more was needed to produce a dynamo; and there Browne's genius took a turn possibly too modest. His failure to coordinate the facts he had gathered has been often noticed and variously explained, but whatever the explanation, the fact is patent that he did not keep his mind long on a problem before his fancy, or wit, or poetry took hold of his pen and changed the subject. To an inquiry both constructive and at the same time methodical no topic confined him, not even the final causes that, by his theory, he might have been pursuing. His *Garden of Cyrus* illustrated his vagaries. It showed enough traces of Hermetism or cabalism to warrant some kind of consistent speculation in the manner of Dr. Fludd, or perhaps an excursus in the number mysticism that attracted him. For no reason that plainly appears except the pleasure of it, he worked at random, canvassing nature, counting fives. He exhorted others to carry on the work by counting fours. The search for fives was not the whole of the *Garden,* perhaps not even an important part, but it was the only trace of a thread running through it and Browne's ostensible excuse for writing it. Such "ocular observations" afforded delight. They afforded, moreover, the "surest way to trace the labyrinth of truth." Outside the grand passages of his poetry Browne liked to think small. He had no ambition to be a Boyle or a Newton; he made it his business to "match and parallel" the more obvious pieces of nature.

With perfidy to Bacon's principles he echoed, in passages that have been sometimes misread, the old Socratic commonplace. He left to others the "more general pieces of wonder" like the tides and the Nile. His humble speculations had "another method," the study of himself. As a physician he had a right to call his science self-knowledge, but a more militant and ambitious naturalist would have chosen other language. For Browne all science was humble, but for his own part in it he was content, in science as in heaven, to bring up the rear.

If he could carry himself thus circumspectly in nature, where zeal itself invited him to feel secure, it seems gratuitous to suspect him of doubts about God's existence or the essential truth of scripture. Contemporaries may have been right in scenting a serious heresy in his kind of natural magic, though not one that many of them would have understood. "You see," said Ross, on catching him up for having mentioned his early mortalism, "what a bad schoolmaster the philosophers' stone is." He was indiscreet, no doubt, being a physician and *ipso facto* half an atheist in esteem, to write of religion with a jest on his lips; but the fanatics could hang him for no one of his timid conclusions in dogma. Digby tried. Ross tried even harder. The Protestant heresy-finder, criticizing *Religio Medici* and Digby's criticism of it, dealt far more gently with the Catholic than he could see fit to do with a Pope-loving alchemist and astrologer, obedient to traditions that the church had added to scripture, charitable to heretics and heresy. But guilty of no atheism in any sense of the word. On that score Ross made the best kind of witness to a truth that another Anglican physician and pacifist wrote of his colleague: "*Religio Medici,* though the world atheism call, The world shows none." Its author seems, of all the world, the man most likely to take seriously nature's "Dehortation from Immoderate Curiosity in Divine Mysteries," as still another doctor called it. Like other physicians annoyed by the standard slur on their religion, Browne pointed out that a student constantly baffled by the mysteries of nature had no difficulty believing more than he could explain in matters above nature. His delight in

pointing out small puzzles in divinity furnished, in his
day, an accepted means for devotion to honor mysteries.
The age liked paradoxes; it never doubted that God's
word contained much that appeared illogical; it derived
pleasure as well as instruction from whole collections of
"orthodox paradoxes." Ralph Venning's quickly went
through five editions. Browne wasted his time, then, if he
meant to teach doubt by finding the eternal generation of
the Son incomprehensible or by mentioning the notorious
fact that God planted two trees in Eden before there were
any trees. If he had infidelity to insinuate, he compromised
himself to no purpose by confessing three youthful heresies, two of small consequence. The third, mortalism,
which tended to abolish spirit and spirits, he explicitly
attacked in a later work. Mortalism ill suited one as confident as he of witches and prophecy. Surely atheism,
like ecstatic mysticism, exceeded his ambition, for atheism
should begin in Sadducism, abolishing spirits. It was damaging enough, and took courage, for him to own the superstition in his makeup, but superstition had at least the
merit of being the reverse of atheism. His submission to
the fundamental articles of faith, doubtless as ingenuous
as Robert Boyle's, would probably have been questioned
by nobody if it had only been as dull. But his very humor
would have kept him from amending the wisdom of Christian antiquity. If the holy story was inconsistent and paradoxical, that was the way he wanted it.

Out of his humor grew his measure of charity, though
it was hardly enough to qualify him as a great pacificator.
He had no ambitious plans of any kind, and hence none
for compromise, resolution, or accommodation in religious
disputes. He could suggest only the peaceable spirit that
he had been born with. A sense of humor might have
taught the church better than to persecute a bishop who
believed there were Antipodes, and the bishop better than
to risk arguing the nugatory point. The doctor found his
own way to religious truth not by divinity, but by experience. As a peacemaker he left Hooker and the moderates
Falkland, Hales, and Chillingworth to their elucidations
and took, as one has written, the "nearer way—the way of

the poet rather than the philosopher." In poetic theology he could take with him his Hermetic dreams. He owned that his was the way of the "Platonist" rather than the Aristotelian, that he loved "an allegorical description of Hermes" better than a metaphysical definition and *lux est umbra Dei* better than *actus perspicui.* "Where there is obscurity too deep for reason, 'tis better to sit down with a description, periphrasis, or adumbration." Undoubtedly the poet was prior to the occultist, and Browne went in the first place to the school of Hermes for reasons that kept Bacon away. Yet his reading in the Hermetists would have confirmed him in his aversion to the bold divinity that took away the loveliness of mysteries. He preferred to contemplate an inexplicable reality, and it is easy to think that he joyed in his religion whenever it gave the lie to the severe schools. His tolerant quietism, his mixed Platonisms, and his respect for experimental fact supplied him with every honest motive to believe the impossible because impossible. It cost him little to hear Tertullian's *certum est* without a reservation. It would have cost him dear to cudgel his reason and produce any kind of *Summa* or his biblical scholarship and turn out a *Christian Doctrine.* These were no tasks to set a man who sorrowed that there were no more mysteries for him to believe.

CURIOSITY AND THE EDUCATORS

In the occultists' holy and pansophic dream for education Milton declined to participate with Comenius. Writing ostensibly for the Comenian Hartlib, he drew the rules of conduct for this world almost defiantly from the pagans, whence came indirectly his ideal of humility. With these he mixed the vocational training insisted upon by the more mechanic successors of Elyot, taught his pupils (one of them remembered details) substantially as he theorized for Hartlib, and in so doing further educated himself. Our record turns, then, toward *Of Education*, but first to the latter-day humanism of popular didactics, for it was this writing that the tractate resembled, imperfectly but distinctly.

As Peacham's fellows began to water learning thinner than Elyot and Ascham, much thinner too than Milton, the guidebooks for public service—essays, meditations, courtesy books here lumped without strict regard for merely literary distinctions—taught with continued zeal the Christian righteousness of knowing for the sake of doing. A little chastened, but still confident, the educators carried to the nobility and gentry—more and more often the latter—an eternal fight against the lazy doctrine of genteel ignorance. In this war downright illiteracy had no friends unless they were some who hid behind the argument that a gentleman should be but *mediocriter doctus*. But a new skepticism sometimes treated the venerable cult of learning with some irreverence. For instance, the educators often shuddered that Louis XI, as Guicciardini quoted him, had wished that his heir apparent might know no more Latin than *qui nescit dissimulare, nescit regnare*. The learned Sir Thomas Browne, in one of his skeptical moods, could not forbear a jibe at the pedagogues. He would have chosen a better sentence, he thought, but otherwise he could see nothing wrong with the king's principle. Among the essayists we may read a few who feared pedantry as much as did Dudley, Lord North; and here we might recall Miles Sandys' reluctance to teach women anything beyond rudiments, because "learning in woman is like a sun dial in a grave." The arguments for ignorance that Lando had advanced were kept before the public if only by educators who answered them, or arguments like them. The debate held a kind of rhetorical fascination. Bacon set down in *De Augmentis* a series of "Antitheses," or topics that might be developed according to his pro and contra headings. One embracing "Atheism" and "Superstition" grew into a familiar pair of his *Essays*. Similarly, he outlined a pair on ignorance and learning but never wrote them, thus depriving us of a Baconian defense of ignorance. On behalf of both topics, John Cleland published parallel columns of opposed argument. He went on to endorse learning. Not so Owen Felltham, whose "Of Curiosity in Knowledge" raised the question whether the progress of learning had done more harm or good and inclined to the former view. His motive is not clear, for the stripling's solemn pronouncements on reason and learning in other essays would clear him of anti-intellectualism. Something of the sort can be said for other courtesy writers and essayists. Faith in learning remained unshaken, but not the old faith in bookishness. Sometimes a lover of paradox overstated his disillusionment in a tribute to ignorance.

Lord North suffered too constantly and garrulously from melancholy to be taken at his word when he held Montaigne responsible for his neurosis. It seems that reading the *Essays,* with their moral mortification and their crying down of delights and presumptions, had "nipt" him in his "first spring." More confidently we can give the Frenchman some credit for his lordship's zeal against pedantry, for from that source Cornwallys and other English essayists inherited the prejudice. Lord North more bitterly than most of the educators lashed at curiosity while he taught young men to use women and books with discretion. He once phrased a precise definition of the sin to include synonyms usually applied only to the decorative arts: "sedulous consideration; ostentation; daintiness." They expressed Lord North's idea of curiosity in learning. Often in this critical vein the essay caught a strain of Montaigne or of Bacon; sometimes from its kindred art form, the devout meditation, it took a measure of Bernard's humility. The piety sometimes appeared in oddly mundane context; the Baconianism, such as it was, missed Bacon's organon and emerged as vocational practicality; the Pyrrhonism flowed quickly into humanistic dogma. All strains concurred to give the courtesy writing of the seventeenth century a tone of skeptical caution and to limit enthusiasm—to inspire at least as much gloom as might become a serious stock-taking. Henry Peacham kept discouragement out of his *Compleat Gentleman;* the gentry need inspiration, not arguments to excuse indolence. But in other writing Peacham could take his text from Ecclesiastes and soberly grieve that the presses poured out unreadable quantities of unprofitable books, so that a man might wisely inquire whether printing had been for the best.

Virtually all the educators must be accounted inheritors of the humanistic tradition. Though they hedged their creed with mingled skepticisms, they still believed that virtue could be taught, and that reason, rightly cultivated, learned to abhor vice. They continued to affirm the dignity of man and of self-knowledge. "Whither can knowledge bend her force more excellently then, than for man to look upon man?" demanded Cornwallys. "This knowledge is beautiful; other, this omitted, is curiosity." Their faith embraced the political wisdom of broad culture and the beauty of well bred holiness. Presently we shall extract from all this literature a miscellany of truisms that few or none contradicted. In the meantime, we should not omit to hear from two educators who cannot be numbered among the humanists—one, an eccentric of more interest than importance, David Person; the other, a significant rebel, Francis Osborn.

The Scotch schoolmaster Person took on several characters in his *Varieties* as he "incited" his reader to study metaphysics, alchemy, and what not. But as he assembled his hodgepodge of often sensational information, he regarded himself most frequently as a spokesman on behalf of the traditional natural science, and thus he measured curiosity by something like Bacon's rule, not that he had it from Bacon. The master vice, curiosity, could never be eradicated from man's depraved nature, he argued; it could be only controlled. And the study of nature afforded its safest and pleasantest outlet. A reverent investigator of matters obvious to the senses could not break the old law *Non altum sapere* as the student of "contemplative" mysteries easily could do. The "clergy and gown men" who daily upset the world figured as the eminent and last sinners in the section that Person called "Of Curiosities." He listed abundantly their contemplative questions that "wonderfully distracted the peace of the church"—all of them scholastic or Popish. But Person as a natural historian was the kind of conservative who demanded a stable earth, a single world, and elemental fire as fiercely as Du Bartas; and when a question threatened the *status quo* in science, it too became in his eyes "contemplative" and therefore curious. Here he collected more illustrations hallowed by convention: the reasons for compass deviation from true north, the sources of the Nile, the effect of climate on races, the origin of volcanoes, the size and distance of the stars, and the habitability of planets. His professed respect for natural studies hardly extended to astrology, for all his alchemy, and it scanted astronomy. God played games with the overweening astronomers, he parroted; the Almighty altered the orderly course of the heavens from time to time in order to baffle them. Person often spoke the same language as that other Scotch schoolmaster, Alexander Ross, who said and proved that he liked to walk in the old ways with Aristotle, "hitherto the wholesome food of our universities." The darts that Ross cast at heretics in religion and at Moderns in learning like Comenius, Carpenter, Lansberg, Harvey, Bacon, Browne, Digby, Hobbes— Milton did not escape a reference to the Divorcers—he aimed against innovation, the only single curiosity of which he could find these miscellaneous thinkers alike guilty.

A list of the philosophers whom Francis Osborn championed reads like a list of Ross's victims. In the chronicler Osborn, the literature of conduct found one militantly bourgeois voice of progress. His troubles with the clergy had helped to make him the friend of every man who had bearded the parsons to "embellish this doting age with new notions"—Ralegh, "the first" to "sail aloof from the beaten track of the schools"; Bacon, whom Osborn praised for trivial reasons and understood imperfectly in his positive teaching; Digby, for whom Bacon would have had little use; Hakewill, Selden, Chillingworth, Browne, and Hobbes, together with a dozen others acquainted with intellectual reform in one shape or another. Alexander Ross he abominated as the chief blasphemer against knowledge. To Cornelius Agrippa, whom he had once admired, he showed hardly more kindness: Osborn could see no virtue in the sport of celebrating ignorance for pastime. He valued his own dogma of modernity before any formal skepticism, and therefore sounded more like Hobbes than like Glanvill as he concentrated fire on an implicit faith in antiquity that had blinded man to a world of truth lying beyond "that rotten bar." Some vain philosophy rose out of folly and much out of knavery. Only fools would study astronomy from General Joshua, who could have been no authority, or honestly fear witchcraft. But King James had been no fool, merely an adept in Machiavellian policy. Thus many a lie that tradition perpetuated had been, like witchcraft, invented to cover a cheat or to conceal ignorance. Pundits had stuffed learning with so much meaningless cant that most books suited a dunghill better than they graced a pompous library. When Peacham wrote his ruminations on the making of many books, he thought of the new ones; Osborn thought of the old. Pedagogically, his directions sounded of positivism and utility. Useless and curious knowledge could be measured by its distance from mathematics, the Queen of Truth. A son of the middle class should master a craft, study the real arts and manufactures, and specialize. There was to be no longer an assured place for the Renaissance gentleman, the *uomo di virtú*. Osborn complained that such a universal dabbler served only to cause trouble in the world.

His own doctrines seldom rested upon evidence mathematical in its certainty. He loved conjecture, particularly in theology, and most particularly in points certain to annoy the predestinarian clergy. Being a notable heretic, he naturally favored toleration. Religious persecutors who, in the height of their presumption, "put the forgiveness of God under a bushel" deserved the title of Antichrist more richly than the Pope. They would limit the Kingdom of Christ, the universal church, to one creed, whereas the ratio of head to heel set up in Eden argued a more merciful God. Most of Osborn's speculations we must pass by with Samuel Johnson's observation that small boys might have stoned him for his impertinence; but one of them, in "A Contemplation of Adam's Fall," touches us nearly. Adam, he argued almost *contra mundum*, could have had no more actual knowledge than a child—hence his curiosity, his only weakness. The animal-naming proved nothing, for Adam could have named animals by whim in a state of ignorance. Osborn overlooked, of course, as

no learned divine could have done, the fact that Adam's
reputation as the complete philosopher rested not so much
upon Genesis or upon rabbinical commentary as upon Ec-
clesiasticus xvii:3–11. He joined, at all events, with the
orthodox to clear God of having issued a trivial command:
its violation involved curiosity, the only sin possible to
Adam. God checked him in his weak point; another command, like "Thou shalt not kill," would have implied a
depravity in the will. And what was weakness in Adam had
descended, redoubled, to his sons: "Since no heart is empty
of the humor of curiosity, the beggar being as attentive in
his station to an improvement of knowledge as the prince,
it is not unlikely to have been the primary and centrical
sin."

Without turning over the heap of remaining essays and
courtesy books author by author, peering at their Senecan
antitheses built of notebook sweepings refurbished and re-
assembled, let us construct out of the lot a composite set
of rules bounding good learning. As a matter of course,
the educators made their submission to religion, and in so
doing often turned the arts into faithful handmaidens of
learning's prudent queen, Divinity. Conservatively understood, the maxim *philosophia ancilla theologiæ* meant that
the rules of any art or science had to agree with the principles of the formal theology taught in the schools, the
noblest reason for studies, and in a real sense the ruler and
censor of all. We can think of educators who accepted the
medieval saw with reservations, but we here contemplate
a norm. The piety that consisted with courtesy walked the
via media always in doctrine and usually in discipline,
eschewing extremes like atheism and superstition, or like
extravagances of Papists and Anabaptists. Since the Separatist John Robinson kept narrow sectarianism out of his
excellent essays, the Puritanical Clement Ellis stood about
alone as an exception. He admonished the genteel sinner
to be a son of the church only so far as he saw "her willing
to continue his Saviour's spouse." Ordinarily, a gentleman would scruple to read controversial theology, and
would never study controversies for ornament. Curricu-
lum-builders who retained logic out of Aristotle dropped

the commentators and the scholastic method of objecting against truth.

Grammar, the disciples of humanism chorused, was a means, not an end. Its extreme and foolish cavils could "break a wit in pieces." Cornwallys despised rhetoric, but permitted a gentleman to know at least how to join nominatives to verbs grammatically. If the educators feared pedantic excess in literary studies, they trod yet more gingerly when they approached the natural sciences. Astrology they utterly condemned; impious in all men, it could teach a prince only superstition and cowardice. For the sake of fortification, architecture, and navigation they prescribed some mathematics and a little astronomy short of figure-casting, though Cornwallys wanted less astronomy than would make one calendar. Brathwaite permitted the gentleman enough science to exclude ignorance. The doctor would need somewhat more and likewise the minister, who would use it for sermon-illustrations. Only so far as it served a vocation could science be safely reckoned among the means to self-knowledge.

Deference to that ideal and to Socrates, who first turned philosophy from heaven to self, had become cliché in the literature of courtesy in Italy before translators brought it to England. It remained canonical so long thereafter that it was 1672 before an aristocratic courtesy book, full of the gloomier skepticism, besought young gentlemen to shun logic, rhetoric, and all contentious learning to pursue experimental philosophy, by interesting definition the "Spagurical and Cartetian." While the Merry Monarch was yet a lad he was admonished in all sobriety to keep a commonplace book, buy no impropriations, and to study nature with diffidence and a moral motive. The prince would never know God except by knowing himself, or himself except by his own corruptions: "The height of all philosophy, both natural and moral, is to know thyself, and the end of this knowledge is to know God."

The ancient debate between action and contemplation (study, not ecstasy) became as stylized in the literature of conduct as that between ignorance and learning, and a given writer's decision about as predictable. Contemplation in this writing exalted knowing for the sake of knowing, whereas the educators accounted nothing of "all this book learning that cannot be put to use." For Socrates and Plato, Boethius and Augustine, the contemplative life transcended all goods as the privilege of those destined to glimpse truth; the elect mystics and monastics of later centuries esteemed Rachel the fair, or devout contemplation, higher in God's favor than Leah the fruitful. If we credit Leah's rise to dominance wholly to the Protestant Reformation or to the new science, we leave out of account a branch of humanism older than either, the influential literature of courtesy. Castiglione did not write to train scholarly recluses. As humanism restored the earthy, classical sense of the word contemplation, the active life gained favor among educators like Guazzo, who argued it to be so far preferable to the contemplative life as society (with its rules of courtesy) surpassed solitude. The very titles of English courtesy books reveal how often in the seventeenth century action and contemplation meant no more than public and private life, and what educator trained men for the delights of country solitude? Beside the mundane sense of the word contemplation the older religious sense persisted and colored the former. Thus both suffered by association with mystics and monastics, as Little Gidding suffered abuse that had been heaped upon monkish idleness. Hall wrote into his character of "The Slothful" the usual prejudices: "He is a religious man, and wears the time in his cloister; and as the cloak of his doing nothing, pleads contemplation." Sportively, Milton permitted an odor of the cloister to hang about his Penseroso, but in good earnest neither he nor his contemporaries found the odor agreeable.

> Monastic walks and circumscriptive walls
> Are fit for plodding wits—

so a satirist began to sing of action, the doer alone being the truly learned man and the fit teacher.

In the mid-region of humanity the dichotomy set the blameworthy extremes of character. Hamlets and Othellos (or Hotspurs) sinned equally against the mean—"As contemplation altogether without action is idleness, so constant action without contemplation is bestial." Milton once substituted Belial and Moloch, and elaborated. The educators made it their business to eliminate both extremes, but excess of contemplation, apparently the graver danger, brought with it doctoral ignorance, mere scholarship, and vain affectation. "Although learning have a private and pleasing end in itself," all of them warned in some fashion, "yet it is but a serving quality, preparing the mind to a nobler end of well doing." King James wrote the doctrine throughout *Basilikon Doron* as he grounded his heir in the rudiments of kingcraft. In this heartfelt conviction the humanistic educators joined Bacon in a common definition of curiosity. "Barren, fruitless, and liveless is that knowledge which is not reduced to action," they preached with one voice against knowledge for its own sake. It endangered the immortal soul. The Earl of Manchester opened a treatise of holy living and dying with the three kinds of life known to philosophy—*activa, contemplativa,* and the contemptible and negligible third, *voluptuaria.* What more perilous in contemplation than curiosity, "the itch of man's soul"? What better witness against curiosity than Bernard? Once again, then, we hear the great contemplative speaking through alien lips, warning men to pursue a life of action and safety.

A single essay of Daniel Tuvil's, "Of Learning and Knowledge," neatly bound together these kinds of half skeptical humanism. The author happened to borrow for this essay generously from Montaigne, as he elsewhere lifted bits from Bacon. But the respectable conclusion of his discourse of action and contemplation he took without credit from the sterling humanism of Sidney's *Arcadia:* "What is contemplation but a glorious title invented only to set a gloss upon a base and idle disposition? In action a man doth better himself and benefit others." From defenses around this practicality he trained his guns upon the same trio of vanities that Montaigne and Bacon had made their targets. As impartially as either, he scotched vanity in the three competing disciplines—nature, dialectics, and literature. "Artists" labored to "discern the motions of the heavens before they learned to compose their own," and Aristotelians disputed "whether privation be a principle," and scholars could "stuff whole volumes quoting divers lections of depraved manuscripts." He left one important hiatus—he overlooked the religious warrant for action. That would make curiosity a sin. It would allow his three forms of it to cohere under one genus. For a new edition, as recent study has shown, he turned his essays into literary "resolves" by adding to each a note of pious determination. The resolution that he added to this one supplied the missing note of religion, and the resolution that seemed to Tuvil appropriate after his plea for worldly action came not from Bacon but from St. Bernard of Clairvaux: "As there is a foolish knowledge, so there is a wise ignorance. . . . I leave God's secrets to himself; I may be *pius pulsator,* but not *temerarius scrutator;* I may knock at God's privy council door, but if I go farther, I may be more bold than welcome."

Thus surrounded by the piety of the useful, Milton went up to the university at sixteen already schooled in the doctrine by which he was to account much of the dons' lore no better than vanity and curiosity. By the time he delivered his first academic Prolusion he faced, or so he said, a largely unsympathetic audience of those sturdiest of conservatives, the generality of college youth, whom he dismissed with a characteristic insult in order to address himself to the discriminating few. Whatever the whole reason for this breach with the students, he made it clear in the pungent asides that he dropped while handling the anodyne topics set for him at the university that he quarreled with the administration for incompetent method, or teaching by debate, and for otiose assignments—topics either in themselves "foolish trifles" (Prolusion vi, "That sometimes sportive exercises are not prejudicial to philosophic studies"), or unsuited to logical debate in prose (Prolusion i, "Whether Day is more excellent than Night"), or ambitious matters wrung, as he wrote in later years, "from poor striplings, like blood out of the nose." For one such topic (Prolusion vii, "Knowledge renders man happier than ignorance"), more substantial than most and once

set for students by Lando's translator, he himself took
credit. From two of his own occasional orations (II, "On
the Music of the Spheres," and III, "Against the Scholastic
Philosophy") and by inversion from VII, we may collect in
embryo some of his lifelong notions of intellectual abuse.
In the important matter of learning, surely, his mature
reflections represented no evolution beyond the progres-
sive unfolding of basic convictions—a judgment to be
premised here for much of Milton's thought.

In the humanities he found abundance of delicate
learning and gowned ignorance. The grammarians and
rhetoricians could not teach even their own "despicable
trifles" without often speaking ungrammatically and child-
ishly, according to a young man who was to vindicate his
right to criticize. We may compare his heated dispar-
agement of Salmasius' profession, a little self-consciously
hedged, as well it might be in view of the grammatical
work that stole some of the poet's own time. At best, he
awarded the wise grammarian honors second to those due
the wise statesman—an honest and considered compliment
to Bonmattei and a piece of rhetoric consistent with Milton's definition of eloquence as "none, but the serious and
hearty love of truth." The master of rhetoric was to note
repeatedly the abuse of an art that Aristotle himself had
made a bag of sophistical tricks for decking out a dishonest
cause. Satan's apostrophe to the forbidden tree comes at
once to mind, or the sneers that Milton wrote to comment
on the rhetoric of Comus and Satan. It would not be amiss
to add the contempt he expressed for the love poetry of
the vulgar amorist, for the rhyming parasite's adulatory
bid for patronage, or, at least twice, for the immorality
and foolishness of the serenading cavalier. Without competent teaching and virtuous application, rhetoric became
a prime vanity. So logic as well. "Queen she is of the arts
if she is handled in accordance with her worth," Milton
wrote long before he devised a textbook to improve her
state. But in daily practice "not men, but just finches" fed
on "thistles and thorns." Or they fell into metaphysics, that
"Lernian swamp of sophisms, contrived for shipwreck and
destruction." No reader of his prose works needs to be told

how often Milton professed to despise "metaphysical fume" or "metaphysical gargarisms" while he accumulated his body of wholesome divinity "without school terms and metaphysical notions." As a matter of familiar fact, he now and then ventured in his *Christian Doctrine* to debate the theologians on principles of first philosophy, but not—at least not consciously—to add his own assumptions in ontology to the empirical facts taught in the sacred volume. He labored, as he thought, to remove what had already been added. He remained all his life, to the best of his honest conviction, aloof from subtlety.

On the subjects of astronomy and natural science he wrote in his early exercises little to the purpose beyond what we are permitted to infer from the unbounded intellectual enthusiasm of his *Music of the Spheres* and *Vacation Exercise*. In both, and explicitly in the latter, he commended everything in heaven and earth and the waters under the earth, past and present, to the seeker after knowledge. Everything, presumably, except the rubbish discarded in *Against the Scholastic Philosophy*. But if the rest was good, it was not all equally good. In his third Prolusion we read the humanist's proper subordination qualifying a rhapsody of enthusiasm for natural knowelge. "Nor let the most minute little star be hidden from you," the orator exalted science. "Let not your mind suffer itself to be hemmed in and bounded by the same limits as the earth." Yet he gave ethical philosophy a still higher place, and divinity the highest of all: "Finally, what is after all the most important matter, let it learn thoroughly to know itself, and at the same time those holy minds and intelligences." What he subordinated he hardly prohibited, either in the *Prolusions* or in *Paradise Lost*.

The black beast of scholasticism hounded him all his life. Beside Popery, the great horror of religion, it prowled as the bogy of his intellectual and cultural world. The two were but different aspects of the same evil—stagnation and superstition. By the mere word he sometimes meant what Bacon called contentious learning; sometimes, simply reaction. He came to associate the thing with all vestiges of medieval thought and feudal institutions; he could see it before him everywhere, supporting outworn pedagogy, prelacy, the canon law and unintelligent literalism in exegesis (when both opposed the reform of divorce), censorship and the Stuart monarchy. After the Stuarts came back, it supported its spiritual father the Pope. But while Milton was a student, it meant education by quibbling. A country is chiefly adorned by two achievements, he observed in his third Prolusion, by *præclare dicendo* and by *fortiter agendo,* to neither of which had the word-battles of the doctors ever contributed anything. The writings of the scholastic divines had no literary style; constantly stating and refuting, they led nowhere; they cultivated in their authors neither graces nor virtues. In Milton's later years scholasticism continued to bear all the blame for error religious and intellectual. The whole work of Reformation and advancement was a work of restoration, clearing away the wreckage it had left, reestablishing morality and politics on principles of classical sanity and doctrine on pure scripture.

Sometime in these green years, while he marshalled exuberant Latinity to express what a critic has called the boundless expectations of the full Renaissance, he met the paradox of learning's inferiority to ignorance and once planned to maintain it. He left the evidence in his seventh Prolusion, that uninhibited pæan to knowledge that has been contrasted with the more judiciously chastened expressions of his later years and taken to mark the most optimistic stage of his evolution. An academic oration would be slight support for a conclusion so weighty even if Milton had not told his audience frankly that it had been his real wish to defend ignorance. According to his own story, he himself proposed a debate on the merits of ignorance, presumably in order that he might have the pleasure of the paradoxical side. But whoever it was who took up his challenge claimed that side of the argument, leaving Milton without excuse to write a youthful piece of cantankerousness, and critics without a topic of delectable speculation. We can be sure that Milton had meant to play the skeptic in classical dress, for what he actually left us specifically "either disproves or mitigates or counter-

balances both that Socratic ignorance and the cautious uncertainty of the Skeptics." The exercise that he had his
heart set on writing may not be quite lost, for it is not impossible to restore, from the arguments that he answered,
the oration that he expected his opponent to deliver and
that he himself had perhaps already outlined. Preparing to
speak on either side, he would have opened somebody's
defense of ignorance, and the likeliest that a determined
search has turned up seems Pierre Charron's in *De la
Sagesse*. We must borrow the skeptic's modesty and abstain
from declaring that it was Charron and no other whom he
had open before him or in his head for refutation; but
Milton wrote no arguments that Charron had not somewhere countered, Charron wrote none that Milton overlooked, and the sequence in both is remarkably similar.
Let us then substitute Charron for the opponent that
Milton faced, and hear in summary both what the young
poet actually said and what he had wanted to say.

Charron. (1) The first aim of education is wisdom, not science and art. *Milton*. (1) The first aim is to know God aright,
as one can do the better by knowing all creation. *Ch*. (2) The
second aim is to "form the judgment, and by consequence the
will and the conscience, rather than to fill the memory." Wisdom and learning are quite different things. Many foolish and
wicked men are learned; learning is the mother of heresies;
two thirds of the human race manage very well without learning. *M*. (2) The premises are granted; their cogency denied.
The degenerate many corrupt a few of the learned; conversely,
one learned man or family has been sufficient to reform a
whole state. The medieval night of Popish ignorance is proof
that where no arts at all flourish, divinity and morality perish
together. *Ch*. (3) Learning in and of itself cannot make a man
happy in private life, or do anything to assist his probity.
M. (3) Let us "acknowledge of our own accord that virtue
without knowledge is more conducive to a happy life than
knowledge without virtue," but where they are joined, as
they most frequently are joined, the cultivated intellect leads
the subservient will down the road to private happiness. *Ch*.
(4) The well-being of a state owes nothing to knowledge—
witness the happy condition of primitive Rome, of Sparta, of
the Indies, and of the Turkish empire. Their prosperity bears
out, inversely, the curse laid upon Adam's curiosity, and the

words of St. Paul and the Preacher. Licinius, Valentinian, Lycurgus, Mahomet, and other lawgivers banished learning, because it can only "make us more humane and courteous, but not more honest." *M.* (4) The *leaders* of the Romans always sought glory in letters as well as in arms; the learned Lycurgus was the source whence much Spartan virtue sprang. As for the Turks, their polity bears its condemnation in its face. The power of learning to lift a barbarous people from primitive rudeness is not to be despised. *Ch.* (5) Learned men are ridiculous, clumsy pedants, proverbial "mere scholars," bad-mannered and, in competence of real knowledge, inferior to plodding aldermen. *M.* (5) The argument that "the majority of the more learned class are hard to please, boorish, uncouth in manners" is conceded. Above the inanities of polite society they seek higher conversations. Surely Plato's under the plane tree were preferred, and justly, before all fopperies. *Ch.* (6) Excess of learning is our disease. Because it is a means to get fame, reputation, riches, it becomes a staple of sordid chaffer. Parents buy it at any price, neglecting for it all other training. *M.* (6) Learning is, indeed, a valid claim to distinction in private life. Innocent self-interest is no vice. *Ch.* (7) Ignorance is a better antidote than learning against misfortune. Life is too short for art. Those who would persuade us that death is a refuge from evil commend nothing other than ignorance, for death is the perfect ignorance. *M.* (7) Life is long enough for real learning. The defenders of ignorance, it seems, would drive men lower than the brutes, which are respectably learned and even reasonable; lower yet than the trees and rocks, which gave oracles and heard Orpheus with pleasure. Will ignorance then "be permitted to find repose in that Not-Being of the Epicureans"? Not if we allow evil a positive reality. *Ch.* (8) Learning is quarrelsome, presumptuous, contradictory, servile—dominated by Aristotle, Cicero, and Bartolus. *M.* (8) The vain arts of grammarians, rhetoricians, logicians, metaphysicians, and lawyers are not learning.

   Ch. (9) Learning is not absolutely to be condemned. Were it consistent with wisdom, were matters so arranged that men turned their speculations into practice, to the purposes of human life, the advantages of learning would be unspeakable. *M.* (9) Agreed—"if one could both know the useful arts and properly choose the useful in the arts," if one could "wisely omit the foreign, the superfluous, the useless."

Thus Milton and Charron came by diverse routes to the same end—utility. Perhaps no more important conclusion can be drawn from Prolusion Seven.

The early works demonstrate at what age Milton knew perfectly that the man who studied for the sheer pleasure of studying was curious, but he was newly established at Horton before he happened to call the sin by its usual name. Two drafts survive of a little essay on himself which he cast in the form of a letter to an unnamed friend, plausibly assumed to be Diodati. Both replied to a playful accusation of vain conceit in study. If any man had reason to meditate seriously upon the action-contemplation rhetoric in the air, to search his motives carefully, it was Milton at Horton. In the first draft he admitted some personal vanity, but alleged the usefulness—to him—of his labors as proof that he was innocent of "an affected and fruitless curiosity of knowing." In the revised copy he mended both his virtue and his style. He minimized his vanity and denied that he had committed an "unprofitable sin of curiosity." The stereotype lodged in his mind shaped here and there a phrase prophetic of his later poems. Texts condemning subtle and controversial theology he wrote in his early hand under the rubric "Curiosity" in his *Commonplace Book*. In a letter of 1637 he used *humile sapiamus* to mean "Let us rise cautiously," or perhaps "Let us taste moderately"—the theme of Michael's lecture to Adam even more importantly than of Raphael's. Dedicating his first divorce tract to a Parliament engrossed in "dependencies and independencies," he remarked man's disposition to "search after vain curiosities" while neglecting matters like domestic liberty which nearer might concern. While he studied

> Serious to learn and know, and thence to do
> What might be public good

and taught his pupils in the same spirit, he constantly followed the rule as he interpreted it. When he wrote out for Hartlib a program of studies modeled, and rather closely, on the one he taught, he meticulously underscored the utility of each course, allowing in theory nothing sim-

ply because it happened to be traditional. He justified
languages so far as they conveyed "solid things," and held
his offerings to Greek, Latin, Hebrew, and a smattering
of Italian—minimal for ideas of most importance. The
mere grammarian in these had a poor funeral. Natural
sciences and technologies, to be taught by daily practitioners who would appear as guest lecturers, he carefully
applied: meteorology and anatomy, for example, to help
the student take intelligent care of himself or, if need
should present itself to some future Essex, of an army.
He would offer astronomy of an elementary kind in preparation for seamanship, and mathematics as far as trigo-
nometry, but not for intellectual discipline alone. As early
as the seventh Prolusion he had scoffed at the "empty
little glory of demonstrations." Rather, he would satisfy
the inescapable requirements of fortification, architecture,
engineering, or navigation.

Yet he weighted his hypothetical curriculum heavily toward the other practical science—ethics. Early in their
course the boys were to study classical morality along with
rhetoric out of Plutarch and Quintilian, "to inflame their
zeal for study." As soon as they grew mature enough to
profit, they might undertake formal ethics, and, quite late,
the study of logic. Thus he would handle logic in accordance with her worth. He allowed no dusty view of utility
to crowd out the *belles lettres* that some zealots had slan-
dered, though he recommended to Hartlib for the average
student less of that kind of learning than he wanted for
himself. As either listeners or performers, the students he
planned for were to learn music, another of the arts that
polish life but useful as well "to compose the soul." Picked
up in leisure, it would steal none of their working hours.

Such fidelity to the ideals and principles professed by the
essayists and courtesy writers can be taken to add to the
probability that Milton had read at least some of their
works. He would have found there the controversy between self-knowledge and natural knowledge, whose rival
pretensions he undertook to harmonize. There too he
would have found practicality, knowledge for doing, the
disputed ground claimed by both moralists and naturalists.

And above all, he would have found there the unprofitable student *qui scire vult ut sciat*. His curiosity became the subject of many a colloquy in the years when abstract, scholastic rational science was giving ground, first to the practicality of well doing, and ultimately to the practicality of well having. The coincidence of this anti-curiosity preaching with the progress of utilitarian positivism is obvious— as coincidence. Deterministic historians of the cycles might tell us that the preaching and the progress were but twin births of time. Some of us, naïve enough to think causally, may conclude that the preaching was both cause and effect. Doubtless, men preach to justify their actions, and in so doing modify the morality of others.

But the preaching that bent Milton toward the doctrine of utility taught only one form of intellectual sin. There remained for his guidance a store of medieval piety holding learning within her place as handmaid to religion and, what was not the same thing, to divinity. Except briefly in *Lycidas* he hardly touched in his youthful writings the question of a minister's learning, which therefore need not occupy us until later. In the matter of religion and laymen's learning he early showed himself entirely orthodox and, as I intend to make good, remained so. He challenged the sanctity of no learning that respected the precedent claims of morality and practical religion. Like any Christian humanist he sheared the bondwoman and bade her wait upon her mistress. In *Of Education* he set the "determinate sentence" of scripture above all conclusions of human ethics, and in God's law would his charges meditate Sundays and nights. By all their learning they achieved the great end, "to know God aright," striving to imitate him by possessing their souls of true virtue, thus repairing their damage sustained in Adam. He added that complete education equipped the student to discharge his nearest duties, "all the offices of peace or war."

These two statements have been reconciled easily enough, but not, I think, in the exact relationship that Milton had in mind. To write fruitfully of education he would have thought it necessary to write of it in its causes, that is, to define it, to capture its essence. Let us consider that his two famous remarks were perhaps not two definitions, "medieval" and "modern," but two causes. For his essay in definition he needed the four Aristotelian causes—material, formal, efficient, and final—or more exactly three of these. In *Of Education* the efficient cause would have been "discreet teaching" in profitable order, or good method. This his own rules permitted him to touch lightly, for in his textbook of logic the efficient cause might be absent from a definition. The material cause would have been the subjects in his curriculum. The form of an *art*, we read in his rules, was not arrangement, as we might expect, but "the teaching of some useful matter." In his Ramism he insisted repeatedly that formality partook of finality. We are therefore permitted to take an ability to execute offices as the form, or formal cause, of a complete and generous education. The ultimate final cause, the prime end, Milton clearly labeled, and placed it first, as our educators set up objectives: to help man conquer original sin and imitate God as nearly as possible in virtue.

From a commonplace that educators of various religious tempers took for their literary gambit it is hazardous to deduce anything narrowly doctrinal about Milton's religion. It fitted easily into Puritanism and Anglicanism, Calvinism and Arminianism. It proved nothing startling about Milton's spiritual alteration, least of all that he said in *Of Education* anything that he took back in his *Christian Doctrine*. In the religious treatise he left out learning and social aims when writing of Christian regeneration because he there dealt with faith, saving faith, a concern both private and irrelevant to learning. No doctrinal work could have treated learning and society under the head of Christian redemption. Why a social reformer decided to write of doctrine in the first place is another question, but the answer is not a spiritual about-face if Phillips came at all near the truth when he dated the beginnings of the *summa*, or of something like it, about as early as *Of Education*. Finally and most importantly, Milton said nothing in the early tractate of salvation by learning or social service. He fell even short of some contemporaries in making reason and learning propædeutics to faith. He claimed for learning at the highest this, that it conduced to virtue. Moral virtue, then, if joined to the higher and entirely distinct grace of saving faith, made up a perfection lacking in mere naked faith. The elder John Brinsley, strict Puritan educator, had long preached Milton's doctrine, which no conservative or "legal" Calvinism would have contradicted.

MILTON AND THE ORTHODOX ON
FALSE PHILOSOPHY

Milton's later manner of reconciling learning with piety, entirely usual for the most part except in perhaps two of his works, gives occasion here to review normal opinions gathered from the preachers, for an age can profitably be studied in its platitudes. The poet himself surely deserves our admiration where he adorned a conventional theme, and our closest attention where he altered it. When he thought as a Christian of learning and philosophy got by the feeble light of nature he remembered as easily as the preachers that the Apostle had warned of philosophy and vain deceit, and in an electric passage of *Paradise Lost* proclaimed what thousands had mumbled. We contemplate here not the angel Raphael's lecture on curiosity, but the lines in which the poet himself appraised the arts of hell. Variously as apologists applied a text (Col. ii:8) written probably of Gnostics in the church at Colossæ, good exegetes plausibly supposed that St. Paul had spoken of Athenian philosophies, and by extension any unsanctified learning, as vain. Milton interpreted the warning broadly in the *Christian Doctrine* and *Likeliest Means,* where it damned metaphysics and school divinity, and more narrowly in his two epic poems, where the bare letter of his paraphrase spoke against historical Hellenism.

The anti-paganism of *Paradise Lost,* so far as it went, accorded perfectly with that of catholic Christianity. Before real apostasy became usual, all speculation professed to work obediently within the vertical frame of faith, reason, sense—or grace and nature—different in kind and graded downward in nobility. Nearly always it relegated the natural man of antiquity to the same limbo where Dante found Virgil, or where Augustine would have found Virgil. The stern compulsion saddened Erasmus and some other humanists, especially those whose Protestantism abolished limbos. A few Papists whom Trent reproved, Zwingli and Oecolampadius notably among early reformers, and a handful of English rationalists rebelled, agreeing to save worthy pagans on Milton's "Arminian" ground, that they deserved salvation. Certain of the sectaries who leaned toward mysticism—universalists, Quakers, and apparently Familists—thought that God's mercy might extend to some pagans. But the great majority of Christians forbade the ancient moralists to hope, and none confidently encouraged them. When one Calvinist preached of grace he justified God's death sentence pronounced upon the pagans by repeating the tale of their blindness, vanity, superstition, and persecution of Christians. He preached with such bitterness, he said, because he feared the peril of unsanctified learning, Christ's greatest enemy and "the only pillar of the devil's kingdom." If he had been a Quaker, he would have been more charitable to pagans, but less charitable to their learning.

For learning when sanctified became, by his divinity as by many men's, an ornament of grace and, since the learned parson held a good living, indispensable to Christ's very church—a transformation not curiously to be inquired into. The lustration by grace cleansed a science that could be sanctified by two other arguments. One was the Hebrew origin of pagan wisdom, the other the divinity of nature's light, or the candle of the Lord, as Solomon, Whichcote, and some others liked to call it. Milton certified its divinity and its relative dimness. Neither would rationalists too highly esteem nor simple dogmatists extinguish that light: Arthur Dent, who pointed Bunyan and many plainer men a narrow pathway to heaven, rejoiced to find in the philosophers the usual "ruins" of the "excellent frame and building of man's first creation." The preachers, like Aquinas before them, deduced reason's divinity from their assumption that Adam in blessedness had been a most learned philosopher. They liked to measure the distance of the pagans' fall by contrasting unregenerate learning with Adam's, as they could do by supposing that Adam had known everything that frustrated man would like to know. In rhapsodies, too, on the perfect knowledge that angels enjoyed and that glorified saints could expect, they had the freedom of their own dreams. Sir Thomas Browne, with a bit of a twinkle, praised them for their piety.

Fallen angels retained more knowledge than fallen man, but by sin less knowledge and power than the good angels. The topic had of necessity been threshed out in the literature of demonology and witchcraft as well as in divinity proper. "For their knowledge, that it is exceedingly great in itself, is without all question, they being of the same substance with the other angels," the "virtuous father" of Milton's Lawrence wrote of the devils in a treatise sometimes cited as authoritative. But by the analogy of natural man he deduced that they knew not everything in science, less in revealed theology, and nothing at all in unrevealed matters, like future contingents, except as God chose now and then to permit. In *Paradise Regained* (1.445–454) Milton expanded what he had already written in the *Christian Doctrine* on Satan's abilities and limitations, probably following his favorite authority, Zanchius. When John Webster, to overthrow Glanvill, wrote similarly in his chapter "Of the Knowledge and Power of the Fallen Angels," he admitted that the devils knew much; but it suited his argument against the spirits to limit their "spurious, erroneous, fallacious" knowledge. Satan and his brood could not know, for instance, the mind of a man who kept his mouth shut. This common bit of demonology, consonant with Augustine and the Talmud, obliged Milton's Satan to eavesdrop. Another bit consisted neatly with the poet's fable. It was the devils' custom "to sing melodiously" and "with their impure mouths" to "meditate and talk of holy scriptures."

Though the fallen angels of *Paradise Lost,* "wounded in their naturals and deprived of their supernaturals for sin," had good warrant from theology, it was not of angels that the poet most seriously wrote, but of natural man, who receives not the things of the spirit (I Cor. ii:14). Of unbelievers all the preachers spoke about alike, regardless of creed: "We cannot deny too much to nature; we cannot ascribe too much to grace." To regenerate Christians one Calvinist promised an increment in even their natural knowledge. To the mere natural man and his worldly merits Henry Hammond's Arminianism, on the other hand, could offer only picturesque abuse. In their sulphurous language the preachers obliquely complimented learning, the natural man's proudest boast. "If anything in the world were worth respecting, it must needs be man," one mounted to his otherworldly pitch, and if anything worthy in man, then surely his soul's ornaments. They were as nothing in the sight of God; rather, as natural, they were "exceedingly corrupted," or as another finished the same sentence, "deadly and damnable." The glorious Stagirite himself provided no more than enough worldly perfections to feed the flames of hell. A dram of devotion in the day of judgment would outweigh a pound of discourse, "one work of mercy turn the scale to the whole library of Aristotle," prophesied Thomas Drant of Shaston. "The mere moralist," the mere "civil judiciary," though stored with learning, expressing "in action and civil honesty the absolute portraiture of Aristotle's moral virtues," could be without grace "but as a rotten carcass stuck over with flowers, magnified dung, gilded rottenness, golden damnation." For readers of *Paradise Lost*, Henry More's words are apposite. Fallen nature made a brave show; she framed curious conclusions in religion or cavils against it. Sometimes she betook herself to poetry and wrote melting elegies, bloody hymns of battle, amatory sonnets, or drinking songs. Such powers resided in the mere natural man.

More's was the lesson that readers would have found in Milton's account of nature fallen, though angelic, in Satan. Rotten carcasses richly furnished with choicest gifts, his devils matched and surpassed the noblest achievements of antiquity and the Renaissance. Yet in them nature sinned outright, warring against Jehovah, or by consequence, missing its regenerate potentialities. To the active life the infernal powers, with their restless Balboas, contributed little that was distinctively and peculiarly classical beyond

the greater part of their military science and their march-
ing with wisely moderated courage to Spartan flutes. To
contemplation and liberal exercises they brought pure
Hellenism when, in a happy mingling, Milton blended
Olympia and catholic Christianity to enrich what might
otherwise have been the sterile convention of epic games.
In one contemplative detail he may have modernized the
ancients, though it could be easily matched in the classics:
Stygian philosophers reasoned of "foreknowledge absolute." In other respects he reproduced only the gifts of
Athens. His reference to the epic is clear in the following
lines (II.548), and his intention to include tragedy after
the punctuated cæsura can be established by comparing
the language of *Paradise Regained* iv.261. The devils sang

> With notes angelical to many a Harp
> Their own Heroic deeds and hapless fall
> By doom of Battle; and complain that Fate
> Free Virtue should enthrall to Force or Chance.

To smile that Milton set his devils composing poetry or
debating the problems of philosophy that he himself
solved by scripture is to miss his important point. Their
song was incomplete, "partial"; their metaphysics inconclusive; their ethics ultimately unsatisfactory—not his own
so long as all was hers who, from God, brought it nightly
to his ear. His mere natural spirits, cut off from grace,
soonest lost their way in the wandering mazes of first philosophy because all metaphysics, by his prejudice, was
fume. They succeeded better, but only a little better, when
they turned to ethics. In *Paradise Regained* (IV.351) Christ
found unregenerate philosophy in error throughout

> *Unless* where moral virtue is express'd
> By light of nature not in all quite lost.

We may compare, too, the passage in *Samson Agonistes*
(657) where Milton disposed of the classical *consolatio*,
a form of Stoic rhetoric perfected by Crantor and imitated
by Plutarch, Seneca, Cicero, Erasmus, and their disciples—

> Consolatories writ
> With studied argument, and much persuasion sought
> Lenient of grief and anxious thought,

> But with th' afflicted in his pangs their sound
> Little prevails . . .
> *Unless* he feel within
> Some source of consolation from above.

Hell could not admit the exception:

> Of good and evil much they argu'd then,
> Of happiness and final misery,
> Passion and Apathy, and glory and shame.

Though with its "pleasing sorcery" their heathen morality could charm

> Pain for a while or anguish, and excite
> Fallacious hope, or arm th' obdured breast
> With stubborn patience as with triple steel,

it had neither part nor lot in the divine promises. Accordingly (II.565), St. Paul had called it

> Vain wisdom all, and false Philosophy.

As Bishop Hall had written of tranquility, "Not Athens must teach this lesson, but Jerusalem."

We cannot explain the bitterness of the lines against learning in *Paradise Regained* by the commonplaces vitalized differently in *Paradise Lost,* or by any others, as I shall try to confirm while rounding out this account with some of the truisms played upon in the brief epic. Nothing would better correct the reading of *Paradise Regained* IV.285–364 as pious convention than to study—and study in their original settings—the unimpassioned platitudes to be isolated next, for these are the true commonplaces. Yet upon this base of received doctrine Milton reared his lethal argument against out-of-place Hellenism. The argument therefore seemed plausible and "epic," and hence artistically fit, because by bits and in contexts alien to Milton's it had become public property.

In deducing the arts of the pagans from the Jews, for example (IV.338), he drew upon a theory that nobody would have dared openly to scout, inasmuch as none of the Fathers had denied and most had affirmed it. Josephus had traced learning from Adam through Abraham to Pythagoras and Plato. Philo of Alexandria had allegorized

Moses until he could find the teachings of his beloved
Plato in the Old Testament. The Fathers therefore saw
no difficulty in supposing that both accounts were right,
that to Plato the truth had indeed descended. Milton had
certainly read as much in Clement and "in that Eusebian
book of evangelic preparation." He had equally surely
met the theory in later writers. When Theophilus Gale
wrote four volumes largely on it, he supplied only details
to document a fact that had been long accepted and sometimes fancifully trimmed:

> Pythagoras by his father was a Jew;
> Circumcised: known and taught by Ezekiel too! . . .
> From speech with God Moses' face did shine:
> Plato having read Moses seem'd divine.

The authority for the biographical detail escapes me.
Clement refuted the patristic legend that Ezekiel taught
Pythagoras, but he acknowledged Plato's debt to Moses
and did not deny that Pythagoras had learned what Ezekiel
might have taught. The whole idea endeared itself to Cambridge Platonists, for it bound Platonism to God. If Plato
had not thence learned his doctrine of unity, then—and
Lord Brooke hoped the better—the devil taught him a
half truth. The Jewish origin of pagan wisdom left little
for merely natural light except the usual "sparkles" in the
form of common notions, *noemata,* bare axioms. After
Lord Herbert had raised his Deism upon the tiny concession, Dryden became one of the learned who found it safer
to deduce even common notions, at least in religion, from
the Jews.

Josephus did his part to stereotype the simplified history
employed in "progress" essays—facile records of piety and
learning from their beginnings through their vicissitudes.
Since this kind of history is importantly glanced at in
Paradise Regained, we may appropriately consider it here.
Examples abound, but it may be most familiar to many
in George Herbert's "Church Militant." Planted in Eden,
religion passed to Noah and Solomon, moved westward to
Egypt, and thence (because arts and prowess had been
evangelic preparation) to Greece and Rome. *Ergo* was

transformed into *Amen;* the Roman army converted. But
sin set out at the same time from Babylon and traveled
the same road to Rome, picking up on the way the creatures of Antichrist—the petty deities of Egypt, the oracular
infallibilities of Greece, the wealth and stateliness of
Rome, or new Babylon. Thence sin sent out ambassadors
to make the world the Pope's mule. Denham retraced
some of this popular history but brought it down farther
in his "Progress of Learning." Adam taught Abraham, and
through him Chaldea, Egypt, and Greece; the Greeks
added poetry from Moses and David, and worthy ethics
from their own seers. Soon squabbling sects blasted the
tree of knowledge, which yielded only sapless leaves until,
about the time of Jesus' birth, learning revived in Rome.
"Once more to Paradise restor'd we seem'd," but not for
long. The Papists rose to assault heaven like the Giants
of old, to set up their own wrangling schools, and under
Hildebrand to conquer the temporal world. Satan taught
them to honor ignorance as devotion's dame, but balked
of complete victory by this ruse, tried another—learning.
With Luther, Loyola, and printing came other monstrous
sects, and with their disputes, Denham's skeptical conclusion: "Sublunary science is but guess."

For any one of Milton's comments on heathen culture
in *Paradise Regained* we may establish a tradition among
his enlightened contemporaries, or what is equivalent, in
the Fathers, whom every educated man knew. The Fathers,
like Milton, deplored the bawdry of Greek poetry and
myth, and none more eloquently than the fine humanist
Clement of Alexandria. Milton had read his *locus patris-
ticus;* he knew the Father's sources; and he addressed
readers taught the Clementine lesson by other good classi-
cists. We may not agree entirely with those who thought
Zion's songs in general lovelier than Ionia's, but Milton
had found them so in 1641, long before he wrote Christ's
literary judgment. Among the audience that accepted the
indefectibility of scripture, hundreds had written piecemeal or entire what Milton objected against the philosophers in his verse and prose. St. Paul's "correspondent"
Seneca could not live up to Christ's principles or his own.

There may have been an echo of Cyprian in the sneer at
"proud, inconstant Stoics," whose tedious talk was but
vain boast. It was mere nonsense, said Milton and legions,
for them to hold all sins equal or to prate of apathy:

> The Stoic overwise no passions felt;
> The Skeptic in uncertainties still dwelt.

Nobody needed a classical or patristic source for the proposition that the wisest pagan knew only that he knew nothing, ubiquitous as it was. Almost any of the Fathers or
their modern imitators could have matched Milton's
school-by-school criticism of pagan philosophy, which used
the labor-saving device of rejecting only the ethical *summum bonum* of each sect. But out of deference to entries
from Lactantius in his *Commonplace Book,* we may pass
by the crabbed Tertullian or the scholarly Clement to
consider the Christian Cicero in his third Book, *De Falsa
Sapientia.*

Lactantius condescended to refute the ancients like a
school philosopher so far as his emotional temper and ora-
torical style allowed. Philosophy had betrayed its weakness by multiplying sects, but the apologist thought only
four of the schools well worth criticism. The Epicureans,
who claimed credit for destroying polytheism, had only
substituted atheism, their absurd atomism, and a debilitat-
ing ethic. The Stoics did better in several respects, but
forgot that man requires happiness along with virtue. And
they erred in holding all sins equal. The Skeptics like
Arcesilaus refuted themselves in holding real knowledge
impossible. As for those princes of philosophy, Socrates
and Plato, the former did well to check speculation and
philosophic pride, but (here we read primitive Christianity) he kept his eyes too fixedly on the earth. Plato's vile
communism of wives and children spoke for his whole
philosophy. Lactantius was plainly no "source" for *Paradise Regained,* but rather one of a company who made its
doctrine familiar and hence suitable for epic poetry. His
sentiments became a staple of learned and rational apologetics against atheism. Probably the modern work most
esteemed in this kind was Philippe de Mornay's *De la*

Vérité de la Chrétienne Religion, the translation of which, started by Sidney, was finished by Arthur Golding in 1587. By simple method, Mornay showed how much Christianity the light of nature had taught the pagans, as he could do by cautiously picking quotations. He glorified reason; he honored faith by allowing it logical in its lower propositions; and yet he sternly held the best of ancient thought, measured by the only true philosophy, primitively inadequate. The peerless gentleman of England's Renaissance apparently found no fault with his critique of philosophy. The Epicureans pursued a paltry good. The Stoics held a higher ideal if only it had not reigned chiefly in their imagination. Aristotle placed his highest good in public and private happiness, the former no end in itself, and the latter attainable only by religion. "The deepest of our knowledge, saith Socrates, is ignorance." Out of France came another notable evidential work, by Moses Amyraut, with a quotation from Lactantius, *De Falsa Sapientia,* on the title page, and an entire second Part given to confuting the schools.

It would be tedious to hear many of the enlightened Englishmen who depreciated the schools of philosophy, but our concern with Milton suggests that we call George Hakewill, enrolled among the Moderns for rejecting the notion that history is but a record of decay. If Milton's verse essay *Naturam non pati senium* is fair evidence that the young poet had actually looked into Hakewill's book, he found there little Baconianism, but a reverent account of providence throughout history sustaining or improving the heavens and the earth, also the human frame, intelligence and art, and above all, morality. Roman wickedness proved unanswerably the impotence of classical ethics and the moral superiority of modern Christians, professing a religion powerful to expel vice. Hakewill had more to say than *Paradise Regained* of Moses' preeminence above the pagans as a lawgiver. The pagan codes encouraged sin. Sometimes they were merely silly, as when Solon absolved all debts, or worse, as when Lycurgus legalized adultery. Among the legal theorists, Plato permitted promiscuity, Aristotle abortion. Among the philosophers, the

Epicureans hindered virtue, and the Stoics, by holding all sins equal, encouraged vice. Sir Thomas Browne, though not precisely a humanist in all respects, was surely no foe of classical erudition and no bigot when he wrote that Aristotle and the Stoics could not live by their own ethics; the Skeptics confuted themselves, and so on. Therefore, he urged, "Sleep not in the dogmas of the Peripatus, Academy, or Porticus. Be a moralist of the Mount." For a third witness, we may hear a humanist worthy to be mentioned with Milton, Jeremy Taylor, "whose finest works," in the language of an unenthusiastic editor, "are darkened and disfigured by a vainglorious display of classical shreds and patches, many of them drawn from those sources of impurity which the Apostle forbids to be once named among the saints." Truly, in the access of his iniquity, Taylor dared to bring to his Christian writings the assumptions, the spirit, and even the very language of the ancients, as anybody who has come to his *Holy Living* or *Holy Dying* fresh from Plutarch, Seneca, and Cicero must acknowledge. The imitator of Stoicism and the *consolatio* suffered no discernible pang when he, too, named the chief fountains of ancient error and lamented that Christianity had been contaminated by contact with the weakly wrangling schools, which every "witty man" (speculative thinker) and "philosopher" (scientist) in Taylor's day thought he had "reason and observation enough easily to reprove." Not the philosopher or the scientist, however, so often reproached the ancients with their poverty as the mere Christian:

> Peace Epicure, cease Stoic, and the rest
> Of ancients, to make known what makes you blest:
> Your chief goods are but empty dreams, but mine
> A real vision, glorious and divine.

These representative utterances *contra paganos* may have some interest as criticism of learning in the age of Bacon and Boyle. We meet them at every turn—in Burton, Baynes, Sydenham, Abbott, Montagu, Ashmole, and writers of less distinction. They should be reckoned with, doubtless, as unintended contributions to the progress of empiricism, Hobbism, and experimental science. In Theophilus Gale, learned criticism of the ancients easily spilled over into Restoration skepticism. But these sermons on the pagans are not, as one may see here, the stuff of *Paradise Regained,* and in context they appear less so. Neither Hakewill nor the apologists Mornay and Amyraut proclaimed scripture's sufficiency in Milton's angry voice. The rest wrote briefly, incidentally, and for the most part perfunctorily. As Tillyard has noticed, Milton gave more space to his anticlassical outburst than to any other section of his poem. He built his whole argument thither, as to a climax, and wrote his "obscurantism" at white heat, whereas scripture and theological tradition for the story of the Temptation did not require him to write it at all. So far as scholarship knows now, only Milton among commentators who extended and claborated the biblical story dreamed of a temptation by learning. His own theses, as usually explained, did not oblige him to damn Greek art and letters along with pagan thought. The distant "parallels" here set down do little to elucidate *Paradise Regained* except to establish the existence of a real problem. We may leave it for the time being to follow Milton's steady course through some tempests of dogma.

Chapter III

DOUBTFUL DISPUTATIONS

Knowledge and Zeal

A READER steeped in the prejudiced language of ecclesiastical controversies might be tempted to describe Puritanism in flower as the triumph of curiosity over vain philosophy. It began in schism; it flourished amid a medley of heresies. *Plerumque schisma in hæresin eructat*—the revolution justified the adage. At any point in its course the ascendant clergy, fortified behind one scholasticism or another, saw disaffected radicals in the van misguided by ignorance and presumption. Before the Civil Wars the Anglicans called the Puritans' mutinous stirrings curiosity; and when the word in its political sense had dropped out of use, the "arrogance, self-ends, and peremptory schism" called Independency remained to challenge the right of one church to exalt itself over another. It was no excess in knowledge, this curiosity and pride of the advance guard, but rather a manifestation of zeal without knowledge. In sober fact, none can safely deny that for about a generation after Martin Marprelate the Puritan divines actually enjoyed a diminishing advantage in learning; at any rate a candid Anglican or two admitted as much. We need not here weigh in a sensitive balance the learning of Puritan and Anglican at mid-century, or name in the ranks of the sectaries the men of birth, breeding, and education. Facts have little to do with the stereotypes of calumny. Radicals of any kind are often accounted giddy, and in theology, where so much learning goes into the rationalizing of fixed dogma and institutions, the radical must seem to the conventionally learned deficient in mere knowledge.

On account of his supposed ignorance the Puritan could not be conceded the right to an ecclesiastical opinion. He invaded the privilege of the learned caste. It was the busybody's first crime against order, against the sacred code of obedient place-keeping, that he violated the Mount by contemning God's priesthood and temples. The lay schismatics, instead of walking in their callings as Christ bade, meddled with *arcana religionis et imperii*, rifled the Ark, framed a church after their own fancies in the wilderness of New England. Some, out of a Pharisaical conceit of their superior holiness, separated themselves like the Donatists of old. In such forms the "preposterous humility of the proud Puritans" exasperated King James. But unlike the heretics cursed with too much wit, always the "silly schismatics" offended God and the church "in having too little." Hence the early Puritan seldom heard himself compared with Adam. He was more often a Lucifer, aspiring above his sphere. In hundreds of sermons he was Uzzah, the dull zealot struck dead for steadying the Ark. We may better appreciate Milton's fine scorn of traditional pulpit learning if we remember that he himself belonged to the ignorant party. We know, of course, that the Puritan of whatever shade cherished his own vision of true order. We know how tirelessly Milton worked to make the spheres sing again as once they sang. He too abhorred Satan's insubordination and Adam's. But there was wry humor in his pen when to the proud bishops he held up as warnings Adam, Lucifer, and Uzzah.

The ignorance thought to support rebellion would naturally be encouraged, in turn, by private revelation, for its critics could not conceive that schism might be the teaching of reason, scripture, or tradition. Thus it was assumed that radicals were victims of enthusiasm, an ignorant and factious reliance upon the spirit. During the social and ecclesiastical revolution enough of the underprivileged gravitated toward the extremists to confirm the prejudice behind Robert Burton's question: "What are all our Anabaptists, Brownists, Barrowists, Familists, but a company of rude, illiterate, capricious, base fellows?" Puritans somewhat more conservative than these invited criticism by the very rigidity of their scripturalism, for they mocked the human reasoning which, in Anglicanism like Hooker's, had rationalized idolatry. "Carnal reasoning they cannot abide," a curate exclaimed petulantly while lecturing proud Pharisees who would neither kneel at a church door nor hear him explain why they should kneel. A great nonconformist of the Scotch Kirk shrugged aside the imputation of ignorance as common but irrelevant. If his adversaries were learned, what then? God would as soon confound them. If Puritans were ignorant, what matter, so long as they were right? The day was to come when his party, fallen to the conservative rear, would stand grimly on its learning and deplore the progress of heresy among the mystical illiterates.

It may help us to read the late heresy-hunters more judiciously if we remember that their very Genevan Model of church-government had once been called a fancy of ignorant enthusiasm. How the Puritans were expected to maim the arts, to kill instead of shearing the bond-woman, to pull down schools and universities, we must hear when we come to consider the learned-ministry controversy. To smirch the ignorant fanatics Peter Studley, the unpleasant minister at Shrewsbury, was willing to stoop low with a story of his acquaintance, the notorious Enoch ap Evan. The maniac had been arrested for murdering with an ax his mother and younger brother because they took communion kneeling, and executed after Studley (so he gloated) had compelled the "hypocritical" wretch to kneel before he would give him his own last communion. He was no ordinary madman, by Studley's diagnosis, or learned enough to be any kind of heretic; he was "only a silly, ignorant, and downright English Puritan." A Catholic priest took the widely publicized murder as the principal occasion to address a book "To the Unlearned but Well-Meaning Puritans," accommodated to those "defective and illiterate in the elements and main principles of learning."

The curiosity of schism, of nonconformity or separation, wicked in itself, might lead into an evil that Enoch ap Evan missed. The Anglicans and conservative Puritans needed small insight to perceive that division in church discipline must lead to division in doctrine, and that schism must issue in the arrogance of major heresy. His-

torians remember Bishop Hall's prophetic warning to
Brownists that they must, in consistency, either return to
the Church of England or go "forward" to the Anabaptists, for if the English church was no true church their
baptism into it was no baptism. In 1631 Hall reported
to Laud eleven congregations of sectaries in London, by
1641 eighty, while the Archbishop published a catalogue
of the horrible doctrines that Puritans had loosed by dis-
obeying his demand for uniform discipline. After the
handful of doctrinally pure Brownists in the Westminster
Assembly struck up a political alliance with the milder
heretics, Independency became in Presbyterian thinking
the passive tool of heresy. All wanton wits preferred it to
synods and classes, Thomas Edwards truthfully reported
in his first major work against congregationalism. In the
sequel, *Gangræna*, he declared that there were not fifty
pure Independents in the country. Rutherford said not
one. The unholy marriage of error and church-autonomy
was the Presbyterians' wail so long as their Covenant had
life, and after it was dead and buried. Baxter was raising
it futilely when the Presbyterian classes were hopelessly
decayed and Quakers and Ranters in swarms bore out
the worst that had been predicted of Brownism.

Coercing Christians into uniformity seemed to Milton,
from the very first, a cure worse than this disease of variety,
for all truly Protestant opinions had their origin in scripture. The trunk, however it might branch, grew single
and sturdy. When in his Presbyterian phase he dealt with
sectarianism, he did not openly palliate the evil beyond
shifting the responsibility for it from Puritanism to prelatry. Like Cheynell, like John Hales and the moderates,
too, he blamed Laud for imposing things indifferent, thus
driving sincere Christians into schism, whence they fell
into heresy. But his earliest words on the heterodox often
carried an un-Presbyterian kindness, like his somewhat
later "Anabaptists and Familists, if we understand them
not amiss" or Arminians who "perhaps out of a vigilant
and wary conscience except against predestination,"
phrases that betray a man ready to listen sympathetically
to novelties and just possibly, like Lord Brooke, convinced

already that the Bible tolerated Baptists. In days when he still seriously misunderstood Arminius he publicly displayed uneasiness about making God the author of sin, his great and lifelong objection to Calvinism. On better grounds than his kindness to sectaries we may conclude that he had long been an Independent in principle, or even that he fought for an Independency by the practical expedient of backing Smectymnuus and the most radical effective party. What Assembly presbyter, already ordained by a bishop, for example, would have challenged episcopal ordination on the ground that it transmitted the power of Antichrist? Or would have spoken cordially of lay preaching? Or would have seriously supposed that classical ordination meant the "full and free election" of presbyters by congregations? Milton did so in his earliest polemics; and as soon as we have extracted from them what he wrote on unnecessary ministerial learning and the separation of church and state, we shall have, from 1641, all his Independency in germ.

About this same year some worried conservatives began to notice that two of their mutually exclusive dogmas had collided. Heresy could not be the outcome of ignorant schism and of philosophy too. Tertullian's ancient saw about philosophers, the patriarchs of heresy, therefore passed quietly out of currency, and a few writers marked its passing. For some years already it had been only the ancient heresies that philosophy sired. When the spirit of Tertullian was on a preacher, he raked the older heresiologies and displayed his erudition in a sonorous roll: Carpocrates, Cerinthus, Ebionites, Valentinians, Apollinaris, Eutiches. Perhaps he added a Hackett and Coppinger from Camden's *Annals*. But the modern errors traced by popular mistake to John of Leyden and David George— that is, the doctrines of Anabaptists and Familists—were the brood of folly and ignorance. Preachers who denounced such errors, even preachers like Knewstub, Denison, and Featley who wrote specifically against them, showed not much solid information. Ordinarily, an "Anabaptist" in James's reign was an enthusiast politically turbulent, a "Familist" a kind of mystic insidiously quiet and hypocritical, a "white" wolf in Stephen Denison's terminology; and before the Civil Wars these two terms generally covered all the novel, "ignorant" heresies. The heresies of a rational stamp—neo-Arianism and neo-Pelagianism—counted as antique survivals; they were occasionally reckoned as the spawn of ignorance, but less often. When Ephraim Pagitt wrote his heresiology he began historically at the beginning, but brought his work down to include the modern heresies swarming in the 'forties. Hardly had it appeared than the sport of killing bygone errors became in itself a form of intellectual vanity. Thomas Edwards assured his reader that his own study did no such thing. Fuller's Faithful Minister refuted no dead heresies, no doubt because Fuller was bedeviled by palpable Baptists and Quakers, not philosophers. While Daniel Featley was a young rector he preached to an academic audience on Tertullian's sentence, with the ancient muster roll of heresiarchs, and with Cornelius Agrippa as his most modern instance. He told the students that the maintenance of heresy was no work for the dull or illiterate. Before he died he was cataloguing visible heretics who believed ignorance to be the mother, not of devotion as in Popery, but of prophetical revelation. The complexion of old Ephraim Pagitt's world had changed, too. In the year of the Presbyterian-inspired ordinance against lay preaching, he observed that the prophets who would reveal God's secrets and "open and shut heaven" came no longer from the schools of the prophets, but from the mechanic trades. The heresiographers who listed Milton's alleged Divorcers after such prefaces made the poet another of the mechanics. They never saw fit to hint what his book displayed—that the Divorcer was one whose learning would have been held in high esteem with Paul.

Learned Protestant divines here and there manifested a reluctance to give up the Roman clergy's privilege of doing the laity's Bible-reading. Some of the ministers who stubbornly insisted that every Christian should scrutinize every syllable of scripture confessed by their belligerent tone that a Bible in every home had its inconveniences. In the opinion of many, the incomprehensible mysteries

that Protestantism adored had to be guarded against scripture itself unless the clergy stood by to read and interpret.
John Robinson the Separatist wished that more laymen
shared the opinion. Fuller begged the fireside expositor,
assumed to be feminine, to skirt all but the plainest texts
unless she could remember perfectly how the learned
ministry had explained them. John Hales in his *Abuses
of Hard Places of Scripture* warned the schismatics that
the scriptures, clear enough in saving fundamentals, were
in nonessentials too hard for them. Opinionated igno-
ramuses grubbed texts or concocted allegories to prove
anything at all. And when in their anti-Popish zeal they
invaded the Apocalypse, they made the Protestant cause
look foolish. The learned knew, too, that many apocalyptic
texts could encourage prophets, as difficulties could make
infidels. A good historian warned that seeming contradictions might cause even the wisest to "admire the purpose
whereunto God worketh," but perhaps did not foresee
that Deists and Quakers would simply look for more reliable media of revelation. Fifth Monarchists particularly
affected difficult scripture, ignoring the common Protestant
dictum that God's word was clear in all points necessary
to salvation. That very principle tended to make large
parts of God's word a curious study, and learned mysta-
gogues had to defend themselves. Joseph Mede explained
that experts might know much that the simple were forbidden to meddle with. Jeremy Taylor, who said the same
thing, would have cared little for Mede's learning in millenarian prophecies. In a chapter on the "usefulness" of
apocalyptic studies, the millenarian Henry More discovered the identity of the true Antichristian church, the extent of reformation to be completed, and the futility of
Fifth Monarchists' hopes. But the incompetent reader of
the prophetic books would altogether miss their sense specifically because he would be *ipso facto* a curious reader.

Orthodoxy screamed so many years about the Anabaptists' and Familists' too sudden path to God's council
chamber that John Smith, Henry More, and Meric Casaubon, who would save Plato and Plotinus but not George
Fox, set up the test of learning, proved in turn by ortho-

doxy, to distinguish vulgar enthusiasm from what we should call mysticism. Hales mocked weapon-salve cures and high-flown enthusiasm with the same pleasant skepticism. When the Spirit interpreted scripture, it interpreted, he supposed, by stirring up men to learn—of the Word, the church, and the schools. "More than this in the ordinary proceedings of the Holy Spirit," the little scholar added, "I yet could never descry." To come so near to denying all new revelation smacked of "Socinian" reason. Jeremy Taylor's unmystical rationalism scoffed at the bold pretense of ecstasies "inquisitive of highest mysteries," and the very notion of rapts and extraordinary revelation infuriated Hobbes. But most divines hedged, for who dared to affirm that God could not add to what he had revealed? An impeccable Presbyterian in a chapter "Of Revelations and Inspirations" avoided this manifest impiety, but explained that a Familist (by his time the word meant antinomian) could not distinguish a dream inspired by Satan from the kind of revelation granted infrequently to right-thinking men in unusual circumstances. William Bridge, a conservative, liberally Calvinistic Independent of the Assembly—"Socinian," a gossiping bishop would have him —assured his more radical brethren that God would not mind if they slowly and carefully tested their revelations by scripture. Such dreams might well be Satan's doing. All these critics, with more candor than tact, frankly discouraged ignorance from disturbing order.

Since heterodoxy was enthusiastic when ignorant, and ignorant, ordinarily, only when fresh and politically dangerous, we may fairly wonder whether any considerable number of legally sane Christians actually depended upon extraordinary revelation for new dogma. The voice that guided Lord Herbert, Sir Simonds D'Ewes, the Protector, and numerous Quakers in practical decisions, that foretold so precisely the death of young Saltmarsh, that persuaded Reeve and Muggleton of their quasi-divinity, hardly added, unless in the last instance, a new article to the creeds. How many prophets delivered extrascriptural *doctrine* as new light? Fox learned directly from heaven what others collected from the Bible—that ministers needed no

universities. God possibly vouchsafed more esoteric truth
to favored tub preachers who never published. Others who
were known as enthusiasts, quite as certainly, preached
some literal word of scripture. To survey every particular
form of their giddiness, so called, would be a useless dupli-
cation. The Presbyterian heresiologies are filled with the
usual horror. Alexander Ross once abridged his studies
in a versified catalogue that included the master heresy
among many others:

> Some say the scriptures are no more God's Word,
> Than that which any holy man doth speak;
> Some look for revelations from the Lord,
> And all the written Word do quite forsake.

Vile opinions might once have been plucked up, he
reminded the Covenanting divines, if only they had kept
their oath. Modern studies have often presented these vile
opinions in a sympathetic light, but for a sample of the
Presbyterian language, one has only to glance through a
Table in *Gangræna:* "A relation of the sectaries in contempt of. . . . Of one who affirmed that he was Jesus
Christ. . . . A great sectary who holds himself able. . . .
Of the pride of the sectaries and boasting in. . . . Sectarian
soldiers beating a man for gathering tithes." And above
all, "A relation of the sectaries' insufferable insolencies
and affronts to authority."

Some of these insubordinate fancies touched Milton's
religion. In order to canvass them methodically we shall
follow a course from left to right across a median of sobriety, from which it may be possible to plot Milton's position. Surveying pride in the purely doctrinal controversies,
we shall move from atheism through the "Pelagianism"
of the rational heresies, hear Calvinism preaching modesty
to Calvinists, and pass in order to the "enthusiastic" sects,
none soberly wise in the opinion of the rest. For some
such method contemporary picture-thinking set plentiful
example.

ATHEISM AND SUPERSTITION

The proposition that true religion is a mean between
atheism and superstition, implied by Plutarch in his essay

"Of Superstition" and elaborated by Aquinas, was honored by preachers and laymen, sometimes in twin essays, meditations, or chapters. Calvinists, whether Puritan or Anglican, might alter one term of the antithesis as new foes threatened, but always they claimed the sacred middle, and by Protestant tradition justly, for many ancient and most modern heresies of Christendom can be measured by their distance from Calvin's theology. Thence the atheist turned to the left, the superstitious (primarily the Papist) the other way, reason being the soul's left hand, faith her right. The extraneous sects described in Henoch Clapham's *Errour on the Right Hand* tended to complicate matters and spoil the neat picture, for the threats to orthodoxy were actually three, as those who drafted the Etcetera Canons of 1640 saw well enough—atheism, superstition, and enthusiasm. To juggle them into a pair, the preachers sometimes laid down a course between heresy and enthusiasm, but then they were likely to be thinking of the ecclesiastical *via* between Popery and Anabaptistical Brownism. When they thought of doctrine before cult, they often lumped together superstition and enthusiasm as a single excess on the right hand opposite atheism.

Thus did Robert Burton, who elaborated upon heresies as forms of curiosity wide of a doctrinal mean. For that matter, the bookish clergyman made himself perhaps the century's best authority on curiosity of any kind. He filled his treatise of personal and social psychiatry preaching a healing sobriety. Adam's intemperance had bred fears, sorrows, and excesses, the very stuff and essence of melancholy. Earlier authorities who had found studious wits susceptible to the disease had used none of the detail that Burton lavished illustrating curiosity, men's "itching humor to eat of the forbidden fruit," and their vanities in religion, humanity, science, philosophy, and politics. A generous dash of Pyrrhonism took the harsh bite out of his disenchantment and some heat out of his religious zeal. When the mood was upon him in his bookish ivory tower he could dream constructive Utopian dreams for society, but far more often a sad laughter reduced him to detached contemplation, criticism, Stoical preachments, and something like Montaigne's irresponsibility: "Happy is he [who] is not troubled with state matters, . . . inquires not . . . whether Peter were at Rome, or Constantine's Donation be of force; what comets or new stars signify, whether the earth stand or move, there be a new world in the moon, or infinite worlds, etc. He is not touched with fear of invasions, factions or emulations." Into this context he introduced, for he acknowledged no predecessor, his closing section on religious melancholy. In a sense he was wrong in claiming priority; the approach to heresy-whipping through psychological instead of historical inquiry was tried before Burton wrote, and after him in forms not of his suggesting. Bishop John Abernethy, whose name he honored, used it in his masterpiece —an incredibly tedious and scholastic mapping of the mind, its objects, and the "blindness" or "madness" incident to each area, down to "The Gangrene of Heresy" and its four "blinds": reason, philosophy, tradition, and enthusiasm.

But nobody besides Burton so sweepingly identified heresy in general with melancholy in particular, or so neatly arranged the devious doctrines. "For method's sake," he proceeded, "I will reduce them to a twofold division, according to those two extremes of *Excess* and *Defect,* Impiety and Superstition, Idolatry and Atheism." On the side of excess, of zeal without knowledge, he sorted with the Papists and pagans all schismatics and the enthusiasts who, by special revelation, "perceived God's secrets." With atheists speculative and practical, ancient and modern, he included Averroists, fatalists, deists (whatever he meant), and desperate persons distrustful of God's mercy. On this ground Milton was to count predestinarians as little better than atheists. Burton, being one of the predestinarians, returned dutifully to the orthodox center only to beg the faithful to let God's decrees alone, lest the unnecessary and morbid fascination of his wrath tempt them to name others or themselves as reprobates. His therapeutics had the sanction of both Calvin and the seventeenth Article of his church.

A biographer has called it strange that a layman should beg of Baxter in 1658 a treatise of divinity showing error on both sides and truth in the middle, but it was not strange to Baxter, whose pacific habit it was to seek truth there always. It looks as if the mystical scholastic deliberately planned his controversies to radiate from a neutral center of "mere Catholics" addicted to no sect or party, "though the vulgar call them by the name of Presbyterians." After his Christian apologetics against atheists he engaged in order the Baptists, antinomians, and Quakers; finally, the Papists and prelates. From not quite the same center Henry More wrote against atheism in 1653, enthusiasm in 1659, and Popery in 1664. After superstitious ceremonies ceased from troubling, in the middle decades an interval ensued when Popery might become another shade of Arminianism and by its doctrine rather than its discipline cross over the center to stand in "one confederacy" with atheistic Socinianism. The Covenanting divines who concurred in the *Testimony* of 1647 left it out, calling by name only antinomians of various shades on the one hand and, on the other, certain rational heretics like Arminians, the Divorcer, R. O. the Mortalist. A more usual Presbyterian scheme guided Samuel Rutherford: "The Papist and the Arminian on the one extremity enthroneth nature. . . . The Familist, libertine, and Antinomian on a contrary extremity and opposition, turn man into a block" not in humility, to be sure, but "to comply with all presumptuous, proud, fleshly men, walking after their lusts." Naturally, no sect gloried in mere fanaticism or admitted that it stood apart from religion's true center. Papists held the correct position between Judaism and Gentilism. A Protestant editor built with pains a moderate spot between legalism and Familism for the century's most irrepressible mystic, Dr. John Everard. The point is that public opinion induced him to do so.

Viewed from our own day, the course of the dogmatic Reformation looks generally clear enough: the half measures of Calvin (to omit reformers less influential in England) lay in the direction of more radical tendencies incorporate in the enthusiastic groups of the Primary Reformation. Political inertia in the English Reformation, because it was achieved from the top down, retarded the church so that its polity did not catch up to Calvin's until much of the populace had already gone far beyond. The lagging political ascendancy of the Genevan Model was therefore brief and accidental. But throughout our whole period the half measures of Calvin in doctrinal reform made a pleasing orthodoxy for a church that invested intermediacy with peculiar holiness. The half measures in both that most seriously displeased the advance guard can be quickly told. The Reformation had asserted the right of the believer to be his own priest—and Geneva had left a clergy schooled in priestcraft, arrogating to itself the exclusive exercise of sacramental offices. The Reformation had declared for salvation by faith—and Geneva had left remnants of a fearful legal bondage, in the church and in daily life. The seeds of antinomianism planted by St. Paul could not grow in its shadow. Accordingly, in England, from leveling the episcopal hierarchy it was but another step to abolishing the priestly caste. As it was inevitable that many would continue the work of abolishing cere-monies by spiritualizing the very sacraments, replacing baptism in spittle, first, and later in water, with an im-material baptism, so it was inevitable that they and others would move from salvation by faith to salvation by faith alone. Because so many earnest Christians took this path to, or toward, Quakerism, there have been early and late a few critics to assume that the same path late in his life became Milton's, in theology or in hermeneutics as in church-government; and indeed the hitherto accepted read-ing of *Paradise Regained* would make some such *volte-face* necessary to assume. At the same time, the contrary drift of the poet's religion and its uniform tenor in other works make the hypothesis exceedingly uninviting and altogether too rash to adopt for a poem otherwise explicable. Some confusion may clear away if we hold eternally to the plain and easy distinction between doctrine and discipline. In Milton's *Likeliest Means* George Fox might have found some crumbs of comfort, though no rich diet. So might John Biddle the Socinian, on the other hand, or any other enemy of the Black Coats. The circumstance is irrelevant to dogma, for *Likeliest Means* was a work of discipline.

In doctrine the Reformation had set up scripture as the sole authority—and Geneva had left a forensic system of theology, sanctified by an upstart tradition and petrified in confessions and catechisms. In the retreat from Rome had fled some like the Sozzini, Ochino, Acontius, or in England Chillingworth and Thomas Firmin, who followed St. James and moral reason instead of St. Paul and ecstatic holiness. For these, whether they accepted it or not, the first reformers had left what had once perhaps seemed a thing indifferent, the "Jesuitical tenet"—so Paul Best called it—of Trinitarian dogma with its inescapable elements of antinomianism and largely vicarious atonement. Within these two streams, one tending toward intuitive religion and Sabellianism, subordinating Christ's humanity, the other toward Deism and Unitarianism, subordinating his divinity, every Christian could find to right and left, forward and backward, much frightful presumption and curiosity. On which side of the doctrinal *via media*, the rational or the intuitive and pietistic, scripture settled Milton's religion in his declining years would be too easy a question to raise again concerning an Arian and an Arminian if he had not written *Paradise Regained* to suggest, to some readers, Socinianism by its human and merely exemplary Christ and, to others, pietism by its stern renunciation of reason and the world. But if his latter faith mingled confusedly the mystical and the antimystical, the legal and the antinomian, the immanent and the transcendent, then he had indeed renounced his reasonable God. The gulf that sundered these oppugnancies was real, and it was held too constantly before his eyes for him to suppose that the sacred library could teach both ways and make sense.

The atheists and Socinians on the extreme left transgressed more damnably in abolishing mysteries than the superstitious Papists in multiplying them, a point on which faggots have thrown sufficient light. Yet except for a brief essay on the natural proofs of God's being and attributes, required by the plan of his *Christian Doctrine*, Milton

nowhere spent his energy refuting atheists, in whom he
saw less menace than in the common and dangerous predestinarians, who doubted God's ways justifiable by the
rules of human right—

> Just are the ways of God
> And justifiable to Men;
> Unless there be who think not God at all,
> If any be, they walk obscure;
> For of such Doctrine never was there School,
> But in the heart of a Fool,
> And no man therein Doctor but himself.
> Yet more there be who doubt his ways not just.

These, from first to last, occupied Milton's pen. We can
read in the lines if we please (and if they were written
late enough) the natural irritation of a rational Christian
exasperated to hear his Arminianism, Arianism, rational
pantheism, materialism, soul-sleeping mortalism, and even
religious toleration continually identified with atheism by
those who would hide God's light under a bushel. When
Chillingworth preached sermons on "The fool hath said
in his heart," he too set out to prove, unlike Burton,
Donne, and an army of preachers on infidelity, that most
atheism by far was not intellectual or notional, but a de-
fection of the heart. So a militantly rational Christian
might well argue. In Marlowe's generation the Jesuit Robert Parsons and Protestants who stole sermons from him
had not insisted on the point.

In spite of the enormity of atheism and the constant
thunder of the pulpit, the English in half a century turned
out nothing to compare with the fifty-odd important treatises of Christian apologetics that *le libertinage* evoked in
France. Bishop Martin Fotherby's scholastic fragment long
stood preeminent and almost alone, unless we include
Nosce Teipsum with its reprints as an antidote to Hobbism
and heresies touching the soul, or rank with these the English translations of Mornay, La Primaudaye, and Amyraut.
In 1653 Henry More countered Herbert's natural religion
with an evidential work of philosophy, and two years later
Baxter rose against Lord Herbert with the evidences of
revealed religion. In some parts of his treatise he attacked

both atheists and, at the other extreme, extrascriptural enthusiasts. He held competently enough to the neo-Aristotelian round: God exists, he is to be worshipped, Christianity (of the author's persuasion) has a better claim than other religions to possess a true copy of God's will, which vouches for God's existence. If this circle of reasoning had not been largely discredited among Deists, there would have been no need for a Descartes, but Baxter was not likely to fight one kind of atheism with another. Where his out-of-date logic would not serve to convince, his preaching must: "If the devil did not win most souls by silencing reason"—he meant obedient reason—"hell would not have so many sad inhabitants." On the other hand, by the "dark premises" and axioms of nature—he meant undisciplined reason—the wisest man could never know what the silliest woman could learn by reading the right book. Baxter saved one of his closing chapters, "The Arrogancy of Reason," to drop his logic and mount the pulpit for a bout with a multitude of impious and blasphemous questions. "What an abundance of 'why's' hath an arrogant infidel," he exploded, and launched into the appropriate discourse on God's *arcana imperii*. In his own good time God would answer such questions with brimstone.

Cudworth's great evidential work against all fatalism broke off before it collided with the Stoics and predestinarians. The completed section, against Hobbes and the rest of the materialists, stands as a piece of question-begging as elaborate, learned, and devout as any in a literature necessarily written to prove premises by conclusions drawn from them. For all his mending of Descartes' ontological proof, Cudworth was no Aquinas and his Platonized cosmology no dialectic. By this Plastic Nature, his pacific compromise between the theists' overworked God and the Deists' too busy nature, he sought to woo apostates with a vision of intellectual beauty, not with demonstration. His invention seemed to him the best explanation consistent with the being and character of God; therefore he found evidence for God and his attributes in so lovely a handmaid. Again, he could not wholly concede to the "mechanic Theists" that philosophy ought to let final causes alone because Descartes had called them an excuse for prying into God's secrets. Without at least the general concept of teleology an important proof of God failed and ushered in again the fortuitous concourse of atoms. Because religion needed the argument from design, final causes had to be a placet of philosophy. Since, then, causes were final as well as efficient, the universe had design and God existed. It was too plain that Cudworth saw eternity, or its logic, as a great ring of pure and endless light. Scolding could not replace the missing propositions, though the philosopher dealt his pious insults freely. Atheists lacked man's natural shame; they denied the very axioms of thinking, thereby obliging the respondent to prove the axiomatic. Or they put bold queries for no purpose except to embarrass: If God made the world, why? If for his glory, how for love? Cudworth assumed at the threshold that it would be "a great part of confutation" merely to state such impiety; and with great learning he heaped up the "puffy show of wisdom," like "the giant Orgoglio in our English poet," blown up with nonsense and contradiction. His critics wounded him by pointing out that the statement of a shameless argument made no part at all of confutation, and that he had raised more arguments against religion than he had well answered.

Henry More did his sometimes foolish best to stop the holes in the standard arguments with new evidence from strange sources, even from natural science. He spent a lifetime collecting a patchwork philosophy "to draw an exoteric fence, or exterior fortification about theology." What materials he put into it and in what order are generally known—Platonism in many forms to stop materialism; a mended Cartesianism, to establish God's existence; cabalism, to give God all possible credit for sound human learning; apocalyptic exegesis, to display the truth of God's promises; and whatever opinions of the Royal Society he could use to prove the rest of his foregone conclusions. With pride he wrote at the end of his most ambitious evidential work: "I think I have ransacked all the corners of every kind of philosophy." To protect the Apostles' Creed he brought out of his plunder three concepts alien to dangerous modernity: his account of *a priori* knowledge, a purposeful direction in nature, and a world of extended spirit. In his *Antidote Against Atheism* he abundantly supplied, with bad science, final causes in detail where Cudworth left a discreet blank. He confronted Cartesian dualism and Hobbesian materialism with his spiritual cosmology, contrived of a preexistent soul, coextensive with the body; and a penetrable Spirit of Nature, coterminous with the physical universe. "Assuredly," he wrote, "that saying is not more true in politic, 'No bishop, no king'; than this in metaphysic, 'No spirit, no God'." And here once again he bent his science to devotion by making his Spirit of Nature account for gravity, sympathetic vibration, and whatever phenomena the Royal Society had not yet explained. For the charts and logbooks of his spirit-world he rifled scripture, cabala, neo-Platonic myth, and old wives' tales, gathering other men's truth, but not with what we should be likely to call an open mind. Much like Milton justifying God, More once took up in his *Mystery of Godliness* the *données* of the Gospel story each by each, proving every detail rationally necessary.

Obviously, only a properly "circumstantiated" reason would serve his turn, and it was a clipped and shorn reason that passed the philosopher's tests. The energy that he might have used prohibiting objects he gave to defining the faculty. In his Cambridge days or soon after, the common distinction between carnal and regenerate reason which every Christian must hold in some form seems to have struck him with the force of a revelation, for in *Psychozoia* and ever after he hinged his entire philosophy on it. Mnemon, or Spirit, he called religion's true authority in his not quite Spenserian verse-allegory of the creeds. It easily routed Popery and church-authority (Corvino), Calvinism and the Protestant tradition (Psittaco), and worldly reason (Graculo), chattering school questions, beating out subtleties, and hugging as greedily as the others its dominion over men's consciences. To make clear what he did not mean by Spirit, he contrasted that other "spirit" of the antinomian sects, or "naked faith disjoin'd from purity," in the person of Glaucis, daughter of Psittaco—yet hated of Psittaco worse than of Mnemon. The problem was a delicate one for a Platonist and a cabalist who tried to leave the impression that he had attained beatific vision. It is delightful to read Henry More and Thomas Vaughan quarreling, each accusing the other of enthusiasm. But on the simple matter of antinomianism, More was always firm. Whenever he fixed a wall between logic-chopping intellection, or "dry" reason, and the divinely philosophical, "incomplexionate" reason, he set up conditions both theological and moral. Reason formed no part of God's revelation, but "the oracle of God" could be heard only "in a good and holy man." It is instructive to read in another place More's propositions proving that no revelation truly from God could oppugn God's knowable attributes, clear natural truth, rational morality, or established government. Assuredly, before a philosopher could seek truth with incomplexionate reason, he had to learn submission and obedience. More's principle left enough reason to cure the "disease" of absolute skepticism, but it charted a unique course for the intellect to travel between axioms and revelation. Deviation betrayed the complexionate reason. Like other mysteries, that of godliness had to be believed in order to be understood.

And at last Arminians' incomplexionate reason grappled with Socinians, or with bold scripturalists like Milton, at the point of the grand mysteries. Where Milton's Bible taught him, so far as he could urge scripture, to remove gratuitous illogic from the Creed, More's theology taught him to explain why God had seen fit to be obscure. The mind of man had all mundane truth for its province; and if those "great pretenders to reason," the Socinians, could keep one sanctum inviolate, they would show themselves the more reasonable by their respect for God's privacy. A man truly wise would know enough not to thrust himself into the presence. Jeremy Taylor would have counted with many as one of those great pretenders to reason, for to More's simple Arminianism he added a Pelagianism that came near abolishing original sin. Coleridge objected that it tore down the whole Christian theory of redemption. Being such a rationalist and a noted tolerationist in the bargain, Taylor naturally took his place among the "Socinians" of gossip. But he enlarged reason only as a moral faculty, to make man entirely responsible ethically; no more than Baxter or More would he condone a cognitive reason unbridled in dogma, and in many a rule and precept he bade weak philosophy keep its appointed limits. The Socinians in particular, by the judgment of a man who went far toward being one, were "highly to be reproved for their excess in the inquiries of reason, not where she is not a competent judge, but where she is not completely instructed." And yet this Pelagian divine, who gave little honor to tradition as a ground of faith, knew as well as Milton that Trinitarian theology belonged more precisely to tradition than to the Bible that Protestants held by.

Between the last sacrifice of a unitarian to the legally acceptable metaphysics in 1612 and the rash of unitarianism that broke out in Presbytery late in the century, historians have pointed out few Englishmen demonstrably guilty of Milton's detestable heresy. The undiscoverable remainder had good reason to dwell anonymous. What could become a capital offense by the Presbyterians' Blasphemy Act of 1648 remained rank enough to strain the Protector's larger tolerance; it was the Biddle affair that finally, to Milton's disgust, provoked Cromwell to let slip his Triers. The "horrid and mighty monster of all heresies," as Laud called Socinianism, numbered far more honorary than active adherents by lending its name to religion that resembled it in any tenet. Laud himself, for denying absolute predestination, became Socinian, if not a Socinian, in Cheynell's index. Tillotson's much-quoted remark about the practice of branding every rationalist a Socinian held almost as true in his father's generation. To exalt "proud merit," or oppose man's free will to God's free grace, subtracted like Socinus from the fullness of satisfaction in God the Christ. To suggest, against all antinomianism, that Christ himself promulgated new laws smacked of the Racovian Catechism. To plead for religious toleration was to argue like the Polish rabble. Speaking of pretended liberty of conscience, Tuckney explained

to Whichcote that the age knew too much about Socinianism to confine it to disbelief in a coessential Trinity. As
for that peculiar tenet, nobody, Catholic or Protestant,
denied it to be logical; reason was its curse, for it fetched
divinity out of human wit, or it set *ratio recta* "opposite
to universality of tradition and the main stream of sound
antiquity." The Socinians, for their part, could find nothing opposing them but this very tradition of antiquity—
surely not scripture. Though Biddle and Milton no doubt
relished the moral religion that flowed from unitarianism
as a consequence, both earnestly denied, and with an excellent case, that they learned their doctrine from reason
rather than from scripture. Socinians regularly rested their
case on the Bible, comprehensibly interpreted. An impression runs current among Milton's critics, some of
whom have not pretended authority in objective study of
the scriptures, that the poet reached his doctrinal positions
by ratiocination and then collected texts to support them.
The premises granted, the rational direction of his heresies
would make him a kind of Deist in spite of himself; but
the premises must not be hastily admitted before a theologian more detached than Bishop Sumner can comment
the *Christian Doctrine.* Meanwhile, one may be forgiven
for asking what uninstructed reader, ignorant of Christian
tradition, his mind doctrinally a *tabula rasa,* could rise
from mere study of the scriptures ready to formulate the
Athanasian Creed?

Our own biblical scholars, with whom I profess no unusual familiarity, might object more strongly to Milton's
aim—to keep the tenor of the Bible while reducing it to
method—than to some of his particular heresies. St. Paul,
St. James, Amos, Job, collectively, reduced to method! Yet
Milton had his faith in God's consistency for his warrant,
the "marrows" of divinity for his precedent, and more
good scholarship than he had read to concur in some of
his unusual exegesis. Thomas Fuller and Jeremy Taylor
shocked nobody by suggesting that scripture did not contain all the received dogma of the Trinity. Nobody supposed that scripture taught the doctrine except by logical
consequence. One may read the best single text, John

xiv:16, and judge for oneself. Certain Catholic controversialists deliberately pointed out that scripture alone would overthrow the holy doctrine. They meant, of course, to commend the councils and church authority that Milton repudiated, and to discredit the bare letter. On Milton's premises the very Catholics discredited a superfluous subtlety. I would not be understood to meddle with the proposition that God may progressively reveal truth through his church. Milton denied it, and when a Catholic demonstrates that the *Christian Doctrine* is un-Christian by comparing it with Aquinas and the Anglican prayerbook he grotesquely begs the question. In matters of faith, Rome could not turn illogic into a religious mystery by calling it one; only scripture could do that, and the only article that it called a mystery was the Incarnation. In this positive exegesis Milton and Hobbes read alike. And here where he stopped, his way barred by the flaming swords, our untrammeled rationalist, our supposed manipulator of texts, preached to Socinians, Papists, and sober Christians his longest sermon on curiosity in doctrine. If men would only "acquiesce in the simple truths of scripture, unencumbered by metaphysical comments," there would be no more argument, no more heresy. The Bible plainly expressed all essential doctrine, and plainly declared it to be essential. On the evidence of clear scripture Milton utterly rejected the merely natural, the Socinian, explanation of Christ's satisfaction. If Protestants could only content themselves to abide by scripture alone, he thought, the necessary would appear, the mysterious remain inviolate, "and we should be fearful of overstepping the bounds of propriety."

And let us add that if he had not respected what he said, and tried to live by it, Socinianism would have afforded him a less mysterious religion than the scripturally derived Arianism that he stopped with. When he came to it first is a sleeping question and irrelevant here. That he never retreated from it is patent in the "Socinian" Exemplar-Christ of *Paradise Regained* and in the long, earnest, unqualified defense of the antitrinitarians that he made public in 1673. Anything that he wrote in his *summa* on the

cardinal dogma of the Trinity and left standing in a treatise that he was reworking all his life must surely be accepted as his last word. By the end of the century two
sorts of Christian had prominently drawn away from in-
stitutionalized religion—the Deists and the Quakers. Milton's unique scripturalism—or biblicism, as some may
prefer—yet a third way, set him apart from both. If we
accept the invitation to link him doctrinally with either,
his Arianism born of scholarly literalism must leave us
wrestling with a hopelessly untenable theology too freakish
for the comprehension of Charles Blount or George Fox.

Sympathy with those who had suffered beside him in
the heresiologies and a wish to spread sympathy among
those who shared enmity to Rome undoubtedly spurred
Milton to study his medley of questions more pertinent
to religious freedom than to saving doctrine. But we have
his word that he first settled his convictions by scripture
and read the heretics later. And in the face of his stubborn conviction that whatever Antichrist persecuted was
probably truth, he managed well to abide or interpret by
the plain places as Augustine bade. His earliest public
"error," divorce, strained the Sermon on the Mount to
fit a Bible studded with contrary texts; but whether he
brought Christ down to the Law or restored to the Gospel,
as he thought, the true message of Christian liberty, his
conclusions have been allowed by communions free of the
medieval canon law. If their drift has been away from scripture, Milton can still be acquitted of grave curiosity in
a point of doctrine, for the divorce question belonged
largely to matters merely civil, where reason properly held
the right to dictate when scripture spoke doubtfully. So
too some moral questions in the ethical second Book of the
Christian Doctrine, where scripture seemed at times an
afterthought corroborating classical morality. (A Catholic
critic calls this the only Christian part of the treatise.)
Still another matter more civil than doctrinal was polygamy, which nevertheless followed more clearly from scripture. One will search in vain for a clear text against a
practice clearly permitted in both Testaments. Not only
the humble zealots who acted upon the permission, but

some respectable Anglicans who did not, could read the Oriental drift of the Bible on the point. It is putting words in his mouth to assert that Milton therefore advocated harems. The Gospel revoked no civil permission of the Law, and hence neither divorce nor polygamy; but by the same token, biblical permission would hardly impose polygamy upon moderns whose civil laws forbade it so long as polity and not religion wrote the laws.

That cardinal Puritan tenet repudiated by Milton, the Sabbatical Sunday, affords an analogy. The Apostolic Lord's Day, Milton and Taylor determined, fell on Sunday, but whether weekly, monthly, or annually, neither could learn from the Bible. The day was never prescribed, as the clergy had a too plain interest in prescribing it, or invested with Mosaic rigors. Milton left Christians to observe it every Sunday if they found it expedient to do so, provided they understood that they chose freely. It is an earnest of the irenical intent running through the *Christian Doctrine* that he went out of his way to say a kind word for the Seventh Day Baptists. They erred, he thought, in their too legal Saturday-keeping, yet did better than legalistic Sunday-keepers. As for the more distinctive practice of many Baptists, immersion of adults only, part of which got into *Paradise Lost* (xii.442), but not as a prescription, most Christians will probably allow it to have been the Apostolic interpretation of scripture, as did Calvin.

In theology Milton strayed perhaps further from Protestant tradition than from the Bible. Scripture for the mild pantheism that he embraced only to account for creation (he made no other use of the doctrine, and never came near Fludd's ecstasies) is thin and inconclusive, to be sure, but no thinner than biblical proof of creation *ex nihilo*. His monism, creation *ex Deo*, eternity of matter, and traducianism—his Christian materialism—countered Deism on the one hand and predestination, with its latent Manichæan dualism, on the other. Yet so agreeable a consequence required the warping of no scripture. At any rate, his rational deviation from the received doctrine of God's transcendence seems about as scriptural as the orthodox

dogma, and so it had seemed to rabbis and other good
authorities. His theory of the natural generation of the soul
with the body and the orthodox opinion are both extraneous to a book that says nothing at all of the soul's origin,
but Milton chose the only explanation that, as Overton
had pointed out, would consist with mortalism. In this
soul-sleeping he had a pretty firm textual anchor for the
consistent remainder of his ontology. Scripture (Philipp.
iii:20–21), orthodoxy, and Milton agreed that the body
and soul would rise together, but the New Testament neglected to utter a distinct syllable on the state of the soul
between death and the general Resurrection. Papists filled
the gaps with the legends of Purgatory and Christ's Descent into Hell. It seems to have been suspicion of a mercenary motive for Purgatory that drove Luther and some
Lutherans to adopt psychopannychism, and we know what
Milton thought of Purgatorial cupidity. What has not
been remarked is that he used his mortalism to belie both
Purgatory and the Descent into Hell. A few more Protestants might have participated in his heresy if they had not
misunderstood it to be mere Sadducism, denying the Resurrection. The gap in the New Testament that Papists
filled with their legends he himself filled with pertinent
texts from the Old, which could not be supposed to disagree in a question touching ultimate reality. His Old
Testament texts had been written before Jewish belief in
a Resurrection became general. Since in the Old Testament, certainly before Daniel (xii:2), the soul slept per-
manently, and in the New, rose with the body, Milton's
now naïve harmonizing (it slept temporarily) cannot confidently be ascribed to mere philosophy.

The mother of all extrascriptural curiosity, the Roman
church, seen now as a subtle, overphilosophical teacher of
free will, now as a dismally obscurantist tyranny, broke
bounds in two directions at once. In disputations with the
Jesuits and more violently in their pulpits, preachers
damned the antichristians for staining the grace of God
with the puffed-up merits of man, or for abridging the
dignity of man with the arrogant doctrine of blind, implicit faith. The Papists multiplied mysteries without ex-

cuse and maintained their great mystery of iniquity by shutting out learning. At the same time, their too wise divines presumed to solve problems that sobriety would not touch. The curiosity of medieval scholasticism, it was forgotten, had been whipped before the Reformation, and by Rome herself at the Council of Trent, so that a Protestant controversialist could collect Catholic witnesses to its futility. The sixteenth and seventeenth centuries had reason to blame speculative divinity for everything amiss, and the commonplace quarrel with scholasticism furnished them an excuse to father their troubles upon Popery, for it had been the schoolmen who "first" mixed philosophy and religion. When Thomas Hobbes said so—and he said it as often as possible—Bishop Bramhall flew again and again to the defense of the well-nigh friendless schoolmen, whose exact method alone could resolve controversies. For his doctorate in divinity Bramhall had defended the thesis that the Papacy and its subservient divines had caused all the controversies of Christendom.

Elizabethan clergymen had inherited and transmitted the cavils of the early Reformation. Forgetting Philo and the Fathers, they made the schoolmen authors of allegories, iniquitous displays of human wit. The schoolmen had corrupted the language of the Holy Ghost into barbarous and desert terms, or debated "subtleties without the circle and compass of the world"—whether an ass might drink baptism or a mouse eat the Lord's body. To later preachers were handed, already listed in collections of commonplaces, convenient sermon-examples of "good" and "vain" questions, the latter surviving from the night of doctoral ignorance. A Scotchman's chapter "How Curiosities Have Wonderfully Distracted the Peace of the Church" drew curiosities only from Popery, important dogmas and petty quibbles together: whether God can lie, whether he could create accidents without substance, whether angels are individuals or species, to what heaven the ouranographers believe Enoch was rapt. Scholastic ouranography should not have moved Milton to wrath, though critics have often remarked that his own was a little less precise than Dante's.

The Moderns from Bacon to Glanvill who belabored

Aristotle and reaction often spoke the language of religion to cry down vain philosophy. The educational reformers of Parliamentary times—Hartlib, Dury, Petty, Hall, and others—often quoted St. Paul against learning "nice or fantastical." The intellectual revolution has been so familiarly chronicled that Thomas Hobbes, defender of the faith, may suffice for our single example. He could find a way to include the philosophies of the Greeks (for the Athenian schools could not claim geometry), the traditions of Jews and Papists, all myths and all supernatural illumination under his pious curse, but especially the medieval universities with their jargon of separated essences and occult qualities: "If such metaphysics and physics as this be not vain philosophy, there was never any; nor needed St. Paul to give us warning to avoid it." The Popes had been its chief authors and beneficiaries. His ban, falling upon Scholasticism historically defined and upon more philosophy besides, prompts the observation that the schools, like the Familists and Socinians, had lent their name. Writing his *Advancement,* Bacon apparently thought of historical Thomists and Scotists when he described Scholasticism as unprofitable matter endlessly divided. Elsewhere he used the term more broadly. Debating Knott the Jesuit, Chillingworth too defined school divinity as idle questions and "distinctions that exterminate reason and common sense," illustrating with stereotypes of calumny like angels on a needle point and mapmakers drawing heaven. But the quite distinct sins of either subtlety or presumption could make any divinity scholastic, and its date mattered little. Chillingworth added that some Protestants fixed the value of Christ's blood at that of exactly so many souls, and by no means one soul more. This seemed to him to be scholasticism, and a "fearful, dangerous curiosity." Protestant theology had brought, true enough, its own scholasticism, of which Laud's Oxford Statutes of 1636 can be taken as a fair specimen; and sometimes "school divinity" meant the theology taught at the universities. But we need not think academically every time we read the word. The measure of it was a leaden rule, a nose of wax. In most language of popular detrac-

tion the term meant simply curious divinity, particularly
that of an old-fashioned sort.

Some gnarled topics of early inquisitiveness, like the
origin of the soul, carried more than their share of the
general disrepute, and Protestants who pursued them dutifully labeled them curious, occasionally at length. A favorite was exact angelology. Though generally looked upon as
a Popish effrontery, it had not been esteemed by all Catholics. Pulci's learned demon Astarotte, it may be remembered, had been a chieftain among Seraphim (xxv.159)
without knowing half the things that pseudo-Dionysius
and Gregory wrote about. On the other hand, Zanchius
and Salkeld, acknowledged authorities, with Mede, More,
and a respectable company, wrote learnedly of angels for
Protestant readers. Less formidable theologians dabbled
superficially, diagramming the hierarchy, or guessing with
Zanchius that the angels fell in pride for refusing to worship Jesus. But marshalling the angels in ranks remained
an incautious pastime. Fuller liked to use it the way Milton used plural worlds, as a symbol to stand for all curiosity. So he used it twice, each time with the same quip:
rather than believe the bold angelologists, let us go to
heaven to confute them. Searching for every crumb of
revealed truth—nothing more—Joseph Mede scolded Protestants for being unduly incurious about angels, their
names and orders. Protestants deserved only a part of his
reproof, for, as a matter of fact, angelology fascinated them.
But inasmuch as they had rejected St. Denys and his over-
bold commentators, it is not remarkable that Milton, meticulous as usual, deliberately made Uriel a seraph at one
moment and an archangel at another.

The same church that produced so much evil subtlety
had been to the first reformers a sink of ignorance, and
the rise of the Inquisition made her the only politic and
calculated obscurantism outside the Turkish empire. The
fates of Bruno and Galileo (Vanini's martyrdom to atheism elicited no sympathy) made for Protestant detractors,
and other material in abundance gave point to *Areopagitica*. Sir Robert Dallington exposed the reason why the
Inquisition had deleted embarrassing pages of Guicciar-

dini's history. Junius, complimenting John Casimire on
having procured a copy of the *Index*, added with relish
that Casimire had also uncovered a Spanish "plot" to expurgate the Fathers, dropping all anti-Catholic passages;
and from Junius' edition the story became current. Jeremy
Taylor twice put it to use in controversy. This kind of
propaganda, taken with the everlasting "evidence" of ignorance in the lower Roman clergy, constantly persuaded
Protestants that "Licinius, Caligula, Caracalla, Domiti-
anus, Papists be enemies to thy understanding." Whoever
first said that ignorance is the mother of devotion, Eliza-
bethans quoted the remark as one that Henry Cole had
made in the course of an abortive public disputation, and
for generations it was repeated as approved Catholic doctrine. Pious ignorance and overwise divinity presented no
real paradox: the Papists enclosed "all learning within the
walls of their clergy, setting forth Lady Ignorance for a
great saint to the laity, and showing her unto *them* for
the true mother of devotion."

The numbing stupidity thrown around an arrogant
pretense of infallibility enabled Rome to fasten on God
things he never wrote. On the doctrine of Purgatory, or
counting the mansions in the Father's house, King James
preached to Bellarmine the earliest curiosity sermon we
can be sure Milton read; for with a loyal glance at the
king's wit, the young poet opened his own long war against
Antichrist. Where Rome, the common enemy, demanded
not too much reason but too much faith, Arminians joined
hands with James and the orthodox. In multiplying mysteries and imposing them as fundamentals the Papists tied
God to their sacraments, Chillingworth told Knott without much originality. By their eucharist in particular they
violated Augustine's rule forbidding the question How?
where God permitted only What? The Trinity and the
eucharist, under the phrase "hypostases and sacraments," in
Milton's textbook of logic symbolized all scholastic divinity. Since most of the embattled preachers angered by
transubstantiation or the Immaculate Conception brought
nothing new to these questions but their rhetoric, we shall
pass them by, for the rich flavor of their clichés evaporates

from our idiom. A most important occasion to denounce the Mass arose when La Milletière argued before the young king that the Anglican doctrine of the Real Presence was a treacherous quagmire on which to lay a *via media* in England. John Bramhall did what he could with his scholastic plane that smoothed the knots of controversy; then he betook himself to homily that Papists might learn, "Secret things belong to God." Faith was "minced into shreds and spun into niceties" because curious wits could not "content themselves to touch hot coals with tongs." The Papists anatomized mysteries by reason as a child might dip the ocean dry with a cockle shell. Transubstantiation goaded Jeremy Taylor to write with unusual length, heat, and platitudes on the proposition that in mysteries faith would ask What? and curiosity How? Bernard, Cyril, Justin Martyr supported this major. Scripture and reason gave him his minor: Christ had not told how his blood became wine—"It is behind a cloud and tied up with a knot of secrecy." Therefore, he concluded, "Let us lay our finger on our mouth, etc., etc." On this solitary point, where the Papist came a little closer to literalism than the Protestant, the scripturalist had to fall back on reason. By an ancient saw, a Christian would wink with the eye of reason in order to see better with the eye of faith, but Taylor thought it likely that here he would see only spots before his eyes.

Milton was too good a scripturalist to call the Pope Antichrist, whose identity would not be certainly known before the Last Things; but he deferred politely to the identification, for Antichrist of a certainty kept his "chief kennel" in Rome. Hatred of everything distinctively Popish in thought and practice drove him to the life-long intolerance of Catholicism that we can read in his early lines on the Gunpowder Treason or in his very latest tract on unity. For his prejudice he alleged the usual grounds: the "spiritual Babel," upheld by ignorance of scripture, imposed an ecclesiastical as well as a political tyranny, "both usurped, and the one supporting the other." Indifference to scripture, God's revealed will, made Popery the only true heresy, or the greatest; and much of the trouble had

begun when Constantine caused the Kingdom of Christ
to be adulterated with things of this world. The emperor's
mythical Donation (somewhat oddly Milton never distinctly called it a forgery in his many allusions to it) sym-
bolized the work of Antichrist so frequently in his prose
that we may at least suspect a Popish significance to details surrounding *donation* as a legal term where we meet
it in his poetry. Valla and the Reformers had left the word
practically no other association. When Michael unrolled
the future before Adam, Milton seemed to hark back to
what he had called the Papist: "the only heretic, who
counts all heretics but himself." After a new Covenant
for redeemed Israel, according to the angel's predated view
of history, the remnant lived for a season with gainful
labor, free government, and approved religion until Nimrod the Upstart rose to arrogate dominion, ruling others
in despite of heaven while claiming to hold his sovereignty
from heaven, accusing others of rebellion, himself and
his crew guilty of the true rebellion (XXII.30–39). In
some of these details, extraneous to both scripture and
Josephus, Milton drew Nimrod very like a type of Antichrist. Adam pertinently remarked the difference between
God's true "donation" and Nimrod's usurped empire, an
encroachment upon both man and God (69, 73). Thus
the lesson directed at tyrants may have been deliberately
meant to brand them as antichristian. So far as Milton
wrote *Paradise Lost* to assert dogma (if the æsthetic critics
will turn their heads while we fetch a little dogma thence),
he wrote it against Calvinism on the one hand and Popery
on the other—the latter more openly. The anti-Calvinism
of the poem needs a supply from the poet's other works,
for what Milton said of free will he actually said of Adam's,
so that his teaching could, and apparently often did, pass
for sublapsarian orthodoxy. It could never have passed for
tepid Protestantism, even though the poet, too much of
an artist to scream at Rome, only once and in jest spoke
literally of Antichrist. The friars, indulgences, rosaries of
the great Folly in Book III, suggested perhaps by Ariosto's
anticlericalism, are obviously Popish, but the ecclesiastical
argument may not end with these. The rest of the *exempla*

in the Fools' Paradise (III.463–473) may comment more
significantly on Rome—the revolted Giants, neither divine
nor human, popular as the type of Antichrist; the builders
of Babylon, easily new Babylon, fortress of usurped power;
the fools Empedocles and Cleombrotus, types of superstition, who in misguided zeal to heaven did that which
heaven never required at their hands (Is. v:2). Other lines
in the poem are militantly Protestant. The antichristian
character of Hell's great Sultan, reigning amidst the
trappings of Popery, is generally conceded. And Milton
brought his poem almost to a close by drawing Antichrist according to the lineaments of Popery (XII.506–540).
Critics who have perceived *Paradise Lost* to be a poem
importantly ecclesiastical have found no reason to think
it consistently so, as it likely would have been if its historical sweep had been narrower and later. But in those
places where Milton looked at Catholicism he saw the
same presumption that he described in the wisdom-folly
antithesis in his *Christian Doctrine*. Wisdom he there defined as knowing and doing the will of God, plainly, by
the context, knowing the Bible and living by it. To it he
opposed false conceit of wisdom, "prying into hidden
things" like Eve or Lot's wife, and finally "human or carnal wisdom." But the prime folly, out of which grew the
rest, was ignorance of God's will. Thus Milton on folly, in
what is surely our best commentary on the Paradise of
Fools.

THE ELUSIVE MIDDLE WAY

Papists, Jews, philosophers, Anabaptists, Socinians—all
the "civil judiciaries" or "justifiers of themselves" on the
rational side of orthodoxy—met, as we have noticed, in
strange confederacy to discredit "common Protestantism,"
the sweet and comfortable doctrine of predestination. As
they surveyed pride they found the orthodox conspicuously guilty of it on the point of infallible assurance. Milton, too, rejected Calvin's reading of II Peter i:10, necessarily, but without ridicule, possibly because Catholics had
been pounding against the *certitudo salutis* from the time
the Council of Trent set them the target. How, the Papist

wondered, could the Protestant be so arrogant as certainly to know himself one of the elect? God's judgments and man's heart being inscrutable, how could he know that his assurance of salvation came not from his own logic? The hundreds of properly instructed Protestants who took up the challenge knew that they were far more humble to collect their assurance by God's plan than by works, as did the proud Papist, whatever his assurance could be worth. To suspend Christians in perpetual anxiety, something a Calvinist would never do, was "to strive with God under the shadow of humility." Arminians strove, nevertheless. No mortal, or no Arminian mortal like Jeremy Taylor, could certainly know his election—his own or his neighbor's.

For their sin of exalting man, the free-will men drew solace from the knowledge that they had not dishonored God. Strype recorded Anabaptists in Kent back in 1549 teaching that predestination was a doctrine fitter for devils than Christians, and the opinion had gained ground by 1581. It invaded high places with the Cambridge revolt in the 1590's. Soon thereafter Anabaptists, as it seemed to D'Ewes, began to change their name to Arminians; others observed the Arminians to "jump with" the Anabaptists. Either way, an apprehensive parson feared that "the world" had begun to "flock after Arminius." If he spoke statistically, he alarmed himself needlessly for the moment, for Samuel Hoard's manifesto of the high-church Arminianism in 1633 everywhere spoke of the author as a "dissenter" for holding absolute reprobation to be "a mocking denial of God's gifts," and a God who decreed sin "worse than the devil." But in 1647 Zephaniah Smyth, a Black Coat, wrote for a crowd of what he called Levellers in Suffolk an uncompromising sermon of absolute reprobation, "because this is a doctrine not often insisted upon and at this time denied." When he tried to deliver it he was interrupted by the High Constable and hooted by the citizenry for his devil's doctrine not fit to be preached.

For saving God's sorely impeached goodness without sacrificing his Calvinity the half dozen theologies of compromise that floated about satisfied relatively few English-

men. The compromising Baxter seems to have followed
Amyraut with a theory of limited universal grace somewhat broader than Calvin's, and it has been shown that
some in New England followed Cocceius and Ames into the
federal theology. Professed dissenters, instead of patching,
were more likely to drop absolute predestination altogether and take either the way of Quakers and universalists (Origenists)—widening the bounds of God's mercy—
or that of Taylor's *Deus Justificatus* and all other Arminianism—enlarging the power of man's rational integrity. Of
the great majority who abided by the sublapsarian theology of Dort, some pacifically left doctrine to one side and
preached a way of life. Perkins early showed the moral
way. All the faithful accepted a subtle theory to save God's
goodness; he was the author of sinful actions, but not of
the sinfulness in the actions. When an alleged antinomian
wrote "soberly and modestly" that God was the author of
both, the Assembly arranged a book-burning. All softened
reprobation with the Scotist distinction, hateful to Milton,
between God's reason and man's. This they formulated
in the theory of the double will, according to which God
held out redemption to all men by one hand and withheld
it from most by the other. To prove as much they reveled
in the moral contradictions of the Bible, stories of God's
putting evil in men's hearts, permitting evil contrary to
his laws and promises, or rewarding evildoers. William
Twisse, ablest of the Upper Way, piously accused God of
many sins, but he would not admit that God could contradict himself. In some fifty pages, to the everlasting glory
of the Almighty, he collected one formidable instance after
another of God's sins—committed, permitted, and commanded. Everything, in short, except duplicity: God
merely commanded one thing and purposed another, and
any opinion to the contrary was "sottish" and "most averse
from sobriety." Where reprobation occasioned the double
will, assurance-seekers could find small comfort in the Calvinists' empty guarantee that the secret will could not contradict the revealed (could not, that is, by a harmony evident to God alone) or in word-play that merely altered
terms. When Richard Resbury answered John Goodwin's

Arminian logic with a euphemism, for instance, the secret and revealed wills became the "decreeing will, or will of intention," and the "declaring will, or will of administration."

A Catholic demanded to know how the hidden will could be called secret when so many knew so much about it. Predestinarian theology made so bold with the dread *arcanum* of all divinity that a Calvinist anticipated an objection: "Is it not lawful then in any condition to meddle with the hidden and secret counsel of God?" Three questions, he decided, might be asked with modesty: Why is the secret will so called? What does it mean to practical holiness? How does it give peace by accounting for evil? To practical holiness the secret will contributed most when left secret; this point his opponents would have yielded. In answer to his last question they would have liked a simple *O altitudo!* better than Calvinists' meddling. A Royalist physician whose temper may be judged in his unstinting praise of Sir Thomas Browne shrank from the question and from a dualism that some called Manichæan:

> Sin is defined what's contrary to God's will;
> Yet abridge ours, and he's the cause of ill.
> What God doth preordain, sure his will is:
> If then the sin be done, the sin is his.

But how then could God be just in punishing guilt?

> Hath God two wills, one secret, one revealed?
> Good in appearance, is he ill concealed?

He retired humbly from the work of justifying God's ways as his rugged rhymes for peace embraced a religion that exchanged "aery mysteries" for "orderly zeal."

Milton laid down a plain and important rule of sobriety to purge the doctrine of the double will. He allowed God, as any believer must, a secret will—

> Some I have chosen of peculiar grace
> Elect above the rest; so is my will—

but free only to good. An act of mercy, but only an act of mercy, needed no justification. For absolute reprobation

there could be none. Fortunately, scripture spoke of predestination, election, and reprobation, but nowhere of
predestined reprobation. Where scripture left off and reason had no license to multiply mysteries, unreason had
less than none. Milton held an unjust God little better
than no God, and that God unjust who refused to be
tried by the rules of human justice. In *Paradise Lost* he
drew a circle within the circle of the *Christian Doctrine,*
the larger embracing the biblically defensible opinions
that he invited Christians everywhere to respect, the other,
in its few admonitions, the indispensable and saving doctrines. He taught the essentials pointedly enough: to
"serve and fear" a just God who held himself accountable
to man, to hold "faith not void of works" in the divinity
of Christ, and to obey the moral law as revealed to the
Jews, illuminated by the Gospel, and corroborated by the
light of nature. In some such articles he might have formulated evangelic religion, which he once "told in two
words, faith and charity; or belief and practice."

But one who staked all on scripture saw religion fall to
the ground if God's morality failed in God's written word.
As a scholar Milton knew that the Bible could be found
factually in error, but its mistakes in that kind belonged
to the Holy Spirit's penmen and hardly imperiled religion.
That God had flaunted his own unrighteousness in the
sacred histories the Christian poet denied with all his dedicated power of reflection. Where he met obstacles in his
labor of exculpation, like the difficulty of justifying God's
ways to serpents (*P. L.* x.169), he leveled them as best he
could before leaving them with "More concerns us not to
know." Original sin, too, the visiting of the father's guilt
upon the children, he found hard to justify syllogistically;
but nothing in scripture forbade him to try, even if he
had to go at last to the ancients and nature's bare precedent for piacular punishments. We do not need to seek afar
those against whom Milton for so many years defended
God. It would be doing Hobbes and the few philosophical
determinists too much honor to imagine that he opposed
them in particular, especially when in his *Christian Doc-*

trine he identified his antagonists as clearly as he could
do in a work that called no erring Protestant sects by name.
"For the purpose of vindicating the justice of God," he
might, he declared, in some wild fancy allow determination in natural and civil things (materialism's more trivial
error) if he could save the human will free in matters of
morality and religion. Calvinists, as all readers would have
understood, allowed the will free in natural and civil
things, but held it powerless to do good in the sight of God.
"It is *entirely*" on this latter opinion, he concluded, "that
the outcry against divine justice is founded."

Touching predestination he dared to ask, foolishly on
Calvin's premises, "Why should God foreknow particular
individuals?" To suppose that God did so could only raise
futile questions. "Without searching deeper into this subject," he was content to know that God "predestined to
salvation all who should believe." The kind of secret will
dimly revealed in the story of Pharaoh and the other stories
of God's aid to sinners or his putting evil into the hearts
of men, he did what he could to explain rationally away.
The learned Rivetus might conclude that God did in some
fashion "dispense" and there give up the question, but it
behooved a Christian to wrestle with the problem if
prompted by the right motive, to remove "absurdities"
that reflected "against the purity, justice, and wisdom of
God." He doubtless had in mind the Calvinists trium-
phantly demonstrating God's patent wickedness when in
Samson Agonistes he reckoned the deniers of God to be
few—

> Yet more there be who doubt his ways not just,
> As to his own edicts found contradicting.

In numbers, certainly, the Calvinists, and perhaps the
scoffers raised up by their errors, headed God's enemies
who thereupon gave "reins to wandering thoughts," care-
less of his glory, piling up contradictions in their perplex-
ity. Milton's Chorus agreed with them part way, though
we need not take its perplexities for his own: God's justice was a *datum* to be accepted on faith, even when the

Almighty behaved questionably, for who could bring him
to trial, or

> confine the interminable,
> And tie him to his own prescript,
> Who made our Laws to bind us, not himself?

"Down reason, then"—William Twisse and the rest of
Job's comforters would have gone no further, but Milton's
Chorus finished the sentence—"at least vain reasonings
down." While reason could still absolve God from guilt,
it had work to do; it was the vain reasoning that doubted
God's ways justifiable to men that must down. Mere human morality had no case against God for having driven
the Nazarite into the arms of the Timnian bride:

> Unchaste was subsequent, her stain not his.

If God moved Samson in mysterious ways, to a Timnian
woman or to suicide, reason had a simple choice: to render
a moral verdict in God's favor and support it by logic, or
to render the same verdict and be silent and assenting,
confessing its own feebleness as an advocate. It was the
course that Milton laid down in the eighth Book of *Paradise Lost* for all speculative thought. By way of homely
analogy we might consider the valve that permits water
from a pump to flow one way only.

In studying to defend their theology at the points of
reason, tradition, scripture, and consequences, the better
predestinarians agreed to surrender the feeble outworks
to carnal logicians at the first push. Predestination was
"only attributable to the will of God," the "rule of all
reason in the creature." It "explained" that folly and impotence which prevented Henry Vaughan's reprobates in
"The World" from soaring to the ring of light: God had
merely willed that only the bride-elect should enjoy it.
Let Arminians keep their tenets "plausible enough to cor
rupt reason, and set out to the best advantage of wit and
art," their "new model of God's counsels framed in man's
brain" still found no support in scripture. The creed of
SS. Paul, John, and Augustine could not be called reasonable in the vulgar sense, but God spoke, and his voice

silenced all inquiry, or nearly all. The godly, "soberly" attributing evil *actions* to God, might concentrate profitably upon the good use he made of them and there drop the matter. After losing heavily the argument from reason, predestinarians scored perhaps a trifling advantage in the battle of scripture-texts, and won easily the argument from Protestant tradition. Since Arminians dragged the Apostle over to their own side, they could, notwithstanding, feebly return the charge of brash novelty and date the Lower Way from A. D. 400, the Upper from 600 or 800. In the long run, as the Popish threat in Arminianism faded into oblivion, all the "immoral" fruit that the free-will men had early predicted from Calvinism ripened abundantly in the form of antinomian religion. Thus the Arminians won the argument from consequences and with it their most important victory. Hammond turned all his thunder upon the lawless extravagances of "fiduciaries," orthodox or antinomian. Any Christian innocent of curiosity would accept gratefully the vagueness of the Articles of the Church of England, forget about predestination, and devote himself to holy living. Like Henry More, who made his Glaucis the daughter of Psittacus in *Psychozoia*, Goodwin accurately enough deduced from the Calvinists' imputed righteousness the antinomian corollary that God saw no sin in his children. The orthodox, in detesting the consequence, imitated the stepfather who marries the mother and tries to beat the children out of doors.

For the factual record, it is not inaccurate to say that antinomianism grew out of Calvinism, for much of it sprang thence. We might reckon up many instances—Tobias Crisp moving from Arminianism to the opposite extreme through Calvinism, John Eaton graduating from Pagitt's tutelage, John Saltmarsh collecting his infallible assurance from faith alone. Peter Sterry, "almost" at Zion as antinomian Erbury measured, wrote for predestination and for more determinism besides. Young Vane's disposition to antinomianism seems clearer in his political record than in his incomprehensible meditations, but if he actually embraced it, he also wrote in a moment of perfect lucidity that God predestinated men and angels by name before

eternity, both to mercy and to wrath and for no antecedent cause; and if our reason rebels, who are we to reply
against him? Such theology might accord well with antinomianism. At the same time, we must recall that there had
been Familists in England from the 1570's, hardly claimed
by the predestinarians, and regularly accounted antinomian, whatever may have been their founder's views. If
Seeker and Quaker antinomianism bore any historical relation to the theology of Spirituals set abroad in Calvin's
time, then it appears that two widely separated sources
exuded converging streams.

The interminable predestinarian wrangling, indecisive
and often carried on by men who wore their doctrine only
as a badge of party affiliation—for most Englishmen the
doctrine of predestination eventuated in no distinct and
peculiar consequence of any kind for practical living—
constituted as a whole the century's most obvious waste
of thought. The Arminians most often, for several good
reasons, pointed to the seventeenth Article and deplored
bickering about a nonessential doctrine. Milton set an importance on the controversy unusual for one of his "Pelagian" persuasion. The Anglican divines in particular—
Laud as well as the other doctrinal moderates—wished to
hear no more about the matter. "Adam was driven out of
Paradise for asking too much knowledge," Bishop John
King had early reminded the extremists on both sides,
and "the men of Bethlehem were slain to the number of
fifty thousand for prying into the Ark." Many laymen who
thought of themselves as ordinary Protestants would have
agreed with Davies of Hereford that "curiosity's cat's
eyes" peering into predestination could too easily make
"God our foe, sin's cause, and so a devil," and that it
sufficed to know that he would save all who used the revealed means of salvation. Predestinarians were willing to
drop the subject of God's decrees, but not while heresy
breathed. Their doctrine too clearly belonged to the saving
fundamentals. King James himself certified its importance by pursuing Conrad Vorst as far as the royal arm
would reach and by ordering one of his books to the
flames. Tuckney growled that from all he had heard of

rixæ et lites in the pulpit, God's existence would soon be
a mere speculation. In the late season when Baxter was
about ready to confess the Arminian controversies a contention about words, Presbyterians could still be heard
maintaining their right to dispute for their necessary theology.

Fundamental or not, the argument had the honor to be
one form of curiosity outlawed by royal edict in three
reigns, and Jeremy Taylor looked back on this piece of
kingly wisdom as worthy of Constantine, the emperor who
forbade his bishops to argue about the Trinity. Neither
Constantine nor Charles had much effect. The predestinarian war dragged on, with sharper battles when Montagu, leader of the Anglicans' Romanist faction, threw
his *Apello Cæsarem* to the orthodox at the beginning of
Charles's reign, and again when the Independent Goodwin
redeemed redemption early in Cromwell's. Throughout
this vast literature every writer battled a curious opponent.
"Yourselves can nor relish nor savor anything but only
God's secrets," Bishop Montagu warned the Calvinists,
who could never let the *arcana imperii* alone. One of his
numerous respondents, armed with scripture and tradition, took up this theme of the quarrel: nobody pried into
God's secrets so irreverently as the Arminians. The Church
of England had always soberly kept the one true Protestant theology, as anyone could see by counting heads and
weighing prestige. Montagu should learn to live by his
precepts of humility. In another exchange of the same
futile kind in later years, the Arminian Bramhall was to
find Hobbes following "the mode of these times to father
their own fancies upon God, and when they cannot justify
them by reason, to plead his omnipotence, or to cry *O
altitudo!*"

Predestination can be a reassuring doctrine for minori-
ties like the early Christians under persecution. It has
solaced scattered individuals in better times. To Calvin it
came as the complete answer to Popish works and merit.
But afterwards it established itself as a triumphant orthodoxy. Joy in God's free grace, "the action of predestinating
us to adoption"—preachers liked to ignore the converse—

had paled somewhat by the time Samuel Hoard called his earliest of English replies *God's Love* because it demolished reprobation. Meanwhile within Calvinism itself certain time-honored teachings of caution permitted orthodoxy to approach reason.

Calvin had anticipated that outraged reason would assail his interpretation of scripture at the points he so copiously guarded with *O altitudo!* He would not have foreseen that in time a pragmatic spirit would turn many of the doctrinal enigmas he thus advertised into nonessentials, or that his concessions to reasonable morality would be magnified dangerously for a season by his nominal disciples resisting antinomians. The patriarch had had his own troubles with pietists and spirituals; he too contrived scriptural and rational antidotes for the venom of the *Theologia Germanica* and mysticism unbecoming to the sobriety of Christians. He taught the folly of seeking assurance from God's decree alone, of naming others as reprobates, of preaching unnecessarily and incautiously of reprobation. Having thus laid the ground for a ministry of moral redemption, the good classicist wrote habitually of reason and learning like any other humanist. The Fall had left nature only purblind, and to argue its total blindness and impotence, or to hold the will bound in aught except supernatural matters, was contrary to scripture and common experience. As a consequence of the Fall the mind suffered a predisposition to curiosity, however. Calvin delated throughout his scriptural *summa* its futility in school questions: How was God occupied before Creation? What are the ranks and titles of angels and devils? Overwisdom might venture the curiosity of Servetus, or with almost the same "monstrous impiety" demand the wherefores of God's secret will in predestination. All determinism necessarily bowed with unusual deference before the secret will, as we may read in Hobbes for the materialists or in Lipsius for the Stoics.

Perkins and the rest rebuilt Calvin's chain of fortresses, until futile argument coupled with their own deprecations could only induce laymen to hold the unknowables first as nonessentials and then as idle speculations. Thomas Sut-

ton's lecture on Romans xi:33 (*O altitudo!*), covering the
unreasonable points in St. Paul's creed and Calvin's deriva-
tive, silenced with the Apostle's caveat all "curious and
unnecessary questions." Why did God condemn men for
unbelief, "seeing no man can believe, except God confer
faith on him"? Is not God cruel to condemn men eternally
before they have done any evil? The *O altitudo* could
only betray weak defenses when the men seriously asking
Sutton's long list of unthinkable questions were the same
kind of men who would soon march with Cromwell.
Where the orthodox theologians used it, their theology
was most vulnerable. Yet they used it constantly to turn
religion from dogma to practice.

Without thinking of federal theology, then, or any other
mild departure from the divinity prescribed by Dort, we
can hear the preachers softening or rationalizing Calvin by
extending man-pleasing doctrine from no source but the
Institutes. They gloried in reason except in the very decree of predestination, and invited it to examine matters
supernatural, with the stipulation that only regenerate reason accept. Regenerate reason, "captivated by grace,"
broached no heterodoxy. Wherever salvation made no
part of the question, mere natural reason, both discursive
and moral, had full scope. When a distinguished student
can momentarily forget himself and write without apparent jest of Puritans winning predestinated battles,
there may be some virtue in repeating that Puritans of
every hue allowed perfect freedom in natural, moral, and
civil things, categories that included battles. Thomas
Hobbes and Peter Sterry, on dissimilar grounds, used
Calvinism as one corner of a determinism that went beyond religion, but other names may be difficult to recall.
Preachers welcomed the chance, as moral philosophers, to
mitigate God's austerity, answer Lucretian atheism, and
concede all that the ancients and the light of nature could
justly claim. When we seek the "cause" that shaped an
educational theory or a constitution of civil government,
we shall therefore look more probably to the interests of
Anglican, Presbyterian, and Independent politics than to
the differences between predestinarian and free-will the-

ology. We could explain little about the "Calvinistic" Roger Williams or the "Arminian" John Milton by starting with their formulated doctrines of free grace and free will. Though we have heard Milton declare that he would prefer a natural necessity to a religious, he too left man free, actually, in indifferent things, natural and civil, and cautiously granted him "some" power to do good in the sight of God. Peter Heylyn thought, perhaps wrongly, that all sects would grant as much. In his guarded statement Milton professed himself no Pelagian. He never intended, like some fully emancipated rationalist, that free will should abolish original sin or reduce it to mere imitation of Adam.

If assuring oneself of one's own election was a sin in the eyes of free-will men, assuring oneself of another's reprobation was worse in the eyes of all men, perhaps worse than assuring oneself of one's own damnation. Obviously, this kind of presumption would tend to quench endeavor. It was a bold curiosity for assurance-seekers in Donne's divinity and everybody's to peer, as the cant had it, "into God's books." Calvinists offended if they concluded prematurely that either their own election or their reprobation, decreed from all eternity, made works indifferent. Baxter had certain parishioners at Kidderminster who, hunting excuse for laxity that they would have found somewhere in any theology, posed as fatalists and refused to "use the means." It was pure doctrine, not compromise, that Zephaniah Smyth preached when he reminded his truculent Levellers that particular persons might not be named as reprobates, for secret things belonged to God; nor was it for any man to determine that he himself was a reprobate, never knowing when God might show him mercy. In general, "Whom God hath elected and whom rejected we know not, . . . neither is it necessary that we should know, but yet thou mayest know for thine own particular, that God hath predestined thee to life." The knowledge came through works of faith, but not because of them. William Sclater found some heretics in James's reign peculiarly given to legal works and the habit of identifying the elect thereby. Their leader was the "upstart prophet" John Trask, who flourished about 1617. Trask himself eventually returned to his "holy and tender mother" and opened his penitential work with a chapter of humility; but to his converts, or to one at least, the observance of man's Sunday instead of God's Saturday remained of a piece with the imagination of a world in the moon. The Traskites, of whom Milton once spoke gently, began by holding that the dietary compromise of the first Christian council was still binding, believed like Milton that the observance of the Lord's Day was not, and thereafter, steeped in error, supposed that the company of the elect could be recognized by the outward sign of their Jewish practices. For both the Calvinist Sclater and the Jesuit Falconer the Traskites were wicked examples of the length to which Christians could not go in collecting assurance for themselves and others from works.

In the decades that followed, Calvinists fretted less and less about legalism while they themselves became known as legalists. Faith in a kind of excess menaced them far more seriously than works as fideistic "perfection" grew like a weed and pushed them toward the Arminian way. They herded the faithful with godly warnings along the ethical road to assurance, away from the cruxes of theology, away from antinomian presumption. God's purpose was not to be sought in his bottomless counsel, but "in the means and manifestations appointed for the same" in his word. "Jacob wrestled with the angel at the foot of the ladder: we must not be so hardy as to wrestle with God at the top of the ladder." When an orthodox minister forbade his faithful followers to search the secret will, he forbade them to presume upon their election, for speculation forsaking the daily righteousness of their "vocation." Inasmuch as this form of curiosity strayed from the moral road to assurance, a preacher could write meaningfully: the prying into God's secret will and "the suffering of thy heart to be questioning it, is the cause of most of thy sins." Enlarged, such preaching against antinomian tendencies blended with Arminianism; the very secrecy of God's decree worked, for practical purposes, toward abolishing that decree.

ENTHUSIASM—AN ERROR ON THE RIGHT HAND

Mere antinomianism, unmixed with other aberrations, dared to revise common Protestantism in only one article: it eliminated the vocation step (and the good works identified with it) as the path *to* predestined justification. The orthodox way of vocation, justification, sanctification, and glorification was not exactly lopped, but telescoped. Faith alone justified; the truly believing Christian in a state of grace then loved God and hated sin because God hated it. He honored and kept God's law. He kept the Ten Commandments, for they best defined sin. Inasmuch as the callous sinner could not presume to have saving faith (as by orthodoxy he could not be destined to have it), one may not see at once how this doctrine, probably closer to St. Paul's than its predecessor, could "abolish" or encourage sin if not distorted. Unless *Grace Abounding* is less honest than it seems, Ranters and some others distorted it, but candid critics absolved John Eaton, the first mere antinomian to publish in England, and his doctrine when shorn of wicked consequences. Since the Covenant, the catechism, the Directory, and the theocrats' sacramental offices could be numbered among the legal requirements of the "ministry of condemnation," we may be sure that the Black Coats' fear of immoral consequences was in part bound up with a fear for their own ecclesiastical dignities. In pious modesty, the antinomian, as well assured as Calvin of his adoption, was forbidden to know what measure of faith, precisely, God accepted as sufficient, to judge the estate of others, or to conclude himself reprobate: "Election and condemnation being secret things belong to God." Possibly no antinomian taught that the "perfected" believer literally could not sin. Certainly all taught that God saw no sin in him—and thus raised a scriptural mystery not to be discoursed upon by reason. If legalists could hold reprobates powerless to do that which God considered good, then antinomians might put the converse without soaring higher above reason. What they asked thereby was a religion free of Pharisaism; good works performed indeed (whatever slanders malice might invent), but performed freely for love of God, not slavishly, fearfully, or selfishly; repentance in sorrow, not in fear of punishment. The legalist who admitted works to be a part of the faith that saved—Milton did so—offered them in payment for salvation. Protestant or Papist, he presumed upon the light of nature and his own merits.

So each party set up its accusations of pride in the war of name-calling, mostly a fuming about consequences—the notion that free grace must lead to immorality against the theory that legality must result in bondage. Tobias Crisp raised the customary objection to offering Christ payment for his gifts; Stephen Geree countered with the pride of sinners who supposed that they had as much part in Christ as any saint in heaven. Robert Towne discovered in the Presbyterians' legalism the bulwark of natural knowledge and the opinion of men; Samuel Rutherford replied that he had described Popery. The gospel way (the Presbyterian) was the middle way. It was no merit-monger, but it would not, for all that, have God merciful to "dogs and swine," or to those who threw off all external obedience, substituting private enthusiasm for scripture and presumption for faith. It was the antinomians, not the legalists, who made faith the act of a lofty Pharisee. "I confess," the Presbyterian summed the case for rational religion, "this is a hasty, hot work," and "a wanton, fleshly, and a presumptuous work, to lay hold on the promises of mercy and be saved."

Though the camp-meeting religion of the antinomians implied no necessary enthusiasm, it easily admitted it in the vulgar or some kind of mysticism in men like Saltmarsh, Dell, and Erbury, so that most new lights, alleged or probable, shone among the enemies of legalism. In taking his carefully stated position against free grace in Eaton's sense, Milton surely meant to close the door—gently—on the religion of the more mystical sectaries. It bears recalling, if only to the meditations of some who would make a religious poet a religious mystic, that he recoiled from antinomianism as emphatically as from absolute predestination. In dropping the Jewish law, in neglecting Calvin's distinction between the moral and the ceremonial law of Moses, he wrote nothing one way or the

other on the question of legalism. Luther had doubted
that St. Paul meant the Gospel to abrogate only ceremonies, but Agricola would never have called Luther antinomian. If Milton became a "Free Gratian" for such
exegesis, so perhaps did Zanchius, whom he cited to support it. The only consequence that he drew from the
abrogation of the whole Law was Christian liberty, politically defined as freedom of worship by separation of civil
and spiritual powers. The way Calvin's distinction had
been abused would have encouraged him to deny it. Those
who argued the moral part of Moses' law to be still binding had made Sunday-keeping a part of that law, invoking
the secular arm. Milton would have thought of the Blasphemy Act of 1648, punishing mere dissent with fines and
prison, grounded upon the law of Moses, where tithes and
witch-hangings also rested. For some of these reasons, but
emphatically not for antinomianism, Separatists had read
St. Paul again and had found no support for Calvin's
theory that the Gospel revoked nothing but ceremonies.
Early and antagonistic readers of the *Christian Doctrine*
bore witness to Milton's legalism and approved it.

His pacific intention showed once again in his polite-
ness to antinomian textuaries; they had some scripture on
their side, plausibly St. Paul. Justification, he granted
them, came by faith, without the works of the law. But
not without works. Without works of faith, different from
Pharisaical works and more necessary, there could be no
faith. It is delectable to think of Tobias Crisp or Samuel
Gortyn reading the ethical, Aristotelian second Book of the
Christian Doctrine, which outlined the works of faith.
Erasing Moses, then rewriting him by the light of nature
and the Gospel, erased no legalism from theology; it only
permitted Milton to drop the uncharitable and irrational
parts of Moses. That which in Moses the Gospel revoked,
the Holy Spirit, later in time and in a higher degree of
illumination, rewrote in the heart. But in Milton's book
of Christian ethics the light of nature assisted the Spirit
where love of God and more especially of neighbor needed
some wise rule or clear principle of school morality. At the
same time, this theology of works—rational, unmystical,

"Arminian"—left no room for pride in human merit, because even an Arminian's good actions were really God's.
And as John Goodwin discouraged boasting, the sinner
reaped infinite felicity for, by comparison, nothing—like
the fortunate subject who lent his king a pin. Works
helped to excite grace, Milton boldly stated what antinomians abhorred to hear, but only as a tiny spark in
powder released tremendous forces disproportionate yet
answerable. The spark could not boast that it had "earned"
the result, nor the sinner his salvation. The scriptures
spoke hyperbolically of the "perfection" of the new creature in tribute to Christ's satisfaction, not to be the creature's sinlessness. One might therefore embrace the figure
safely as befitting those who purified themselves with
good works to the limit of their ability.

The biblical scholar felt more at ease with the Baptists.
They built their church far from Antichrist and the world,
and framed by scripture its government, doctrine, and
sacraments. In these last they showed a Christian materialism that to the Quaker seemed rudimentary, a betrayal
of early Anabaptist spirituality. The Baptists' materialism
that would not allegorize the Gospel story grew to serious
controversial importance in a time when radical groups
were repudiating John's water-baptism as a retrograde
step into sensual idolatry. Milton early meditated the fact
that Jesus, for some good reason, instituted his sacraments
in matter, and more of such reflection may have helped
him work out his own ontology. The young man who
wrote of the continuity of all being in *Comus* aspired
poetically to rise free above the world of matter, but he
outgrew the prejudice; the monist who wrote of heaven
in *Paradise Lost* glorified *this* world's substance and true
form. To suppose that excesses of spiritual religion had
taught him earthy sobriety would be conjecture, but not
implausible conjecture. Let us conceive some Seeker or
Quaker who understood the sacraments spiritually in
order that he might rid his worship of all unholy dross;
let us endow him with Milton's gifts; and let us imagine
what the mystic might have written of heaven, its inhabitants and their conversation.

Before Masson made him an eclectic of all sects or a sect in himself, Milton was commonly reckoned a Baptist; and it may still be well, if one finds it helpful to classify him, to consider his scriptural excursions into Arianism and materialism as easy extensions of an Arminian Baptist's faith. In their manifesto of 1650 Baptists repudiated antinomianism. In consistency, if not in charity, they did voluminous battle with the Quakers. Milton's unsettled Baptist friend Roger Williams apparently did not consider that the Quakers' thirst for religious freedom entitled them to ignorant enthusiasm under the guidance of a spirit of presumption. The distinction between spiritual and civil power, which Milton had studied from his youth and not under George Fox, had been the Anabaptists' from the beginning. For it as much as for their religion they had burned under the Tudors, and their apostles like Thomas Helwys had done more than other sectarians to hammer it into the English conscience before Baptists began to slip into fat livings under Cromwell.

Sleidan's stories of the Anabaptists' Münster rebellion easily clung to a sect that harbored political theory more distasteful than dangerous to any established English church. Ink-and-paper persecutors for more than a century refused to allow their descent from the godly Menno instead of from the polygamous communist John of Leyden, and vilified them particularly around 1647, though Parliament vouchsafed them a declaration of their harmlessness. The political intransigeance of Fifth Monarchists, which Cromwell had to answer with his treason ordinance in 1653, embarrassed the Baptists, for there had been heralds of King Jesus at Münster, and detraction liked to keep the memory green. It has been easy to show that the new crop of "raised martyrs and changed saints" rose from several theologies, and that Baptists contributed no more than their share. Antinomian mysticism has been put forward as a real cause of Cromwell's worries, and the suggestion seems much likelier than a connection between rebellion and either Baptist theology or millenarian theory. If we run down the roster of millenarians we see names like Hakewill, Mede, More, Goodwin, Twisse,

Hartlib, Caryl, Kiffin, Sterry—and Milton, traveling here in good, but not predominantly Baptist, company. These students of the Bible determined in common nothing more horrendous than that the period symbolized by the Thousand Years of Rev. xx was still to come. If in our own day we habitually think of the Millennium as future, the credit must go to Milton's century. Protestants battling Rome narrowly scrutinized the Apocalypse. As a by-product of their study, they discovered its harmless chiliasm and turned it into a new orthodoxy. Though certain Fifth Monarchists who tried to seize the government for Christ rationalized their rebellion out of prophetic writ, we need not solemnly hold even their own prophetic studies responsible for their ambition. The millenarians' futurism has been not unfairly described as a form of social predestination, a political fatalism, so that a teaching that has been by some accused of inspiring rebellion has been by others held to foster lethargy and inaction. In truth, this academic product of rigorous biblicism was, and is, in itself innocent of any necessary practical consequence.

Baptists, like other men, were often millenarians, but the Baptist manner of teaching that Christ's Kingdom is not of this world could not be reconciled with a grossly carnal expectation of that Kingdom on earth drawn from the Old Testament prophecies. No sectaries stood more staunchly for freedom through separation of church and state than uncorrupted Baptists. None fused the two swords more solidly together or were more fanatically intolerant than Fifth Monarchists. Milton identified the Kingdom of Christ in this world with that church which he, too, spiritualized completely. He expected a future Millennial reign of Christ—that is to say, some glorious interlude in the story of the church—but we should not allow our knowledge of the bare fact to predispose our study of his opinions touching the political here and now. As futurism alone compelled him to no bizarre consequences—that Christ would sit on David's throne as a temporal ruler, that the saints would hold civil authority, that the Glorious Reign was at hand, that pious political effort might hasten it, or that King Jesus would delay only long enough for his heralds to make ready his throne—so it compelled him to no other confusion of the civil with the ecclesiastical power. The Appendix, Note B, offers some comment to suggest that he drew a far different conclusion. The only piece of utopian theory that he wrote and his latest comment on purely temporal affairs placed civil power in the hands of substantial citizens without regard to their estate as Christians. The magistrate might only encourage religion and protect the church from *outward* violence. If millenarians taught this last point, so did thousands who rejected the notion of Christ's personal reign in this world. So do most civilized nations in our own day.

Political slander of the Baptists never deceived Cromwell. Doctrinally, they had long been well-nigh invulnerable. Even Pagitt was constrained to call the Particular Baptists' confession of 1646 "some ratsbane covered with a great deal of honey." He would have found more ratsbane if it had been a confession of the General Baptists. Lord Brooke had already flayed the free-will variety, their communists, and their enthusiasts profaning the spirit; yet for the Calvinistic Baptists, along with the Brownists, he constructed a scriptural defense so convincing that he betrayed to many his own conviction, earned Milton's admiration, and just conceivably settled a new heretic. The Baptist heresy was hard to resist for one who truly made scripture his rule. If Baptists could have been bishops, Jeremy Taylor would probably have been both. The long series of confessions in which they repudiated Münster, the political Fifth Monarchy, Levelling, and unscriptural enthusiasm helped to establish confidence in their respectability. Political slander and textual squabbles apart, the only great pride that calumniators tried to fasten on Baptists was their enthusiasm bred of ignorance; but we need not take too seriously the ignorance—and therefore not the enthusiasm—of Canne, Smyth, Denne, Jessey, Williams, Cornwell, Knollys, and Tombes. Other ministers and their followers may have been simple enough to license Fuller in writing his *Infant's Advocate* down to their understandings. (He would not presume to say, he told them, what God would do about an infant dying unbaptized;

but he knew in God's place what he would do about the
father.) It had long been the practice of Baptist apologists
to attack the established clergy for the kind of learning
that taught them to misread scripture. The godly thereupon recalled that the piety of ignorance and the iniquity
of arts had long been "well known to be the Anabaptistical
tenet" and "the way to banish all learning out of the
church." In Butler's characters the Anabaptist let his children grow up pagans, cried down learning, and in his ignorance saw visions; and so Featley had written of Milton
along with the Dippers. To an attack of the same kind the
Baptist Thomas Collier replied pleasantly that he was not
personally acquainted with any man who professed to experience truth by dreams and visions. When he met such
a man he would regard him as more modest than one who
denied them to be possible.

The railing against sects on the extreme right—right,
that is, as its own century plotted it—discovered no essentially new presumptions. The "perfected" saints left rational ethics for inspired goodness (or wickedness) and
the written word for inspired knowledge. The two errors
went twinned. Long before the days of George Fox, Spenser's Roffy and others tilting at the dragon of Familist
error had left after times little new to say against Seekers,
Ranters, and Quakers. Except for the writings of Henry
Nicklaes and two docile, conformable petitions to the
throne in 1575 and 1608, the strangely inarticulate Familists said nothing in their own defense, so that modern
accounts have been made up from slanders or sympathetically deduced thence. For that matter, most contemporary
Familist-baiters copied still earlier "researches" at one or
more *reprises.* For their submissive conformity to James's
church as a thing indifferent, early Familists could be ridiculed. Or else they could be abhorred as guilty of a ruse
by which they slily infiltrated into the doctoral ministry
and even into the peerage. In those days, apparently, the
Familist and the Rosicrucian were cut from the same
stripe. Later, in Presbyterian times, when a Familist was
commonly any antinomian, the sect included men like
Saltmarsh, Dell, Towne, Crisp, Eaton, and Giles Randall,

if we may believe their critics. Some of these men, as one can see, were or had been Baptists of the enthusiastic fringe. The anonymity of the historical Familists and the vagaries of nomenclature allowed Familism to pass "by degrees" into Ranterism, according to folk history, which may have been right.

For present purposes we may leave the invisible communions tangled. Any or all the confused rout of aberrant Christians, but specifically the historical Familists, might endure the vulgar abuse familiar in Middleton's play, or perhaps we should now say Middleton's and Dekker's. They all followed the theology of "the family of lust and lewdness, termed the Family of Love." Mildly anti-intellectual passages in the *Evangelium Regni* of Nicklaes could be cited to prove Familists as hostile to learning as Anabaptists. Obscurantism became the most detestable Familism or Seekerism (now one, now the other) of Saltmarsh, Dell, Webster, and Erbury, though at least the first two antinomians named also spiritualized sacraments and Webster, like Everard and Pordage, dabbled in occult science. Familists rose above scripture, according to detraction, counting it no word of God, or turned it into a "bastardly brood of allegories" to match the inspiration of creatures "Godded with God." They deified their illuminated elders and, upon conversion, themselves, in whom all prophecies were fulfilled. In their Christ-like and sinless perfection they had no need to pray for pardon. The Seekers, for their part, asked God to woo them with a new dispensation before they would worship, suspending his ordained sacraments the while. Ranters told more loudly than the rest "whither the spiritual pride of ungrounded novices in religion tendeth." Digger Winstanley and all Quakers repudiated a sect alleged to spurn scripture as a pack of lies and, as Butler phrased for all respectability, to make vice the whole duty of perfected man.

Where the Presbyterians had set up a Pope in every parish, Quakers set up a Pope in every breast. Only a history of anti-Quaker diatribe could do justice to the pious indignation they roused with their inner light, sufficient to save pagans and, one calumniator added, the very devils.

With it they replaced human learning and the carnal letter of scripture, for whose sake Protestantism had encouraged learning. Since in the Bible itself they discovered "the word of God" to mean prophetic inspiration, they invited horrified zeal to prove that the Bible contained the whole word of God. The commonly recognized problems of editing it—problems of contradictions, vowel points, doubtful canonicity, uncertain authorship, and variant readings—in the seventeenth century made for Catholics and Quakers alike. The latter's most nearly learned champion gleefully dropped the whole bundle into the laps of scripturalists to discredit the written word and exalt the light. One of their authoritative prophets formulated their distinctive doctrine in a considered statement: the scriptures, a valid revelation, could be added to by the spirit, provided only that the additions not contradict the written word. We perceive at once that "not contradict" and "agree with" are hardly equivalent; irrelevant additions would not contradict. The formula came within a hair's breadth of matching, to the letter, the Black Coats' definition of enthusiasm: "A testimony of the Spirit, and voice unto the soul, merely immediate, without any respect unto, or concurrence with the word."

In its indignation before the Quakers' spiritualized insubordination, zeal almost neglected to load sins upon their antinomianism. In spite of the kindred Ranters and the Muggletonians, who Quakers thought drew persecution down upon them, in spite of their "perfection," and in spite of some early instances of public disrobing, the Children of Light suffered little moral censure; but gossip made up for the oversight with talk of witchcraft and concealed Popery. The pride too, not altogether doctrinal, which possessed the simple flock furnished a *cantus firmus* for various descants. It explained their "thou"-language and their rudeness. "You'll think it strange," wrote Baxter to a prospective convert of theirs, "that pride should be the very master of sin in them that go in so poor a garb, and cry out against pride so zealously as they do." But, like the Papists, they made the light of nature a saving light, and they claimed absolute perfection. Worst of all, in the

opinion of Baxter, whom they had howled at in public,
they reviled the church and ministry of sixteen hundred
years' standing. *The Perfect Pharisee,* Thomas Welde called
his exposé of Quakers' sinless perfection, their suprascrip-
turalism, their disdain of visible sacraments, and their un-
civil churlishness. Every one of these errors and alleged
errors, including the inner light, which Williams declared
could "outdo the Pope in pride," received a check from
Milton, the bad manners among the rest. The poet declared
that Jesus Christ, as prophet of the church, taught God's
whole will and his final will. Thomas Ellwood may not
have noticed that he met some bad Quakers among Milton's good angels. They studied science to the glory of
God; they used ratiocination like men, only more quickly;
they had too little mystical intuition to perceive God's
secrets as Bernard believed them to do; and they paid
decently ceremonious respect to superiors.

In this survey of pride across the doctrinal map, I have
been at pains to plot Milton's position as that of a con-
scientious and careful scripturalist—erring sometimes, it
may be; possibly "only vaguely Christian" where the Bible
is so—resisting extrascriptural presumption in its Popish,
Presbyterian, and enthusiastic shapes. Where an argument
of the moment drove the exegete to infer meanings not
put in the express words of the text, he bridged its gaps
with that ethical reason which, in a regenerate Christian,
he called spirit, so that all his conclusions, however derived, set him on the side of a ratiocinative religion. His
reason repudiated Calvinism and its antinomian extension; his biblicism excluded the intuitive devotion of
Seekers, Quakers, Ranters, and the like—those Christians
whom I designate collectively as spirituals. The truism is
of such importance to the study of the poet's inner life that
it might well be called the key. For if Milton ever reached
the point where he yearned for the God of Saltmarsh or
Fox, we must posit in him a change that wrenched his
deepest roots.

All the bits of tangible evidence I have seen alleged or
hinted are these: (1) anti-intellectual passages in *Likeliest
Means* and in *Paradise Regained,* that " quietistic, Quaker-

like poem"; (2) the invocations in *Paradise Lost;* (3) Milton's friendship with Ellwood; (4) the direction and drift of religious evolution in his day; (5) his individualistic aloofness from visible communions; and (6) a solitary line in the *Christian Doctrine.* With the first and most plausible proof I purpose to deal fully in its place. The others hardly deserve attention except perhaps the last. Imploring the Spirit not for new truth, but for "answerable style," would have been doctrinally orthodox if John Calvin or John Biddle had written the prayers; they showed more Christianity but no more Quakerism in Milton than in Homer or Virgil. One gathers from the factual record that Milton taught Ellwood, not Ellwood Milton; and to convict him of pietism by association is idle guess. He also ragged a serving man for the fooleries of the conventicle, and in defending oath-taking he wrote pointedly against a tenet held most prominently after 1650 by the Quakers. In ecclesiastical polity the Puritan revolution drifted, carrying Milton, toward freedom, individualism, and disestablishment. In doctrine it drifted simultaneously toward Quakerism and Deism, leaving Milton with his Bible. I do not know how to relate his solitary worship to his religious development, being ignorant of his record for church-attendance in youth and the direction that his solitary meditations took. Contrary to much learned comment, I cannot find that he would abolish organized religion or the ministerial order or, in any event, that the congregational churches he planned resembled in any respect the general assemblies of the faithful convened by George Fox. If the question should be asked why a dogged scripturalist never wrote in his *summa* against the doctrine of the inner light, the answer is that he did so. Everything that he wrote for scriptural sufficiency against the Papists opposed the illuminated brethren, even though charity for the harmless individualists forbade him to name them. He made a point of naming no Protestant sects. And now let us deal with the possible Quakerism in one line of the *Christian Doctrine.*

In hermeneutics Milton stated and often reiterated as

his own the undervalued theory of all Protestantism that
God's truth had been

> Left only in those written records pure,
> Though not but by the spirit understood—

the orthodox reverse of the Quakers' rule, which deliberately held the written records secondary to an additive
spirit. No Christian, I suppose, would have imagined the
Holy Spirit inferior in its nature to its own dictation, nor
for that matter, the inner spirit. Familiar is that passage
in Bacon's "Of Truth" ending, "Still he breatheth and
inspireth light into the face of his Chosen." God reserved
the continuing illumination by his Spirit for his latest
and greatest, his Sabbath work. But in any one of Adam's
posterity, Milton explained to the illuminati, the spirit
abode in limited measure, intermittent and doubtful. The
Apostles enjoyed a clearer revelation by their advantage
in time—except in instances where their own writings had
been corrupted by Romish scribes with a strong motive
to alter. (He likely suspected them of having tampered
skilfully with Christ's pronouncement on divorce.) Our
own scholars deplore the Masoretes' destruction of variants from which we might restore the true text of the Old
Testament; they receive gladly the garblings in the New
Testament writings, descending to us in four textual types
with more than a hundred thousand variants, as the best
safeguard against undiscoverable corruption. To Milton,
the textual difficulties in God's latest and highest revelation presented a puzzle and a danger.

He perceived that Papists could use the familiar uncertainties to justify church-authority unless he could make a
strong case for what they called a private spirit of interpretation. In one place, then, he exalted that spirit, the internal ground of faith. It offered firmer footing than the
external ground in that a mere natural man, lacking the
spirit and provided with only the uncertain manuscripts,
could fall a prey to doubt, whereas the spiritual man could
not be easily deceived. To him the doubtful readings
offered no difficulty, for he could discern the Spirit's
intent. He had a guide more certain than the church.

Through the garbled passages he had the spirit, a teacher clearer than scripture itself. Such was the context into which Milton introduced a remark which, out of that context, could be taken for a piece of Quakerism: by committing the New Testament to the uncertainties of Romish scribes Providence doubtless meant to teach "that the spirit which is given to us is a more certain guide than scripture, whom therefore it is our duty to follow." An eminent scholar has asserted without references that Milton in the *Christian Doctrine* "several times" exalted the spirit above scripture. My best reading shows only this one remark to be conceivably relevant, and I cannot but think that a solitary sentence would be, at most, evidence of a passing mood rather than of major apostasy. But in its place it fit the debate between Christian liberty and hateful authority (not between the letter and the spirit) with the scholar's meaning, not the enthusiast's. Milton wrote of Bible-reading, and commended as uniform and incorruptible a spirit that interpreted, not one that added. Nothing obliged a reader to believe that such a spirit either taught new truth or altered a jot of accurately reported dogma. The spirit that guided a Christian through the daily business of living was conscience (*P. L.* iii.195; xii.486–497), and it performed no unusual functions.

The spirituals' sublime faith bred strong souls; not a man of Cromwell's time dwarfed George Fox, not even John Milton. But before Milton, with his particular cultivation, could approach the God of the spirituals he had to renounce the God of intellect and rational justice whom he had served with all his energy in happier times. The God of the *Christian Doctrine* consisted with the best principles of humanism and reasoned liberty; there was a God whose word could be studied by scholarship, whose ways could be rationally defended and to a remote point explained, whose goodness rewarded man's efforts as man judged them good. If, after the book stood substantially finished, Milton altered his faith, he confessed to himself or revealed to us the inadequacy of Christian humanism to sustain his spirit in evil days. I cannot see how we can do other than accept the spectacle of a defeated old man throwing himself in craven surrender upon a God who would have none of the Milton we know. It is a spectacle afflicting, profoundly ugly, and so unlikely as to demand the clearest evidence. To set against the renegade from scripture and reason, we have another Milton, who embraced early the justice of God, the dignity of man, the inseparability of virtue and freedom; clung with grand and stubborn dogmatism to his axioms, "developed" by recognizing and confessing the consequences of his own doctrine, and ended his course in unruffled serenity. Where the jerks, irruptions, disappointments he met inspired doubts and rebellion, he purged them quickly in art and controversy. When a party played his principles false, he changed his party, not his principles, until, lonely at his altitude, he found his party small, scattered, yet still secure of its eventual triumph. This is approximately the Milton that Professor Hanford, if I understand him correctly, has reaffirmed of late. The dream of an unworldly church, woven into his politics and into his religion, was Milton's long before Fox had his first opening from heaven on the subject. It is clear in *Lycidas* and still clearer in the anti-prelatical tracts. Perhaps he did not then know how it was to be achieved; perhaps he naïvely hoped that the Presbyterians, once in power, would work out a way to build Christ's Kingdom, the church, free and apart from the temporal state. When they took the wrong turning, he switched his allegiance to Independency. By the time it too had gone the way of the world he had learned that any form of state church would have to be abolished, and toward that end he wrote *Likeliest Means,* not for a new principle but with a new plan. It is coincidental, and of no great importance to readers of poetry, that the spirituals favored disestablishment. It would be of the greatest importance as the mark of a great faltering if Milton had embraced pietistic doctrine.

We know how firmly and consistently he refused to admit Popery to full legal toleration. We can find him at least lukewarm toward the motion of tolerating enthusiasm. Listing those heretics for whom he was publicly about to beg charity in 1673—Lutherans, Calvinists, Anabaptists

(mere Baptists by the sequel), Socinians, Arminians—he
showed no solicitude for the spirituals, but only for sects
whose opinions were "founded on scripture." There were
in London many of the Quakers whom he omitted and few
of the Lutherans whom he defended, but Milton burned
with more zeal for scriptural unitarians than for either.
Engrossed in those controversies that had long seemed important to him, he probably forgot his Quaker neighbors.
By his oversight he betrayed no animosity but only a lack
of real interest in the harmless (and therefore not intol-
erable) enthusiasts who had so often filled London prisons.
He would have had some excuse to fortify his religion on
the spiritual front, as against the Papists, once ranting had,
by all reports, reached dangerous proportions and the antinomian extreme that he had feared in the *Christian Doctrine*. Here is a spiritual gem that appeared in 1659, the
year of his plan for a free church: "From my seed-spring
within me I say this unto you, that there is not any [sent
directly] by the spirit of inspiration or revelation, but only
myself to bear record and testimony that John Reeve and
Ludowick Muggleton are the last commissioners that ever
shall appear in this unbelieving world, I say from the Lord
Jesus, I having the same spirit of revelation that gave the
commission." Harmless, of course, in comparison with
organized Popery, and far more innocent than the Presbyterians' Blasphemy Act of 1648. The Parliament had en-
acted in 1650 a milder act for the suppression of all who
asserted their equality or identity with God, or held that
eternal majesty dwelt in the creature. In a court of rude
justice it could easily have been interpreted to punish a
Muggletonian like the one quoted. In 1659 John Milton
complimented the Parliament on "its prudent and well de-
liberated act." This "intolerance" is significant to us for its
spiritual direction only; Milton plainly meant that the act
was prudent in its plausible definition of blasphemy when
compared with the act it replaced. One would like to think
he did not know that George Fox and other Quakers had
been suffering under the prudent act.

Chapter IV

THE PEACEMAKERS' MODESTY

NONE of the embattled preachers discouraged metaphysical curiosity to urge in its place Christian morality with more earnestness than those moderate divines who labored for reconciliation. On this ethical account it is both proper and usual to trace the spirit of sixteenth-century humanism in Falkland and his associates, in Cambridge Platonists, in conciliators like William and John Forbes, James Usshcr, and John Davenant. From the direction of their humanism we approach the intellectual sobriety that Milton's Raphael taught in *Paradise Lost*. In its moral and often "Arminian" bias, their divinity and Milton's coincided. In matters ecclesiastical, Milton parted from these loyal sons of the church and the devout skepticism by which they meant to do her good. Therein the more conspicuous pacifists, but not usually Milton, anticipated the Restoration Pyrrhonists. To be sure, many controversies would in time have come to rest in skeptical apathy without the peacemakers; yet if these enemies of all fanaticism did not hasten the process, at least they helped to make a virtue of it.

When Milton first wrote of what he would later call "fume, or emptiness, or fond impertinence," he too wrote of sins against religious peace. Sometime before 1639, according to the likeliest dating, he entered in his Commonplace Book the rubric "Curiosity," and illustrated by collecting under it three passages on nonessential wrangling. One was Theodoret's story of how Constantine tried to silence Arius and Athanasius, his metaphysical bishops. The popular commonplace stands as a symbol of pathetic futility. An early Anglican coaxing Puritans to conformity; an early Baptist pleading for toleration; an orthodox and harassed Independent, urging less heat on all sides of

157

his middle way; Jeremy Taylor, sequestered Anglican, preaching moderation to Presbyterians, whom he was to find as deaf out of authority as in—each used the story without much success to urge peace on terms that seemed good in his own eyes. Whoever delights in criticism's little ironies can find one in Bishop Sumner's revised translation of Milton's *Christian Doctrine*. Meditating the heresies there written of the Trinity, the clergyman was so forcibly struck by Constantine's words in Theodoret on the evils of curiosity that he found it "impossible not to quote them as a caution to future speculators on this holy mystery." With Milton's Commonplace Book still in darkness, he could not know that the poet himself had read and even copied Theodoret. While controversies blazed with fury and freshness, every man who fed them paper saw himself as a peacemaker and used Constantine's sentiments, if not his words. They expressed one article of religion on which all agreed. And when Englishmen in large numbers turned at length from controversies with a cynical shrug, Constantine's doctrine justified their indifference.

Outside these irenical pleas the earlier seventeenth century produced no remarkable volume of skeptical writing. Here and there a detached mystic or quietist extolled unknowing without polemical intent: Henry Vaughan, for example, possibly tutored by Cornelius Agrippa, told of being lost in the mazes of natural knowledge and, worse, of self-knowledge; and George Herbert wrote in the same strain. But if we reviewed all the merely philosophic doubters, Pyrrhonic or Academic, of our sixty years, and added Donne and Ralegh for good measure, the company would not be impressive. Burton might head many a reader's list, with Browne or even Bacon close behind. Young Glanvill, almost outside our chronological limits, advertised his dubiety with some diffidence, but actually came no nearer than Browne to doubting all things though plain sense. Here and there satirists like Wither and Bancroft, or essayists like Cornwallys and Dudley North, borrowed matter as well as form from Montaigne. Cowley wrote an early poem on the proposition that there is no knowledge; a drop of skepticism always served him, as it had served Ralegh and Bacon, for a solvent to set learning forward

in new paths. Porphyry's tree of absolutes, which in Boethius' Latin had helped to pattern so much scholastic
thinking, figured in Cowley's poem as Eden's forbidden
tree. Richard Whitlock, M. D., quoted Charron and John
Donne to justify standing in the old ways, but he too
stopped far short of systematic doubt. An elastic enough
definition of the skeptic could extend this roster; but since
our theme is not skepticism, but curiosity and skepticism
in irenical writing, we may close these few or occasional
Pyrrhonists and open a treatise by the first Englishman,
the first so far as I can discover, to declare himself a skeptic
in all things not directly of the faith—Robert Greville,
Lord Brooke. Our neo-Platonist and Academic skeptic
was more notably tolerant than his Presbyterian coreli-
gionists, though not so tolerant as *Areopagitica*, for its own
obvious reasons, implied. He set bounds about his tolerance and his skepticism whenever either threatened his
Calvinism, which he did not live to outgrow. A connection
between his doubt and his charity seems likely enough,
though he wrote them in separate books and left us to
guess which caused the other.

If Cherbury's *De Veritate* can be called the first work
of metaphysics or epistemology by an Englishman, then
Brooke's *Of Truth* must be the second. The two works
had little in common except their titles. The former, intended as an escape from Pyrrhonism, said nothing of
curiosity. It displayed the real potentialities of mind properly analyzed and matched, faculty by faculty, with fit and
knowable objects. Brooke apparently intended his treatise
as an escape from Lord Herbert. Nathaniel Culverwel,
who preferred Cherbury to Brooke and his unpromising
doubt, perceived the antithesis. The skeptic anticipated
Cudworth in rejecting the prevailing faculty psychology
as he brushed aside all distinctions between knowledges,
all Cherbury's compartmentalized epistemology, all subtle
definition and analysis in the study of the mind, for a Platonic oneness of intellect. Into this unity, with God as the
sole ground, he knit up all the established dichotomies of
mind and soul, understanding and its objects. It has been
thought that the rhapsodic Peter Sterry may have had
something to do with a philosophy that defined Good as

Being and evil as privation, and made God the immediate cause of all effects. In utterly denying second causes—the end of the Aristotelian's quest—Brooke loosed the golden chain tied of old to the throne of Jupiter. More accurately, he tied there not the highest link, but all the links.

True wisdom, then, lay not in cause-hunting, so long and fruitlessly pursued, but in contemplation of the Good. Brooke would have reminded his philosophic readers here about equally of Plotinus and of Pyrrho, or perhaps of the earlier Ænesidemus in his Eight Tropes against causality; but he searched for support among the more reputable Moderns. Comenius, another unifier, he thought agreed with him, and likewise Bacon, who had expunged "doctrinam fantasticam, litigiosam, fucatam, et mollem; a nice unnecessary prying into things that profit not"—things like the mystery of nature. True, the Advancer had sometimes trifled with causes "as for entertainment," but his serious philosophy had escaped the tyranny of causality as cleanly as that of Plato or Ficino, and had thus pointed the way to sobriety. Mere intellectualism would always come to vanity, as Ecclesiastes predicted. After centuries of futile study, what modern Adam could name the creatures according to their natures? Natures could be known only in their causes, and these God had reserved for his *arcana imperii,* "which to meddle with is no less than high treason." Sir Walter Ralegh took his place in Brooke's miscellaneous collection of witnesses, along with Bacon and Ficino, because he had contributed to wisdom an aphorism: "The cheese wife knoweth that runnet curdleth cheese, but the philosopher knoweth not why." One thinks what satisfaction he could have taken in Ralegh's translating Pyrrhonism if the *Skeptic* had been in print. The matter-of-fact lawyer, Sir John Davies, got into this strange company because he, too, knew how to resist the forbidden tree by keeping the old rule *noli altum sapere,* and Brooke quoted the lines that opened *Nosce Teipsum:*

> Why did my parents send me to the schools,
> That I with knowledge might enrich my mind,
> When the desire to know first made men fools,
> And did corrupt the root of all mankind?

Neither Davies' excursions into self-knowledge nor Bacon's into natural knowledge commended these divergent scientists to a skeptic bent only upon skimming from their writings a composite sermon against curiosity. When John Wallis answered him, he reminded him that Bacon had called system-builders web-spinners. The distinction between true and false was real enough and should incline Brooke to practice some of his own sobriety.

Peacemaking could do with modesty less thoroughgoing than Brooke's metaphysical obscurantism, though not without some rebuke for curiosity and dogmatic pride. Such an argument could be turned to serve dogmatism itself—that of the "forcers" on the one hand or that of the schismatic tolerationists on the other. The Laudians in power or the Presbyterians who succeeded them often acknowledged that the fundamentals of faith, the articles necessary for salvation, were few and hard to know. Since the great wits in all ages, entangled with matters confessed to be nonessential, had been driven to an *O altitudo!*, an Anglican demanded, "Why should we not all be wise unto sobriety, and let God alone with his secrets?" That is to say, be soberly wise and conform. The Presbyterian Samuel Rutherford, the great enemy of religious freedom who replied to Goodwin, Taylor, Williams, and kindred spirits, could not understand why they or any man should cavil if the state's new church imposed certain articles that he and all considered to be uncertain and nonessential. Milton once exposed the *non sequitur:* imposition made the articles essential! Rutherford admitted that some trifling subtleties of the schools, though sinful, could not be made illegal; yet the magistrate had to be empowered to punish errors that somebody would call venial. The whole business of determining what truths were irrefragable and necessary "bordered with God's secrets" anyway. Hardly was the Restoration accomplished when Stillingfleet was writing in the same strain for peace at any price. "Curiosity, that greensickness of the soul," had too long been "the epidemical distemper of the age" for any Savoy Conference to think itself infallible. With a courage that he was to repent later, the young churchman examined every rival constitution in turn and showed that not one could claim to be *jure divino*, hoping thereby to forestall an Act of Uniformity. But he frankly exhorted all Christians to indifference and submission, whatever worship might be imposed upon them; and if readers should think him a skeptic, it was, he assured them, "the very thing" that he had been "so long in proving of."

The sectaries for toleration, that is, for the right to dogmatize unmolested, doubted the infallibility of persecutors; otherwise they required little of the skepticism taught by the stiffly dogmatic Rutherford and the somewhat more temperate Stillingfleet. They made their contribution to anti-intellectual divinity by attacking pulpit "learning," but their politically inspired pamphlets, to which we shall return, hardly deserve to be called skeptical. The "persecuted" Christians as a body inclined toward fanatical certainty, not doubt, and begged toleration chiefly for the sake of truth, not peace. The mystical Saltmarsh accordingly found in his irenicon sweet uses for diversity, for without it how could the Christian try all spirits as God commanded? Men needed only enough skepticism—his word—to remember that carnal interest often affected preaching and not believe "too suddenly." Saltmarsh has often been called a Seeker, one of those Christians in whom Calvinists detected an "Arminian" uncertainty. Like Milton in *Areopagitica* he asked freedom because all earnest sectaries held to some valuable truth. The Independent needed the Baptist; both needed the Seeker for his godly criticism; and all needed the Presbyterian, though one infers not desperately. To determine whether we have in Saltmarsh a true skeptic is to dispute of terminology; what we can see at a glance is that he did not argue, like Hales and Taylor, that human frailty asks charity because any dogma may be in large measure false.

The historically important tradition of doubt was best served by a band of peacemakers who did not include Saltmarsh or Milton. These were the comprehensionists, the men willing to accommodate disparate opinions within a broad visible church. The communion sought might be as elastic as that which Burroughs enticed the sects into or as farflung as the international church to which John Dury would admit all Christians except Socinians. The Presbyterians of liberal temper, like the younger Brinsley, and conservative Independents of the established national church asked combatants to sacrifice some truths, even useful truths, for the sake of peace. Whoever preached a degree of visible unity to an already divided people had to minimize the importance of divisive doctrine, and thus in some measure to sacrifice doctrine to discipline, dogma to cult, the notional to the visible.

Moderate Anglicans turned the critical light of their learning this way upon the pretences of authority and that way upon the inspired certainties of fanatical ignorance. With scholarly wit John Hales chaffed the enthusiasts, but held them no more responsible for rending the church than those prelates who loaded its public forms with private fancies. The so-called Socinian confessed his own share of Adam's desire to know too much, prescribed for himself and others the "Christian modesty to participate somewhat of the skeptic," and in so doing taught devout diffidence to Stillingfleet, Baxter, and the company of Restoration divines who studied his irenicon. Jeremy Taylor's even more explicitly made intellectual frailty an inducement to peace. What any man thought he knew by fallible reason he could not presume to impose upon another; and whoever turned to follow some other authority simply added another man's errors to his own. All that reason, our feeble best, permitted Christians to hold as certain was the Apostles' Creed (which as everybody knew had permitted Arianism of old, else the next two creeds would not have been necessary). Taylor's broad irenicon provided for the fullest comprehension within and nearly universal toleration without the national church; in charity it matched Milton's. But because it was the work of a comprehensionist, it rested upon a stronger argument from weakness.

If Benjamin Whichcote's surviving work is a measure of the whole, we have in him that rarity among conciliators, an arbiter who sincerely placed his own mild Calvinism among the nonessentials and abstained from controversial dogma. We have only Dr. Tuckney's word, unimpeachable though it is, that he had heard Whichcote preach against the rationalists and his honest assurance, possibly mistaken, that had his friend lived he would have finished his book against the Arminians. If it had been Whichcote's regular custom to preach sermons on depravity and imputed righteousness, the elder Calvinist would never have mourned that one of the faithful should speak much of "divinest reason," call Plato to witness for Christ, and curiously seek to define fundamentals in the interest of peace like some Socinian. Since God and good men were alike reasonable, it followed for men like Whichcote and Chillingworth that good men would not disagree about a fundamental doctrine. It also followed that whatever good men disagreed about could not be fundamental. "To multiply questions," ran one of Whichcote's aphorisms, "is not the way to improve religion: the zeal of man should be turned from curiosity of speculation to honesty of practice." To him, as to Hales, the scriptures taught latitude by favoring here one and there another side of a controversy. God, who alone knew how to resolve the apparent inconsistencies, had placed many of the resolutions among his arcana, leaving to men the ancient rule *nolite altum sapere*. A Christian might nevertheless, for the advancement of knowledge, publish whatever he had diligently and prayerfully discovered, provided that the author and the reader took for their motive to peace the fallibility of everything outside scripture. Infallible passion and interest, masquerading as zeal and conscience, imposed catechisms and confessions; and when they did so, Whichcote's skeptical rule worked another way for unity. As Baxter said when looking back on the Act of Uniformity, what the Cambridge divines had thought too trivial to impose, they found too trivial to stick at when imposed. Whichcote's disciples learned well their master's lesson: "Peace and goodwill among men is of greater consequence than any private apprehension."

A divine bound by many ties to the Cambridge men of latitude, Richard Baxter issued five major works of conciliation within twenty years after the Restoration, not, in these works, pointing out the peace-breakers' mistakes in theology, but expounding only the rules of love and fellowship. Possibly it was not long after 1660 that he wrote, too, what he published much later—his chief work of anti-intellectual devotion, *A Treatise of Knowledge and Love*. In this book he distilled pure the devout nescience that he mingled in other writings with his formidably scholastic divinity, for the author of *Saints' Rest* had a less devotional character, that of "Priest" Baxter, the Black Coat, abused by the spirituals for his learning and logic. He ranked with Perkins and Taylor as a moral casuist and owned, appropriately, that he held "higher thoughts of the schoolmen" than Erasmus and other humanists had done. The blend of pietist and schoolman in his nature helped him to spend his life working and writing to bring Protestantism into some comprehensive Worcestershire Association. In this labor his coaxing required his skepticism and his controversies his forensic divinity. In pacific enterprise he always phrased his own mild Presbyterianism and Calvinism to sound like his nearer neighbor's religion, constantly following a dream of visible union. When late in life he had lost some hatred of Papists, forgiven the Baptists, repented his excusable harshness to Quakers ("Miserable creatures," he once saluted them), apologized for his pun on Vanity and Sterility, and leaned as far toward Arminianism as his elastic orthodoxy would stretch, he was still at odds with Owen and the Independents. Congregational autonomy was not the kind of unity that he understood by his favorite motto: In things necessary, unity; in things doubtful, liberty; in all things, charity.

In specific proposals for education Baxter and Milton served much the same cult of utility. For the sake of piety and the relief of man's estate, both men encouraged the building of schools, and both commended about the same curriculum. We find differences, of course. Conscious of heresies, Baxter hedged with rigid safeguards the study of nature, the little of it that he permitted. God, he thought, could better be studied in his works of grace. He would have no boys tempted to embrace ancient atomism, the absurdities of Paracelsus and Boehme, or novelties of Lord Herbert, Gassendi, Henri le Roy, and Hobbes, worst of the lot. Loyal to the ideal of a "learned" ministry, he naturally thought first of education as a preparative for the pulpit. Ministers would need it to refute heresy—Socinianism on the one hand and various "Familisms" on the other—and to that end would need logic, metaphysics, and formal divinity. Baxter had once come near declining ordination because he had not the university degree that became a duly qualified minister. Perhaps by way of compensation he sometimes spoke with innocent pride of his reading in the poets, divines, historians, philosophers, and scientists.

When he contemplated the danger to his own soul in such erudition, he felt himself "much better in Herbert's Temple," and thanked God that he had arrived at a *nihil scitur* instead of Hobbism. In *Faith and Love* he called much of his reading a devilish snare, "the cheat of souls, the hinderer of wisdom, and"—next spoke the peacemaker—"a troubler of the church and the world." He pushed skepticism almost to the extreme of Pyrrhonism and commended to the Christian reader a select bibliography of "laudable books" by Cornelius Agrippa, Sánchez, Glanvill, and others, for further tutelage. Yet utter nescience he would not insist upon: science was possible, even though everywhere inadequate. From Pyrrhonism he rescued two sorts of verity—scripture and empirical fact with its immediate consequences. From St. Paul's condemnation for vanity he exempted vocational studies. Beside a page or two on these exceptions he set some two hundred on "Falsely Pretended Knowledge," reducing to vanity all sorts of learning not obviously vocational—physics, metaphysics, medicine, politics, history, and much theology. An early biographer judged that the treatise was better calculated to teach skepticism than humility. Baxter intended no distinction.

Only a dogmatist would venture to assert categorically that Milton was no skeptic, though calling him one seems a little like calling the prophet Isaiah a skeptic. If the word designates only a man who questions much that others believe, it fits Milton, but whom does it not? His distrust of reasoners like, for example, the self-seeking prelates implied nothing like Baxter's distrust of reason. Consistent skepticism he held to be a piece of pagan folly from first to last, in the seventh Prolusion as in *Paradise Regained,* as he could not have done if he had worked long for a present identity of conceit and outward community of worship. When he wrote his organon of progress, *Areopagitica,* his program of free, cooperative research assumed the attainability of absolute truth. Her body had been torn; men possessed her by bits; but given the freedom to bring their bits together, they might once again behold her entire. Scripture in its untried purity gave him the primary certainty of empirical fact, certainty of a kind impossible for "scripturalists" who read at second hand by Calvin's or another's eyes. It permitted him to assemble many sectarian fragments of truth in his *Christian Doctrine,* and his unwillingness to impose them on others cannot be taken to show his own lack of confidence in them. Things of "plain sense," axioms of thinking, accurate processes of logical discourse, the doctrinal infallibility of scripture—these pillars sustained his thinking on a broad base of certainty, but with a proviso. God had planted in man his umpire Conscience, and only if man used it well could he attain light after light. Right practice, the end of every philosophy that discouraged notions by doubt, had been Milton's point of departure. Who loved liberty had first to be wise and good, he wrote often to Salmasius, and who loved wisdom, he wrote in *Comus* and earlier, had first to be good. If prizing self-knowledge and self-control above all philosophy and rational piety above all speculation means skepticism, then Milton participated so far, but not necessarily further. It would be idle to deny his affinity in moral religion with Taylor and Whichcote, Socrates and Erasmus.

If the title humanist has any meaning in the seventeenth century, surely Jeremy Taylor of all men will wear it unchallenged. Not many years ago it was the humor of some critics to deny it to Milton as inconsistent with his "Puritan" idealism, much like a logician who would make the terms red and round mutually exclusive. It can do no harm to test such logic by these two men who resembled

each other so remarkably in their classical erudition, their
rational morality, their Stoical philosophy, their "Socinian" religion, their often parallel exegesis, their irenical
charity. Any distinction between them more significant
here than the color of their hair can be narrowed to a finite
difference in political radicalism. In orders and emotion-
ally attached to Anglican uses, Taylor subscribed Erastian
and Royalist, with a little prejudice to his tolerance. When
it arrives, any clear and final definition of the humanist
will be welcome, but it will surprise a few if it makes the
sine qua non of humanism an Erastian and ritualistic
religion or even conservative politics.

Taylor and Milton thought alike in much; and like Milton in the wisdom-folly antithesis of his doctrinal treatise
or in Raphael's lesson to Adam, his fellow humanist deplored intellectual vice that drew attention from faith and
living; "Inquire not into the secrets of thy God, but be content to learn thy duty according to the quality of thy person or employment." Thus Taylor taught in *Holy Living*
as he wrote like a Stoical Plutarch converted to Christianity and school-method, exhausting the personal, social, and
divine virtues of sobriety, justice, and religion. It was the
doctrine that he preached from his pulpit and, as bishop,
begged his ministers to preach, expounding only necessary
scripture, and that for edification, wrenching no texts,
pressing no allegories, squaring all by fundamentals. "Often speak of the four last things," he admonished. "These
are useful, safe, and profitable; but never run into extravagances and curiosities, nor trouble yourself with mysterious secrets." The minister had a special duty to learn all
he could of divinity and humanity, else how could he refute heresy? How better could he learn to recognize the
trivial questions? The truly learned minister would know
that "theology is rather a divine life than a divine knowledge," and in knowing this would hold the key to all mysteries. Taylor's simultaneous devotion to reason and to
obedient piety entangled him in no contradiction so long
as his Pelagian God and his Senecan morality bade the
same. Ideally, reason came from God; yet in any living
man it served concupiscence as often as not; and until

the preaching of holiness could restore both holiness and truth, men would be led by passion and interest. They would persist in error so long as they found error convenient. Thus by moral as well as by intellective skepticism Taylor accounted for the disparity of doctrine in a fallen world and the folly of expecting unity by discourse. "Let us now try God's method," he urged. "Let us betake ourselves to live holily, and then the spirit of God will lead us into all truth."

So attractive did this kind of divinity appear in factious days that Calvinism itself leaned toward it. We have already considered how, as a vociferous minority of saints pushed on into antinomianism, the worried Calvinists searched for morality in their own theology and found it in God's dictum that they should be saved by labor in their vocation. Thus the religion of Presbyterians approached Arminianism and in time often drifted into unitarianism. We traced earlier the connection between Calvinists' moral preaching and their tabus shielding God's decree. Now we may appropriately notice that, within the confines of orthodoxy, their morality undermined with a most important skepticism the *certitudo salutis*. Back in the sixteenth century, Catholic criticism of Calvin's "absolute and loose faith" had laid before Protestants the need to preach less of God's decree and more of the good works by which a Christian might assure himself that God had already chosen him. The old-fashioned way of asking the elect to bear their certainty with modesty and good works would not, the latter-day preachers feared, insure good works where antinomian faith alone sufficed to inspire certainty of salvation. It behooved them to shake the confidence of the most secure dogmatists of all, the assured saints. Inside Calvinism and out, the "legal" teachers, as antinomians called them, all but blocked the road to the *certitudo salutis* with safeguards to keep the presumptuous from trying to go to heaven on their election. This orthodoxy accommodated nominal predestinarians like Whichcote and Baxter, with more taste for morality than for detached metaphysics.

Tom Fuller called this moral Calvinism the new temper,

and shrewdly judged it to be the prevailing temper when
in 1647/8, the year Zeph Smyth was hissed, he published
his remarkable *Sermon of Assurance.* The Royalist betrayed, debatably, the time-serving that Heylyn accused
him of by dedicating it to the regicide Sir John Danvers.
Still more to the point, he blazoned on the title page the
fact that he had been preaching the sermon for fourteen
years. Plainly, the deprived minister, living precariously
on a series of London lectureships, wanted the conquering
powers to know that if he had erred in serving Charles,
at least he had never fallen into heresy, Arminian or antinomian. This piece of what he thus published as unassail-
able orthodoxy he opened with the schoolmen impudently
arranging the angels, thereby setting the proper tone of
caution. Most of his commonplaces would have passed
safely in an earlier generation. The text (ii Peter i:10,
"Give rather diligence to make your calling and election
sure") "stabbed" the error of meddling in other men's
election. The order of the words reproved as well the "preposterous curiosity" of setting election before calling: men
were not to launch into the profound mysteries and bottomless depths of predestination at first dash, but to begin
soberly with their calling or vocation. They were explicitly
commanded to seek assurance; they could not be arrogant
as the Papists would make them if they did so. And assurance was no pious fraud: some might attain it. But from
the reverend divines of the past Fuller had parted in one
matter—he made a notable point of it—not insulting their
memories, but thanking God that his own age, standing
on their shoulders, had clearer truth. He would not make
assurance of salvation the very ground of Christian religion as they had done. If Christians properly collected
their assurance from this syllogism, Fuller argued,

> Major: he that truly repents . . . is surely called,
>   and by consequence elected before all eternity. . . .
> Minor: But I truly repent. . . .
> Conclusion: Therefore I am truly called and elected,
>   etc.,

all the difficulty would be in the minor. And by means of that difficulty he was able to hold out to Calvinists an assurance almost as difficult and dubious as that demanded by Arminians. Christians could, no doubt, by working achieve acceptable repentance, but God might even so withhold assurance for his own good reasons. The favored few, to have it, would have to work without ceasing. The sermon opposed two errors common to rigid orthodoxy and its antinomian progeny: that true faith always brought assurance, and that loss of it signified lack of saving faith.

It is easy for us to see after the fact that the preaching of a morality largely shorn of religious dogma fostered natural religion and so marked a step toward the distant future of no religion, but the humanistic divines had no such intention and no choice. It would be unjust to hold them, or Milton, accountable for a development probable without their divinity. No teaching could have been in its setting more admirably sane, balanced, and therefore historically fleeting than the blend of Platonism and Puritanism with which the Cambridge latitudinarians hoped to recover Christianity as pure as it had been before Aquinas. Whether Calvinist or Arminian, each of the school taught with Whichcote: "nothing is more spiritual than that which is moral"; and the Socratic article in their confession, as in Milton's, took away vain philosophy by ranging the *ratio recta* under the instructed will, practically if not theoretically. For more than a century English humanism had been saying often enough that knowledge without virtue is dangerous—not quite the same thing as saying that real knowledge without virtue is impossible. Religion too had deduced true thinking from true belief, but the new philosophy liked to draw it from good behavior. Only thus could Whichcote's essentials of religion have been the doctrine agreed upon by good men, or John Smith's "thin, airy knowledge" got by mere speculation have sprung from wickedness. Virtue conditioned truth, Smith explained by sound psychology, in that "while we lodge any filthy vice in us, this will be perpetually twisting up itself into the thread of our finest spun speculations."

Where the Apostle wrote, "The natural man receiveth not the things of the spirit," Smith interpreted him to mean that the vicious man cannot think straight. Cudworth persuaded himself, like Taylor, that righteousness alone could so clear the intellect that sophistry and syllogistical wrangling, no longer needed, would quietly disappear. Henry More devised an elaborate psychological machinery of Boniform Faculty and Divine Sagacity to account for the vain philosophy of the vicious. If impurity of spirit destroyed the Divine Sagacity, a man could neither discover truth nor profit by true teaching.

Two members of the school on occasion took advantage of the orthodox road to the *certitudo salutis* which liberal Calvinists had broadened to include an ethical religion. John Smith, the purest Platonist and best Calvinist of the Cambridge group, if we except the peripheral figures Brooke and Sterry, kept his ethics faultlessly within the formula that his hearers understood. A gospel faith, he wrote like the Presbyterian Rutherford, was the middle way between the legal righteousness of absolute free will and the antinomian fideism of internal apprehensions. The orthodox Protestant had nothing to fear but a presumptuous misuse of God's decree. Let antinomians prate of salvation for the soul unripe, true faith would not "pursue an ambitious project of raising the soul immaturely to the condition of a darling favorite of heaven." Heaven required assurance, but with the proviso that the Christian take heed "to moderate his curiosity of prying into God's Book of Life, and to stay awhile until he sees himself within the confines of salvation itself." If he would but labor in his vocation, he would not then need the dim starlight of theology or care to pry into heaven's secrets and to search the hidden rolls of eternity. Ralph Cudworth poured some new wine into these same old bottles when he too preached to Parliament of the legal arrogance on the one and the antinomian presumption on the other side of gospel faith. Privately, he probably did not believe that Calvinism held the gospel center, though the Presbyterians who had left him in his Cambridge living would have so understood him. He accommodated his message of

peace and morality to his hearers. With "leaves of controversies lying thick about," he preached to the Commons
obedience, exhorting them to trade their intellectual persuasion of adoption for obedience to God's revealed will.
They would find it easier and safer, he told them, to labor
in their calling, to look within rather than above. If within
they could find God's image, then they might speculate
with some allowance, provided that they remembered how
easily our fallen, fallible intellect could spin cobwebs and
"sapless opinions." Pointedly to discourage Parliament
from making "this or that opinion, this or that form, the
wedding garment" and sentencing the rest to outer darkness, Cudworth cautioned his hearers not to soar too high
lest their wings be scorched, or climb lest they be struck
down like the giants. He preached an obedience that would
not paralyze thought but purge it, curbing speculation and
insuring charity for all that consisted with virtue.

From Cudworth's liberal humanism, preaching ethics
in the name of rational religion and to that end deterring
speculation, it is a plain and easy step to Milton's. One who
has read these pages will be already familiar with Raphael's
lecture in *Paradise Lost* (VIII.1–216) to inquisitive Adam,
soliciting his thoughts with matters hid. He probably
knows too what would have surprised Milton, that critics
have taken apart the conventional and innocuously didactic passage looking for the poet's unconscious meanings,
evidences of frustration or deepening religiosity, his prejudices against astronomy or the new science. I have already
assembled some parallels to document the generally accepted conclusion that Milton did not write a large and
important section of his epic merely to condemn astronomers. If he held such animus against them *qua* astronomers he omitted to mention it while he was exonerating
them in the *Christian Doctrine*. It was Ptolemaism that
most amused the angel, if we read literally his hoary jests
about scribbling over the sphere with cycle and epicycle;
this kind of star-knowledge, at least, Milton had approved
by teaching it out of Manilius and Holywood to his students. Raphael taught it generously, and newer theories as
well. If we observe the poet's syntax, the angel hardly used

imprudence in astronomy *per se* as even a symbol. Having
had his ponderous fun with the heavenly fabric that God
had left, as in play, obvious to man's disputes, he twice
warned Adam to go by no means *further,* or intrude into
the affairs of planet-dwellers, whatever astronomical theory should triumph:

> But whether thus these things, or whether not, . . .
> Solicit not thy thoughts with matters hid,
> Leave them to God above, him serve and fear;
> Of other Creatures, as him pleases best.

And again:

> Be lowly wise:
> Think only what concerns thee and thy being;
> Dream not of other Worlds, what Creatures there
> Live.

But into even this solitary piece of positively forbidden
conjecture we need not read more than an injunction from
searching God's intentions curiously. By his original question, Why luminaries so great, bright, and numerous?,
Adam implied that the Creator probably intended to people them, as we can see by the angel's rejoinder.

The critic who once wrote of Milton as a poet difficult
to disable, in that he could develop with fresh brilliance
the tritest of themes, said no more, surely, than that Milton succeeded as an epic poet. It became him to hint, but
not to parrot, a long tradition of profitable homily, a tradition represented by the moralists Socrates and Sir John
Davies, who praised self-knowledge with a conventional
jibe at star-knowledge. Such moralists have been legion.
We may think, as we read Raphael's lecture, back to Erasmus (whose book Milton mentioned in the sixth Prolusion) and his astronomers retailing eclipses, stellar dimensions, and multiple worlds—and we remember that the
grammarian made them only one regiment in a fools' army
that included grammarians, lawyers, and divines babbling
the oppositions of science. Robert Burton found the astronomers no longer guilty of major imprudence once he
bethought him of other "gigantical Cyclopes," the theologians who invaded God's secrecy. In a passage strikingly

like Raphael's discourse he reproved curiosity, not star-gazing. Though he ran through the competing astrono-mies with his usual eager interest in such things, he entered his long bill of particulars against pagans, heretics, school-men, and enthusiasts "of God's privy council." Close to the Anglican's preempted center of the humanistic tradi-tion, George Herbert admonished oversubtle—but not as-tronomical—divines who curiously explained the Presence in the sacrament:

> Then burn thy Epicycles, foolish man.
> Break all thy spheres and save thy head.

The Socratic commonplace, which made astronomy al-most as statutory in Book VIII as Homer had made the epic invocation in Book I, was poetically a happy accident. It is not easy to think of another science—natural, moral, or theological—that Adam could have intruded upon so effec-tively. Doctrinal and ethical questions of fate and freedom, passion and apathy, never dramatic, were inappropriate before Adam knew sin. Angelic orders would have sym-bolized curiosity, but Raphael had a practical reason for expounding angelology without hindrance—to show Adam his attainable reward—as he had for narrating the conflict in heaven to warn him of the enemy and of God's punish-ments. More of such discourse would have been tiresome. Any historical question suitable for Adam, like Faust's "Who made the world?", had been answered in scripture and so fell within bounds; what God had been doing earlier hardly made a question worthy of our philosophical sire. Astronomy remained, and it gave Milton a pat occa-sion to display the learning required of him by the rules of the Renaissance epic, the kind of learning, too, that Gabriel Harvey, in discreet Latin, once censured his fa-vorite epic poet for lacking. Measured by any obvious utility, the subject matter could become unprofitably curi-ous. Milton had taught astronomy for practical use, and he knew that in farming or navigation, whether heaven moves or earth "imports not if thou reckon right." Even astrologers and almanac-makers reckoned by either sys-tem, and Milton knew at least the venerable name of

Blaeu, whose most famous treatise taught mariners to use globes by both. Conveniently for Milton's purpose, learned astronomers had often been reminded in variations on Proverbs xxv:2 and Ecclesiastes iii:11 that God toyed with them for pastime; and in popular myth they had been associated with Alfonso, the astronomical king who regretted that he had not been at Creation to help God with good advice. At one point (74–75) Raphael may have glanced at the apocryphal blasphemy.

And finally, the Socratic *exemplum* must have come to the poet as a godsend when he remembered his own astronomical problem. If he had been so convinced of Ptolemy's accuracy (with amendments) that he could let Raphael endorse it from heaven, he would never, to say the least, have nodded toward Copernicus. In all conscience, he could not allow Raphael to call the lovely framework of his poem fact; yet as a poet he could not suffer him to call it fiction. The curiosity lecture served all ends with economy by shutting off discussion. Astronomy was not only for Milton, as someone has said, simply the most obvious curiosity; it was just about the only one suitable. The poet had pretty clearly decided so and started writing toward the angel's topic when he early gave to Eve a curious astronomical "wherefore" (iv.657); and his likeliest real, though rationalized, motive in moving Ariosto's lunar paradise to the outer shell of the world would have been to steer Satan away from the moon. Otherwise he would have had to know positively facts about moon-dwellers that Raphael could not legitimately tell Adam.

For him to omit altogether a discourse on curiosity from a thoughtful song of Adam's fall would have been inconceivable even if he had wished, and he had no good reason to wish. In his second Prolusion a very young Milton wrote Adam's story with mythological names, imitating the Latin practice of Bembo, Erasmus, and many humanists: the thieving Prometheus, he it was who, by his audacity, had disabled posterity from hearing the music of the spheres. It was the task of learning and morality to repair the damage. In one place in the *Christian Doctrine* he mentioned Adam, Eve, and Lot's wife as types of curi-

osity, and in another listed Adam's aspiring to God's attributes among all the major crimes that our grand parent
comprehended in a single lapse, much as he dramatized
falling Eve's several and distinct sins. Countless preachers
displayed their ingenuity in multiplying Adam's. Their
innumerable subdivided and detailed lists answered, and
not always unconsciously, an ancient Manichæan error
which Augustine had refuted with a similar analysis of
apple-eating. Mani would have argued matter to be evil
in itself and proved it so by Genesis; for unless Adam was
punished for touching evil, then God set an outrageously
high price on apples. In many a catalogue of sins written
to show wherein Mani, or his disciples, had missed the
point, seventeenth-century preachers always listed intellectual sin as Adamic error and nearly always called it
curiosity. Conversely, every sort of disagreeable opinion
was damned with a reference to Adam. The pages cited
in the notes here are filled with them. As a great preacher
phrased it, the times were "sick of Adam's disease." All rash
discoursers plucked the forbidden fruit, and Cudworth,
thinking perhaps of a rabbinical legend, swore that he
had caught them shaking the tree. John Norris in fun accused Henry More of carrying it away.

But though Milton, writing of Adam, had no choice but
to write of curiosity, and next to none but to illustrate it
with astronomy, we are not therefore permitted to think
that he wrote Christian humanism perfunctorily and without complete sincerity. Our critics will properly sift all
his conventions for whatever they may reveal of the unique
Milton, even while they remember that in this passage
circumstances caution them not to overdo. They may perhaps sift too fine if they draw from Raphael's sermon on
a text from Socrates evidence of the poet's discouragement
and altered faith in reason and learning. Altered from
what? If the humanist who subdued learning to the service
of a moral utility in the Prolusions and Of Education later
lost confidence in learning, the fact must be proved by
better evidence than Raphael's orthodox caution against
trivial speculation. Some recent studies have so well fitted
the angel's lecture to the poet's normal opinions of knowl-

edge that they have left no labor of harmonizing. Such
efforts can succeed with *Paradise Lost*. They have not, I
think, succeeded with *Paradise Regained*. I happen to believe that in neither poem are we obliged to find an em-
bittered Milton reversing himself, but I doubt that the
earlier cautions of Christian and classical Socratism amount
to the same thing as the later rejection of classical learning and poetry. The two passages differ so entirely that a
single explanation can hardly fit both. Let us then confine ourselves for the present to the restraint of speculation in *Paradise Lost*.

If we reduce his poetry to flat preachment, Raphael
taught self-knowledge as the beginning and end of wisdom. Other knowledge, this omitted, was curiosity.

> Yet what thou canst attain, which best may serve
> To glorify the Maker, and infer
> Thee also happier, shall not be withheld—

so the angel promised to execute his commission and fur-
nish Adam knowledge within bounds. No niggard in the
performance, he proved that knowledge for daily living
might, when joined with virtue, rise to God and embrace
the universe, and with no proviso that Milton in ardent
youth would have lamented as a burden. Humanism has
never acknowledged any criterion but that by which Adam
learned to judge the drift of thinking—utility for right
action:

> Apt the Mind or Fancy is to rove
> Uncheckt, and of her roving is no end;
> Till warn'd, or by experience taught, she learn,
> That not to know at large of things remote
> From use, obscure and subtle, but to know
> That which before us lies in daily life,
> Is the prime Wisdom.

Whatever served the prime wisdom as handmaid, best
served to glorify God and infer man also happier; whatever asked at large of things remote was "more," and therefore "fume, or emptiness, or fond impertinence." Here
surely is nothing for tears unless it is that our civilization
forgot the lesson and followed strange gods, whose serv-

ice has been something less than perfect freedom, until
we find ourselves

> in things that most concern
> Unpractis'd, unprepar'd, and still to seek.

The study of man cannot take all knowledge uncriti-
cally for its province. We cannot honor Milton as a humanist, his religion and politics apart, without honoring
him also for his warning. If we must still have him a naturalist as well, we must accept his science as he offered it—
in the service of God and of the human spirit. Nonsense
itself could not make him out a passionate Baconian; but
his physical studies, though occasionally touched with occultism and frequently lagging behind the newest discoveries, proclaimed him no enemy of natural science. Three
or four times he insisted upon its dignity by pointing out
that Adam in innocence named the animals according to
their natures. Eve named the flowers. If one fears that he
did not know what delighted Bacon, that the story sanctified naturalists, one can read (viii.439) his own clear
declaration.

As if by carefully predetermined pattern, Milton introduced three angelic tutors into *Paradise Lost,* teaching in
as many faculties. One professed astronomy, among other
sciences, and taught an ostensible angel. A second professed history, philosophy, and divinity, and taught vulnerable Adam, little lower than the angels. A third taught
handicrafts, physiology, elementary ethics and politics, and
the bare essentials of religion to fallen Adam. Original
sin and natural infirmity required such a *scala intellectus*
to correspond with the *scala virtutis.* Let us begin at the
top. When a young cherub (young in order that Satan
might plausibly seek education and ask questions, a cherub
because the cherubim burned with the fire of intellect as
the seraphim with love) attended Uriel's astronomical lecture (iii.694–735), he heard nothing but Bacon's best piety:

> Fair Angel, thy desire which tends to know
> The works of God, thereby to glorify
> The great Work-Master, leads to no excess
> That reaches blame, but rather merits praise,
> The more it seems excess.

There he found no quantity of learning stinted, no subject matter discredited. The student (so far as his precep-
tor knew, for upstart passions in the face had not yet betrayed him) stood in blessed condition, already secure in
self-knowledge and self-control; only the worship that God
required limited his permission to know. As Uriel bound
natural knowledge, though angelic, to the service of faith
and worship, he anticipated Raphael with an important
warning, couched in the language of Ecclesiastes iii:11,
"No man can find out the work that God maketh from
the beginning to the end." Exegetes understood the verse
causally, that is, "from efficients to finals," and so Uriel
admonished the cherub (III.707). What created mind
could comprehend the wisdom—here, the purposes, ends,
intentions—of created things since God had "hid their
causes deep"? The poet showed by his plentiful teleology
in every science that he had not gone all the way with
Descartes. A religious philosophy older than Descartes—
we have read it in Donne—forbade the cherub to seek
causes and Adam to hypothecate Selenites unless their
study of finality saved both man's dignity and God's glory.

To human depravity at the foot of our ladder the angel
Michael taught self-knowledge in a context of original
sin. The poet can never be sufficiently praised for his account of the means whereby fallen man might regain to
know God aright—education. Students have discerned his
theories of pedagogy in the last books of his epic, but
something might still be said of the wit, in the high sense of
the word, that converted without distortion the Old Testament histories, adding little, preserving their sequence.
Unobtrusively they became a systematic course of study
in Christian ethics; the Law became what the Apostle had
called it, a schoolmaster to bring us to Christ. Beginning
with things obvious to sense and ending with the clear
teachings of the spirit, the angel showed Adam first the
ravages of sin on the body and the remedy in *nihil nimis*,
then moved by method from the individual soul to society
and thence to history, tracing the consequences of immorality, irreligion, and idolatry. In vision first and then by
lecture he accounted for tyranny in the state and corrup-

tion in the church, pointing the remedy always: obedience to the will of God revealed in scripture and confirmed in conscience. Learning this obedience, Adam learned a lesson more valuable than all science, natural and supernatural (XII.575), and by adding works of virtue, patience, temperance, and charity answerable to his high knowledge, possessed his inward Paradise in happiness.

Milton puzzled some readers by writing, apparently only months apart, two poems of comparable length on the subject of Paradise Found. Criticism has pointed to a small difficulty in the presumed overlapping of *Paradise Regained* with the two books closing the precedent epic, and to a greater one in the negative, pietistic, unworldly teaching of the later work. The latter hopelessly contradicted the Christian humanism of the former if Paradise was to be regained in the one poem by working piety, right conduct in this world, wisely moderated use of its gifts; and in the other, by utter withdrawal and renunciation. *Paradise Lost* taught the means of salvation: faith not void of works in God and in Christ crucified. It taught man how to use the means in private morality, public service, and active charity. Of this doctrine *Paradise Regained,* by the usual modern reading, explained or extended nothing. It was rather the *Christian Doctrine,* with its "legalistic" humanism, that confirmed all. The ethical and practical second Book of the treatise in particular mapped a road to personal salvation only artistically abbreviated in *Paradise Lost.* In due time we shall look to find in *Paradise Regained* the salvation of the Kingdom of Christ, while, with proper regard for a difference, we leave *Paradise Lost* to teach the salvation of man. There is no difficulty if the one poem edifies the individual, the other an institution. In the matter of learning, Michael taught Adam his rudiments in humanity and religion without forbidding any knowledge serviceable to the fundamental wisdom. *Humile sapiamus:* let us savor in moderation. Knowledge, like food, required temperance (VII.127); and Adam achieved temperance in knowledge by learning, in profitable order, what obedience prepared his vessel to contain. Unless Milton wrote confusedly, the more Adam might grow in grace toward his former innocent state, the more knowledge he might comprehend within the bounds of self-knowledge, Uriel's mild yoke ever remaining.

At the feet of Raphael, Adam in blessedness could expect more advanced instruction, but he sought knowledge *haud passibus æquis.* Or his thirst for knowledge outran his zeal for worship. He asked his dubious question inopportunely and therefore irrelevantly, and he asked in the wrong spirit. By contrast, the first time in the poem (vii.95) that he begged his heavenly guest for more light on visible nature, its origins and structure, matters that "nearer might concern," he pleased the angel by seeking

> What we, not to explore the secrets ask
> Of his Eternal Empire, but the more
> To magnify his works, the more we know.

By the language of his antithesis Milton made it plain that searching the *arcana imperii,* the secrets of the Eternal Empire, meant not knowing this or that science, or too much of it, but knowing for the sake of knowing or for the sake of carping. Philosophy will hardly show us why the stars should be a topic higher or more recondite than, say, the spirit-world, which the angel graciously explained fully at Adam's request. But once warned by Raphael's lecture that he needed to study perfect obedience because he stood in mortal peril, Adam was in no case to open the question period foolishly with the digressive topic of astronomy. Let us recall that our grand parent provoked the angel's reproof by asking how an otherwise frugal nature could "create" with superfluous disproportion so vast and excellent a universe to light this "punctual spot" of earth (viii.23). As an answer, the angel's ensuing lecture on rival astronomies migh seem irrelevant if we could not so easily supply Adam's unspoken cavils. One was a criticism of divine economy, like Eve's earlier

> But wherefore all night long shine these, for whom
> This glorious sight, when sleep hath shut all eyes?

Adam erred more seriously than his mate in that he impugned not only the wisdom of God, but also the dignity of man by his criticism of man's dwelling. Tutored by paganism, skeptics had filled out part of his ellipsis: was not man presumptuous in Montaigne's and Charron's account to suppose that he was the cause of all creation, situated at what one of their imitators called

> The stair foot of the world, and sediment
> Of nature?

Adam as needlessly and more seriously tangled himself in God's designs by his invidious praise of the stars, inasmuch as his grumbling about wasted planets argued them inhabited, hinted at Seneca's *non nos causa mundi sumus*, and thus raised a host of speculative problems. To this irrelevant and irreverent teleology the Miltonic angel replied with the best that finite reason could offer—in astral bodies "great or bright infers not excellence." Then he drew the very veil that Satan (ix.679) was presently to tear away in an apostrophe:

> O Sacred, Wise, and Wisdom-giving Plant,
> Mother of Science, Now I feel thy Power
> Within me clear, not only to discern
> Things in their Causes, but to trace the ways
> Of highest Agents, deem'd however wise.

Speaking in his own person Milton guessed freely enough about plural worlds. But speaking through the angel he chose to be reticent because he used the worlds to stand for God's designs. Inquiry into those hidden purposes might distract thought from immediate problems, hinder obedience, and dissuade from worship. In this bad sense Raphael placed final causes beyond the reach of "scanning" inquiry (viii.74), but dealt freely with God's intentions wherever his reason could justify them. Raphael, Michael, and the Chorus in *Samson* all declared God's ways justifiable and gave man free rein to do the work of justification, not to undo it. When reason ran counter to its permitted course it had no franchise at all. From the angel's lecture on the stars Adam could have learned considerable astronomy, but he might have stood had he learned the duties of a Christian humanist: to know for the sake of well doing; to grow in knowledge by building *gradatim* upon this prime wisdom and upon a constant faith in the total rightness of God's universe.

Chapter V

PHILOSOPHY AND VAIN DECEIT

SOME ISSUES IN THE LEARNED-MINISTRY CONTROVERSY

IN closing an earlier chapter I seconded the judgment that the anti-intellectual lines of *Paradise Regained* (IV.285–364) should not be read—indeed, cannot be read—as mere commonplace, adding elsewhere my opinion that the lines bear no immediate kinship to Raphael's warning in *Paradise Lost*. In that poem, and emphatically in its eighth Book, Milton taught Socratic humanism; in its sequel, the anti-humanistic principle of scripture's absolute sufficiency. In both, to be sure, he taught a sobriety. But sobriety was a virtue that we have heard claimed for every opinion under his sun, so that to find this common principle we must climb to the thin heights of abstraction. Alone, a bond so tenuous will hardly permit us to mention the two passages of "obscurantism" in the same breath. What we can match with *Paradise Regained* to our better instruction may be *Likeliest Means,* where Milton took the stand to which his earlier politics had committed him. He denied that a minister was no minister unless learned. The learned-ministry controversy and his position in it deserve study. And if, as I think, the Christ of *Paradise Regained* made that poem importantly ecclesiastical by setting an example for the church and its ministers, we shall find it doubly important to understand *Likeliest Means*. Our road to the tract lies through the reformers' ancient quarrel with a learning that stultified.

It goes without saying that the sectarian clamor against universities and "able, orthodox divines" amid which Milton had his official being was not simply a crusade for the advancement of ignorance; nor were the contrary pleas for universities, ordination, and tithes—three inseparable props of the learned ministry—a counterblast against igno-

184

rance, though they seemed so no doubt to the entrenched clergymen who wrote them. We may be quite sure that if universities could have taught a sectarian divinity, and if ministers had been ordained on the strength of that learning, the favored sect would have found no mystical reason to brand learning with the mark of Antichrist. But, "Have not those fountains ever sent what streams the times have liked?" Roger Williams asked rhetorically, "and ever changed their taste and color to the prince's eye and palate?" In the liberal *Oceana* we can see what he feared. Harrington thought the Bible stipulated universities, else how could the scriptures be searched or Catholicism opposed? In his tolerant republic all ministers might preach freely, and none might hold state preferments; yet his church had its "national part," and universities served that part. Since it seemed inevitable to Harrington that a national church would require school divines, Williams could justly assume that school divines would inevitably require a national church, and that it would be a forcing church. Harrington indeed directed that the universities should review all assemblies of ministers. Milton and Williams had good reason to doubt that university divines and true liberty could well consist, when England was to need two centuries to attune the jar. To the Commonwealth's "ignorant" divinity as a source, democratic sentiment has been often credited. It seems almost demonstrable, however, that democracy or a leveling spirit often came before the doctrine. Where leveling touched church-polity it taught the rebels a simple fideism that would make the reactionary "learned" priests unnecessary. The numerous Baptists can be offered as evidence that the hen sometimes preceded the egg. Those scripturalists were not necessarily enthusiasts, their religion mystical, or their apostles unlearned; yet as schismatics, sometimes Levellers, they were uniformly anti-intellectual. Numbers of them, as Baxter credibly witnessed, then advanced from their schism and their scripturally defensible "heresy" into enthusiasm. Without aspiring to cleave political thought sharply into civil and ecclesiastical in an age when settlement of the church entered into every political question, I intend to

dwell upon politics, or ecclesiastical polity, as the leading
motive to "ignorant" divinity. The connection has not
gone unnoticed by students of early radical movements.
The great solitary mystics of the Middle Ages rose above
their school learning for the sake of beatific vision. Late
controversial "mystics" took a stand for Christ against Antichrist, the great enemy of the church. In the early seventeenth century that broad debate swallowed up almost
every issue known to thought. Those who depreciated
learning in order to drive it from the pulpit were often
respectably learned Christians. Yet, as remarked earlier,
the disintegration of the church resolved itself, as always
in the language of vituperation, into a struggle between
the ignorance of the learned and the meddling presumption of the ignorant. It had been so when St. Paul warned
of philosophy and vain deceit while Tacitus, Pliny, Celsus,
Lucian, and Porphyry were soon to write of all Christians
as ignorant. It had been so when the Oxonian Wyclif,
using Eve for his example, damned the universities and
their degrees in divinity while schoolmen sneered at simple
Lollardy and Wyclif's ignorant fanaticism. It had been so
when Huss, Luther, Melanchthon and the rest denounced
the antichristian universities while a grave Catholic historian related that Carlstadt, Melanchthon, and their followers had burned their books and betaken themselves to
the mechanic trades.

In the secondary reformation of the English church,
Separatists and nonseparating Puritans preached anti-intellectualism scant or extravagant according to their degree
of radicalism. The more conformable Puritans, planning
to take over rather than break up the national church,
needed only a little of it. Geneva and Zürich had declared for ministerial learning and founded universities as
divinity schools; backed by secular authority, Calvin had
repudiated the mysticism of spirituals and the ignorant
fanaticism ascribed to Münster Anabaptists. Papists, notwithstanding, hunted evidence of Protestant obscurantism
and found it in the annotated Geneva Bible, where it numbered among the locusts of Revelation ix:3 the doctor of
divinity. Abhorring, like Wyclif and Milton, both that

locust and his title, the earliest Puritan manifesto, the
Admonition, by Field and Wilcox, regularly doomed the
masters and doctors whenever it ran through the antichristian hierarchy. From all the second printing except the
preface, presumably added late, the offending words "masters and doctors" had been methodically deleted by somebody. By Thomas Cartwright, we may guess, for it was he
who defended Puritan learning when Papists in their
Rheims Testament deplored the Protestants' stand against
divinity degrees; and his own *Second Admonition* nowhere objected to the doctorate. Some early Anglicans who
tried to associate all Puritans with Brownists and Anabaptists failed to give moderate Puritans credit for such care
to protect learning from zealous extremists, but Meres
more temperately ranked the factions in iniquity: "As the
Anabaptists abhor the liberal arts and human sciences: so
Puritans and precisians detest poetry and poems."

If later Puritan preachers and lecturers had learning, at
least they forbade a parade of it in the pulpit as if Greek
and Latin had been the Urim and Thummim of their
sacred fraternity. Early and late they denounced the abuse
of heathen philosophy and "ethnic" quotations, and employed both sparingly, so that as Puritanism rose pulpit
oratory declined. The celebrated Puritan John Preston,
D. D., royal chaplain, roundly delivered that a man might
estimate his degree of sanctification by the pleasure he
took in an unadorned sermon. Moderate Puritans blessed
only the ignorance that clothed their own religious sim-
plicities, and there a little sufficed. In Marprelate days they
ridiculed the establishment not for having learning, but
for lacking it. In 1589 the church was too often guilty as
charged, and the harassed lexicographer Bishop Thomas
Cooper would not attempt to deny it. But in fifty years an
Anglican could write truly, "Blessed be God, that cloud
was never better blown over." In these years, whatever the
Puritans wrote in criticism of education they normally intended for the better enlightenment of the ministry. A
good humanist of the Scotch Kirk, Andrew Melville, wrote
Latin verse *contra Larvatam geminæ Academiæ Gorgonem*,
or, *Anti-tami-cami-categoria*, only to deplore the way the

bishop-ridden universities were being manipulated to the prejudice of real ability in favor of wealth, titles, and re-action. The author of *Lycidas* might have written it. Soon Milton was to add his moral censures of the universities. Against the license that D'Ewes and others found there a crusade came to a head in the time of Charles's first Parliament. Its criticism in later years and from other pens took on a significance not originally intended. Bitter enemies of England's theological seminaries loudly demanded smaller schools nearer home. Thus morality placed a weapon in the hands of sectaries bent upon breaking into bits the monopoly-holding universities.

Unlike the sectaries who would replace the two universities with scattered colleges, more ingenuous reformers brought their proposals—and there were many between Elizabeth's reign and Gerbier's academy or the projected university at Durham—to add schools. In 1659 and again in 1660 Milton suggested additional schools and used the moral argument. It has been thought that as early as *Of Education* he described the kind of foundation which would better distribute learning and teach youth at home, away from the vicious life of Cambridge. At both stages of his development Milton came somewhat short of the extremists. His early projecting for Hartlib wrested no divinity-teaching from the universities; his more radical Independency did so, yet nowhere suggested melting down two schools to make others.

The radical Independents inherited their antipathy to a budge aristocracy in the church not from Cartwright and the Puritan center, but from Robert Browne and the Separatists of the advanced wing. The earliest "Puritans" to oppose the idea of a national church aimed heavy blows at its ministerial seed plots, objecting to more evils than the granting of degrees in divinity. Henry Ainsworth, who owed none of his own learning to universities, took exception to Popish customs like the celibacy of students, and deplored the study of pagan authors further than linguistics required. The foremost Hebraist in Europe, as Leyden had saluted him—if it was indeed he who wrote the Brownists' *Apologie*—recommended to divinity students only those studies serviceable for understanding scripture, which he declared "fully sufficient for all instruction." If he had written fifty years later he would have known better than to add that such studies might be useful to refute heretics, for that argument was to become the stock excuse for university-trained divines. Already "heathen tales and testimonies" stuffed too many sermons and wasted too much time. To the charge that his churches sought to overthrow universities, the Separatist replied that he would have them multiplied tenfold, "the corruption of Antichrist being removed."

The heresiologists Robert Burton and Robert Baillie rightly credited the Brownists with "large invectives against universities" as "worse than monasteries," with opposing tithes and divinity degrees, and wrongly, with a general disposition to burn the heathen philosophers. The evidence usually came from the lawyer Henry Barrow. When Dr. Some wrote against him, the Anglican's first chapter stoutly defended universities. Fuller, exaggerating a bit but alleging Some as his authority, shuddered to remember how Barrow and Greenwood had moved Queen Elizabeth to abolish Oxford and Cambridge. What Robert Browne in truth once asked in a letter to Burghley—Strype printed it as a curiosity—was that her majesty remove wasteful methods from teaching and university learning from the ministry. The angry churchmen who cited Barrow's *False Church* and *Refutation of Gifford* seldom troubled to state the Separatists' educational position fairly, while for some decades their victims held their peace. As soon as the presses were unbound, the sectaries renewed the ancient war, and criticism of the universities gathered from Barrow's writings by some professed friend of Independency was reprinted. Barrow had retched at manners, morals, and politics out of Aristotle instead of scripture; and at time wasted on elenchi, topics, and tropes. He cared not to be told that when the Ephesians brought together their curious books and burned them the books were of conjuring; for no conjuring could be more dangerous than the curious books of the Popish universities, upholding the Beast. He would hear no lawful art condemned as in itself evil—and nearly all the sectaries could honestly say the same—but demanded for schools what he wanted for churches: independency; that is, a school for and controlled by every congregation.

Though moderate Puritans and the Anglicans alike plumped for ministerial learning, it was generally the Anglicans who wrote the long rhapsodies that droned from hundreds of pulpits. On the slightest occasion or none, they forsook their announced texts to insert these digressions, which would now seem as pointless as dull if the preachers had not sometimes accounted for the vainglory. Thomas Adams, whose Puritanism has been exaggerated, complained that a minister dared not quote a Father or a poet lest the fanatics cry out against his poisoned eloquence, as if all this were not "spoils of the Gentiles and mere handmaids unto divinity." Bishop John King once chanced to use a bit of Stoicism to prove anger a sin, and launched himself into a dozen pages scolding those who cried, "Pull down schools and universities!" Always, against the extremists who would kill the bondwoman instead of shearing her, the apologists maintained that only learning could refute heresy. Egeon Askew's apology *Of Secular Learning in Sermons* formed a part of a larger work wooing dissenters back into the fold, and so excused the divines for being erudite. How could they be wrong, Askew demanded with Mornay, Zanchy, and all the scripture he could muster, if they converted atheists by the only authority a natural man respected? Many preachers, echoing Jerome and hence Philo's and Origen's allegories, welcomed Hagar if forbidden to meddle above her mistress. They quoted Æneas Silvius on the lovely face of human learning, fairer than the morning or the evening star; or after Eusebius, Socrates, or Theodoret, recalled Julian's edict forbidding learning to Christians because, as the wicked Apostate had turned a proverb, "We are being wounded by our own feathers." The clergy had to explain away a medley of uncomfortable texts, like Adam's sin and the Preacher's weariness or Tertullian's *Quid Athenis?* and the scourging that Jerome suffered in a dream for reading Cicero. Constructively, the preachers could point to Moses, well learned in Egyptian lore; to Solomon, wiser than the children of the East; to Daniel, well seen in the cunning of the Chaldeans; to St. Paul, whose much learning and pagan quotations harmed neither his sanity nor his piety; to Zenas, Luke, Apollos, Dionysius. All this argument went to prove the scholastic premise that nothing true in philosophy can be false in divinity. So Bacon wrote, with much scripture, in his *Advancement of Learning,* and Bacon's defense served also to guard bishops, Puritans, and Assembly Independents against their dread and common enemy, "contempt of the ministry."

Milton, too, was to find use for this cento of scripture and Fathers; he had copied some of it into his own Commonplace Book. But he had abominated the use to which the tithe-gathering persecutors had been putting it when, not loving presbytery less but hating prelatry more, and detesting hirelings, he reentered the lists against the bishops in 1641. From its earliest sessions he had followed the Long Parliament's debates on ministerial maintenance. Even as the reforming members, beginning timidly, meditated only abolition of deans and chapters, he would have heard how some mild Culpeper had urged the senate to do nothing drastic enough to jeopardize learning. Milton wasted no anxiety on the learned priests who were "progging and soliciting for a new settlement of their tithes and oblations." He hated their "piddling tithes" in 1641. What he then wanted instead is not equally clear, except that it was something modest, equitably distributed, doubtless at that stage of his thinking a state maintenance. He assumed that a ministry so rewarded could achieve that solid and disinterested learning that he valued all his life, even for the pulpit. But while he lent his youthful pen to Smectymnuus he upheld two principles of the unworldly church that ought not to be transferred to his old age: a minister should, ideally, volunteer his service *gratis,* and God did not absolutely require that he be learned. His statement of the former sounded much the same when he wrote it early as when he repeated it thus in the *Christian Doctrine:* to avoid suspicion and scandal a minister did best to live by his private income or his private resources; if

he found the ideal impossibly burdensome, he had a scriptural right to live by the gospel so long as he lived modestly
and without puling that he had an expensive education to
pay for—a plea which to Christ and St. Paul "seems never
to have occurred."

Very early in his career Milton openly sneered at the
medieval notion that learning stood or fell with the ministry. And when he heard learned fools and hypocrites
whine that without bishoprics and deaneries young ministers would lose their motive to study, he thought back to
Socrates and St. Paul and exploded with impatience. The
hirelings who advanced such a plea dishonored learning.
If mercenary fathers would not put their sons to school
without reckoning up the gain, let them keep their base-
born issue at home. God could raise up noblemen or other
fathers of independent means to give sons to the church.
He submitted once that God could make some use of
tradesmen. The young man touched upon the fornication
of money with clergy-learning somewhere in each of his
early antiprelatical tracts, always in these accents: the
prelates "never lin pealing our ears, that unless we fat
them like boars, and cram them as they list with wealth,
deaneries, and pluralities, with baronies and stately preferments, all learning and religion will go underfoot." The
very heathen would have thrown out such greasy sophisters, as respectable Englishmen would have done, except
that, by capturing the universities, the bishops had perverted the mind of the nation. For himself, before a place-
seeking cleric, he preferred "a plain, unlearned man" to
edify him toward a godly and happy life. What would it
avail England to have a hireling ministry "though never
so learned"?

The difference between these early tracts and *Likeliest
Means* is no difference of principle, but of political experience. The evils that Milton at first took to be accidents
of prelatry inhered, the clergy was to convince him, in
any state religion. Whenever in his private meditations
he took the short step from fixed stipends to pure voluntaryism, he had finished his education in ecclesiastical polity. We cannot know the exact date, but the Presbyterians

began to teach him much wisdom of the serpent while he kept his ear on the Parliamentary debates and found the conscript fathers ever lagging in the reformation that God and liberty expected. When he addressed in 1643 a Parliament all but "tired out with dependencies and independencies, and how they will compound, and in what calends," he wooed the members to forsake the "swoln visage of counterfeit knowledge" that had corrupted church and state. When he next addressed them he had reason to confess, ironically, that real learning stood in fair way to be trodden down as the bishops had prophesied, and to warn of the "mystery of ignorance and ecclesiastical thralldom" grown afresh in new disguises. The following year he had been goaded to inflict some fine irony along with his own new light and real learning on the Parliament itself. He reminded the misguided legislators how they had been zealous to do nothing about tithes (for thus we may safely construe his meaning from a parallel in *Areopagitica*) and so to "wipe off the imputation of intending to discourage the progress and advance of learning."

It was in *Areopagitica* itself, his clearest summons to intellectual freedom and progress, that he precisely wrote his contempt for hireling philosophers into the proper context of his own passion for knowledge. He caught up grimly the scriptural chant of the prelates, but not to their purpose. If the senators dawdling over tithes so valued learning, let them take his newest advancement of it, written in a bold and broad spirit to fit God's plans for England. And if they liked the bishops' old texts when presbyters mouthed them, let them now hear applied truly the same scripture: Moses and Daniel were learned in the lore of the Egyptians and Chaldeans; the classicist St. Paul quoted the poets in holy scripture; early Christians so well mastered heathen learning that the Apostate complained of wounds by such weapons. That the freedom he sought stood for real learning Milton went on proving to Parliament by rebutting the familiar texts for ignorance—the devil whipping Jerome in a dream for reading Cicero (it was no angel, else the Father had been whipped for reading Plautus); Solomon finding much reading wearisome

(if it had been sinful the inspired sage would have used
stronger language); the Ephesians burning their curious
books (their *magices artes,* as the Syriac version read). On
Adam's curiosity this time he commented as his argument
required: we are not Adam; we share his doom and, unlike
the innocent Adam, must know good by knowing evil.

He turned wrathfully upon the hirelings who had perverted these words of God. Not a motion to distribute
justly the revenues of the church but had always incited
the prelates to cry out that "all learning would be forever
dashed and discouraged," as if "the tenth part of learning stood or fell with the clergy." By drily inserting the
decimal in this context he threw in the teeth of the legislators their reluctance to meddle with the sacred tyranny
of tithes, as he made indisputably clear in the sequel. As
in *Tetrachordon* but at plainer length, he went on to remind the senators how sordid was the clerical argument,
how foreign to the true spirit of learning. Parliament had
shown itself sufficiently loath to dishearten the false pretenders to learning, but ever ready to discourage the "free
and ingenuous sort" of truth-seekers. The intrusion of the
tithe-gathering parsons into *Areopagitica* shows how heavily they bore upon Milton when he was thirty-five and how
near he then stood to *Likeliest Means* in all that concerned
freedom from tyranny and superstition. If in his oration
he touched only incidentally on the fiscal question, it was
not there his argument. And now let us scrutinize more
narrowly the question of money as an issue in the learned-
ministry controversy. Milton had been listening to pre-
latical plaints from the days when Lancelot Andrewes
discovered, as a vicar put it, "an indissoluble combina-
tion between sacred manners, sacred means, and sacred
revenues."

TITHES AND CLERGY-LEARNING

Puritanism had risen linked with fiscal debate, though
Marprelate was probably not the first in England to jeer
at the bishops' subterfuge that they could not buy books
unless they held two or more livings. Against tithes as an
institution Puritans on the hither side of Separation at first

raised no objection, but only against the abuse. William Vaughan, who damned stage plays in general and Marlowe in particular, bared the grounds of their discontent. He hoped that he would not be taken for a Puritan if he pointed out that Welsh parishes yielded tithes worth a hundred pounds a year, out of which a curate was paid twenty nobles. After yearly procurations, fifteenths, and other exactions, the cleric could spend five pounds. What respectable scholar, Vaughan demanded, would accept the beggarly annuity? Conforming Puritans and Anglicans alike generally found the source of poverty and clerical ignorance in the impropriations that had made tithes a negotiable security for laymen's investments. Later, the Puritan lecturers and certain ministers, underpaid and hopeless of relief, instead of preaching dutifully against the "simony and sacrilege" of impropriators, began preaching against paying tithes into the treasury of Antichrist. The arguments they drew out of Selden's book gave the vested interests strong motives for suppressing the jurist's proof that the creaking system was not *jure divino,* though Selden nowhere proposed another system. He himself observed cynically that the lecturers stole from the ministers as the friars had been wont to do. As an Erastian he found learning indispensable to the minister—to refute heresy, naturally. An Anglican despised the disaffected parsons who preached against tithes, caring nothing if they ruined the faithful. What recked it them? They were sped if they could gain easily and quickly by screwing themselves into popular favor. Meanwhile the able minister, after spending a lifetime in study, could keep his family like some inferior tradesman. Contentious tithe-payers vexed Burton when they trampled on learning. In spite of the rebels, prædial tithes were paid readily enough on the whole, though often impropriate; but personal tithes would never be collectable so long as Puritanism discouraged payment. "Nonconformed great ones," city merchants, and skilled laborers therefore rolled in Puritanism and untaxed wealth, swaying their mechanics toward schism. "Indeed it is this filthy lucre hath occasioned so many babblers in our church," roared the rector of Pokington. Money or the lack of it induced preachers to "bray at universities for a morsel of bread" and exclude all arts from the pulpit.

When the Presbyterian babblers seized the widowed whore Plurality, together with her traditional honoraria, they left unaltered the time-tested method of paying the clergy and the episcopal defense of it. The abolition of deans and chapters supplied enough revenue to relieve the worst oppressions, and if Presbyterians or Independents showed a real mind to do away with tithes, impropriators blocked them. A history of the paper controversy exceeds the scope of these remarks, confined to the union of money and learning. Of effective legislation there is nothing to tell. The Long Parliament at first contemplated some relief of ministers from unnecessary tithe-suits. More rigorous compulsion of payment became necessary after 1644, when the "illegal" imposition of presbyters was met by nonpayment and the pamphleteering quickly grew in bulk. Cromwell vacillated. His Instrument of Government promised reform, but afterwards zeal languished, and the last act of the expiring Second Rump enabled vicars to recover their prædial tithes.

The legislators might have left the national church dominant by virtue of the paymastership if they had pooled tithes and paid salaries. Such a plan might have done very well by "learning," but Peter Heylyn, the "highest" Anglican living, could see nothing rising therefrom but a "gross night of ignorance, and Egyptian darkness." The conservative clergy dared not give up their tithe-rights, settled by ancient laws, to let an Independent government control the purse-strings. So long as the able, orthodox divines could sue for tithes, they might make shift to live, preaching to empty steeplehouses while live religion gravitated to the gathered churches. The Presbyterians knew the value of security; and Anglicans awaiting a brighter day backed them, still pleading their learning like Thomas Fuller, who had a better right than most. They saw the unrest for what it was, a political revolution against their feudalism. One of their best propagandists traced all the horrors of the Peasants' Revolt back to Anabaptists' voluntaryism. Let once the learned ministers be discouraged by poverty, he warned, the more popular illiterates would replace them. When that happened, "assure yourselves"— he addressed the country gentry—"the Levellers will begin with your copyholds, and conclude you have no right in the creature because you belong not to the monopoly of saintship." Gerrard Winstanley, the Digger, had indeed already damned together copyholds, tithes, and antichristian clergy-learning; and the Levellers proper trailed not far behind. Richard Overton in particular, beyond reasonable doubt young Martin Mar-Priest, pitted his wit against theocrats too proud to imitate the Apostle's tent-making. "Indeed, I cannot much blame our presbyters, considering their breeding," he mocked; "for we must consider that our presbyters are university men."

The Levellers' pure voluntaryism had been the practice, and therefore the preaching, of the Brownists from the beginning, as of the Baptists and the communions beyond them who excluded their ministers from livings in the national church. Their zeal to overthrow state-support altogether promoted toleration by the likeliest means, disestablishment. Commonly they suggested like Milton that a minister without private means learn some lay calling in order to be not wholly dependent on his sacred vocation and thus obliged to preach willy nilly, with or without a spiritual call. Tithers had no choice but to sell pulpit-ware to buyers who had not the privilege of refusing it. The sects all assumed, however, as did Milton, that a truly reformed minister would normally live by gifts. To the learned incumbents howling in protest they made two answers: one, that they did not need, *as ministers,* the kind of learning they collected for, and two, that they did not have it: "For all that I can understand, these [Presbyterian] clergymen were born stark naked as well as others; their education at schools and university (to say no more) is no better than their fellows'."

In the tithing controversy we have most clearly to do with unadulterated politics, from which religious doctrine flowed consequentially. A society in transition from graded feudalism to more nearly level democracy, or as the late Thorstein Veblen liked to phrase it, from barbarism to savagery, must clip the prerogatives of the military and priestly castes, the former enterprising in its own esteem, the latter learned. Though the doctrinally sound Independents and some Baptists settled for tithes or favored mere reform of tithes, Baptists in general continued firm in their opposition to all forms of state-support and constituted the largest body of voluntaryists. Their more turbulent antinomians passing into Seekerism so called, like Erbury, Webster, Dell, and Saltmarsh, the popular Army preachers; less important heretics like Salmonists, Coppinists, Muggletonians, Ranters; at last the Quakers, who emptied many Baptist churches—all shared the voluntary principles of the early Brownists and a common antipathy to a learning that filled tithe-barns. Saltmarsh returned money that he had got by state-hire, and taunted theocrats with their learning. Erbury and Webster, sectarian reformers of the universities, once joined to debate a Presbyterian, an Independent, and a renegade Baptist on the intertwined questions of learning, ordination, and tithes. It was to smite the Black Coats that the Quakers first rose out of chaos; and for all their professed indifference to political matters, the Friends in virtually every one of their publications poured vitriol on the state's hireling ministry, pointing to Apostolic times, when ministers with expensive education had not been merchants chaffering to get their money back. It is idle nevertheless to impute such doctrine for distinctive Quakerism, when George Fox and many in the mobs that persecuted him hated equally the gospel-taxation, speaking the language of learning and the Beast.

Roger Williams set forth the arguments of *Likeliest Means* while Milton was still busy with *Areopagitica*. He saw that toleration, as distinct from comprehension, must lead toward disestablishment and at any point in its course raise the problem of ministers' maintenance. In the New Testament he found two solutions: voluntary contributions or, failing these, labor of ministers in a secular calling. The doctrine necessarily plunged him, like Milton, into the question of learning. Tongues might be necessary for scripture-study, but men like Ainsworth the Brownist had managed to get them without going to the shop of Antichrist. So said Milton. Williams went on to add a touch of Seekerism that we do not find in Milton: a new dispensation might dawn, bringing by miracle the same linguistic gift as the first Pentecost. What he had written in defense of toleration he had to repeat at length when he attacked directly the national, parishional church. Gathered churches with excellent prophets promised the colonial Baptist-Seeker more good for the missionary work of conversion ahead in America than a state ministry bound to Popish territorial divisions. The voluntary ministerial labors of lawyers, physicians, soldiers, and tradesmen had been fruitful, but "how many hirelings have preached for years without a convert?" Among the fruitful he naturally remembered his coreligionist "that despised and yet beloved Samuel Howe," the cobbler Baptist, who had been not long since buried in the very highway, attended by hundreds. The tradesman had made himself the ablest of textuaries, being "without human learning, which yet in its sphere and place he honored." Unlike Howe, Williams hinted yet again at what he may have awaited, the miracle of a new Pentecost, but on that wistful hope he rested no arguments. For his divinity he may have waited on the spirit. With certain of his languages, we know, he could seek a more pedestrian help from John Milton.

If the prelates had feared for their universities and tithes when Brownists were scarce, the Presbyterians had better reason when Brownists "much increased" and "cried down the maintenance of learning." The new presbyters, never as popular as they had been as lecturers, quickly had to learn how to fight for their money and dignities by piously defending the liberal arts. The only fiscal reform they cared to hear of would reinforce the existing system, check impropriators, and collect personal tithes. The Independents who had in mind measures more radical figured in Pagitt's book as those who "to overthrow learning" would "overthrow the maintenance." Their kind of meddling flouted the mediate call ordained by

God for latter-day ministers. If tithes occasionally supported idleness, did not legacies do as much? Only learning could stop the spread of heresy. If tithes were taken
away, and ministers had to beg or go into trade, with no
means to keep their sons at a university ("if there be
any"), in a generation the church would be without the
learning by which Pemble, Ames, Twisse, and Kendall
had kept the ancient and orthodox faith pure.

As the Presbyterian argument, so went that of Erastians
and of Anglicans in opposition. The most garrulous, devious, and disarming of their books bore the innocent title
An Humble Apology for Learning and Learned Men. Edward Waterhouse, who wrote it, glorified the Anglican
clergy in a bromidic courtesy book after the Restoration.
Even in the critical year 1653 he confronted the Barebones Parliament frankly as an Episcopalian conscious of
only temporary eclipse. He opened his work innocuously
with a thankful sigh that he handled no controversial
theme, that he carried no firebrand in his pen, and for
more than forty introductory pages ran through the standard apology for learning. But for it, heretics would carry
the field, and so on. In the beginning, God had given the
arts, and tediously Waterhouse traced their history from
the Jews down to the English universities, proud monu-
ments to learned bishops. At the end of another fifty
pages of such history he came to the point: "Episcopacy
interred, what remaineth to learning but the universities
and tithes?" We may forbear his final hundred pages
on tithes. Sir Henry Spelman as legal counterpoise to
the weighty Selden particularly heartened the clergy-mer-
chants; Milton acknowledged him the ablest defender of
decimal arithmetic. But the lawyer's mind when framing
popular propaganda obeyed partisan passion. God had
planted the interdicted tree in the very midst of the Garden to signify that he had reserved knowledge to himself,
that is, to the priest. He had appointed tithes as a means
to that end. True, some ministers enjoyed more revenue
than others, but only because they had been longer in the
service or at a university. All this meticulous logic Spelman incorporated in an open letter "To a Person of

Quality," assuring him that he might safely educate his son, inasmuch as the Parliament had shown no disposition to compound or abolish tithes.

ORDINATION AND LEARNING

As academic dignities supported the clergy in avarice, so also in glory, or ministerial prestige. Milton often declared this second mark of Antichrist, surviving from the Middle Ages—

> Then shall they seek to avail themselves of names,
> Places and titles, and with these to join
> Secular power.

The badge of caste, legal ordination in the national church, raised a controversy and gave clerics an additional reason to chant glorias to their trinity of learning, class-distinction, and political interest. Before the Rebellion, while bishops clung to their earldoms, any clergyman great or small might pretend to a share in nobility and doctoral respect, even a starveling bachelor of divinity who had little else. Contempt of the ministry grieved the Puritans awaiting their party's triumph, and success was to teach them no humility. When Thomas Hall opposed the unordained preachers with learning's arsenal of weapons, and added that to tolerate lay preaching would bring the ministry into contempt, the Baptist Thomas Collier pounced on the exposed weakness: "I thought where I should take you at last. Oh, you love honor as well as your profit, to have the cap and knee, and to be called of men 'Rabbi'; then it goes gallant, and pleaseth the heart of a proud Pharisee."

In the early years of the century there had been enough unordained Puritans lecturing and enough Separatist and Baptist laymen preaching to keep Anglicans explaining that both a spiritual call and adequate learning made the true minister. The simple laymen pressed into service by Jesus and the Apostles set no example for Stuart times, when the church had plenty of more learned men. When, as always, ignorance meant schism, no uneducated Christian deserved the imposition of a bishop's learned hands or might preach without it. Bishop Boughen, inspired

with the confidence of orthodoxy, warned in his visitation
sermons that monolingual preachers innocent of a university filled the ranks of the giddy schismatics, and God
would not pardon their affront to ordination and learning.
He took his warrant for both out of Calvin because the
culprits honored his judgment above "any canon or injunction of the Church of England." When the old order
changed, the Presbyterians tried to follow Calvin: they
bound an ordaining classis to test a candidate for orthodoxy and for learning. But Boughen was unhappy; he still
doubted the social acceptability of the new theocracy. The
ordinations were "mere nullities" and the new presbyters
would be what they had been before, "shopmen or worse."

Shopmen or not, the new aristocrats quickly sheltered
themselves behind the old fortifications. Even before
the accidents of war saddled the English church with
the widely despised Presbyterian Covenant, Thomas Edwards the heresy-hunter could not understand how particular congregations, unfit to judge of learning, could
expect to choose their pastors at will among the button-
makers and others "low in parts." Early and late the
Assembly divines, though not uniformly distinguished
for learning, sang the bishops' old song: no heterodox
enthusiast could be learned; no qualified minister could
be ignorant; no learned and qualified minister would
oppose the statutory ordination. The "gifted" layman
who preached could know that his spirit came from the
devil, for God's spirit kept men within bounds. Parliament
assisted God with its ordinances of April 26, 1645, and De-
cember 31, 1646; but the machinery set up for classical
ordination never functioned, nor its tests for learning and
orthodoxy. In many areas classes were never organized,
and those set up, though they stood legally until 1657,
soon fell into neglect. It became virtually impossible for
many a new minister to be ordained legally. Congregational approbation, permitted for lay lecturers as early as
1641, was never seriously interfered with; and wholly
unauthorized lay preaching, unless scandalous or blasphemous, suffered prosecution usually in pamphlets. In
the long run respectable Independents of the Assembly

came to look back with disapproval on past efforts to keep a "Popish" distinction between laity and clergy. In the end they held, on the subject of ordination, Milton's mature opinion. Though they preferred a congregational ceremony wherever feasible, and though it was "not for all to preach without ordination, nor for any to preach ordinarily without approbation," still they acknowledged that some might preach occasionally without either if qualified not by piety and learning, but by "piety and gifts."

Milton's long silence on church-policy between the antiprelatical tracts and *Of Civil Power* has been probably ascribed to his diffidence before a question that had already embarrassed him—and, we may add, would infallibly do so again, though perhaps not in the same way. Once he had finally concluded what many Christians now take for granted—that a church not of this world cannot be a state church—he found himself obliged, for the sake of an ultimate good, to defend some present nuisances. He expected that religious progress would in time bring forth a ministry godly and sober. But he can be forgiven for procrastinating about writing for disestablishment when it seemed at the moment that it would unleash two evils foreign to his nature—mere ignorance and antinomian enthusiasm. It is easy enough for us to belie the picture that the satirists drew of a spellbinding mechanic who, like Satan, preyed on Eve first, or of the hulking tub preacher who ridiculed unburned books and the ordained ministers who read them. But the satirists told a half truth. Enough idiotic preaching found its way into print to signify that much more did not. The guarded permission of lay-lecturing in 1641 enfranchised, for example, the trouble-making prophet James Hunt, who ended his preaching in Old Bailey. His muddled antinomianism in prose and bits of doggerel survives in two illiterate pamphlets, where we may hear ignorance railing at Cambridge, challenging Greek and Latin to climb down from the pulpit. The bookseller who first printed Hunt gaily supplied a woodcut of the prophet, tub and all. When we think how Milton must have felt about this lunatic fringe of Independency, Christian charity notwithstanding, we must admire him for the risk he took of being identified with it. Ridicule drew no fine distinctions. One who seemed to side with ministerial "ignorance" could never hope to make his exact position clear to those who did not already agree with him.

Somewhat uncomfortably, too, for a scholarly Arminian, many of those who agreed with him were the antinomians whom he charitably corrected in the *Christian Doctrine.* A few were Ranters, to whose extravagances, we have noticed, he seemed to prefer the Independents' Blasphemy Act. And between Ranters and Quakers in the 'fifties, Milton would probably have seen no great difference. The earliest Friends redoubled the piety that some mystics had already found in unknowing. The spirit first came upon Fox to tell him of wicked universities, and when Cromwell thought of building a new one, Fox protested against such worldliness. His Children of Light served the cultus of ignorance so vociferously that Cambridge delighted to honor them and their founder with a beating whenever they visited the academic precincts. One of the Friends accused the universities of direct complicity in a campaign of persecution. In the second generation Penn supposed that his predecessors had meant only to deny what Milton denied—the indispensability of learning in divinity. But almost any Quaker tract from the first generation, picked up at random, will contradict him by its very tone. We shall hardly read there the usual disclaimer paying tribute to learning confined within its proper human sphere.

Whoever would measure the distance between Milton and the Friends must read for himself at large in the latter's books of the "wisdom from beneath" pitted eternally against the spirit. The earliest Quakers had, to be sure, not only their inner light as a motive to suspect learning, but some other motives as well: their social rank, humble for the most part; outcast sectarianism; and an untutored ministry that labored *inter pares.* George Whitehead in matter and manner not precisely Miltonic exposed them all when he wrote his own life. He confessed to having wasted his first years in vanity, in "fine books and foolish

clauses." But the light shone within him though he knew
it not. When he was fourteen in 1652 it pleased the Lord
to send some Quakers his way. He straight forsook the
learning in which he had surpassed many others; he forsook too the steeplehouse at Orton and those blind hirelings whom he was later to taunt with going to Oxford to
find out what fishermen had meant. Since Milton did not
respect all that ignorance taught, if we may believe Richardson's story of the offended serving man, and since he
fully declared in the *Christian Doctrine* that a minister
truly followed his sacred calling if he learned whatever
languages and arts might help him understand scripture,
we have no right to suppose that either Whitehead or
Hunt had mastered all that Milton thought belonged to
the faithful herdsman's art. Beside a national church with
a Canterbury, a Westminister Assembly, or a Committee
of Triers, they were simply the lesser of two evils. Just
before the king came in he warned the backsliders that
they would soon enough wish back the preaching tub once
they had tried the powdering tub.

The men who taught in Milton's spirit, with or without
a tithe of his learning, we shall find most easily among the
Baptists. We have heard Roger Williams, whose quantum
of Seekerism affected his Independent politics not at all.
We can hear the same Baptist scripturalism from his unlearned friend Samuel Howe, author of *The Sufficiency of
the Spirit's Teaching without Human Learning* (1644).
The Calvinistic Baptist, an intelligent cobbler thoroughly
skilled in the scriptures, was no mystic or fanatic. Nevertheless, he too suffered ridicule in his own wretchedly
printed book. The anonymous stationer provided a caudal
"sonnet" in this style:

> Cambridge and Oxford may their glory now
> Veil to a cobbler if they know but How.

The cobbler begged Christians to cease pinning blindly
their faith on the sleeves of the learned when a peddler
might, by the grace of God, interpret with better authority.
The learned, not the peddlers, had made scripture teach
falsehoods—that men must come together in churches of

lime and stone, that they must pay tithes, that Christ's
church must be national. In prose scarcely more elegant
Milton taught the same. Let learning once be brought to
impose its human conclusions upon the mind of God in
scripture, it became "detestable filth, dross, and dung."
Yet in religion itself this much-ridiculed obscurantist
granted tongues valuable to translators of scripture, an
admission too liberal for Quakers and the erudite Henry
Stubbe. And outside religion he quarreled with no good
learning at all. Like Milton he declared that mankind
needed it to repair the damage suffered in Adam. "Well
sewed, Sam!" jeered Thomas Hall. "These stitches will
hold." In Howe and the Baptists generally we shall find
solid reason complaining only that science falsely so called
spurned Christ's laws of ecclesiastical polity. The church,
the universities, and the magistrate banded together for
the suppression of truth.

So testified another Baptist writing for "lay" preaching—Thomas Collier, fairly to be counted with the competent band that included Jessey, Knollys, and Tombes. In
the learning of these divines certain simple conservatives
could find the vain philosophy that the Apostle spoke of—
a twist of debate that may remind us of a point in the
Americas where the Atlantic lies west of the Pacific. One
of their orthodox but unlearned opponents pretended to
be amazed that such men should oppose ministerial learning, though it is plain in his pages that he knew the reason
well enough. Some of our own historians who loftily pa-
tronize the sects cannot be too often urged to put themselves in the dissenters' place and to take their view. An
exclusive national church maintained schools primarily to
train ministers; these schools indoctrinated young men in
the art of holding on to power; the well-meaning clerics
then arrogated to themselves burdensome privileges and
claimed them by right of one virtue, real or fancied—their
learning. Collier growled at their assumption that every
tradesman was ignorant and every presbyter learned, but
refused to argue the point. Who had learning, who had
not, mattered not at all to Christ. He passed on to some
other questions in the political debate. If the Presbyterians

could permit ministers to teach professionally in the schools, he could see no reason better than false dignity why they should not work at another trade. The examples of Moses, Daniel, and St. Paul might sanctify learning, but Collier read nothing in them against the congregational ordination that went stigmatized as lay preaching, nothing that substituted university gifts for spiritual gifts, nothing that justified the mystery of iniquity by which the Presbyterians had been spoiling men with their own kind of vain philosophy. In every sect—"libertines" or antinomians, Separatists, and even the despised Familists—Collier found a partial truth more estimable than the oppression that identified itself with learning. Ecclesiastical polity alone drew into this controversy John Horne, an Independent who had not digressed from orthodoxy far enough to be even a Baptist. To a refutation of Tombes and his doctrine of baptism Horne appended a set of arguments to prove what the learned Tombes would have known, "That the study of philosophy (though lawful to be known, and in some points useful), yet is not necessary to the preachers and preaching of the Gospel."

If we once lose sight of politics we shall hardly steer a true course through some cross-currents of paradox. Disputants who worried the question of learning—mystics against legalists, skeptics against dogmatists, Ancients against Moderns—espoused now this side and now that in the learned-ministry controversy as their politics guided. The quarrel, bound up with the question of toleration, cannot therefore be resolved into some more familiar abstraction or given some merely philosophic name. It was essentially and distinctly the learned-ministry controversy. But though the issue stood logically apart from some other divisions of thought, practically it overlapped some of them far enough to deceive an unwary historian into assigning an argument to the wrong debate. In Alexander Ross, to illustrate with a religious and intellectual conservative, we have an Ancient disinterested almost beyond suspicion of politics, not that the Presbyterian schoolmaster loved heresy or undervalued the Covenant. He attacked men like Hobbes and Wilkins for their sin of modernity in science; in theology,

he and Wilkins generally held alike. Hobbes ran contrari-
wise true to form in berating the Aristotelian cobwebs
and the sorry state of the universities, though without
meaning to strip divines of their orthodoxy or its learning.
No libertarian, he meant only to hand over to the state
both the parsons and the schools they had too long controlled. Seth Ward and Cromwell's brother-in-law, John
Wilkins, held university livings in the national church
and defended the meliorating universities as constituted,
that is, as divinity schools. If their livings influenced their
arguments, it can still be said to their credit that they disputed on a high plane, with unusual urbanity and good
sense, and that the mathematical divines themselves saw
no inconsistency, because they followed Bacon in the conviction that theology and natural philosophy move amica-
bly in separate spheres. They quite properly brought their
science to the promotion of the infant Royal Society on
the one hand, and their conceivably interested theology to
a lukewarm defense of Aristotle and school divinity on the
other. For an Ancient loyal to Independency we might consider Henry Stubbe, who became an adversary of the Royal
Society vocal enough to have won the applause of Alexander Ross had the schoolmaster been then alive. Stubbe's
own learning, which he owed to Vane, entitled him to a
post in the Bodleian until he forfeited it by writing—with
a most scholarly bibliography of scripture, Fathers, and
divines in all ages—to overthrow Aristotle, universities,
degrees in divinity, tithes, and the established church. In
this instance, let us observe, left-wing Puritanism repudiated Aristotle and school divinity from motives that
had nothing to do with "modernity" or the new science.
We might expect that a good skeptic like Richard Whitlock, M. D., would have shared with Stubbe some doubts
about learning, since he too liked the old ways and agreed
with Charron that ignorance endeavoring is all our knowledge. But the conservative physician quickly developed
some certainties when faced with radicalism like Stubbe's
Independency. He could take Copernicus or leave him,
because all was opinion; but in 1654, when the able divines badly needed succor, he published his dogmatic

essay " Learning's Apology." Whatever the physician might doubt, it was not God's delight in academic preachers "to break in pieces the forgeries of error, which then flourisheth, when knowledge and art wither." The first enemy of learning that he could discover had been the Dipper Pharaoh, antagonist of the learned Moses.

Nathaniel Culverwel's *Light of Nature,* posthumously published in 1652, made perhaps its best sense in the learned-ministry controversy. The author has been several times described as a kind of apostate from Cambridge Platonism, and certain it is that the traditional Aristotelian showed no consistent respect for "Platonic fancies." His discourse showed itself deficient, too, in the kind of rationalism that its title and even its hedged endorsement of Lord Herbert promised. When Presbyterian orthodoxy frowned on reason, Culverwel trembled—and left all the real questions where he found them. Whatever license reason enjoyed in platitudes, it enjoyed in Culverwel's deceptively rhapsodic tribute, no less and no more. To understand why he honored nature's light with nothing more substantial than compliments we probably do well to remember the political situation, for his oration seems to have been originally designed to steady Cambridge students. Two prefaces tell us that the work was first delivered orally in the chapel at Emanuel, possibly piecemeal in something like its present form, possibly in some earlier draft. The author may have added much for the printer, but his Chapter 27, on the pleasantness of reason, ending with an incitement to study, remains in particular pure oratory. And in its setting it was topical.

In 1646 the Presbyterians, Culverwel's associates, were taking over the universities in order to indoctrinate a new crop of ministers. By their Scruple Office at Oxford and their ejections at Cambridge they dominated the latter university completely by 1647 and the other effectually by the next year. Cries naturally rose from the extreme conservatives: the Knipperdollings of the age had "broken the heart strings of learning" and committed depredations worse than the Vandals'. The partisan exaggeration has been exposed, but it is certain that the war and reconstruction interrupted the scholastic routine. Independents, the radicals especially, set up their own wail. They could see nothing to approve in a mere change of masters, since the Presbyterians, like the bishops, were about to prescribe the doctrine of the schools whence would come the bachelors of divinity whom the same Presbyterians would approve and ordain; but they took advantage of a lull in education to fill many pulpits with their own supporters. All radical Independency meanwhile took up the doctrine of Howe and Williams to protest the Presbyterians' obvious strategy. At the very doors of the universities they proclaimed the doctrine of scripture's sufficiency.

We may therefore suspect that Culverwel's original point lay in his incitement to study, and that he held aloft the candle of the Lord in order to shed light on the beauties of the curriculum that the "Seekers" Dell and Erbury would persuade divinity students to neglect. The agile Calvinist teetered cautiously between atheism and enthusiasm, abasing reason with counsels of modesty where it threatened to broach a truly rational theology, glorifying it with hosannas where fanatics might plead the spirit. Carefully he reminded the youth before him that when the absolute philosopher named the animals in Paradise his candle had even then been a diminutive light, which, "aspiring to be a sun, has burnt dimly ever since." Some men would "still stretch out the hand to the forbidden tree"—the astrologers, seeking knowledge beyond what angels have; the "blundering antinomian," the "vagabond Seeker," and the "wild seraphic, set on fire of hell." Truly the light of nature was "a feeble, diminutive light." Yet dimly as the candle burned, God himself had lighted it. Only blasphemy could say that the Word of God opposed right reason. Papists said it, or sectaries and skeptics, but sober Christians (Presbyterians) knew that the light teaching us to respect the "eminent, refined part of mankind" was certain, directive, pleasant—and peaceable. Faction was the work of private revelation. Though in all this Culverwel allowed the light of nature nothing but what he could have found in John Ball or John Calvin, his surviving brother Richard grew apprehensive, as he wrote a preface for the work, that readers might misunderstand. Nathaniel in life, he said, had been reputed vain on the score of his intellect, and his very title might sound Socinian. But if he had written of nature, the preface reassured the orthodox, readers had no cause for alarm, for he had taken care to demonstrate the shortness of reason's line, the depth of God's bosom secrets, and the need to wink with the eye of reason in order to see better with the eye of faith. Nathaniel's sparkling sentences had indeed justified Richard's platitudinous confidence.

Aside from the solidity of Seth Ward and John Wilkins, the routine industry of Edward Leigh (who made a gesture of applying his directory of the learned world to the controversy of the moment), and the oratory of Culverwel, nothing distinguished the conservative apologists for ministerial learning, or disguised their interest. Their titles are familiar, or easily available. Among them we find a defense of enlightenment, or enlightened heresy-hunting, by Joseph Sedgwick, another by Robert Boreman, D. D., who wrote also for tithes. Thomas Hall, B. D., contributed several, among which his *magna opera*, *The Pulpit Guarded* (1651) and *The Schools Guarded* (1653), may fairly stand for the whole genus. The former guarded the pulpit against lay preachers, assumed to be Arminians, Socinians, or "libertines"—in any event Separatists, responsible for all error. Because Hall replied directly to the Baptists Howe and Collier, he opened with some thirty heretical tenets of the Dippers and the Antipædobaptists, exhuming their long folk history of extravagances and mystical obscurantism, the root of heresy. Errors thus spawned in pious ignorance had been spread by laymen preaching contrary to the practice of even the wiser Independents, who knew that to the ordained alone God had given the custody of the keys and of learning. In Hall's abundant and heterogeneous marginalia, which included Moses, bishops, and new presbyters for learning, the sectaries would not have been surprised to see Rutherford's writings against toleration. For Hall, the Presbyterian inquisition expressed the very essence of enlightenment, and great was the "pride and wantonness" of the age to tread all that learning underfoot. When he later guarded schools against Sam Howe and John Webster, he conceded the iniquity of mingling Aristotle with the highest mysteries, but only the Popish schoolmen had been guilty. Learning could be abused, to be sure—by heretics, astrologers, atheistic naturalists, paganizing humanists, flowery preachers— but neither this occasional abuse nor an occasional ignorant presbyter made against divine Presbytery. Hall took pains not to disguise his real interest in learning: for the manifold superiorities that he enjoyed he thanked openly and ingenuously the God who had created him a Christian, a male, and a leader.

The Universities and the Sects

The radical Independents striking at tithes and ordained dignity through learning would have been doctors treating symptoms if they had spared the universities, the nurseries of theocracy. But not all critics of the universities welcomed association with the sectaries. John Wilkins laughed at the strange fellowship leagued against Oxford and Cambridge, for at the schools that Hall guarded were leveled three distinct kinds of criticism—broadly, the humanistic, the Modern, and the ecclesiastical. Milton's most youthful diatribes represented only the first, or at best the first two, and in these even conservative parsons could indulge with impunity. Dr. John Boys, Dean of Canterbury when Milton was young, sounded like his admired Bacon, so often found in his well stuffed margins: modern universities were "the old schools new plastered," and divinity professors spun the old webs. But when Dr. Boys thought like a learned and loyal Anglican he could find no dross in those clear fountains. So long as the universities' medieval function of divinity-teaching remained generally unchallenged, sincere reformers took that high responsibility for granted and made it a plea for their own schemes of betterment. Learning as renovated by the imperfectly Baconian or Comenian reformers Dury, Hartlib, Petty, and the essayist John Hall would yet have been a learning dominated by the Presbyterian clergy.

The remaining kinds of criticism were in time to leave the universities no longer the divinity schools that they had been when founded. Toward curricular reform Hobbes voted in the main with Hartlib and the rest, but by way of administrative reform the absolute Erastian would have deposed the governing parsons. Bramhall shrewdly perceived that when Hobbes quoted scripture against the traditional curriculum, and damned the parsons who purveyed it, he was forging some political fetters to restrain the clergy—all the clergy, to be sure, with heaviest shackles for the sectaries. In digging up the seed-plots of theocracy, Hobbes took a leaf from the sectaries' book, but there his indebtedness ended. The unsparing anticlericalism that he and many others shared promoted what is correctly called the secularizing of education.

The same phrase may not be entirely appropriate to ecclesiastical criticism of the universities, in that it achieved without taking thought whatever secularization it ultimately brought about. The sectaries consciously aimed (if one may coin a word) directly at de-universitizing the ministry. We may read their reason toward the end of one of Thomas Hall's prefaces, where the Presbyterians urged right-thinking people to rally behind the universities as the schools led the fight against the sects. The radicals had no choice but to fight a war already declared against them, but they did not therefore want all education secular or require that their own ministers be unlearned. In a series of five pamphlets on this topic William Dell, the notable antinomian Baptist (or Seeker, if one prefers the term for an antinomian who had gone beyond water-baptism), once proposed the "right reformation" of learning by replacing the universities with a chain of small schools. Like Milton, he maintained that twenty could then learn instead of one, and at home, away from vice. Away from Episcopalians and Presbyterians, too, as he made clear in many other places. He expected that his schools would teach divinity, a scriptural divinity. If his projected divinity students worked at a secular calling while they studied, they would learn to do so while they preached, until such time as their devotion should earn them support by gifts. We find

Dell, who held the mastership of Caius and Gonville, at variance with the thorough obscurantism that inspired Fox. Dell would expurgate some classics, as any teacher of young students might do. Otherwise, he would teach the usual languages and professions. Ward and Wilkins, who saw his drift more clearly than some modern students, agreed only that England needed more schools, not other schools.

In 1653 it looked as if the sectaries might overthrow the universities, the third fortress of privilege after tithes and ordination. Anthony à Wood, Baxter, and the first-hand observer Pauluzzi provide us with the essential fact that in the councils of the Barebones Parliament proposals similar to Dell's precipitated a crisis. Milton looked back with approval on those deliberations. Less sympathetic observers went on expecting, or pretending to expect, that universities were momentarily to be abolished. In 1656, for instance, the title page of a collegiate verse-anthology proclaimed that its contents had been written "before the dissolution of the universities." Baxter chose to believe that Cromwell himself set the dismal work afoot in order that he might step in to save civilization and so justify his dictatorship. According to Anthony à Wood, Parliament engaged Webster, Dell, and Horne to write against schools, a not unlikely or especially reprehensible commission. Though it has been discounted, Wood's allegation is confirmed by the dates of the attacks, and should doubtless be allowed until contrary evidence is discovered. The ensuing pamphlet exchange, like the bold preaching of Erbury at Oxford and of Dell at Cambridge against divinity-teaching, has been so often reviewed that nothing needs sampling here except what may, by analogy, help to fix the intention of Milton's *Likeliest Means*.

In their assault on the universities the radical Independents only continued a war against tyranny that had been prosecuted by schismatics, not by mystics—by Baptists more violently than by Familists, by Brownists as vociferously as by heretics. The purely mystical virtues of unknowing still entered only tangentially into the controversy. I have quoted from the *Bloudy Tenent* Roger

Williams' political animus against ministerial fountains obedient to the whim of the prince. He enlarged the argument in his *Hirelings* (1652). He had learning enough to declare convincingly that his own respect for it had nothing to do with the matter. Schools ought to be maintained, but not *in ordine ad ministerium*. The ancient sins of Europe's monastic universities, forbidding labor and marriage, provided critics like Williams and Stubbe with arguments, not motives. The title of scholar, Popish degrees and ceremonies, students' proud laziness—these were sacrilege in a minister, though plainly not the radicals' real worry. Dell too, in writings not yet noticed, went back to early Protestantism for his thunder against divinity degrees. And indeed, if these had been removed the theocrats would have been embarrassed to find another worldly badge so pious-seeming and venerable. To town and gown at Cambridge Dell denounced the false teachers who crept into the church by the familiar route of "academical degrees and ecclesiastical ordination." They detested Christ's true government, which forced nobody; they disowned ordination by unction of the spirit, which might chance to fall upon a tradesman; they reviled antinomian religion. For these reasons he labored to dissolve the two errors of Antichrist, "making the universities the fountains of the ministry" and "making the clergy a distinguished sect or order, or tribe."

No grudge against learning induced him to strike at the mystery of iniquity in its "head and heart," the universities. To arts he gave all honor except as they made themselves preparatory to Christ. If the universities could bring themselves to "stand upon an human and civil account," to educate for the commonwealth instead of the church, he had no more to say. If they refused, the celebrated Army preacher threatened them with the day of God's wrath, when they could choose which way they would turn—to Aristotle and the heathen; to Thomas and Scotus and their cold divinity; or to the secular arm, deluded and seduced by their wiles for so many ages. A theocrat marveled that Dell, professing learning and blessed with noble ancestors, could betray his class; but Dell gloried in his rightness and the gratitude of farmers. It was the farmers' grain and livestock, we must constantly bear in mind, that "learning" carted away. His own task, Dell thought, was the hardest work of reformation, to dispatch the soul of Antichrist that had outlived the body. John Wilkins described Dell as an angry and frantic man—a just estimate if by his frenzy we understand the prophetic sincerity that warmed the hearts of Cromwell's soldiers.

Another Army preacher, John Webster, a sometime physician, schoolmaster, and what not, Wilkins esteemed a charlatan followed by ignorant persons who admired his superficial learning. This estimate, too, seems accurate enough, and a caution to the modern critics who have found in his vaporings important testimony to the advancement of the new science. In purely ecclesiastical tracts, where he wrote much like Dell, he sailed respectably under his true colors. But where he wrote like a Modern, and voiced what Wilkins called "the old, trite cavils of Bacon and Gassendus," his more reputably scientific opponents were able to show in parallel columns that he had lifted them verbatim from the printed pages of his betters. In his best known book he tried to dignify his sectarian criticism of the schools with constructive suggestions for their curricula. As an occultist he naturally found the universities deficient, like that Samuel Hering who wanted Parliament to set aside two colleges for the teaching of Boehme. But Wilkins, not Webster, testified importantly to the true advancement of science when he assured the sectary that Oxford respected Aristotle but did not require that he be studied, that no Ptolemaist could be found among her astronomers, that she took up quickly and freely examined all reputable discoveries. One may doubt that Oxford would have been the better for adopting Webster's unintelligible jumble of grammar, cryptography, mathematical symbolism, and cabalistic alchemy. With a fine lack of discrimination the critic exalted Porta, Paracelsus, Helmont, and his beloved Boehme beside Bacon and even Hobbes. He admired Digby, Fludd, and everywhere the Rosicrucians. He advertised himself the friend of Ashmole, Lilly, Booker, Sanders, Culpeper, and regretted that he had no space to defend properly the judicial astrology that the universities had so lamentably neglected. Weighing this farrago, Wilkins easily proved that Webster knew nothing of the universities or of the subject matter that he would amend, but he would not, he declared, have used him therefore with less respect if he had not thought him a "vulgar Leveller" bent upon discrediting the universities for political reasons.

Webster revealed himself in his opening pages to be what Anthony à Wood called him, "one who endeavored to knock down learning and the ministry both together." That is to say, he attacked the schools, possibly at the request of Parliament, for political reasons. We may not admire him as a reformer, but we are obliged to grant him the enthusiasm he professed for secular learning. Constantly he sang its praises, and plausibly, because the learning he commended was for laymen. Again and again he outdid Williams and Dell in stripping it from ministers. He too forbade the schools to teach divinity or confer degrees in it. Unlike some more liberal sectaries, he would not concede that erudition inspired in a minister anything but pride, unless it was the competence necessary for the handful of men who translated scripture. Whatever the schools could teach laymen was carnal and therefore for laymen only; it pulled a minister down. If the mystic allowed ministers a little less cultivation than did those who would only keep them out of the corrupt academies, he still agreed with his friends on the more important theme: he confined religious obscurantism to the pulpit.

Milton's unflattering opinions of the universities, like his periodic pronouncements on clergy-learning, can be read where others have collected them. He was probably younger than thirty-four when he developed fully his doubt that divinity-teachers could ever fetch themselves up to the forefront of religious reformation. No sooner had he clearly perceived that prelacy, surviving from Popery, blighted education than he lost, he said, an admiration for the universities that had never been great. The scholastic barbarism that had offended him as a militant young humanist he would have at last clipped with some-

thing like the Barebones Parliament's wholesome and pre-
ventive shears, for in control of the pulpit, scholasticism
could perpetually hinder the advancement of piety and
learning. If we insist upon identifying humanism with
conservative politics and denying reformers a place in the
movement, we must leave Milton, young or old, out of it;
if we admit reformers we should allow Milton the privilege of fighting scholasticism with active measures.

By 1659—and doubtless some years earlier—he had
chosen disestablishment, the complete separation of church
and state, with the prerequisite separation of Oxford and
theology, as the likeliest means to destroy tyranny and
legally enforced superstition at a blow. An admirable demonstration that he never achieved quite the secular thinking that should go with a perfect separation of the two
swords will stand without the author's observation (passing and incidental) that *Likeliest Means* "repudiated"
learning. We find nothing in that work urging ignorance
upon any layman, or demanding it of any minister who
could content himself with human learning as a human
accomplishment. We cannot prove by the tract that he
thrust ministers out of what he had once called their "holy
and equal aristocracy." Laymen, we read in his *Christian
Doctrine*, might "as convenience required" preach and
perform sacramental offices, and teaching elders appeared
in *Likeliest Means,* but not as a regular institution. In
both works he projected a distinct ministry, congregation-
ally ordained, and professionally well equipped. He once
accepted in principle what divines had so copiously written of ministers' qualifications, adding that their preaching had been mainly better than their observance.

LEARNING IN THE KINGDOM OF CHRIST: MILTON'S FINAL STATEMENT

It behooves us now to examine narrowly what Milton
actually said of learning in his treatise of 1659, as we may
call a work published in two sections, one, *Of Civil Power,*
dealing with force compelling and the other, its sequel,
with hire corrupting. *Likeliest Means to Remove Hire-*

lings, the sequel, concerns us only so far as its fiscal arguments against state hire led him into the problem of education for the pulpit. Especially in his closing section, which he might have entitled *Diluntur Sophismata,* he scoffed at the clergy's anguished cry that learning and tithes would go down together. If the civil state would properly use the funds it held in trust for the church, he retorted, the money would scatter schools and libraries up and down the land. This same plan insured the freedom of the courts in his political utopia of the next year, where he urged Parliament "to spread more knowledge and civility" by multiplying university colleges as well as grammar schools.

Such was the state of Milton's "obscurantism" on the eve of the Restoration. He meant the clergy to share in his proposed enlightenment. In *Likeliest Means* he argued that his more abundant schools would carry competent learning to divinity students in outlying areas where learning had been scarce, and that when poor students sought education for the pulpit, they might have it in return for their covenant that if they preached they would stay home to preach. Thus he schemed to tether the benefice-chasers who roved here and there seeking always richer livings. While his students worked at languages and scripture for their sacred calling, he expected them to study a secular vocation, not necessarily to live by, but to fall back on if they lacked voluntary gifts or discovered late that they had no call. He honored the preaching tradesmen who discharged two offices for the wages of one, but he expected that they would be too scarce to supply the church; pastors would ordinarily live by gifts. As for learning, he seemed reasonably sure that as the schools stood at the moment a clergy unlike the Levitical castes of Rome and Edinburgh would often include those who had never "come near commencement or a university."

A shift without tarrying to pure voluntaryism could be made workable at once, he urged, with certain interim provisions, which have too often been read as his everlasting model for the church. For the latter, we have the *Christian Doctrine.* In *Likeliest Means* he dealt with the immediate problems of conversion. If tithes had been suddenly cut off, most of the flourishing city churches would have survived easily, while many country pulpits would have been left vacant, for the unpopular Black Coats could not count on gifts. Milton therefore argued that voluntaryism presented no problem in prosperous communities, and could not be so burdensome to even the poorest as the lifetime incumbency of a hireling. Well-to-do congregations would share the expense of sending out itinerants to preach Christian fundamentals and to gather churches—in barns if necessary, according to the poet who was to float his Garden into the Persian Gulf in order to extirpate superstitious reverence for steeplehouses. In a year or two of residence these could arm teaching elders with the English Bible and enough knowledge of the faith to carry on their work temporarily, confirmed by an occasional apostolic visit. The fundamentals of religion required no learned disquisitions. Christ taught them to the poor and simple, and those who first taught after him were "unlearned men"—

Plain Fishermen, no greater men them call.

If the lay teachers needed more tools, "somewhere" could be found a wholesome body of simplified divinity, plausibly assumed to be the one that lay substantially complete in the reformer's own escritoire. Though Milton expected his ideal minister to know more than these stopgap missionaries, he held still his old opinion that knowledge in a minister should be its own reward. The hirelings who expected a return on their academic investment plainly appeared no "true lovers of learning, and so very seldom guilty of it."

The very ignorance of the learned divines contradicted their doctrine of learning's necessity; but if he conceded them learned, what concluded they hence? For their tithes they pleaded their expense at school, when half of them had held scholarships and the rest, except those who had fled parental control for a university and riot, could cover their whole outlay with one year in a good living. But he was not disposed to allow the doctrine that imposed

universities on ministers when he could find no such
teaching in scripture or common sense. Logic, as taught
in the schools, served statesmen and lawyers. Ministers
needed little of it, and few, for that matter, studied it. If
they needed languages, they had no need to go to a university for them; and most could do without them. Most
preachers needed the English Bible and books to the value
of £60, or about the cost of the minister's essential library
that Baxter catalogued in his *Christian Directory*.

To divines prepared with the old retort that heretics
could not be refuted without the "entangled wood of antiquity, fathers, and councils," Milton spoke as he was to
speak again in *Paradise Regained:* let them show the erring
ones that their argument was either not in scripture or
against it. Or let the state build the libraries that he suggested, and if God raised up champions in controversy,
they could find their books there.

Nothing of this was for Milton a strange point or new.
We have read much of it in *Areopagitica,* which is commonly taken to mark the full tide of the reformer's intellectual enthusiasm. If we recall what he there said of tithe-
gatherers' learning and compare the early oration with
these lines from *Likeliest Means,* we shall find only a difference consistent with his argument of the moment and
with his improving grasp of practical issues:

I have thus at large examined the usual pretences of hirelings,
colored over most commonly with the cause of learning and
universities; as if with divines learning stood and fell, wherein
for the most part their pittance is so small; and, to speak freely,
it were much better there were not one divine in the university, no school-divinity known, the idle sophistry of monks, the
canker of religion; and that they who intended to be ministers,
were trained up in the church only by the scripture, and in the
original languages thereof at school; without fetching the
compass of other arts and sciences, more than what they can
well learn at secondary leisure and at home.

Where arts are in any way evil *per se,* or evil in ministers,
they are undoubtedly evil when studied at home. Milton
went on to insist, lest he be misunderstood, that he spoke
in no contempt of learning, but of its cheats—falsehood,

pharisaism, ambition, and the avarice of pluralities, fees, and tithes. We need not suspect his disclaimer. He would withdraw young divines from the universities, where they were being fed school divinity—surely no important subtraction from learning but rather, consequences considered, a most fruitful addition. Laymen might still frequent the academies. Ministers might compass all the human learning they could master without neglecting or perverting their high calling.

And thus we come in sight of *Paradise Regained* with its Learning Temptation, the ultimate object of our journey through the learned-ministry controversy. If Milton's meaning in his brief epic justifies this ecclesiastical approach, then it must follow that his poem has been misunderstood, at least in modern times. And yet in its most puzzling lines it teaches only the doctrine of his ecclesiastical tracts. Not in metaphor, but in straightforward assertion, Satan offers Christ arts and philosophy as indispensable to preachers and preaching. In no metaphor at all, Christ refuses human arts because he knows scripture and, knowing God's word, needs for his ministry no inferior learning. We shall return to this exchange, but in the meantime it may be well to answer a question likely to be asked. How can this or any episode in Milton's austerely unified poem instruct the church unless all the other episodes do so? We shall not stray, actually, from the matter in hand if we pause to consider that throughout the debate in *Paradise Regained* Milton wrote for the church.

His argumentative Christ is hardly the Son the creator honored early in *Paradise Lost*. By virtue of the Mediatorial Office (1.28, 188) Christ is now incarnate as the Prophet, Priest, and King of redeemed mankind. His first task in this Office is to raise Eden in the wilderness (1.7), to found his Kingdom separate and apart from the kingdoms of the world. Unless his triumphant logic is verbiage wasted on Satan alone, he acts as our great Example and speaks for our instruction. A reader sensitive to poetry will not be likely to find Milton's poem a sermon, though it has now and then been censured for teaching a bit too much doctrine. Indeed, it has been this doctrine, not the poetry, that has given the critics most of their trouble. It will probably not be necessary, then, to persuade them that the work was written, at least incidentally, to teach somebody something. Here I intend to concern myself with nothing higher than its didacticism. I should not know how to measure it, but that we may have misapplied it I have suggested in one of the journals, where I have given reasons that we shall not review here for thinking that Milton meant the Head of the Christian church to set a pattern not primarily for the Christian layman, but for the church and its ministers.

A reader content with any ecclesiastical reading will possibly not quarrel with the whole of this one: Jesus refuses to build his church on worldly supports. Obeying God's will, the only Puritan directory of worship, he rejects idolatry, money, worldly eminence, clergy-learning, and civil traffic with the kingdoms of the world; then, for his obedience to God's revealed will, he suffers persecution. In the end he rises triumphant over Satan, sin, and death. Let us grant some hypotheses only long enough to observe their convenient consequences. If Milton wrote thus, or approximately thus, he demanded the same otherworldliness that all his life he had expected of the church, but never of the Miltonic Christian. If with his right hand he wrote thus, he made his brief epic as intelligibly sequent to *Paradise Lost* as the history of the Christian church is sequent to Calvary. We may remember that he all but closed the earlier poem with a précis of church-history. And to return to our hypotheses, if he used the word *Kingdom,* a cardinal term in *Paradise Regained,* in an early and technical sense, we must surely misunderstand his whole poem if we define it loosely in some modern sense. If that way we have fallen into a circle of error, we shall then hardly break out of it by reading and rereading the poem; rather, we shall have to dwell first with seventeenth-century theology long enough to define *Kingdom.*

To this topic I have largely devoted an Appendix, documented in notes that supply a bibliography for further inquiry. A reader may wish to examine it critically before accepting the following premises—by the Kingdom of Christ Milton in maturity meant only the true (invisible) church of Christ; but he wrote *Paradise Regained* to define the Kingdom of Christ—and the obvious conclusion.

From the minor the word *only* is missing because the poem must not be denied its moral and political implications or its manifold beauties as a human drama. As we limit the minor, so we must limit the conclusion; but if the major holds, then the poem must deal with the church so far as it deals with the Kingdom, and further where evidence of another kind appears.

If the word *church* in the major needs defining *a priori,* the *Christian Doctrine* tells us what we need to know. The Kingdom-church begins on earth as the Kingdom of Grace; exalted at the Second Coming, but otherwise the same church, it becomes the Kingdom of Glory. Strictly defined, this church is the invisible body of the elect known (not necessarily foreknown) to Christ. This community precedes and determines a visible community and its acts of worship, or the universal visible church with its particular churches. Visible churches rise out of the invisible church. In them lurk some hypocrites, unavoidably, but Christ knows his loyal subjects. As Prophet, he gives laws to his church, teaching by scripture; as Priest, he offers himself to be its sacrifice. As King, he rules it and defends it against its enemies—Satan, sin, and death. In Milton's Arian theology Christ has no function more important.

Whether the poet took the Kingdom, its nature and limits, for his principal theme one can best judge by reading the text of the dispute on which he focused his poem. As Edward Dowden once observed, and perhaps many another unhurried reader, the bone of contention between Christ and Satan is not, or not simply, a soul, but a Kingdom. Christ is tempted in his official, not in his private capacity. He is offered Satanic gifts because without them he cannot rule his Kingdom. He refuses them because he can. It may help us here to glance at Satan's campaign in a bald outline for which the poet himself (1.97, 178) furnished the topics:

    I. Fraud: deception by disguise.
      A. The pastoral garb.
      B. The angelic pose.
   II. Snares.
      A. *Vita voluptuaria.*
        [1. Illegitimate sensuality.]
        2. Sensuality plausible to reason.
      B. *Vita activa.*
        1. Riches.
        2. Glory.
        3. Political might.
        4. Imperial sway and its perquisites.
      C. *Vita contemplativa.*
        1. Art.
        2. Philosophy.
  III. Terrors.
      A. Threats of suffering to come.
      B. Violence.

In one stratagem, his first, Satan offers no gift and hence no specious prop for the Kingdom, but his trick is made churchly by some other circumstances (Appendix, Note B). The rest of his lures and threats—or eight of his nine or ten devices—explicitly touch the Kingdom and are debated as its blessings or its bane. The Banquet, for example, which by marks of several kinds (Appendix, Note B) may be known for sensual idolatry, is offered as a boon to which Christ's lordship entitles him. Wealth, the Tempter pleads, is the means to kingship and thence to glory, just as sovereignty over Rome or Parthia will guarantee the safety of David's throne. Human learning will prepare Christ for monarchy. Persecution must befall a would-be king who refuses Satan's help. To each of these arguments in turn, as one may read in the lines here cited (Notes), Christ replies to the advantage of his own unworldly Kingdom. If each of Satan's gifts in turn is so offered and rejected, then it should follow that the Temptation is consistently ecclesiastical.

From some broad directions that enfold the debate, it may appear as well that its message is predominantly so.

Satan is first roused to mischief when the Baptist proclaims and the people acknowledge their new King. He hastens to pervert him before his coronation. To offer fallacious guidance, he seeks the Mediator where he is communing with the Spirit in the wilderness, learning how best to accomplish his ministry—how best to publish his Three-fold Office. The Tempter's strategy in his three assaults, and his whole object in the Temptation, is clear to Jesus, who reveals it to us (IV.494): if Satan can induce Christ to accept anything worldly at all, then Israel's King will seem to hold all his authority from Satan.

In arranging lures the poet ascended an ethical ladder, and thus Satan comes last to the highest—learning, or more exactly clergy-learning, the fairest and most plausible bait known to Antichrist. Against Satan's plea for ministerial learning, and countering it point by point, Christ maintains two theses. First, human philosophy cannot teach what it does not know. It cannot be indispensable to God's revealed truth, since at its Hellenic best it falls short of wisdom precisely where a minister needs wisdom. The philosophers could know nothing of creation, original sin, or man's impotence without grace. How could they teach truly of God and the soul? Their books are not therefore sinful, but in the Preacher's meaning "wearisome" perhaps, dangerous "trifles" if taken for "choice matters" by men shallow in themselves (IV.285–330). Second, the oratory, the political thought, and especially the bawdy poetry of Greece will not civilize, will not delight leisure hours better than Hebrew song and story. They will not "form a King" so well or so plainly as holy scripture (331–364). We must understand the "light from above" on which Jesus relies (289) as the written word of God, not an inner light independent of scripture. Satan has urged human arts on the ground that all knowledge cannot be found in the Hebrew Bible—"in Moses' law, The Pentateuch or what the Prophets wrote" (225). Jesus replies that for his ministry scripture is fully sufficient. Neither the offer nor the refusal speaks of another kind of light from above, or of a light within.

Satan's two arguments for philosophy as *ancilla theol-*

ogiæ (IV.229 ff.) had been the stock pleas of every prelate and presbyter jealous for medieval prerogatives:

And with the Gentiles much thou must converse,
Ruling them by persuasion as thou mean'st.
Without their learning how wilt thou with them,
Or they with thee hold conversation meet?
How wilt thou reason with them, how refute
Their Idolisms, Traditions, Paradoxes?
Error by his own arms is best evinc't.

First, to be socially acceptable ("hold conversation meet") and escape contempt; second, to refute heresy, Christ must wound the pagans with their own feathers. At any rate, the ministry of Christ must do so. Actually, Jesus himself is to meet few pagans. We have read the answers in *Likeliest Means:* scripture best relutes heresy. Scripture, too, can supply all the culture that a minister will need for his calling. We know that Milton wished ministers trained to read the Bible intelligently, and this reading they could do without having mastered all the liberal arts and school divinity. Should arts once be accepted as *prerequisite* to Christ, then all the abuses of universities, academic appointments, and hirelings' divinity would follow.

But as always, Milton distinguished carefully between learning itself and the dogma of learning's necessity. Leaving secular learning out of the question altogether, he permitted even ministers to be learned if they pleased. The difference between Satan's position and Christ's is the difference between must and may. Christ himself is not unwilling to be thought learned. "Think not but that I know these things," he begins, thereby exculpating the arts; yet he can preach without them and found a Kingdom on scripture alone—"or think I know them not; not therefore am I short Of knowing what I ought" (286). If he neglects the last point, he opens the door to Antichrist and hirelings, who will, in turn, provoke the secular arm to persecute truth. The spiritual minister will be no enemy of good learning, then, if he simply counts it a thing indifferent in the sight of God. So speaks to all impure churches Jesus Christ, the church's one Foundation, the true fountain of the ministry, our royal priest and prophet, a priest forever after the order of Melchizedek.

APPENDIX

Note A. How Milton's generation normally conceived the Kingdom of Christ and what the historical Jesus meant by the Kingdom of God—in Matthew's phrase, the Kingdom of Heaven—are two widely distinct questions. Only the biblical meaning seems obscure enough to cause dissent among the historians of dogma whom I cite (Notes). In two or three logia (e.g., Matt. xvi:18 and xviii:18–19—possibly interpolated), it is the church. The Kingdom, or City, of God is regularly the church, though not invariably, in the New Testament epistles and in primitive writings like the Shepherd of Hermas. In our own day, Roman Catholics and some sects of Protestants, in particular those Fundamentalists who oppose pre-millennialism, identify Christ's Kingdom on earth with the church militant. Many other Protestants respect the opinion of Albrecht Ritschl that the historical Jesus applied his Jewish metaphor to a real community of persons bound not by laws but by love. In some such fashion eminent historical critics in Protestantism qualify the merely ecclesiastical definition; none that I have read utterly reject it. The difficulty arises, of course, from the circumstance that if in the Gospels we take the Kingdoms of God, Christ, and Heaven to be the same, as moderns generally do, we can take that Kingdom to be either inward or outward, present or future, the community ruled or the rule itself, and find scripture-texts to justify our opinion.

When we come to the topic of what succeeding generations have thought Jesus meant, we find the historians agreed. After the primitive writings the view of a Kingdom-to-come prevailed for a time in the form of chiliasm, sometimes grossly material. The Lord delayed his return so long, however, that with Augustine the Christian world exchanged its idea of a returning Christ for that of a conquering church, a Kingdom "at hand." Augustine's great work on the Kingdoms (*civitates*) of God and the world made chiliasm a heresy. His opinion that his own church was Christ's Kingdom and that it lived already in the millennium became dogma seldom challenged until long after the Reformation. The New Testament epistles regularly use πόλις or a cognate as equivalent to the βασιλεία

of the Gospels, and Augustine chose his title apparently from
a verse like Hebrews xii:22–23, in which text both he and Milton correctly understood the *civitas Dei* to be the church.
Protestants have sometimes thought that he wrote of an ideal
instead of an actuality, but their question touches only his
civitas. Where he spoke of the *regnum Christi* on earth (xx.9)
his unequivocal language has obliged even a recent Protestant scholar to confess, reluctantly, that he meant the hier-
archical establishment. *Civitas* or *regnum*—under either name
early readers would have known the church.

Working within this orthodoxy, certain medieval pietists
drew between the ideal and the empirical a distinction that
was to give Protestants their concept of the invisible church,
which the Reformation normally understood to be the church
meant in the Apostles' Creed. Thus even, or perhaps especially, the most radical reformers could retain the Roman
creedal statements. For their polemics they rejuvenated the
slumbering doctrine of Christ's mediatorial office. Luther declared Christ to be the sole High Priest and King of his church,
and a few Englishmen followed Luther's twofold division of
the office. After some early hesitation Calvin added the Lord's
third title, that of Prophet; and thereafter Catholics heard
themselves condemned on all sides for what George Herbert
called making a jest of Christ's three offices. Priestly inter-
cessors and the daily sacrifice of the Mass convicted the Roman
church of denying Christ's eternal and sufficient priesthood.
By traditions and new dogmas she robbed her true Prophet
of his right to teach, in scripture, the Father's whole will and
his final will. Her Papacy mocked Christ's kingly office whereby
the sole Mediator rules his church and shields it from its enemies—Satan, sin, and death. Thus wrote Lutherans, Calvinists,
Anabaptists, and Socinians—or, in England, Anglicans, Puritans, and sectaries.

All could distinguish the Kingdom that Christ ruled spe-
cially as Mediator from his natural Kingdom, the universe of
angels, men, and lesser beings, which he ruled as Creator. In
this latter character, with no reference to the church, Milton
introduced him early in *Paradise Lost*. Christ's *regnum naturale* became a term about equivalent to the Kingdom of God,
a phrase used only seldom of the church. Matthew's phrase
Kingdom of Heaven was variously applied until the annotated
Geneva Bible settled its meaning; thereafter it normally meant
gospel preaching. In the *Christian Doctrine* Milton equated
the Kingdom of Heaven, which the Baptist proclaimed to be

"at hand" (*P.R.* 1.20), with the church on earth. Late in *Paradise Lost* (xii.444–551) he found occasion to write of that same Mediatorial Kingdom, of its great enemy Antichrist, and of its Millennial triumph (460) here below under the Lord's Glorious Reign. Divines who looked to the future for the Millennium knew it as the time when Jesus would sit on the throne of David.

For his peculiar realm on earth Christ ruled only over the church militant (or suffering and militant), that Kingdom of Grace which, after his return, he would catch up into his Kingdom of Glory as the church triumphant. In this fashion, by a single church in two stadia, the orthodox divines reconciled biblical texts for a Kingdom-present and a Kingdom-to-come. By 1660 scholarly divines, a majority if we may believe certain witnesses, had determined, like Milton, that Christ's reign of a thousand years (Rev. xx) lay in the future and not in the past, where, by Augustine's reckoning misunderstood, it would have ended sometime after A. D. 1000. These millenarian futurists could not agree whether Christ would be visibly present with his earthly church, whether the Glorious Reign on earth (if on earth) would be spiritual only or accompanied by material benefits, whether preparatory heralds could in any way hasten the Lord's coming. But all their theories preserved the essential conception of a Kingdom-church. After reading the Psalms and other Old Testament prophecies, they conceded alike that Jesus had not yet sat on David's throne, but he had sat on a higher one. Under spiritual rule his Kingdom had begun at his Nativity, Baptism, Temptation, Crucifixion, Ascension—or, at the latest, at Pentecost—as the orthodox preterists had taught variously. The futurists in effect gave the continuous Kingdom-church an additional stage between the Kingdoms of Grace and Glory, though at least one of them claimed the Glorious Reign for the Kingdom of Grace in order to safeguard the ancient twofold distinction. Another, never doubting that the whole church from the beginning was the Kingdom that Christ ruled as God, went so far as to question that Christ had yet ruled as man.

The Jesus of *Paradise Regained*, the Saviour of mankind (iv.635), is just entering upon that Mediatorial Office to which Milton and everybody assigned the Kingship. His earthly paradise for Adam's chosen sons is "founded now" (iv.613). Urged by Satan to seize prematurely some of the temporalities promised him by Old Testament prophecies (e.g., iii.351 ff.), Christ, who knows well (iii.189 ff.) that his

Kingdom must begin in suffering, replies that he can wait (III.182, IV.146). If he is ever to enjoy a reign on earth that will be carnally political—and we are never assured that Satan's exegesis is correct—it must be purely a birth of God's own time, not something to be seized or to be prepared for except by obeying God's revealed will. How the millennial Kingdom (IV.147) will come about can never be revealed (IV.153). The new King's task is clear. He must achieve whatever has been promised by refusing all temporalities, as God commands. Here we read Milton's repudiation of all millenarianism politically tinged. These lines suggest that he owed his own futurist eschatology only to an academic and disinterested study of prophecy.

Not millenarianism but Erastianism, popularly so called, strained somewhat against the idea of a Kingdom-church. The more thoughtful Cæsaro-Papists of the Church of England perceived early that the Puritans' Kingdom "not of this world" could become an awkward *imperium in imperio*. Both Puritans and Anglicans had to explain to Separatists and to Roman Catholics alike why Christ's monarchy in the church could be shared by the prince and not by the Pope. Anglicans had to explain why Rome's defective church, outside the Kingdom, was a false church, from which separation was mandatory; and why their own admittedly defective church, inside the Kingdom, was a true church, from which separation was a sin. Sometimes the very paradox made them charitable to Rome. Thomas Hobbes perceived the likeliest means to remove rebel theory from his own state church. The church, he delivered flatly, using Papists for his whipping boys, was not the Kingdom at all. God's Kingdom had been rule over a peculiar people, the Jews. Christ's would begin only at the Second Coming. The philosopher's unheard-of novelty aroused indignant protest, contributed to most vocally by the good Anglican bishop, John Bramhall. Though few in the Church of England were Erastians by conviction, Hobbes's idea had probably crossed some other Anglican minds, and the fact that none expressed it outright testifies to the vitality of belief in a Kingdom church. If we try, we can find a hint of that belief in Hooker's writings, but we must search. The apologist usually avoided the metaphor of the Kingdom in favor of the Head-Body analogy to figure Christ's ecclesiastical headship. Henry Hammond thought it probable that Christ exercised his headship by virtue of his prophetic office, since the Kingdom in scripture is not always the church.

But none held with Hobbes, advantageous as Anglican apologists would have found his superficial exegesis. Instead, they argued that since Christ, king of his church, ruled also the world of nature, he might use things of this world, including the magistrate, in the administration of his church. All was Christ's. Milton, if I understand him correctly, urbanely disposes of this argument in *Paradise Regained* (II.379) after Satan urges Christ to accept the creatures because he, as Lord of all, has a right to use them if he chooses. Christ, following only God's will, replies that he has an equally good right not to choose.

With the mild exceptions mentioned, all the conservatives except Hobbes, so far as I know, either held their peace about the Kingdom or accepted the orthodox statements, however they might interpret them. The surface unanimity of Christians concerning the identity of Kingdom and church in Milton's age is not, I think, disputed by special students, but some testimony here, besides what is collected in the Notes, may be appropriate. The Rheims New Testament may suffice to speak for Catholics, since their agreement on such a point can be assumed. Among Anglicans, Bishop Edward Reynolds knew how to distinguish between the *regnum naturale* and the Kingdom that was Christ's "by donation and unction from the Father, that he might be head of the church." When Bacon wished that a treatise might be written on unity in the Kingdom (*civitas*), he described a work on church-peace. A more important pacificator, John Hales, preaching on the text "My Kingdom is not of this world," confessed Jesus to be Lord of all creatures as well as King of Glory; but Hales confused no kingdoms. As Mediator, Christ ruled "his Kingdom of Grace," otherwise "his Church, his Spouse, his Body, his Flock, and this is that Kingdom which . . . is not of this world." Bishop Hall agreed with Hales, and so did Dr. Donne. "We behold," wrote Donne, among his copious utterances on the subject, "the Messiah, the anointed High Priest, King of that church, which he hath purchased with his blood."

The Kingdom of Grace was to that of Glory as the acorn to the oak, wrote Richard Baxter, whose Puritanism never permitted him to doubt that the church was both kingdoms. Conservative Puritan opinion, like the Catholic, being official orthodoxy, can be predicted, for Calvin himself had written, along with much else, these quotably brief words: "Forasmuch as the church is the Kingdom of Christ, . . . [it cannot] be without his Scepter, that is to say, his holy Word." Whoever read God's word in the annotated Geneva version found the Rod in Psalm cx (the chief Old Testament allegory of Israel's King) explained as "the Word, assembling Christ's Kingdom, the church." We may pass over other notes to the same effect in order to observe Note f on Matt. xi:11, which explained gospel preaching as the Kingdom of Heaven, and the headnote to Mark, which designated John the Baptist as the first gospel preacher. His "office" John would transfer to Christ at the opening of *Paradise Regained* (1.28, 188). English commentaries on the Temptation usually, perhaps always, drew lessons for the church among other teachings. Whenever, in prose, Milton explained the Temptation as a whole, he applied it ecclesiastically. Here we might recall John Bale's anti-Popish interlude on Christ's combat or the wholly ecclesiastical *Tragedy* by Bernardino Ochino, whose early temptation scenes resemble both the gospel story and Milton's poem. Several of the commentaries, notably those by William Perkins and Thomas Taylor, had been conspicuously ecclesiastical, and a larger number had made a point of Satan's attempt upon the very head of the church. They had the support of the Genevan note (i) on Mark i:14, closing the Temptation, which glanced at the kingdom of preaching and thereby set grave authority behind the notion that the trial in the Wildnerness founded the kingdom. Milton's God explains his plan (1.155 ff.): Christ is to learn the principles that he will need for his warfare against sin, death, and Satanic strength. A preacher might have put the familiar matter another way: God will have the Son tempted in order to exercise him in his kingly duties.

The further we move away from Hobbes toward radicalism the more ardently we find the sects enamored of the Kingdom-church and the scripture-texts proving it unworldly. In the Notes will be found a representative band of Separatists, Baptists, Independents, and Quakers to illustrate. But the intelligibility of Milton's poem rested upon the base of received doctrine to be found in catechisms and handbooks. "What is the Kingdom?" demanded John Dod, and expected catechumens to answer: "First, the government of his church in this world"; and "secondly, his last judgment in the world to come." William Ames made an equally precise identification in his widely studied *Medulla*. In this same genre of summary divinity the Independent John Owen inquired: "Wherein doth the kingly office of Christ consist?" His answer was Calvin's and Milton's: "In a twofold power; first, in . . . ruling in and over his church; secondly, in . . . subduing his enemies." As Prophet,

Christ, taught the church his Father's whole will. Finally, I would quote from that popular reference work for preachers, *A Complete Christian Dictionary*, by Wilson, Symson, and Bagwell, words that stood unaltered through at least seven editions between 1612 and 1661. The Kingdom of Christ is "his regiment and rule, which he (as Mediator) hath and exerciseth over the Church, inwardly by his Spirit, and outwardly by his word."

I have already had occasion to allude to the passages in the *Christian Doctrine* where Milton, too, defined the true church and identified it with a Kingdom which, even with its millennial future, moved through the usual two stages of Grace and Glory. There he wrote of the Threefold Office with Christ the Mediator as Prophet, Priest, and King of the church, teaching it God's whole will. As King, Jesus governed and preserved, "chiefly by an inward law and spiritual power, the church, and . . . [conquered and subdued] its enemies." This much was common among Protestants. The rest belonged more peculiarly to Milton:

The preeminent excellency of Christ's Kingdom over all others [is manifested in that] he governs not the bodies of men alone, as the civil magistrate, but their minds and consciences, and that . . . by what the world esteems the weakest of all instruments. Hence external force ought never to be employed in the administration of *the Kingdom of Christ, which is the church.*

Later in his own *medulla*, as in *Paradise Lost*, we find the story of the church carried into the last days. At Christ's return Satan will be bound, then released to persecute for the last time. During the millennium of Satan's captivity—some long but indefinite time—Christ will reign on earth and will judge the quick and the dead. At the end of time he will surrender the Kingdom to God who will then be "all in all."

Note B. The mediatorial Kingdom which runs through and binds up *Paradise Regained* is so confidently and extensively defined in the *Christian Doctrine* as the church that the chance of its meaning anything else in the poem may seem *a priori* negligible. We doubtless ought to examine it, nevertheless. To depart from a definition so ancient and familiar, Milton would have had to explain his novelty. Instead of any such apology in the poem, we find orthodoxy reinforced by a number of literal and direct references to preaching or the church, and these surely validate the treatise as a reliable key to the poem. One, already discussed at length, is the long and plain Learning Temptation. Others that seem to me clear and explicit beyond probable objection I have considered elsewhere (*PMLA*, LXVII [1952], 796 ff.) and shall rapidly enumerate here. For one instance, Christ is coaxed to accept *false guidance* (1.336) while he is planning his ministry of gospel preaching (1.185, II.113). The First Encounter ends as Satan professes his delight in Christ's preaching and offers an ecclesiastical excuse for listening—the "atheous priest" (these lines recapitulate the topic of the scene preceding) is still a priest, tolerated by God (1.475–492). Similarly, after the early temptations in the Second Encounter the Tempter pays a kind of choric tribute to one from whom the greatest priests and prophets might learn wisdom (II.12–16), apparently another summation intended to comment upon the scene foregoing. Again, Jesus defends his plans for inward rule (II.465–472) by preaching (473–476) in lines closely parallel with those just quoted from the *Christian Doctrine*. Still later, Satan reveals his own political drift when he invites Jesus to hold temporal power like the Maccabees, who did so "though priests" (III.169). Anglican polemics once made good use of Judas Maccabeus as an exemplum.

If Milton had not intended the Kingdom to bear the accepted definition that it had borne in his own *Christian Doctrine,* he could hardly have expected a reader misled by this kind of language to find out heresy and understand his poem. If he had intended heterodoxy, he would have had to shun orthodox associations.

Once given the ecclesiastical Kingdom of Grace for his theme, a reader will find other churchly details almost as obvious as those mentioned. When Christ is first enticed to distrust God and to rely for maintenance upon the stones of this world, his Tempter is disguised as a true pastor (1.315). The uncasing of Satan that follows his second masquerade develops, on his side, a standard antichristian argument: a church or minister may be impure without being false (1.358–396). The proposition had shielded Catholics and later Protestants against "pure," Donatistical schismatics crying, "Come out of her, my people!" In passing himself off as an *angel* of light Satan acts the role demanded of Antichrist by all who debated Rome (see Notes). Posing as a true angel, though tarnished, he claims oracular infallibility—a routine metaphor in anti-Catholic polemics. To all, Christ replies explicitly (esp. 456–464) in the name of Protestant scripturalism. God will not teach by Satan's oracles, but by the words of Christ, interpreted by the spirit.

Early in the Second Encounter we approach the Devil's Table, under which metaphor scripture itself (I Cor. x:21) figured idolatry. The phrase and Milton's use of it take us back to St. Paul's long and fiery sermon against meats sacrificed. New Testament passages against idolatry are scarce. This one made a great text for Protestantism, especially Puritanism, and Milton in his tracts used it repeatedly. Here once more he pointed his drift by his whole conduct of the Banquet scene and by alluding explicitly to the Apostle's sermon (II.329). It appears from the altogether theological terms in which Christ rejects Satan's feast (II.259, 321, 380 f.) that food is not the issue. If it is equally clear from the circumstances that I have discussed elsewhere, or others, that the topic debated is idolatry, then I should suppose that the poet's meaning may be something like this. The true church of Christ is not always visible in outward worship. A Christian will participate in the service offered him if it can be justified by God's law (II.259, 321), for by scripture there is a true and spiritual mode of worship (383 ff.). But adversity may deprive a Christian of his worship and the church of its visibility without Christ's body's wasting (256).

The tuneful chant in a theatrical grove (II.292–300) may be worth a passing remark, for the picture seems drawn to suggest a steeplehouse, probably a cathedral. The Tempter spreads his omni-sensual feast in shade "High rooft and walks beneath." The brown aisles converge centrally in a "woody Scene." Innocent enough, perhaps, until we read that to a "superstitious" eye the architecture might betoken a favored haunt of divinity. Thus Satan has planned, for apparently Satan and not nature has been the builder ("it seemed," 295). An altogether peripheral question might be asked about the parenthesis (295) "Nature taught art," usually understood as a general aphorism. May the compressed language mean rather that the grove seems innocently natural and disarming because Satan's artifice, or art, has studied and imitated nature? That is to say, "Nature's own work it seemed *because* nature had (here) taught art?" We may leave this for the more significant fact that Greek myth cooperated with the Old Testament to associate groves with idolatry. Milton and his generation interpreted *asherah* in the Old Testament to mean 'grove' (*P. L.* I.403), an unchallenged mistranslation that runs through the Authorized Version. Any grove, and surely one Satanic and "superstitious," appropriately set the scene for a service of idolatry.

NOTES

The paragraphs in which these notes are grouped correspond with those of the text. Notes are further particularized by line-references placed after the catch phrases printed in boldface.

To avoid counting, one may read a line-number as an approximated fraction of 40, the normal number of lines on a page. A note numbered 12 will refer to text roughly one third of the distance down its page. In that vicinity the eye will readily pick out the catch phrase.

Editions are specified frequently, so that each note should be either sufficient in itself or usable after a short glance up the page. Dates of first editions appear in brackets where two dates are supplied.

Abbreviations:

DA	*Dissertation Abstracts*
ELH	*English Literary History*
HLQ	*Huntington Library Quarterly*
JEGP	*Journal of English and Germanic Philology*
JHI	*Journal of the History of Ideas*
LACT	Library of Anglo-Catholic Theology
MLN	*Modern Language Notes*
MLQ	*Modern Language Quarterly*
MLR	*Modern Language Review*
MP	*Modern Philology*
N & Q	*Notes and Queries*
P.	*Publications*
PMLA	*Publications of the Modern Language Association of America*
PQ	*Philological Quarterly*
RES	*Review of English Studies*
SP	*Studies in Philology*
St.	*Studies*
TLS	*Times Literary Supplement*
UTQ	*University of Toronto Quarterly*

CHAPTER I

1   In . . . **moral allegory (1)**—*Pathomachia* (1630), 5-6, 23, 34. **Allegory of self-deception . . . Puritan (21)**—Daniel Dyke, *The Mystery of Selfe-Deceiving* ([1614] 1633), 181. **Every influential . . . writing (25)**—Curiosity a topic in commentary on the Decalogue and the Creed: John Hooper, *The X Holie Commandements* [1548], in *Writings*, Parker Soc. (1843), I, 326-330; and see, shielding predestination, ch. xvii ("Of Curiosity"), 419; [John Dod], *Exposition of the Ten Commandements* ([1603] 1609), 42, 95; Nicholas Bifield, *Marrow of the Oracles of God* ([1620] 1640), 42, *The Beginning of the Doctrine of Christ* (1630), 47, and (on the Creed) *The Rule of Faith* (1626), 21, 46; Samuel Crooke, *The Guide unto True Blessednesse* ([1613]

PAGE

1 1640), 98. In comment on the Lord's Prayer: Lancelot Andrewes, *Meditations on the Lord's Prayer,* in *Ninety-Six Sermons,* LACT (5 v., 1841-), V, 397; William Wischart, *Exp. of the Lords Prayer* (1633), 146. In renunciations, summary divinity, casuistry: Christopher Wilson, *Selfe Deniall* (1625), 173-175; John Downe, *Selfe-Deniall,* in *Certain Treatises* (1633), 16-17; Jeremiah Burroughs, *Moses His Self-Denyall* (1649), 188; Isaac Ambrose, "Self-Denial," *Media,* in *Works* (1701), 82 ff.; Richard Baxter, *Self-Denial,* in *Practical Works* (23 v., 1830), XI, 127, 283. Jerome Zanchius, *Confession of Christian Religion* (tr. 1599), 30; John Downame, *The Summe of Sacred Divinitie* (1630), 163, 233-234; William Ames, *Marrow of Sacred Divinity* (203) and *Cases of Conscience* (49 = [59]) in *Workes,*

2 1643. In charactery, satire, didactic verse, and the emblem-literature: Samuel Rowlands, *Looke to it: For Ile Stabbe ye* (1604), in *Gwendolyn Murphy,* ed. *A Cabinet of Characters* (1925), 20-21, and see 54, 58, 76, 163; Thomas Fuller, "The Controversial Divine," *The Holy State* (1642), ed. facs., W. G. Walten (New York, 1938), 63, and see 56-60; Samuel Butler, *Characters,* ed. A. R. Waller (1908), 66. *Satyræ Seriæ* (1639), Nos. 2, 13, 15, etc. George Wither, *Abuses Stript, and Whipt* (1613), II, 4, Sig R5; John Stephens, *Satyrical Essayes* (1615), 146-147. Charles Fitz-Geffrey, *The Blessed Birth-Day* (1634), 27. Wither, *A Collection of Emblemes* (1635), 147, 95; Geffrey Whitney, *A Choice of Emblemes* (1586), 28, 78, 157; J[ohn] H[all], *Emblems* (1658), 29 (No. 8). See Rosemary Freeman, *English Emblem Books* (London, 1938), 20-21. The emblematic title page before this volume comes from George Thomson's *Vindex Veritatis,* 1606. **A composer set . . . theme (10)**—Martin Peerson, *Mottects* (1630), e.g., 19. See Fulke Greville, Lord Brooke, *Poems and Dramas,* ed. Geoffrey Bullough (2 v., 1938), I, 279, 287. **Scholars knew . . . pun (19)**—Note, e.g., George Benson's word-play, *A Sermon . . . at Paules Crosse* (1609), 60.

Conventional piety guarding mysteries (28)—Examples fill Walter Montagu's *Miscellanea Spiritualia,* Part I (1648), Part II (1654). **Peace with prudence before . . . speculation (33)**—Lancelot Andrewes, *Ninety-Six Sermons,* LACT (5 v., 1841-), I, 41, 91; Nicholas Gibbens, *Questions and Disputations* (1601), 28, 61, 169; Sebastian Benefield, *Eight Sermons* (1614), 58 ff.; John Day, *Day's Dyall* (1614), 92; Bartholomew Parsons, *The First Fruites of the Gentiles* (1618), 1, esp. 5; John Boys, *Workes* (1622), 277, 366-368; Robert Bedingfield, *Sermon at Paules Crosse* (1625), 3; Robert Bolton, *Walking with God* (1626), 140-141.

3 **Historians . . . have remarked (2)**—Most familiarly, Basil Willey, *The Seventeenth Century Background* (London, 1934), e.g., p. 31, on curiosity as a theme of reflection in the period. Margaret L. Wiley, *The Subtle Knot* (London, 1952), has considered several of the writers who figure in these pages, and has treated them as skeptics. She has not confined the term to acknowledged Pyrrhonists and Academics, or to methodical doubters who ventured criticism of knowledge. See her broad definition, pp. 11-60. A recent commentator on curiosity as conceived in the late sixteenth century is Paul H. Kocher, *Science and Religion in Elizabethan England* (San Marino, Cal., 1953), 3 ff., esp. 63-67, and elsewhere. See Sidney Warhaft, "New Worlds of Ignorance: . . . 1595-1670," *DA,* XIV (1954), 1737.

4 **Pyrrho . . . self-knowledge (29)**—Mary M. Patrick, *The Greek Skeptics* (New York, 1929), 180, notices esp. the influence of the Skeptics on the Stoics. **Hesiod left . . . Adam (31)**—See F. J. Taggart, "The Argument of Hesiod's *Works and Days,*" *JHI,* VIII (1947), 45 ff. J. W. Ashton, "The

4 Fall of Icarus," *Ren. St. [for] Hardin Craig,* ed. Baldwin Maxwell *et al.*
(Stanford, Cal., 1942), 153 ff. Cp. Harry Levin, *The Overreacher* (Cambridge, U.S.A., 1952), 168. Classical exempla, unclassical purposes: e.g.,
Gervase Babington, *[Comm. on] Numbers* (16[5]), in *Workes,* 1615 (Thales
suggests exegetical modesty); John Bridges, *Sermon at Paules Crosse* (1571),
34-38, esp. 38 (Pliny suggests predestinarian modesty). Quibbling . . . science (38)—Seneca, *Epistulæ Morales* xlviii, xlix, esp. lxxxviii, cxvii, and
5 lxxxvii.36. Socrates [renounces "astronomy"] (25)—Xenophon, *Memorabilia* iv.7.4-10. Cp. Cicero, *Tusculan Disp.* v.4.10, and, e.g., Thomas Stanley, *The History of Philosophy* ([1655] 1687), 72.
6 The Fathers . . . texts (27)—Tertullian, *De Anima* (iii) and *De Præscrip. Hæreticorum* (vii), in *Works,* Ante-Nicene Lib. (3 v., 1870), II, 416 and
8-9. Ps-Justin Martyr, *Cohortatio ad Græcos,* in *Works,* ed. cit. (1868), 324.
Clement of Alexandria, *Pædagogus* (i.5-7), in *Works,* ed. cit. (2 v., 1867), I,
366-370. See R. B. Tollington, *Clement of Alexandria* (2 v., 1914), I, 224 n.
Definitions, [288 possible] (39)—Augustine, *Civ. Dei* xix.l. Cp. John
7 Donne, *Works,* ed. Henry Alford (6 v., 1839), V, 250. Allegory of . . .
Hagar, learning (13)—Philo Judæus, *De Congressu Quærendæ Eruditionis
Gratia,* Loeb, IV (1929), 449-551; see also *De Post. Caini* (xxxviii,130), II,
403. Clemens Alex., *Stromata* (i.5), in *Works,* I, 459 ff. Other Fathers in
defense of learning: ps-Justin Martyr, *Cohort. ad Græcos* and Justin, *Dialogus cum Tryphone* (ii), in *Works* (1868), 308, 321; and 87. On Origen's
allegory of the Midianite captives (learning), see George G. Coulton,
Studies in Medieval Thought (London, 1940), 54-55. After the patristic
age (20)—For the theme of intellectual discretion handled by Schoolmen
as well as Fathers, see Arpad Steiner, "The Faust Legend and the Christian Tradition," *PMLA,* LIV (1939), 393-401. Cp. Aquinas, *Summa contra
Gentiles* i.3, and, for Aquinas cited to witness against curiosity, John
Donne, *Essays in Divinity,* ed. E. M. Simpson (Oxford, 1952), 5; John Bramhall, *Works,* LACT (5 v., 1842), I, 22, Note h. See John K. Ryan, "The
Reputation of St. Thomas among Protestant Thinkers of the Seventeenth
Century," *The New Scholasticism,* XXII (1948), 126 ff.
Augustine . . . medieval disciples (30)—On the Augustinian tradition,
see Friedrich Ueberweg, *Grundriss der Gesch. der Philosophie,* Part II, ed.
Bernhard Geyer (Berlin, 1928); for late Augustinianism, Nigel Abercrombie,
Saint Augustine and French Classical Thought (Oxford, 1938), 47, 58-59,
105; and Louis I. Bredvold, *The Intellectual Milieu of John Dryden* (Ann
Arbor, Mich., 1934), 24-26. On the Father's intellectual wanderings, Augustine, *Confessions* (v.10.19), in *Works,* Nicene Lib. (8 v., 1888), I, 86. See
Vernon J. Bourke, *Augustine's Quest for Wisdom* (Milwaukee, Wis., 1944),
8 49. His curiosity sermons: *De Vera Relig.* [L].98; *De Gen. ad Litt.* ii [10].23,
and ii [16].33; *Enarratio in Ps.* viii.12; *Contra Jul. Pelag.* vi [7].17. See
Henri-Irénée Marrou, *Saint Augustine et la Fin de la Culture Antique*
(Paris, 1937), 471-473. The local . . . Abraham's bosom (13)—Vain questions that later preachers would also denounce: *De Gen. ad Litt.* viii [5].9;
Epist. xi; *Civ. Dei* xi.v. Milton on the folly of searching God's early history before Creation: *Works* (New York, 1931 ; 18 v.), IV, 168 (15), and
XV, 3 (3). Plurality of worlds . . . Fathers (23)—A. H. Gilbert, "Milton and Galileo," *SP,* XIX (1922), 239. Augustine condemns magic: *Civ.
Dei* vill.10. See Lynn Thorndike, *Magic and Science,* I, 504-522, 480. Early
Fausts of . . . legend (29)—See Philip M. Palmer and Robert P. More,
The Sources of the Faust Tradition (New York, 1936), 7 ff. Augustine delighted in . . . science (31)—*Civ. Dei* xix.14. See Hugh Pope, *Saint*

240   MILTON AND FORBIDDEN KNOWLEDGE

8   *Augustine of Hippo* (London, 1937), 228-253. **He glorified self-knowledge**
     (32)—*De Trin.* iv.i. On Christian Socratism: Etienne Gilson, *Esprit de la*
     Philosophie Médiévale (Paris, 1944), 214-234.

9   **Luther heard [Bernard] gladly (1)**—See Clement C. J. Webb, *Studies*
     in the Hist. of Natural Theology (Oxford, 1915), 231. **English devotional**
     writers [also] (1)—Helen C. White, *English Devotional Literature (Prose),*
     1600-1640: St. in Lang. and Lit., Univ. Wis., No. 29 (1931), 78-81. **[Bern-**
     ard's] chapters 'De Curiositate' (6)—*De Modo Vivendi* [liv].130; *De In-*
     teriori Domo [xxiv].50. On Bernard's conception of self-knowledge:
     Etienne Gilson, *La Théologie Mystique de Saint Bernard* (Paris, 1934),
     124, 84-85, 91-96, 181-182. For later Socratism: Raymond Marcel, " 'Saint'
     Socrate, Patron de l'Humanisme," *Rev. Int. de Phil.*, V (1951), 135 ff.
     Calvinist [and] Arminian . . . agreed (17)—See, e.g., John Hull, *Christ*
     His Proclamation to Salvation (1613), 153-154; or Milton, *P. R.* iv.309-312.
     Cp. La Primaudaye, cited below, Pt. i, p. 6.

10   **"The beginning of all sin" (26)**—Bernard of Clairvaux, *The Twelve*
     Degrees of Humility and Pride, tr. B. R. V. Mills (1929), 70.

     Form known . . . as the meditation (28)—See H. Fisch, "Bishop Hall's
     Meditations," *RES*, XXV (1949), 217. Joseph Hall, *Meditations and Vows*,
     in *A Recollection of . . . Treatises* (1614), 1, 36; see 909. See Helen C.
     White, *English Devotional Literature*, 216. Henry Montagu, Earl of Man-
     chester, *Contemplatio Mortis et Immortalitatis* (1631), 12-13; Anthony Staf-
     ford, *Meditations and Resolutions* (1612), 1-2; Joseph Henshawe, *Horæ*
     Successivæ, or Spare-Houres of Meditations ([1631] 1640), 250; Arthur War-
     wick, *Spare Minutes; or, Resolved Meditations* ([1634] 1637, repr. 1821), 11.
     Bernard's wish (36)—*Sermon on Canticles* (xxvi.2), in *Works*, ed. John
     Mabillon (4 v., 1896), IV, 156; Daniel Tuvil, *Vade Mecum* (1638, from
     Essayes of 1609), 25; Robert Chamberlain, *Nocturnall Lucubrations: or*

11   *Meditations Divine and Morall* (1638), 87-88. **[Bernard] reckoned up a**
     list of sinners (1)—*On Canticles* (xxxvi.3), *Works*, IV, 235-236. Cp. John
     Robinson, *Essayes, or Observations Divine and Moral* ([1625] 1638), Obs.
     xiv, p. 170; George Benson, *Sermon at Paules Crosse* ([May 7] 1609), 62;
     Francis Quarles, *Enchyridion* (1641), Cent. ii, ch. 8; Robert Aylett, *Divine,*
     and Moral Speculations in Metrical Numbers (1654), 145 (iii, 1).

     La Primaudaye countered Paduan atheism (19)—See Henri Busson,
     Rationalisme dans la Littérature Française de la Renaissance (Paris, 1922),
     475-477. George T. Buckley, *Atheism in the English Renaissance* (Chicago,
     1932), 98-100. **Borrowed Bernard's sentiments (20)**—Pierre de la Pri-
     maudaye, *The French Academie*, tr. T[homas] B[owes] ([1586-1601] 1618),
     Pt. i, 5, 6-7, 17, 66-70; Pt. ii, 574, 589; Pt. iii, 635, etc. **Du Bartas [on**
     curiosity] (38)—*La Sepmaine*, tr. in *The Complete Works of Joshua*
     Sylvester, ed. A. B. Grosart (2 v., 1880), I, 17-113. See Week, I, Day iv, l.
     150; I.ii.973; II ("Eden"), 90, 164, 276, 646, 791-795 ff.

12   **La Primaudaye's doctrine [in] Davies of Hereford (13)**—*Microcosmos*
     (1603), in *Works*, ed. A. B. Grosart (2 v., 1878), I, 77-88. On sources: R. B.
     McKerrow, rev., *RES*, I (1925), 242-244; Ruth L. Anderson, in *PQ*, VI (1927),
     57 ff. On the skepticism of the men discussed here: esp. Paul H. Kocher,
     Science and Religion, etc. (1953), 54 ff. **La Primaudaye's doctrine [in] Sir**
     John Davies (13)—See L. I. Bredvold, "Davies' Source for *Nosce Teipsum*,"
     PMLA, XXXVIII (1923), 745 ff. George T. Buckley, *Atheism*, 107-120, and
     MP, XXV (1927), 67-78. William L. Doughty, *Studies in the Religious Po-*
     etry of the Seventeenth Century (London, 1946), 68-69, notices the Christian
     Socratism of Davies' preface. Cp. Anthony Nixon's title for an outline of

NOTES

241

PAGE

12 psychology—*The Dignitie of Man*, 1612. The [preface] . . . as . . . skepticism (21)—Buckley, *Atheism*, 114-117, esp. 116; Wilbur K. Jordan, *The Development of Religious Toleration in England* (Cambridge, U.S.A., 1932-1940; 4 v.), II, 425; E. H. Sneath, *Philosophy in Poetry: A Study of . . . 'Nosce Teipsum'* (1903), ch. ii, 4-62. Kocher, 57. We should . . . study ourselves (33)—Part I of *Nosce Teipsum* (1599), in Davies, *Works*, ed. A. B. Grosart (3 v., 1869-), I, 43-54.
The words of Sir Thomas Browne (37)—*Vulgar Errors* (vi, 8), in *Works*,

13 ed. Keynes, III, 220. Pietism . . . in the Anniversaries . . . recall[s] Bernard (20)—Thus L. I. Martz, "John Donne in Meditation," *ELH*, XIV (1947), 247 ff. Cp. M. M. Mahood, *Poetry and Humanism* (New Haven, 1950), 112-113. D. C. Allen, "The Double Journey of John Donne," in *A Tribute to George Coffin Taylor*, ed. Arnold Williams (Chapel Hill, N. C., 1952), 94-99. For whatever reason (21)—Donne not normally mystical: Helen C. White, *The Metaphysical Poets* (New York, 1936), 116-119. L. I. Bredvold, "The Religious Thought of Donne," *St. in Shakespeare, Milton, and Donne: Univ. Mich. P.*, I (1925), 193 ff. Michael F. Moloney, *John Donne, His Flight from Medievalism* (Urbana, Ill., 1944), 183-195. Mahood, 121, 151. Montaigne picked the stars, . . . Nile, . . . tides (29)—*Fssays*, tr. E. J. Trechmann (London, 1935), II, 15, and I, 523; II, 83. Cp. Pierre de Charron, *Of Wisdom*, tr. George Stanhope (3 v., 1729), I, 409, 421-422; II, 642-643. Cp. La Primaudaye, *The French Academie*, tr. T. B. (1618), Pt. III, 728; and Du Bartas, Week I, Day II, line 973 (and see I, IV, 150 ff.), in Joshua Sylvester, *Works*, ed. A. B. Grosart (2 v., 1880), I, 35. Cardan's meddling with elemental fire (36)—Jerome Cardan, *De Subtilitate*, in *Opera* (London, 1663; 10 v.), III, 7, 680 (9)-681; VI, 916. The argument . . . that Bacon ridiculed (40)—Bacon, *Works*, ed. Spedding (15 v., 1861), VI,

14 277; VIII, 79. We doubt that . . . dismay (9)—Thus J. C. Maxwell, "Donne and the 'New Philosophy,'" *Durham Univ. Jour.*, XII (1951), 61 ff. The new philosophy in relation to Donne's pessimism (various positions): Marjorie Nicolson, in *SP*, XXXII (1935), 456-457, and *The Breaking of the Circle* (Evanston, Ill., 1950), 83, 102, 137, etc. Arnold Williams, "A Note on Pessimism in the Renaissance," *SP*, XXXVI (1939), 246. Mahood, 112-113. [Donne's] depression, if real (10)—The Anniversaries and their important sincerity: Nicolson, *The Breaking of the Circle*, 69. Hugh I'Anson Fausset, *John Donne: A Study in Discord* (1924), 182. Theodore Spencer, "Donne and His Age," *A Garland for John Donne* (Cambridge, U.S.A., 1931), 191. [Donne's] insecurity (11)—His intellectual poise: Moloney, 58-63. Paul H. Kocher, *Science and Religion, etc.* (1953), 59-60. His mood of disenchantment: Bredvold, "Religious Thought of Donne," 217-218. Hiram Haydn, *The Counter-Renaissance* (New York, 1950), 23, 165. His mood accounted for biographically: Arnold Stein, "Donne and the Satiric Spirit," *ELH*, XI (1944), 266 ff. His mood related to the literary vogue of melancholy: Nicholas Breton, *Melancholicke Humours*, ed. G. B. Harrison (1929), with introductory essay on melancholy. D. C. Allen, "The Degeneration of Man and Renaissance Pessimism," *SP*, XXXV (1938), 202 ff. Lawrence Babb, "Melancholy and the Elizabethan Man of Letters," *HLQ*, IV (1941), 247 ff., and *The Elizabethan Malady* (Lansing, Mich., 1951), esp. 184-185. [Donne's] astronomy [examined in] Cardan, Bruno, Kepler (20)—Charles M. Coffin, *John Donne and the New Philosophy* (New York, 1937), 123, 167 ff.
Satires and essays "On Presumption" (23)—Montaigne, *Essays*, tr. Trechmann, I, 441, 443. Charron, tr. Stanhope (3 v., 1729), I, 408-409; II,

14 642-643; I, 421. On Charron's relationship to Montaigne: Henri Busson, *La Pensée Religieuse Française de Charron à Pascal* (Paris, 1933), 181-182.

15 William Drummond, *A Cypress Grove*, in *Poetical Works*, ed. L. E. Kastner (2 v., 1913), II, 67-104, and notes, II, 344-345, 347, 349. On Drummond's borrowing from Donne: G. S. Greene, in *PQ*, XI (1932), 29; and M. A. Rugoff, in *PQ*, XVI (1937), 85-88. **New magnetic studies (7)**—For Vanini's opinion of Gilbert, see John Owen, *The Skeptics of the Italian Renaissance* ([1893] 1908), 385. Later skeptics against presumption: George Wither, "Of Presumption" (II, Sat. 4), *Abuses Stript* (1613), Sigs R4-R5^{vo} ff. Robert Burton, *The Anatomy of Melancholy*, ed. A. R. Shilleto (3 v., 1893), II, 59-61. See Fritz Dieckow, *John Florio . . . und Robert Burton's Verhältnis zu Montaigne* (Strassburg, 1903), 92-117, esp. 98; R. M. Browne, "Robert Burton and the New Cosmology," *MLQ*, XII (1952), 131 ff., esp. 132, 140, 147. W. R. Mueller, "Robert Burton's 'Satyricall Preface,' " *MLQ*, XV (1954), 33-35, associates the themes of man's vanity and indignity. Thomas Bancroft, *Time's Out of Tune: . . . XX. Satires* (1658), Sat. iv, pp. 25-26. On Bancroft: Raymond M. Alden, *The Rise of Formal Satire in England: Univ. Penn. P. in Philol., etc.*, VII, No. 2 (1899), 240.

16 [Milton] alluded seven times [to plurality of worlds] (4)—For moon-dwellers, see *P. L.* I.21; v.261; VIII.140; and for planetarians in general, III.668-670; 561; VII.621; VIII.126. **Study of [Milton's] interest in [cosmology] (8)**—Grant McColley, "Milton's Dialogue on Astronomy," *PMLA*, LII (1937), 745 n, furnishes references, to which may be added McColley on Milton's astronomical attitudes, *MLN*, XLVII (1932), 319 ff., and "The Astronomy of *Paradise Lost*," *SP*, XXXIV (1937), 209 ff., and *'Paradise Lost': Its Major Origins* (Chicago, 1940), 236-244; Marjorie Nicolson, "The New Astronomy," *SP*, XXXII (1935), 428 ff., and *A World in the Moon: Smith Coll. St. in Mod. Lang.* (Northampton, Mass., 1936), No. 2. **Interest in [multiple worlds] . . . new astronomy (9)**—Thus McColley, "The Seventeenth-Century Doctrine of a Plurality of Worlds," *Annals of Science*, I (1936), 412, 420, 422, 425-426 (n. 184), 428. Cp. Pierre Charron, *Of Wisdom* (tr. 1729, 3 v.), George Stanhope's note, I, 421-422. **Professional astronomers . . . seriousness (15)**—See Burton, *Anatomy*, ed. Shilleto, II, 63; William Boulting, *Bruno*, 141, 145. **Writers . . . argue . . . from . . . geography (21)**—See James Howell, *Epistolæ Ho. Elianæ* ([1645] 1650; 3 v. in 1), III, Letter IX, p. 17, "To Dr. J. D." For casual, routine dispraise of pluralists' speculation to exalt self-knowledge, see, e.g., John Done, *Polydoron* (1631), 200. **Students [have noticed] pleasantry (26)**—Marjorie Nicolson, "The 'New Astronomy,' " *SP*, XXXII (1935), 446-447; *World in the Moon*, 23-24, 40, and *The Breaking of the Circle*, 137; McColley, *MLN*, XLVII (1932), 319-322. **Readers . . . taught to smile (30)**—See Nicolson, *World in the Moon*, 40; Bishop Francis Godwin, *The Man in the Moon* [1638], ed. Grant McColley, *Smith Coll. St. in Mod. Lang.*, XIX (1937), No. 1. **Slang for nonsense (36)**—Note Francis White, *An Examination . . . of a Lawless Pamphlet* (1637), 77, or Sir John Suckling, Letter XXXII, in *Works*, ed. A. H. Thompson (1910), 331.

17 **Donne's youthful Pyrrhonism (24)**—L. I. Bredvold, "Religious Thought of Donne," *St. in Shakespeare, Milton, and Donne: Univ. Mich. P.*, I (1925), 198-201; Bredvold, rev., *JEGP*, XXI (1922), 347-353, and "The Naturalism of John Donne," *JEGP*, XXII (1923), 471-502. On the poet's neo-platonism, see Mary Paton Ramsay, *Les Doctrines Médiévales chez Donne*, (1917), 245 ff., and "Donne's Relation to Philosophy," *A Garland for John*

17 *Donne,* ed. Theodore Spencer, 110-120, esp. 115. **More honest (27)**—
H. J. C. Grierson, e.g., *Cambridge Hist. of Eng. Lit.,* IV (1909), 203-204,
seems to think that Donne's faultless submission covered inner uneasiness.
[Donne's] scholastic education (28)—John F. Moore, "Donne and the
Metaphysical Conceit," *Rev. Anglo-Américaine,* XIII (1936), 290; Joseph
Kortemme, *Das Verhältnis John Donnes zur Scholastik und zum Barock*
(Münster, Westf., 1933), 16-26. His medieval Augustinianism: Evelyn M.
Simpson, *A Study of the Prose Works of John Donne* (1924), 90-97; Ramsay,
Doctrines Médiévales, 245 ff., 337-338; esp. Roy W. Battenhouse, "The
Grounds of Religious Toleration in the Thought of John Donne," *Church
Hist.,* XI (1942), 224-229. Donne and Augustine: Bredvold, "Religious
Thought of Donne," 193-232, e.g., 219. **[Donne on] the mysteries of
Christianity (31)**—*Works* (chiefly sermons), ed. Henry Alford (6 v., 1839),
III, 22-23, 151; I, 9, 86, 313; II, 32, 138; V, 59-75; on God's decrees: III, 227-
228, 236, 261, 450; IV, 584.

Donne [quarreled] as his church (34)—See Grierson "John Donne and
the Via Media," *MLR,* XLIII (1948), 305 ff., repr. in *Criticism and Creation* (London, 1949), 49 ff. T. G. Steffan, "The Social Argument Against
Enthusiasm," *Univ. Texas St. in Eng.* (1941), 41. W. K. Jordan, *Toleration,* II, 42. E. G. Lewis, The Question of Toleration in . . . Donne,"
MLR, XXXIII (1938), 257-258. A. Warren, "The Very Reverend Dr. Donne,"
Kenyon Rev., XVI (1954), 270. **[Donne's] aversions to [mystics, Brownists,
Papists] (35)**—*Works,* ed. Alford, I, 84, 95; II, 371; IV, 415 (against sec-
18 taries); VI, 187; IV, 412 (against revelations and inspirations). **[Donne
loyal to] prerogatives of [pulpit] learning (2)**—*Works,* I, 536 ff.; II, 203,
505-508; III, 152; IV, 415; V, 279; VI, 95-96, 175. **Mild yoke on the pagans
(5)**—I, 297; II, 350, 506-507; 250. **[Study of] creatures . . . without tabu
(16)**—I, 277, 415. **[Donne preaching on] the mind's infirmities (17)**—I,
536; III, 472. **Light struck Saul (21)**—No "ignorant" monastic retirement: II, 187-188, 203, 307; I, 314, 369; V, 56. Cp. Evelyn Hardy, *Donne:
A Spirit in Conflict* (London, 1942), 133. **Reason . . . justified . . . church
(26)**—I, 190, 468; II, 353; IV, 418; V, 175; VI, 42-43.

Donne [on] reason in language [unlike Calvin's] (30)— I, 9, 86, 261; II,
8; III, 22-23; IV, 451, 495, 511; V, 56-60, 65-67. **Predestination . . . election only (35)**—IV, 220, 284; II, 38-39; V, 552; IV, 220, esp. 451. See
Evelyn M. Simpson, *Prose Works of John Donne,* 84, 214-218; A. W. Harrison, *Arminianism* (London, 1937), 136. Election and reprobation from
the beginning: IV, 215; no antinomian abuse of the decree: III, 216; V,
371, 581; VI, 49. **[No] predestination for merit foreseen (39)**— II, 361;
19 III, 309. **[Donne] pried . . . into [chiefly] himself (14)**—Thus Robert
Sencourt (ps.), *Outflying Philosophy* [Hildesheim, 1924], 75; M. M. Mahood, *Poetry and Humanism* (New Haven, 1950), 130; cp. 121; Helen C.
White, "John Donne and the Psychology of Spiritual Effort," in Richard F.
Jones *et al., The Seventeenth Century* (Stanford, Cal., 1951), 359. **One form
of . . . fallen (18)**—Donne, *Works,* ed. Alford, V, 21.

The schools . . . wisdom, too (28)—I, 536; cp. 316, 420; III, 134. **Editor
has remarked (28)** -Logan Pearsall Smith, ed. *Donne's Sermons, Selected
Passages* (1920), xxxiii-xxxiv. Cp. Simpson, 206 ff., 250-251. **He often refused . . . curiosity (38)**—Donne raises, then fences, unnecessary questions: *Works,* ed. Alford, V, 589; cp. 21, 105, and I, 33; II, 16; IV, 73-74,
20 584; VI, 96-97. **Seriously asked . . . in . . . private (4)**—Donne, *Works,*
VI, 317-318; I, 3, 171; IV, 74; V, 64. See Sencourt, 218, 234. **Proved out of
Luther (4)**—On questions of How?, *Works,* III, 84; cp. I, 364-365, III, 202;

PAGE
20 I, 506-507, esp. 567 (Luther cited). On questions of Why?, III, 84; cp. 25. IV, 490-491; V, 371, esp. 327-328 (Luther cited); Donne, *Essayes in Divinity* (1651), 2-3; ed. Simpson, 5-6. **Condemnation of sorcery (33)**—Donne, *Works*, ed. Alford, I, 392. On Donne's occult reading: note, e.g., *Works*, IV, 438, and see Kortemme, 57; Simpson, 195; cp. 98; W. A. Murray, "Donne and Paracelsus," *RES*, XXV (1949), 115 ff. **Nothing [against] natural learning (36)**—Charles M. Coffin, *John Donne and the New Philosophy;* Michael F. Moloney, [*Donne's*] *Flight from Medievalism*, 58 ff.; Hardy, *Donne in Conflict*, 133; Bredvold, "Religious Thought of Donne," *Univ. Mich. P.*, I, 203 ff. **Adam . . . named the animals (39)**—Donne, *Works*, II, 508; III, 182, 288; IV, 528.
21 **[Donne] ranked the philosophers (2)**—I, 261, 287. **Learning [must] serve God (4)**—I, 278; III, 151-152. **"What is curiosity?" (10)**—VI, 96-97; cp. II, 203.
22 **Vanity of learning . . . detail (5)**—Hiram Haydn, *The Counter-Renaissance* (1950), 76-122. Some conspicuous works of Continental skepticism, like *La Gigantomachie* (Middleburgh, 1593) or Paul Perrot de la Sale, *Le Contr' Empire des Sciences* (Lyons, 1599), pay homage to the ass and otherwise recall Agrippa and Bruno, but lie too far from the English tradition to be noticed here. **["Respectable"] mysticism . . . Aquinas (10)**— See Dom Cuthbert Butler, *Western Mysticism* (2d ed., 1927), xiv-xv. George G. Coulton, *Studies in Medieval Thought* (London, 1940), 164. Gerson and "scholastic" mysticism: Rufus M. Jones, *Studies in Mystical Religion* (1909), 306-307. Butler, 182. James L. Connolly, *John Gerson, Reformer and Mystic* (Louvain, 1928), 313 ff. Mysticism somewhere anti-intellectual: Butler, xliii. **Cusa reached the point (19)**—Henry Bett, *Nicholas of Cusa* (London, 1932), 176-188. **Paracelsus . . . cabala . . . manufactured (32)**—Joseph L. Blau, *The Christian Interpretation of the Cabala in the Renaissance* (New York, 1944), 85. Paracelsus joins science to religion: Lynn Thorndike, *Magic and Science*, IV, 630-631; Robert Sencourt, *Outflying Philosophy*, 148-149, 152. **His exclusive piety descended (33)**—Walter Pagel, "Religious Motives in Medical Biology of the XVIIth Century," *Bull. Inst. Hist. Medicine*, III (1935), 97 ff., 213 ff., 265 ff., esp. 100, 110, 120; Paul H. Kocher, *Science and Religion, etc.* (1953), 250-253; A. E. Waite, *The Occult Sciences* ([1891] 1923), 201; W. J. Bouwsma on Renaissance cabalism, *JHI*, XV (1954), 218 ff.; Douglas Bush, *English Literature in the Earlier Seventeenth Century* (Oxford, 1945), 252. Wilhelm Struck, *Der Einfluss Jakob Böhmes auf die Englische Literatur des 17. Jahrhunderts* (Berlin, 1936), 148. John W. Adamson, *Pioneers in Modern Education, 1600-1700* (Cambridge, 1905), 67-68, 126. **Bruno . . . laughter (38)**—John Owen, *The Skeptics of the Italian Renaissance* ([1893] 1908), 294-297; C. Bartholomêss, ed. Bruno's *Cabala* (Milan, 1844), x. R. A. Tsanoff, "The Secularization of the Renaissance," *Rice Inst. Pamphlets*, XVIII (1931), 210. William Boulting, *Giordano Bruno*
23 (1916), 148-172. **Wiegel . . . "much cried up" (9)**—John Wilkins, *Ecclesiastes* ([1646] 1651), 71. Cp. Baxter's comment on Boehme, qu. by William Orme, *Life of Baxter* (2 v., 1831), I, 88. Sparrow translated Boehme: Charles E. Whiting, *Studies in English Puritanism, 1660-1688* (New York, 1931), 321-322; Rufus M. Jones, *Spiritual Reformers in the 16th and 17th Centuries* (1914), 208-234.
   [Baxter on] "Behmenists" (12)—*Reliquiæ Baxterianæ* 1.199 (1696), 74-77. **Translators . . . foreign sources (18)**—Eucherius, *The World Con-*

NOTES   245

PAGE
23 *temned,* tr. Henry Vaughan (1654), e.g., 46. See Helen C. White, *English
    Devotional Literature,* 99-115. On Valdés: Samuel Rutherford, *A Survey of
    the Spiritual Antichrist* (1648), 45-54. On Everard and Randall as trans-
    lators: William Haller, *The Rise of Puritanism* (New York, 1938), 207-212;
    Rufus M. Jones, *Spiritual Reformers,* 239-263. Early German mysticism
    related to England: R. M. Jones, *Studies in Mystical Religion,* 245 ff.;
    Robert A. Vaughan, *Hours with the Mystics* (2 v., 1856), I, 177-315. Note
    Evelyn Underhill, *Mysticism* (1911), 541-562. "Intellectualism, not intel-
    lect" (36)—William Ralph Inge, *Studies of English Mystics* (1907), 32.
24 [Luther] found comfort [in *Theologia*] (1)—Julius Köstlin, *Luthers
    Theologie* (2 v., 1863), I, 133-134, 138, 169. [Luther] to reassure Crom-
    well's sectaries (6)—See William Dell, "The Testimony of Martin Luther
    upon . . . Humane Learning," in *A Testimony . . . Against Divinity-
    Degrees* (1654), 13 ff.; but contrast Luther, *The Comyng of Our Saviour,*
    etc., tr. T. B. (1569), Pref., in praise of learning for its service to the Ref-
    ormation. Antiphilosophical . . . *Theologia* (7)—*Theologia Germanica*
    (xix), tr. Susanna Winkworth (1852), e.g., 60-62. Its influence on Spirituals:
    Maria Windstosser, *Etude sur la Théologie Germanique* (Paris, 1911), 101-
    123. From Spirituals to Quakers: see Robert Barclay, *Inner Life of the Re-
    ligious Societies of the Commonwealth* (1877), 415 ff., 223 ff.; Rufus M.
    Jones, *Mysticism and Democracy* (Cambridge, U.S.A., 1932), 60-142. Calvin
    [called] *Theologia* . . . "venom" (14)—*Lettres,* qu. by Windstosser, 104.
    On Calvin's writings against the Spirituals, see Henri Busson, *Rationalisme,*
    316-344, esp. 336-342.
        Cornelius Agrippa's [occult] devotion (21)—See Elizabeth Holmes,
    Henry Vaughan and the Hermetic Philosophy (Oxford, 1932), 28. **Fore-
    runner of Bacon and Comenius (28)**—E.g., W. K. Whitaker, "Bacon and
    the Renaissance Encyclopedists," diss., Stanford Univ. *Abstracts,* VIII
    (1932), 49-52, suggests kinship with Bacon. For a variety of opinions con-
    cerning Agrippa's motive: Louis I. Bredvold, *Milieu of Dryden,* 29; Geof-
    frey Bullough, "Bacon and the Defense of Learning," *Seventeenth Cen-
    tury St.* [for] Grierson (1938), 14; Lewis Spence, *Cornelius Agrippa, Occult
    Philosopher* (1921), 45; Robert A. Vaughan, *Hours with the Mystics,* II, 38.
25 Agrippa's theatrics: Lynn Thorndike, *Magic and Science,* V, 130. **The
    Bible teaches all things (4)**—Cornelius Agrippa, *The Vanity of Arts and
    Sciences* (London, 1676), 367.
        [Arts are] "the forbidden tree" (32)—Sebastian Franck, *The Forbidden
    Fruit* (tr., London, 1640), 35. On Franck: William Haller, *Rise of Puritan-
    ism,* 212; Rufus M. Jones, *Spiritual Reformers,* 49 ff. Milton on the divine
    origin of good arts: *P. L.* x.216-223; *P. R.* iv.338.
        Petrarch applauded . . . ignorance (39)—"De sui Ipsius et Multorum
    Ignorantia," in *The Renaissance Philosophy of Man,* ed. Ernst Cassirer
    et al. (Chicago, 1948), 47-133; see 29-33, and *Letters,* ed. cit., 76, 93, 97, 125-
26 126, 134. Cp. Valla, *On Free Will,* ed. cit., 180-182. John Owen, *Skeptics
    of the Italian Renaissance,* 107-128. On Valla's leaning toward determin-
    ism: Charles Trinkaus, "The Problem of Free Will in the Renaissance and
    Reformation," *JHI,* X (1949), 59-60. *Scientia inflat* (16)—Lorenzo Valla,
    De Libero Arbitrio, ed. Maria Anfossi (Firenze, 1934), 50-51 (early edd. 13).
    Quoted in part by Georg Ellinger, rev., *Zeits. f. deutsche Philol.,* XLVIII
    (1920), 315-319. In Cassirer *et al.,* 180-182. **Vives [on] learning's hazards
    (21)**—"De Causis Corruptarum Artium," *Opera* (Valencia, 1785; 8 v.), VI,
    8-242; see (iii.5) pp. 130-151. Science commended and hedged: *Vives: On*

26 *Education,* tr. Foster Watson (1913), 166-167. See Watson, *The Beginnings of the Teaching of Modern Subjects in England* (1909), 157 ff. Cf. La Primaudaye, *The French Academie* (tr. 1618), Pt. 1, 17.

Sobriety [in Italy followed] the Revival (32)—Jacob Burckhardt, *The Civilisation of the Renaissance in Italy* ([tr. 1878] 1928), 275-281. **Ascham . . . checked paganizing (34)**—*The Scholemaster* (1570), in *Works,* ed. J. A. Giles (3 v., 1865), III, 161. **Grammarians . . . had more to conquer (38)**— See, e.g., Aubrey G. F. Bell, *Francisco Sánchez, El Brocense* (1925), 45-55,

27 76. **Petrarch [on] action and contemplation (8)**—For the only extant "history" of this important controversy see the translator's introductory essay: Francis Petrarch, *The Life of Solitude,* tr. Jacob Zeitlin (Urbana, Ill., 1924), 25-70. Among late anomalies: Joseph Hall, "A Discourse of the Pleasure of Studie and Contemplation," *Epistles* (3 v., 1608), II, 137-144; or Walter Montagu (Catholic), "The Preheminence of a Contemplative Life," *Miscellanea Spiritualia,* Part I (1648), 398 ff. See notes to my page 72.

Ascham [on] dangerous . . . fashions (16)—*Scholemaster,* in *Works,* ed. Giles, III, e.g., 236. **Praising the abhorrent (20)**—See, on ancient paradoxes, A. S. Pease, "Things Without Honor," *Classical Philol.,* XXI (1926), 27 ff. Cp. Ortensio Lando, "Meglio è d'esser ignorante, che dotto" (iii), *Paradossi* (1564), 13-19. On Lando: Celeste Turner, "Anthony Mundy," *Univ. Cal. P. in Eng.,* II (1928), 1-234; see 90. W. G. Rice, "The *Paradossi* of Ortensio Lando," *Essays and St. in Eng. and Comp. Lit.,* Univ. Mich. (Ann Arbor, 1932), 59-74; Lando summarized, 60; see 67-70. **Notable humanists [and paradox] (26)**—See George Boas, *The Happy Beast in French Thought of the Seventeenth Century* (Baltimore, 1933), 10-17, n 39. **Pyrrhonism [and] paradox (32)**—See Pierre Villey, *Les Sources et l'Evolution des Essais de Montaigne* (Paris, 1933; 2 v.), II, 154 ff. Some Frenchmen take Agrippa lightly: Villey, I, 34-40; esp. II, 163-171, 167. **Man's inferiority to the animals (39)**—In John Woolton, *The Castell of Christians . . . beseeged* (1579), Sigs B3-C2 (with classical refs.), and esp. Godfrey Goodman, *The Fall of Man* (1616), 73-107, extended in *The Creatures Praysing God,* 1622. See Henri Busson, *La Pensée Religieuse Française de Charron à Pascal* (Paris, 1933), 295, 479; John Owen, *Italian Skeptics,* 177 and note; Herschel Baker, *The Dignity of Man* (Cambridge, U.S.A., 1947),

28 298; George Boas, *Happy Beast,* 24. **Erasmus . . . sciences are harmful (18)**—*In Praise of Folly,* tr. H. H. Hudson (Princeton, N. J., 1944), 70-79, xxiv, 43-44 ff., 105-124, 45. For bibliog. of classical paradox-hunters, see p. 2.

[Montaigne's] changes of philosophy (31)—Pierre Villey, *Les Sources . . . des Essais,* II, 321-390. Donald M. Frame, in *Word,* V (1949), 160-161, and see Frame, *Montaigne's Discovery of Man,* New York, 1955. B. R. Headstrom, "The Philosophy of Montaigne's Skepticism," *Personalist,* XII (1931), 262. On his precepts for education: Villey, II, 243-256; Ernest Marchand, "Montaigne and the Cult of Ignorance," *Romanic Rev.,* XXXVI

29 (1945), 275 ff. **Aristocratic academies [follow Montaigne] (8)**—See John W. Adamson, *Pioneers in Modern Education, 1600-1700,* 175-190.

Humility [in] self-knowledge (17)—*Essays* (II, 17), tr. E. G. Trechmann (2 v., 1935), II, 83-84; I, 536-537. **Sirens [offered] Ulysses . . . knowledge (28)**—*Ib.,* I, 482. See I, 494, 496; 440-441, 482; 193, 304. Montaigne not consistently a Pyrrhonist: Villey, II, 142, 152.

Cries of protest [follow Montaigne] (37)—See George Boas, *Happy Beast,* 64-117. **Erasmus had agreed [in deflating Stoics] (40)**—*In Praise of*

30 *Folly,* tr. Hudson, 14; Villey, II, 211-215. **Nature would [teach us to die]**
(2)—Montaigne, *Essays,* tr. Trechmann, II, 511-512. **Man's indignity . . .**
depravity (6)—*Ib.,* I, 440-441; II, 53. Cp. II, 257-272, 267. **Arrogance [in]**
anthropocentric [world] (15)—I, 413, 441; II, 369; I, 533. See Robert
Hoopes, "Fideism and Skepticism," *HLQ,* XIV (1951), 319 ff., esp. 343 ff.
Protestantism sanctified . . . visible activity (33)—See R. Newton Flew,
The Idea of Perfection in Christian Theology (Oxford, 1934), 251-257; cp.
230, 253. **Greville began (39)**—On his "skepticism": George T. Buckley,
Atheism, 114-117, esp. 116; Herschel Baker, *The Wars of Truth* (Cam-

31 bridge, U.S.A., 1952), 152. **Stanza 73 assumed . . . Bacon (16)**—Thus
Geoffrey Bullough, "Bacon and the Defence of Learning," *Seventeenth
Century St. [for] Grierson* (1938), 5; and Fulke Greville, Lord Brooke,
Poems and Dramas, ed. G. Bullough (2 v., 1938), I, 52-55, 291-310.

32 **Doctrine [of] Paracelsus . . . Bacon (4)**—See, e.g., Hiram Haydn, *The
Counter-Renaissance,* 178, 190, 248; or Robert Sencourt, *Outflying Philos-
ophy,* 148-149. **Greville [urged] Bernard's rule (25)**—*Treatie of Humane
Learning,* in *Poems,* ed. Bullough, I, 190.

33 **[Bacon] conceded [self-]knowledge [little] (5)**—*De Aug.,* in *Works,* ed.
James Spedding *et al.* (Boston, 1861-; 15 v.), IX, 14. Cp. Wilhelm Richter,
"Francis Bacon," *Archiv f. Kulturgeschichte,* XVIII (1928), 168 ff. See
Bacon, *Works,* VI, 134; cp. XIII, 147 (xxvi—Man is the center of the world).
He praised ethics (e.g., VI, 162, 314-347); but religion obviated much ethi-
cal inquiry: VI, 314; cp. 395. See Fulton H. Anderson, *The Philosophy of
Francis Bacon* (Chicago, 1948), 165; Adolfo Levi, *Il Pensiero di Francesco
Bacone* (Torino, 1925), 311.

34 **Mind studying mind . . . cobwebs (2)**—*Works,* VI, 122, 131-132. [Mathe-
matically] **better advised naturalists (3)**—See Ernst Cassirer, "On the
Originality of the Renaissance," *JHI,* IV (1943), 49-56. **Projected a "sum-
mary Philosophy" (7)**—*Adv. of L., Works,* VI, 217. See William R. Sorley,
A Hist. of English Philosophy (1920), 22. For Bacon's "metaphysics": *N. O.,
Works,* VIII, 177-178. See Charles M. Coffin, *John Donne and the New
Philosophy,* 22; F. H. Anderson, *Philosophy of Bacon,* 194. For his psy-
chology: *Adv. of L., Works,* VI, 260-261. His mythography: *De Sap. Vet.,
Works,* e.g., XIII, 95; esp. VII, 446. **Made use of some skepticism (18)**—
N. O., VIII, 97-98, 107, 158, 43-45, esp. 52; cp. VI, 276. See Walter Frost,
Bacon und die Naturphilosophie (München, 1927), 65. F. H. Anderson,
"Bacon on Platonism," *UTQ,* XI (1941), 161, and *Philosophy of Bacon,* 279.
Paul H. Kocher, *Science and Religion, etc.* (1953), 53-54. Esp. Moody E.
Prior, "Bacon's Man of Science," *JHI,* XV (1954), 348 ff.
Naturalists . . . could distinguish . . . philosophy and divinity (40)—

35 Adolfo Levi, *Il Pensiero di Bacone,* 56. **[Soul as topic] surrendered to
divines (8)**—Bacon, *Works,* ed. Spedding, VI, 254; esp. IX, 49. Bacon's
Anglican peacemaking deplored subtleties: "Of Unity in Religion," *Essays,*
in *Works,* XII, 89, and *Pacification,* in *Letters and Life,* ed. James Spedding
(7 v., 1861), III, 118-119. See Wilbur K. Jordan, *Toleration,* II, 461. **Paracelsians . . . science out of Holy Writ (18)**—*Adv. of L., Works,* VI, 214,
254-257, 405; *Val. Term.,* VI, 29; *N. O.,* VIII, 91. Contrast VIII, 33-34. See
Levi, 200. **Left the rest to faith (28)**—*Adv. of L.,* VI, 212; *Val. Term.,* VI,
29; *N. O.,* VIII, 35, 478. See S. L. Bethell, *The Cultural Revolution of the
Seventeenth Century* (New York, 1951), 62-64.
Religion . . . commended . . . natural [science] (32)—*Filum Lab.,* VI,
421-423; *N. O.,* VIII, 126. **Religion . . . a mean (35)**—*Works,* ed. Sped-

PAGE

36   ding, IX, 162-163; XIV, 94. **Bacon discouraged . . . final causes (5)**—
VIII, 81, 168, esp. 510. See William R. Sorley, *Hist. of Eng. Phil.*, 27;
Adolfo Levi, *Il Pensiero di Bacone*, 260; Fulton H. Anderson, *Phil. of
Bacon*, 208. Cp. Thomas Hobbes, *Decam. Phys.*, in *English Works*, ed.
Sir Thomas Molesworth (11 v., 1839-), VII, 82. Contrast René Descartes,
The Method, Meditations, and Philosophy ("Principles," xxviii), ed. Frank
Sewall and John Vetch (1901), 311-312. See Edwin A. Burtt, *The Meta-
physical Foundations of Modern Science* (1927), 9. Divinity and "scientific"
argument from design: see, e.g., Thomas Adams, *Workes* (1629), 1118, 1138.
Cp. Bacon, "Of Atheism," *Works*, XII, 132; *Med. Sac.*, XIV, 93; *Adv. of L.*,
VI, 96-97. **Natural philosophers [needed] teleology (23)**—Henry More,
Antidote Against Atheism (i-xii), in *Philosophical Writings* (1712), 37-97.
Cp. Ralph Cudworth, *True Intellectual System*, ed. Thomas Birch (4 v.,
1820), III, 310, and John Wilkins, *A Discourse Concerning the Beauty of
Providence* ([1649] 1672), 6, 87, etc. See Robert McRae, "Final Causes in
the Age of Reason," *UTQ*, XIX (1950), 247 ff.; esp. Herschel Baker, "The
Doctrine of Providence," *The Wars of Truth* (1952), 12-25. **Four causes
37   . . . a definition (1)**—*Val. Term.*, *Works*, ed. Spedding, VI, 63, cp. 220,
and *N. O.*, VIII, 168-169, 205, esp. 485. On Bacon's theory of forms; Spedding, ed. *Works*, I, 68 ff.; W. R. Sorley, *Hist. of Eng. Phil.*, 27-28. A. E.
Taylor, *Francis Bacon: Proc. Brit. Acad.* (1927), 21. William M. Dickie,
"'Form' and 'Simple Nature' in Bacon's Philosophy," *Monist*, XXXIII
(1923), 428 ff. Levi, 248 ff. Ernst Cassirer, *Das Erkenntnis-problem . . .
der neuern Zeit* (3 v., 1922), II, 11-28. **Science . . . said nothing [of God's
nature] (17)**—Bacon, *Adv. of L.*, *Works*, VI, 212. On Pentheus: *De Sap.
Vet.*, XIII, 108-109.

[Bacon's religious] defense of learning (24)—*Works*, VI, 30-31. He
counters the obscurantists' texts: VI, 91-97. Cp. Samuel Daniel, *Muso-
philus*, in *Poetical Works* (2 v., 1718), II, 386. See G. Bullough, "Bacon
and the Defence of Learning," *Seventeenth Century St. [for] Grierson*
(1938), 1 ff. Adam's "scientific" animal-naming: Bacon, *Works*, VI, 30, 138,
310; VIII, 35. Cp. Pierre de la Primaudaye, *The French Academie* (1618
tr.), Pt. II, 343 (text blesses natural philosophy). John Salkeld (dedicates
to Bacon), *A Treatise of Paradise* (1617), 79. Thomas Adams, *Workes*
(1629), 1132. Alexander Ross (ded. to Bacon), *An Exposition . . . of Genesis* (1626), 21. Elias Ashmole, *Theatrum Chemicum Britannicum* (1652),
445-446. Sir Henry Vane, *The Retired Mans Meditations* (1655), 53. John
Lightfoot, *Whole Works* (13 v., 1822-), VII, 20-21. Samuel Pordage, *Mun-
dorum Explicatio* (1661), 59. An important precedent for this divinity:
38   Eusebius, *Prep. Ev.* xi.6, ed. E. H. Gifford (4 v., 1903), III (2), 553. **Elaboration on Proverbs (11)**—Bacon, *Val. Term.*, *Works*, VI, 31; cp. *Paradise
Lost* VIII.78.

Only . . . angels to be spectators (17)—VI, 314; see Adolfo Levi, *Il
Pensiero di Bacone*, 287. **[No risk in] charity of works (19)**—*Val. Term.*,
Works, ed. Spedding, VI, 28; *Essays*, XII, 118; *N. O.*, VIII, 36. **A critic of
the Royal Society (26)**—Richard Graham, Viscount Preston, "The Virtu-
39   oso," *The Moral State of England* (1670), 46. On Baconianism thus satirized: R. C. Cochrane, in *DA*, XIV (1954), 107. **Bacon phrased . . . rule
[of action] (3)**—*Works*, VI, 28, 134; cp. VIII, 48.

Parsons . . . "weakly afraid" (8)—VI, 30-31, 421; VIII, 125-126. **Science
. . . handmaid of divinity (17)**—John Calvin, *The Institution of Christian*

PAGE

39 *Religion* (I.5.2), tr. Thomas Norton (1634), 9. The handmaid of humanity: *Vives: On Education* [*De Trad. Disc.*], tr. Foster Watson (1913), 166-167. On early humanists' tolerance of science: Lynn Thorndike, *Magic and Science*, IV, 386-412. See esp. Paul H. Kocher, *Science and Religion, etc.* (1953), 1-62, esp. 64-65 (and see 146 ff.); repr. from *HLQ*, XV (1951), 101 ff.

Satirists . . . ridiculed (29)—See W. E. Houghton, "The English Virtuoso," *JHI*, III (1942), 54-55; cp. Richard Graham, cited above. **Preachers needed sermon-illustrations (32)**—Nicholas Bifield, *The Rule of Faith* (1626), 149-202. Moralizing on the creatures: John Day, "God's Workes," *Day's Dyall* (1614), 79 ff. Thomas Taylor, *Meditations, from the Creatures,* 1629. William Evans, *A Translation of the Book of Nature into the Use of Grace*, 1633. William Hodson, *The Divine Cosmographer* (1640), 59-61
40 (Adam's animal-naming). More pulpit defense of natural science: Thomas Tymme, *A Dialogue Philosophicall* (1612), Pref., and 59 ff., Humphrey Sydenham, *Five Sermons* ([1626] 1636), 30-31. Thomas Adams, *Workes* (1629), 252-256, esp. 253; and William Burton, *The Rowsing of the Sluggard* ([1595] 1634), 21-22. William Sclater, *A Key to [Romanes], the Key of Scripture* (1611), 107. Paul Baynes, *A Comm. upon . . . , Col* (1635), 85-87 ff., 333. George Swinnock, *The Christian Mans Calling*, in *Works*, (5 v., 1868), II, 415-416. **Fall . . . darkened . . . senses least (15)**—See, e.g., John Abernethy, *A Christian and Heavenly Treatise*, ch. ii ([1615] 1630), 19. **God left [us] the world (21)**—John Wilkins, *New Planet*, Part II of *The Discovery of a New World . . . in the Moon* ([1638] 1640), 234 ff. On Wilkins, note Houghton, "English Virtuoso," *JHI*, III (1942), 202.

Knowledge is as wind (33)—*Paradise Lost* VII.130; I Cor. viii:1. Cp. John Boys (Anglican), *Workes* (1622), 206-207. **Academic question [of] *Nutzen***
41 **[and] *Wahrheit* (1)**—See, for the latter, Kuno Fischer, *Francis Bacon of Verulam* (tr. 1857), 37-40; Spedding, ed. Bacon, *Letters and Life*, I, 4; Adolfo Levi, *Il Pensiero di Bacone*, 166-169. For the former: E. L. Schaub, "Francis Bacon and the Modern Spirit," *Monist*, XL (1930), 416 ff., and others. On, *i.a.*, this argument: B. Farrington, "On Misunderstanding . . . Bacon," *Essays [for] Charles Singer*, ed. E. A. Underwood (2 v., 1953), I, 439 ff. **Scientia inflat (15)**—*Val. Term.*, *Works,* ed. Spedding, VI, 33, *Adv. of L.*, VI, 92; cp. *N. O.,* VIII, 156-157. **[Bacon's] contemporaries could understand (17)**—See, e.g., Robert Bolton, Lenten Serm. on I Cor. 1:26, in *Of the Foure Last Things* ([1632] 1639); John Boys, *Workes* (1622), 277, 785, etc.; Robert Greville, Lord Brooke, *The Nature of Truth* (1640), 142-143.

Ben Jonson remarked [of *N. O.*] (23)—*Discoveries*, in *Works* (10 v., 1925-), VIII, 592. **Three Vanities in studies (32)**—Bacon, *Adv. of L.*, *Works*, ed. Spedding, VI, 117 ff. On Bacon and "delicate" learning: M. W. Croll, "Attic Prose," *Schelling Anniv. Papers* (New York, 1923), 117 ff.
42 **Bacon's "fantastic" learning (1)**—*Adv. of L.*, VI, 125-135; cp. VIII, 91-97, and Idols of the Theatre, VIII, 78. See Levi, 367. **Bacon . . and . . . encyclopedists (13)**—A. E. Taylor, *Francis Bacon: Proc. Brit. Acad.* (1927), 8, and W. K. Whitaker, diss., Stanford Univ. *Abstracts*, VIII (1932), 49-52. **Perfect circles . . . regularity (18)**—*Adv. of L.*, *Works*, VI, 277; *N. O.,* VIII, 79, 124-125, 131. See F. H. Anderson, "Bacon on Platonism," *UTQ*, XI (1941), 161.

[Bacon's] disciples (28)—See R. F. Jones, *Ancients and Moderns: Washington Univ. St. in Lang. and Lit.*, No. 6 (St. Louis, 1935), e.g., 88.

CHAPTER II

PAGE
43   [Sorcery in] a studied definition of curiosity (8)—See, e.g., Donne's, or see François de la Mothe le Vayer, "De la Curiosité," Œuvres (Paris, 1662; 2 v.), II, 464. Magi . . . figures in the past (19)—Eliza M. Butler, The Myth of the Magus (Cambridge, 1948), 143. For bibliog. of writings for and against Paracelsus and other magi: John Webster, The Displaying of Supposed Witchcraft (1677), 8 ff. Mersenne [attacked] Fludd (23)—Arthur E. Waite, The Real Hist. of the Rosicrucians (1887), 289-294; James B. Craven, Dr. Robert Fludd (1902), 130-131, 204-205; Walter Pagel, "Religious Motives," Bull. Inst. Hist. Medicine, III (1935), 299-304. Northumberland . . . his three magi (29)—See Muriel C. Bradbrook, The School of Night (Cambridge, 1936), 10. Francis Osborn recalled (30)—"Of Studies,"
44   Advice to a Son, in Works ([1656-] 1689), 5. A compendious exposure (7)—James Mason, The Anatomie of Sorcerie, 1612.
      Witchcraft . . . not a forbidden knowledge (12)—Thus G. L. Kittredge, Witchcraft in Old and New England (1929), 226. An abundant literature [on witchcraft] (14)—Bibliog.: see these notes, and Douglas Bush, English Literature, etc., 453-454. For primary materials: Montague Summers, Hist. of Witchcraft and Demonology (1926), 316 ff., esp. 330-333. Fear . . . punished . . . witches (16)—Kittredge, 4; Christina Hole, Witchcraft in England (London, 1945), 33. On witches and nature cults: Margaret A. Murray, The Witch-Cult in Western Europe (Oxford, 1921), e.g., 13; Hole, 20-23; Philip W. Sergeant, Witches and Warlocks (London, 1936), 170. On witches and devil-worship: Summers, 1-50; Jules Michelet, Satanism and Witchcraft (New York, tr. 1939), e.g., 3-7. Dee lived quietly . . . except (23)—Charlotte Fell Smith, John Dee (1909), 14-15, 219; Kittredge, 254, 318; Sergeant, 183-227; S. C. McCullough, "John Dee, etc.," So. Atlantic Qu., L (1951), 72 ff., see 74-75. Simon Reade . . . Forman . . . arrests (27)—H. W. Herrington, "Witchcraft and Magic in the Elizabethan Drama," Jour. Am. Folk-Lore, XXXII (1919), 468. Witches [made only] implicit contract (39)—Kittredge, 242; see 316-319 (on Lambe).
45   Faustus . . . asked [and received] un-Ptolemaic information (24)—F. R. Johnson, "Marlowe's Astronomy and Renaissance Skepticism," ELH, XIII (1946), 247. On the Faust of the Prologue and of the pact: Harry
46   Levin, The Overreacher (Cambridge, U.S.A., 1952), 111-112, 119. [Marlowe's] elaborately orthodox fiction (7)—Paul H. Kocher, Christopher Marlowe (Chapel Hill, N. C., 1946), 138-172, esp. 138, 170; and Kocher, "Christopher Marlowe," UTQ, XVII (1948), 115. Marlowe's heterodoxy denied (but hardly disproved): M. Barrington, "Marlowe's Alleged Atheism," N & Q, CXCV (1950), 260.
      Milton's . . . opinion of [sorcery] conjecture (9)—Studied: Wallace Notestein, A Hist. of Witchcraft in England (1911), 248; R. Trevor Davies, Four Centuries of Witch-Beliefs (London, 1947), 170-172. See Milton, C. D., Works (18 v., 1931-), XVII, 133 (14), and 149 (14)-151. Note "sorcery," mentioned, in Tetra., IV, 151 (22). For witchcraft seriously urged as ground for divorce: Henry C. Lea and Arthur C. Howland, Materials Toward a Hist. of Witchcraft (3 v., 1939), II, 929. See I, 68-110; II, 462, 973, 993, on the knowledge and power of fallen angels. Cp. Milton, C. D., Works, XV, 107 (20)-111. On details of demonology in P. L.: W. B. Hunter, "Milton on the Nature of Man," Vanderbilt Univ. Diss. Summary (Nashville, Tenn., 1946), 17-18; "Eve's Demonic Dream," HLQ, XIII (1946), 263; Kester Svendsen, "Milton and Medical Lore," Bull. Inst. Hist. Medicine, XIII (1943), 170-171. Witch- [and heresy-] hunters multiplied (37)—See

46 G. L. Kittredge, *Witchcraft*, 371. **Quakers [and witch-] suspicion (40)**—
47 Notestein, 240 n, and others mentioned in notes to my page 150. **John Gaule
. . . ended . . . Hopkins (2)**—Sergeant, 103; Wickwar, 216; Kittredge,
331; Notestein, 180-187. Hopkins and the Presbyterians: Montague Summers, *The Discovery of Witches: A Study of Master Matthew Hopkins*
(1928), 23, 43-46.

   Elizabeth encouraged [alchemists] (19)—See editor's introduction, Ben
Jonson, *The Alchemist*, ed. C. M. Hathaway, Jr. (1903), 15-90. For some
unsympathetic satirists: Lothar Nowak, *Die Alchemie und die Alchemisten
in der englischen Literatur* (Breslau, 1934), 44-76. Alchemists cozeners, not
wizards: see Herrington, in *Jour. Am. Folk-Lore*, XXXII (1919), 479. On
alchemy as a form of curiosity: Paul H. Kocher, *Science and Religion, etc.*
(1953), 66. **Paracelsus . . . remembered (23)**—For a typical memoir:
Thomas Fuller, "Life of Paracelsus," *Holy State* (ii.3), ed. Walten (1938),
56-60. William Foster, *A Sponge to Wipe Away the Weapon-Salve* (1631), 15.
On the myth: Henry M. Pachter, *Paracelsus* (New York, 1951), 1-16; also
91-97 *(Wanderjahr)*. Paracelsus "pretended" alchemy: see Lynn Thorndike,
Magic and Science, IV, 644-645. On the alchemists' claims to virtue, note
Robert Sencourt, *Outflying Philosophy*, 152, **Patrick Scot [preached to]
"philosophers" (32)**—Scot, *The Tillage of Light* (1623), 21, 2-5, 15, 33, 48-
48 49. **Alchemists in the Royal Society (13)**—See L. T. More, "Boyle as an Alchemist," *JHI*, II (1941), 61 ff.

   Spiritual alchemy . . . of the Cabala (18)—Joseph L. Blau, *The Christian Interpretation of the Cabala* (New York, 1944), 51. F. Sherwood Taylor, *The Alchemists* (New York, 1949), 213-230. **Cabalistic studies . . .
misused for prophecy (24)**—Henry Howard, Earl of Northampton, *A Defensative Against the Poison of Supposed Prophesies* ([1583] 1620), 25 ff.;
John Harvey, *A Discoursive Probleme concerning Prophesies* (1588), 14-17;
note the political motive, 131-132. Other objections to Jewish learning:
Henoch Clapham, *Ælohin-triune* (1601), Ep. Ded., Sig A3; John Lightfoot,
Works (13 v., 1822-), IV, 14-18. **Rosicrucianism . . . would reform (33)**—
See Robert Burton, *Anatomy*, ed. Shilleto, I, 107-108, 135. Cp. Arthur E.
Waite, *The Occult Sciences* ([1891] 1923), 201, and *The Real Hist. of the
Rosicrucians*, 389; Robert A. Vaughan, *Hours with the Mystics*, II, 105.
Douglas Bush, *English Literature, etc.*, 252. Wilhelm Struck, *Der Einfluss
Jakob Böhmes* (Berlin, 1936), 148. The new alchemy a sanctified science:
John Done, *Polydoron* (1631), 85; John Heydon, *The English Physitians
49 Guide* (1662), Pref.; Waite, *Rosicrucians*, 315-386. Contrast Samuel Butler,
Characters, ed. A. R. Waller (1908), 97-108, esp. 97-98; 208; and John Hales,
"Concerning the Weapon-Salve," *Golden Remains* ([1659] 1688), 356 ff.

   [Milton] may have [read] Fludd and Boehme (18)—Margaret Bailey,
Milton and Jakob Boehme (1924), and Wilhelm Struck, *Der Einfluss Jakob
Böhmes*, 237 n. Denis Saurat, *Milton, Man and Thinker* ([1925] 1944),
248-267, esp. 261 ff. **Thomas Vaughan . . . lamented (38)**—Vaughan,
Magia Adamica (1650), 3. Cp. Elizabeth Holmes, *Henry Vaughan and the
Hermetic Philosophy* (Oxford, 1923), 27. R. B., *The Difference betweene
the auncient physicke and the latter*, 1585.

50   **[Occultist on] abuses in professions, arts (6)**—Samuel Pordage, *Mun-
dorum Explicatio* (1661), 89 ff., 108 ff., 283, 285, 291.

   The sermons of Elizabeth's time [against] Doomsday [prophets] (28)—
See Paul H. Kocher, *Science and Religion, etc.* (1953), 76-80, esp. 79. For
the seventeenth century: Victor Harris, *All Coherence Gone* (Chicago,
1949), 113-118, 166, and notes on 229-230. Against the Judgment- and

PAGE

50 Advent-daters: George Benson, *Sermons* ([May 7,] 1609), 59-60; William
    Sclater, *Exp. on Thess.* (1619), on v:1-2, esp. pp. 396-397; Owen Felltham,
    "Progression," *Resolves* ([?1623] 1840), 113; Richard Farmer, *A* [*Pauls
    Crosse*] *Sermon* (1629), 12; John Swan, *Speculum Mundi* (1635), 334-353;
    Sir Thomas Browne, *V. E.* (vi, 1), in *Works*, ed. Keynes (6 v., 1928-), III,
    172-173; esp. Thomas Johnston, *Christs Watch-word* (1630), 82-83. **New
    millenaries joined (35)**—I.e., against exact prediction —of the Judgment:
    e.g., Thomas Brightman, *Rev. of the Apoc.*, in *Workes* (1644), 825; Na-
    thaniel Homes, *Miscellanea* (?1666), 11; —of the Advent: e.g., George Hake-
    will, *Apologie* IV.xii.6 ([1627] 1635), 558-559; Robert Maton, *Israels Re-
    demption Redeemed* (1646), 287; but contrast Sir Henry Finch, *Restaura-
    tion* (1621), 99, and Thomas Goodwin, *A Glimpse of Sions Glory* (1641), 32,
    both computing to 1650. Against such arithmetic: e.g., Edmund Calamy,

51 *Sermon* [1662], in *An Exact Collection of Farewel Sermons* (1662), 30. **One
    scholarly millenarian (2)**—I.e., John Henry Alsted, *The Beloved City*, tr.
    W. Burton (1642), 77-79. On the millenarians: D. B. Robertson, *Religious
    Foundations, etc.* (1951), 44-48; Gertrude Huehns, *Antinomianism, etc.*
    (1952), 127-134. **"Fierce, unnatural zeal" [of millenarians] (15)**—Ephraim
    Pagitt, *Heresiography* ([1645] 1647), 132. Samuel Butler, *Characters*, ed.
    Waller, 45. **Tom Fuller ["predicted"] Advent (19)**—*Collected Sermons*
    (2 v., 1891), II, 235-236. Cp. Joseph Hall, *The Revelation Unrevealed*
    (1654), in *Works* (12 v., 1837), VIII, 506-560.
        Political prophecy [in the manner of] Geoffrey (35)—See Rupert Taylor,
    The Political Prophecy in England (1911), 83-92, 100-107. Madeleine H.
    Dods, "Political Prophecies in the Reign of Henry VIII," *MLR*, XI (1916),
    276 ff. Douglas Bush, *English Literature, etc.*, 50. On prophets: G. L. Kitt-
    redge, *Witchcraft*, 226; S. V. Larkey, "Astrology and [Elizabethan] Politics,"

52 *Bull. Inst. Hist. Medicine*, III (1935), 171-186. On Vavasour Powell:
    Henry W. Clark, *Hist. of English Nonconformity* (2 v., 1911-), I, 381. On
    Venner: Charles E. Whiting, *Puritanism, 1660-1688*, 238-239. On Eleanor
    Davies: Theodore Spencer, "The History of an Unfortunate Lady," *Har-
    vard St. . . . in Philol. and Lit.*, XX (1938), 50. For political animus
    against astrology: William Westerman, *The Faithfull Subject* (1608), 25-26.
    "Curiosity" . . . the root of all divination (17)—Henry Howard, *Defensa-
    tive* ([1583] 1620), Ep. Ded. and 18-25; on political motive, note 1583 ed.,
    t-p. In Francis Coxe, *Wickednesse of magicall sciences* [1561], e.g., Sigs
    A6-A6^{vo}, the prophets are the only tangible magicians.
        "Lyly's . . . approved, etc." (30)—*The Wizard Unvisor'd* (1652), in
    Fugitive Tracts, 2d Series, ed. Henry Huth, 2 v., 1875. Cp. John Melton,
    Astrologaster (1620), 53 (women as clients). John Gadbury, *A Collection of
    Nativities* (1662), Pref., defends astrology against the "politic" critics,
    among others. Astrology weakens civil government: thus Edward Water-
    house, *Apologie for Learning* (1653), 30 ff. **Independency [encouraged] sci-
    ence (35)**—So George Rosen, "Left-Wing Puritanism and Science," *Bull.
    Inst. Hist. Medicine*, XV (1944), 375 ff. **Robert Gell . . . taught . . . More
    (38)**—See Geoffrey Bullough, ed. *Philosophical Poems of Henry More*

53 (Manchester, 1931), xv. **Theosophy . . . counted as . . . heresy (1)**—See
    Nathaniel Homes, *Dæmonologie, and Theologie* (1650), 16, 33-34, 36, 107,
    134, etc. **Lilly recorded the political issue (5)**—*The Lives of . . . Elias
    Ashmole, . . . and Mr. William Lilly, Written by Themselves* (1774), 34,
    83-86, 122, 155.
        Arguments [against astrology] (17)—For bibliog. of contemporary writ-

53   ings against astrology: Thomas Hall, *An Exp. [of] Amos* (1661), 72-73. For
     some modern studies of Renaissance astrology: Johnstone Parr, *Tambur-
     laine's Malady, etc.* (University, Ala., 1953), vii. See Don C.
     Allen, *The Star-Crossed Renaissance*, Durham, N. C., 1941; and Paul H.
     Kocher, *Science and Religion, etc.* (1953), 211-224. [Some, technical,] old as Cicero
     (24)—Theodore O. Wedel, *The Medieval Attitude Toward Astrology:
     Yale St. in Eng.*, No. 60 (1920), 1-24. Lynn Thorndike, *Magic and Science*,
     I, 111-114, 306, etc. C. Camden, Jr., "Astrology in Shakespeare's Day," *Isis*,
     XIX (1933), 26 ff. Argument from current theology: see Hall, 73; John
     Robinson, *Essayes* ([1625] 1638), 30-31; John Raunce, *Astrologia Accusata*
     (1650), 33; George Carleton, *Astrologomania* ([1623] 1651), 181; William
     Bridge, *Scripture Light*, in *Works* (5 v., 1845), I, 438-440. Cp. Sir Christo-
     pher Heydon; *A Defence of Judiciall Astrologie* (1603), 31-32, 58 (chs. i
     and ii entire); Robert Gell, *Stella Nova* (1649), 17-18.

54   Astrologers' premise, [not conclusion, granted] (10)—Allowing stellar
     influence, but not astrology: e.g., Owen Felltham, "Of Divination," *Resolves*
     ([?1623] 1840), 216-217. See Parr, viii-ix. On astrologers: Milton, *Apol. for
     Sm.* and *C. D.*, *Works* (18 v., 1931-), III, 342 (2) ff., 344 (7); XVII, 149-151,
     esp. 151 (6-17). Satan can predict what he plans: thus, e.g., George Gifford,
     A Dialogue Concerning Witches (1593), Sh. Assoc. Facs., No. 1 (1931), Sig
     F; and Henry Howard, *Defensative* (1620 ed.), 86. Confidently . . . the
     satirists (24)—For examples of popular ridicule: Carrol Camden, Jr.,
     "Elizabethan Almanacs and Prognostications," *The Library*, Ser. 4, XII
     (1932), 100-108. Astrology . . . invented by the devil (25)—George Carle-
     ton, *Astrologomania* (1651 ed.), 117 ff.; John Raunce, *Astrologia Accusata*
     (1650), 21 ff. On *sapiens dominabitur astris*: Wedel, 136; cp. John Geree,
     Astrologo-Mastix (1646), Arg. 4. [Astrologers step] "into the chair of God"
     (39)—William Bridge, *Works* (1845 ed.), I, 440; cp. Michael Hudson, *The
     Divine Right of Government* (1647), 51; John Chamber, *A Treatise against
     Judicial Astrologie* (1601), 9, 77, 100; Archbishop George Abbot, *Explicatio*,
     in *Sex Illustrium Quæstionum* ([1597] 1616), 80-104; Geree, 2, Arg. 2; Na-
     thaniel Homes, *Dæmonologie* (1650), 134; Barten Holyday, *Motives to a
     Good Life* (1657), 128 ff.

55   [Astrology] invited [the help of] devils (2)— Chamber, 94-95; Carleton,
     32-36, 56-57, Geree, 7; Bridge, I, 437; Homes, 143 ff.; Raunce, 3, 18 ff.; John
     Gaule, *Mag-Astro-Mancer* (1652), 53 ff. The possibility conceded: Robert
     Gell, *Stella Nova* (1649), 18 ff. A convert . . . wrote of himself (20)—
     John Raunce, *Astrologia Accusata*, Pref., and 19; cf., for thought and
     phrase, George Carleton, *Astrologomania*, 184-186; see Pref., Sig A3b; and
     James I, *Dæmonologie* I.iii (1597), 10-11.
     Milton [on astrology] exonerated . . . astronomy (35)—*C. D.*, *Works*
     (1931-), XVII, 151 (18). Cp. Chamber, 100; Carleton, 36; George Abbot, 85;
     Bridge, 438; Gaule, Pref., "To the Sober . . . Astronomers"; Nicholas Bil-
     lingsley, *A Treasury of Divine Raptures* (1667), Pt. 1, 32. See Paul H.
     Kocher, *Science and Religion, etc.*, 211 ff., and *HLQ*, XV (1951), 108-109.
     [On] Tycho's [curious] measurement (39)—Nicholas Gibbens, *Questions
     and Disputations* (1601), 27-28; W. B., *Philosophers Banquet* (1633), 259;
     David Person, *Varieties* (1635), IV, sec. 2; Robert Bolton, *Last Things*
     ([1632] 1639), 121; Barten Holyday, *A Survey of the World* (1641), 46.

56   Humanistic argument against astrologers: Chamber, 102; Carleton, 129.
     John Gaule . . . left . . . some . . . humanism (12)—Gaule, *Practique
     Theories* (1629), 47-48; cp. his *Mag-Astro-Mancer* (1652), 51-55.

PAGE

56   Artists . . . replied with [Bacon's] humility (30)—See, e.g., Elias Ashmole, *Theatrum Chemicum Britannicum* (1652), 444; Robert Gell, *Stella
Nova* (1649), 18 ff.; Sir Christopher Heydon, *Defence of Astrologie*, Pref.,
and ch. ii; Robert Pricket, *Times Anatomie* (1606), Pref.; John Gadbury,
57   *A Collection of Nativities* (1662), Pref. (Bacon cited). Some "Baconianism"
before Bacon: Heydon, 2-5, and chs. i, ii, x; and *passim;* Francis R. Johnson, *Astronomical Thought in Renaissance England*, Baltimore, Md., 1937.
No excess [possible in natural study] (12)—Ashmole, *Theatrum*, 446. For
other citations of Bacon, see, e.g., 444.

The ill success of [Browne's] critics in [agreeing] (24)—For a review
of the most important before 1931: Olivier Leroy, *Le Chevalier Thomas
Browne* (Paris, 1931), 321-356. On Browne's Hermetic occultism: Edmund
Gosse, *Sir Thomas Browne* (1905), 38 ff., 123 ff. His almost ecstatic religion:
Robert Sencourt (ps.), *Outflying Philosophy* ([Hildesheim], 1924), 104, but
see 166-167. His occultism restricted: Leroy, 163, 214, and Sir Leslie Stephen, *Hours in a Library* (3 v., 1899), I, 269-280. Some later statements on
his "mysticism": Georg Ockerhausen, *Rationalismus, usw.* (Marburg a.
Lahn, 1930), 25-56; William P. Dunn, *Sir Thomas Browne*, 2d ed. (Minne-
apolis, 1950), 20-24, 43, 81-82, 114-122, 132, etc.; Jeremiah S. Finch, *Sir
Thomas Browne* (New York, 1950), 211-213, 272-273. His experiments:
G. K. Chalmers, Harvard diss. summary, "Sir Thomas Browne, True Scien-
tist," *Osiris*, II (1936), 28 ff.; Charles Whibley, *Essays in Biography* (1913),
289; J. Milsand, "Thomas Browne," *Rev. de Deux Mondes*, No. 2, 1858, 676.
Bacon and Browne (esp. *V. E.*): A. C. Howell, in *SP*, XXII (1925), 61;
Alwin Thaler, *ib.*, XXVIII (1931), 87 ff.; W. P. Dunn, *Browne*, 1st ed.
(1926), 15; and see M. E. Prior, in *PQ*, XI (1932), 186-187, and George
Gordon, "Sir Thomas Browne," *The Lives of Authors* (London, 1950), 101.
Cp. Ziegler, 14, and Merton, cited below, 20-23; Dunn, *Browne*, 2d ed., 17,
and Finch, 137, 143-144. His "rhetorical" religion: Dewey K. Ziegler, *In
58   Divided and Distinguished Worlds*, Cambridge, U.S.A., 1943. The vaga-
bondage of his *Cyrus:* Llewellyn Powys, "The Quincuncial Doctor," *Sat.
Rev. of Lit.*, June 4, 1932, 765; J. S. Finch, "Sir Thomas Browne and the
Quincunx," *SP*, XXXVII (1940), 282; Leroy, 364; Dunn (1926), 129 and
(1950), 136. His science limited by lyricism, etc.: Egon S. Merton, *Science
and Imagination in Sir Thomas Browne* (New York, 1949), 4-5, 7-11; Finch,
204. New studies [do] justice to [his] intuitive bent (14)—Esp. Dunn's
second edition. With places already cited, including 81-82, 114-120, see
77-139. G. K. Chalmers, "That Universal and Publick Manuscript," *Va.
Qu. Rev.*, XXVI (1950), 416-420. Note Marjorie H. Nicolson, *The Breaking
of the Circle* (Evanston, Ill., 1950), 113.

Browne . . . and young Dee (25)—See Olivier Leroy, *Browne*, 68-70;
J. S. Finch, *Browne*, 211-213. On the spirit of his religious writings, note
Walter Pater, in *Macmillan's Magazine*, XIV (1886), 10, and *Appreciations*
(1890), 140.

59   He conceded [something to] tradition (13)—Browne, *Vulgar Errors*, in
Works, ed. Geoffrey Keynes (6 v., 1926-), II, 51, cp. 40. See Egon S. Merton,
Science and Imagination, 20 ff., repr. from *Jour. Hist. Medicine*, III (1948),
218-219, on Browne's limited skepticism. Browne "took Montaigne" for a
model (15)—Thus Thomas Keck, *Annotations upon 'Religio Medici'*
(1656), 196-197 and elsewhere. See Louis I. Bredvold, *Milieu of John Dryden*, 40-46; Whyte, qu. by Olivier Leroy, *Browne*, 321. Browne's *hoc scio:
V. E.*, *Works*, II, 39, 40; see 56-64 for some dispensable authors. He would
60   not . . . weep over . . . the Vatican (1)—II, 32-33. See Sir Kenelm

60 Digby's comment, *Observations upon Religio Medici* (1643), 99-112 (cp.
36 ff.), and Alexander Ross, *Medicus Medicatus* (1645), 74-76, with 65-66—
sneers at Browne's professed humility. Ross, *Arcana Microcosmi* ([1651]
1652), title page, with Browne's name in good company. See Olivier Leroy,
Browne, 285-293.
No *sanctum sanctorum* [in "philosophy"] (20)—*Religio Medici, Works*,
I, 18; *Christian Morals*, I, 123. Browne deserted the "severe schools" (I, 17)
when he contemplated final causes: *R. M., Works*, I, 19-20. Sometimes
hunted them in nature: *V. E.*, III, 184-189; II, 259; cp. I, 66. See Georg
Ockerhausen, *Rationalismus und Mystik*, 48; Egon S. Merton, *Science and
Imagination*, 82. Cryptograms in nature (33)—Browne, *R. M.*, I, 75; *V. E.*,
II, 160. See G. K. Chalmers, in *Va. Qu. Rev.*, XXVI (1950), 416-420, 421,
61 esp. 429. On proper study of the lodestone: Browne, *V. E.*, II, 132.
Browne's . . . **failure to coordinate the facts** (17)—See Lytton Strachey,
Books and Characters (1922), 43-44; Olivier Leroy, *Browne*, 186; Merton, 7-
10, 61-65, Dunn, *Browne*, 2d ed., 77-139; in particular, Jane M. Oppen-
heimer, "John Hunter, Sir Thomas Browne and the Experimental
Method," *Bull. Hist. Medicine*, XXI (1947), 17 ff., esp. 31, and G. K. Chalmers, 414 ff. On the mystery of numbers: Browne, *R. M., Works*, ed.
Keynes, I, 17. *Cyrus* [and] **Hermetism or cabalism** (26)—Margaret A.
Heideman, "*Hydriotaphia* and *The Garden of Cyrus*," *UTQ*, XIX (1950),
245; J. L. Blau, "Browne's Interest in Cabalism," *PMLA*, XLIX (1934),
963-964. W. P. Dunn, *Browne*, 2d ed., 121-122, 132. **Counting fives** [**for the**
62 **sake of truth**] (31)—Browne, *Garden of Cyrus, Works*, IV, 124. **The study**
of himself (5)—*R. M.*, I, 20-21; see esp. I, 17 and 158.
Ross . . . **catching** [**Browne**] **up for** . . . **mortalism** (18)—Alexander
Ross, *Medicus Medicatus* (1645), 51; see, on "Popery" and other errors, 1-8,
25, 35, 65-66, 74-76. See J. S. Finch, *Browne*, 117. **Physician** . . . **atheist**
in esteem (21)—Paul H. Kocher, *Science and Religion, etc.* (1953), 239 ff.,
repr. from *HLQ*, X (1947), 229 ff.; J. S. Finch, *Browne*, 12-15. [**Sir Kenelm**]
Digby tried (23)—I.e., to fasten on Browne doctrinal indiscretion: Digby,
Observations upon Religio Medici (1643), 19, concerning Browne, *Works*,
I, 16. For the antiquity of Browne's harmless conceit, note Lynn Thorndike, *Magic and Science*, II, 317. **Another Anglican physician** (31)—I.e.,
John Collop, "On Doctor Brown," *Poesis Rediviva*, 1656. **Still another doc-**
tor (19)—Walter Charleton, *The Darknes of atheism dispelled by the*
light of Nature (1652), 352-355. Cp., on the mysteries in nature: Browne,
63 *R. M., Works*, ed. Keynes, I, 14. His paradoxes in divinity: e.g., I, 28-31;
II, 15 ff., 75-78; III, 261-263; V, 217-220. Margaret L. Wiley, "Sir Thomas
Browne and the Genesis of Paradox," *The Subtle Knot*, 137-161, repr. from
JHI, IX (1948), 319, 322. With Browne's "paradoxes," cp. John Dod and
Robert Cleaver, *Exp. upon the Ten Commandements* (1603), 22-23; John
Davies, *Microcosmos* (1603), in *Works* (2 v., 1878), I, 12; or Ralph Venning,
Orthodoxe Paradoxes [1647], 1652. On "Bacon": A. B. Grosart, *Lord Bacon*
Not the Author of 'The Christian Paradoxes' (1865), 8-24, etc. [**Browne's**]
three youthful heresies (13)—*R. M.*, I, 11-12; see *V. E.*, II, 76. [**On**]
witches and prophecy (16)—I, 38-39, 56; 112; III, 172-173. "Atheism" denied: Olivier Leroy, *Browne*, 113-123. Superstition in his makeup: *R. M.*,
Works, I, 7 (confessed).
64 "**The way of the poet**" [**in religion**] (1)—W. P. Dunn, *Browne* (1926),
51; (1950), 56. See Browne, *R. M., Works*, I, 85-86; and F. L. Huntley, "Sir
Thomas Browne and the Metaphor of the Circle," *JHI*, XIV (1953), 353
ff. " '**Tis better to sit down with** . . . **adumbration**" (8)—*R. M.*, I, 14; see

64 I, 13. On Browne's rationality and his *O altitudo!*: S. L. Bethell, *The Cultural Revolution of the Seventeenth Century* (New York, 1951), 34-36.
[Milton] mixed . . . vocational training (31)—See John W. Adamson, *Pioneers in Modern Education, 1600-1700* (1905), 124-125, for the utilitarian trend in curricula. On Milton's practice: Edward Phillips, *Life of Mr. John Milton*, in *Early Lives of Milton*, ed. Helen Darbishire (London, 1932), 60.

65 Peacham's fellows (1)—On some late and superficial educators: W. E. Houghton, "The English Virtuoso," *JHI*, III (1942), 58-61. On the ideal of public service: Houghton, *The Formation of Fuller's Holy and Profane States* (Cambridge, U.S.A., 1938), 111. See W. Lee Ustick, "Changing Ideals of Aristocratic Character and Conduct in Seventeenth-Century England," *MP*, XXX (1932), 147 ff. A gentleman should be but *mediocriter doctus* (12)—Denied: Richard Brathwaite, *The Schollers Medley* ([1614] 1616), 48; Clement Ellis, *The Gentile Sinner, or, Englands Brave Gentleman* (1660), 165; Edward Waterhouse, *The Gentlemans Monitor* (1665), 342. The saying of Louis XI: Daniel Tuvil, *Essayes* (1609), 12; Henry Peacham, *The Compleat Gentleman* ([1622] 1634), 20, and *The Truth of Our Times* (1638), 18. Contrast Sir Thomas Browne, *Christian Morals* (ii.4), in *Works*, ed. Keynes, I, 123. A few [essayists] feared pedantry (23)—Dudley, Lord North, *Varieties* (1645), 91, 185; Owen Felltham, "Of Wisdom and Science," *Resolves* ([?1623] 1840), 100 ff.; I. B., *Heroick Education* (1657), ch. ix, Sigs G^{vo}-$G3^{vo}$; Edward Panton, *Speculum Juventutis* (1671), 104-105; [Obadiah Walker], *Of Education* (1673), 112. For the "pedantic" Politian, a common *exemplum*, see, e.g., Sir John Davies, *Works* (3 v., 1869-), II, 214. Cp. Miles Sandys, *Prima Pars Parvi Opusculi* (1634), 128 (educating women). Arguments for ignorance (27)—Noticed by Bacon, *Works*, ed. Spedding *et al.* (15 v., 1861), IX, 169 (cp. 162-163); William Vaughan, *The Golden Grove* (1600), Pt. I, Essay 69; John Cleland, *Hero-Paideia: or, The Institution of a Young Noble Man* (1607), 134; Robert Johnson, "Of Learning," *Essayes* ([1601] 1638), 28-37; Edward Panton, *Speculum Juventutis* (1671), 86; Miles Sandys, 139 ff. With the conventional praise of learning (e.g., Barnaby Rich, *Faultes* [1606], 36 ff.), contrast

66 Owen Felltham, *Resolves*, xxvii ([?1623] 1840), 66-68—but for his usual rationalism, see 50 ff., 100, 111, 124, 206-207, etc. On Felltham: Douglas Bush, *English Literature, etc.*, 191.
Lord North . . . held Montaigne responsible (11)—Dudley North, *A Forest of Varieties* (1645), 109 ff., 117-224, esp. 153; 91, 96, 135, esp. 152; def. of curiosity, 119; cp. 185. On unprofitable books: Henry Peacham, *The Truth of Our Times* (1638), 29-30. Cp. *Satyræ Seriæ* (1639), Essays 2, 13, 15 (frequent Baconian "skepticism").

67 "For man to look upon man . . . is beautiful" (9)—Sir William Cornwallys, *Essayes* ([1600] 1632), Sigs S^{vo}-S2.
[David] Person . . . spokesman [for] science (23)—Person (Pierson), *Varieties* (1635), Book IV, "Of Curiosities," 177-203; on the peace of the church, sec. 2. Cp. sec. 7, p. 190. For scientific conservatism, Books I-II, pp.

68 8, 12, 53; v, pp. 58, 70, 81. Cp. Alexander Ross, *Arcana Microcosmi* (1652), Ep. Ded., and *The Philosophical Touch-Stone*, 1645. His reference to Divorcers: *Pansebeia* (1655), 376. On Ross and his learning: Foster Watson, *Beginnings of Modern Subjects*, 384, and "Alexander Ross, Pedant Schoolmaster," *Gentleman's Magazine*, CCXXIX (1895), 459 ff.
Francis Osborn championed [modernity] (22)—*Advice to a Son*, in *Works* ([1656-59] 1689), 152, and *Essays*, 496-497; see Pref. See also 498 (on Ross), 551, 557 ff., 509-512 (on witchcraft), 152 ff. (on bookishness), 84.

NOTES 257

69 Universal dabbler . . . cause[d] trouble (21)—*Advice*, in *Works*, 157.
Being a notable heretic (25)—S. A. E. Betz, "Francis Osborne's 'Advice
to a Son,'" in *Seventeenth Century Studies*, ed. Robert Shafer (Princeton,
70 N. J., 1937), 7; cp. Osborn, *Essays*, in *Works*, 526-527. See "A Contemplation of Adam's Fall," *Essays*, 520-530, esp. 524.
Arts [called by educators] handmaidens of . . . Divinity (22)—See, e.g.,
Robert Chamberlain, *Nocturnal Lucubrations* (1638), 42-43; Clement Ellis,
Gentile Sinner ([1660] 1661), 165 ff. On the gentility of the *via media:* (in
doctrine) John Robinson (Separatist), *Essayes* (1638), 79 ff., 87, 91-92; (in
discipline) James I, *Basilikon Doron* ([1599] 1603), 10, 18-19. See C. J. Sis-
son, "King James . . . as Political Writer," *Seventeenth Century St.* [*for*]
Grierson (1938), 47 ff. With James, cp. John Cleland, *Hero-Paideia* (1607),
107, 100-115; William Ramesay, *The Gentlemans Companion* (1672), 25;
esp. Edward Waterhouse, *The Gentlemans Monitor* (1665), 212 ff., 245 ff.
Contrast Ellis, 173. Against controversial theology: Anthony Stafford, *The
Guide of Honour* (1634), 15, and *Niobe* (1611), 142-143; John Robinson,
71 "Of Disputations," *Essayes* (1638), 79; 148-153. Logic [without] scholastic
method (1)—Cleland, 87-88, 94-95. For skeptical suspicion of logic; Owen
Felltham, *Resolves* ([?1693] 1840), 124 ff.
Grammar . . . a means [only] (4)—Ben Jonson, *Discoveries*, ed. G. B.
Harrison (1923), 71. Conventional distrust of rhetoric: Cornwallys, *Essayes*
(1632 ed.), Nos. 43, 45, 47; Sigs A, C^{vo}, D4, F8^{vo}. William Vaughan, *The
Golden Grove* (1600), Pt. II, Essay 41. Barnaby Rich, *Faultes* (1606), 36.
Satyræ Seriæ (1639), 86 ff. Cp. G-B Giraldi, *A Discourse of Civill Life*, tr.
Lodowick Bryskett (1606), 15; Henry Harflete, *A Banquet of Essayes* (1653),
42 (on literary pedantries). Cp., on pedantry, James Howell, *Epistolæ*
(1650 ed.), III, Letter 8, pp. 13-16. A little astronomy short of figure-cast-
ing (14)—Cornwallys, Essay 45, Sig D3; Henry Peacham, *The Valley of
Varietie* (1638), 116; Cleland, 88 (practical mathematics); Richard Brath-
waite, *Schollers Medley* (1616 ed.), 47.
[Gentlemen not seriously] to pursue experimental philosophy (28)—
But see (late) William Ramesay, *The Gentlemans Companion* (1672), 15
("Spagurical and Cartetian" science). And cp. Margaret (Lucas) Cavendish,
Duchess of Newcastle, *The Worlds Olio* (1655), 69; see 14, 208. Unusual
(early) deference to natural knowledge: *Satyræ Seriæ* (1639), 84-86 (Essay
15). "The height of all philosophy" [is self-knowledge] (35)—Francis
Quarles, *Enchyridion* (1641), Cent. IV, chs. 78, 19, 4, 26. Thus Sir John
Hayward, *Davids Teares* (1636), 125.
Debate between action and contemplation (37)—In Middle Ages con-
72 templation usually triumphed: Dom Cuthbert Butler, *Western Mysticism*
(2d ed.; London, 1927), 291-325. Protestantism and "action" or "calling":
R. H. Tawney, *Religion and the Rise of Capitalism* (1926), 240 ff.; Ernst
Troeltsch, *The Social Teaching of the Christian Churches* (tr. 1931, 2 v.),
II, 471 ff.; R. Newton Flew, *The Idea of Perfection in Christian Theology*
(Oxford, 1934), 251-257, cp. 230. On meanings of "calling" (*vocatio*): R. S.
Michaelson, in *New England Qu.*, XXVI (1953), 315 ff., and his ref. to
Max Weber. [With] humanism, . . . active life gained favor (15)—See
Stephen Guazzo, *Civile Conversation*, tr. [1596], ed. Sir Edward Sullivan
(1925), 32-33, 49; G-B Giraldi, *A Discourse of Civill Life*, tr. Lodowick
Bryskett (1606), 22, 131, 165, 208. The shift in emphasis noted: C. A. L.
Jarrott, in *DA, XIV* (1954), 1709. Contemplation . . . suffered by association
(24)—For sneers at contemplation, note E. N. S. Thompson, "Mysticism in
. . . Literature," *SP*, XVIII (1921), 217-218; cp. Joseph Hall, "The Sloth-

258 MILTON AND FORBIDDEN KNOWLEDGE

PAGE

72 ful," *Characters* (1608), 119, and *Epistles* (3 v., 1608), II, 137-144. For abuse
heaped on Little Gidding: Maurice Hussey, ed. *The Arminian Nunnery*,
in *Church Qu. Rev.*, CXLVIII (1949), 229 ff., and, e.g., Hearne's Langtoft,
qu. by James Bass Mullinger, *Cambridge Characteristics* (1867), 101. "Monastic walks, etc." (33)—Robert Anton, *The Philosophers Satyrs* (1616), 60.
See notes to my page 27.

73 "Contemplation . . . is idleness" (1)—Robert Chamberlain, *Nocturnal
Lucubrations* (1638), 55; cp. 87 (Bernard). *Satyræ Seriæ* (1639), 45. Henry
Harflete, *A Banquet of Essayes* (1653), 6 ff. Cp. Robert Johnson, *Essayes*
([1601] 1638), 28, and, on Johnson and these writers, E. N. S. Thompson,
The Seventeenth-Century English Essay: Univ. Iowa Hum. St., III (1926),
38, 54, etc. **[Bernard echoed as] witness against [contemplative] curiosity**
(23)—Besides Chamberlain (cited), note Henry Montagu, Earl of Manchester, *Contemplatio Mortis* (1631), 1 and 12-13; Anthony Stafford, *Meditations and Resolutions* (1612), 1-2 ff., 70-71, and *Heauenly Dogge* (1615),
1-4 ff.; esp. John Robinson, *Essayes, or Observations* ([1625] 1638) 170 (Obs.
14); see Obs. 13, 19, 60, etc.

Daniel Tuvil . . . borrow[ed] . . . from Montaigne [and] Bacon
(30)—See John L. Lievsay, "Tuvil's Advancement of Bacon's Learning,"
HLQ, IX (1945), 11 ff., and "Daniel Tuvil's 'Resolves,'" *SP*, XLVI (1949),
196 ff., see 139. E. N. S. Thompson, *Essay*, 43-44. W. L. McDonald, in
Eng. Studien, LXIV (1929), 52. For his borrowing from Sir Philip Sidney,
cf. *Arcadia*, in *Works*, ed. Albert Feuillerat (4 v., 1922), I, 58. **His discourse of action** (31)—Daniel Tuvil, *Vade Mecum* [= *Essayes*, 1609] (1638),
[74] 25.

75 Topic . . . once set . . . by Lando (1)—See Merritt Y. Hughes, ed.
John Milton, *Prose Selections* (New York, 1946), xxi and xxi n.

Grammarians [taught] ungrammatically (13)—Milton, *Prolusions* (VII),
in *Works* (18 v., 1931-), XII, 277 (3). On Salmasius: VIII, 95 (17). **Compliment to Bonmattei** (21)—Letters, XII, 31 (11-15). On eloquence and rhetoric: III, 362 (5); *Comus*, 789; *P. R.* IV.4. The serenade: *Areop.*, IV, 317
(21); *P. L.* IV.769. **Logic . . . "Queen . . . of the arts"** (34)—*Prolusions*
76 (VII), XII, 277 (6-10). On metaphysics: XII, 277 (14); III, 273 (9); VI, 78 (22).
The humanist's proper subordination [of science] (22)—XII, 171 (14).

77 **Scholasticism [bore all] blame for error** (14)—*Divorce*, III, 505 (22).
Seventh Prolusion . . . most optimistic (28)—Thus E. M. W. Tillyard,
Milton (London, 1946) 53-56, and see Tillyard in Milton, *Private Corre-
spondence and Academic Exercises*, tr. Phyllis B. Tillyard (Cambridge,
1932), xxxvii-xxxviii. On its origin: *Prolusions* (VII), XII, 251 (10-20).

78 Counters classical skepticism: XII, 281 (13-14). **[Putting] Charron for
[Milton's] opponent** (16)—Pierre Charron, *Of Wisdome* (III.14.13), tr.
Sampson Lennard (1612): (1) 466 ff., (2) 466-468, (3) 468, (4) 468-471, (5) 471-
472, (6) 466, (7) 469, 473, (8) 471, 473, (9) 472-473. Milton, *Prolusions* (VII),
79 *Works*, XII: (1) 253 [26]-257 [25], (2) 257-261 [2], (3) 261 [3-22], (4) 261
[23]-263 [13], 269 [18]-271 [23], 271 [24]-273, (5) 263 [13]-265 [26], (6) 265
[27]-269 [3], (7) 273 [19]-275 [29], 281 [27]-285 [5], (8) 277 [3]-279 [3], (9) 277
[1-2], 279 [6-7].

80 **[Milton's] letter to an unnamed friend** (9)—Assumed to be Diodati:
James Holly Hanford, *John Milton, Englishman* (New York, 1949), 66.
"Unprofitable sin of curiosity" (20)—Milton, *Works* (1931-), XII, 321 (7)
and 323 (23). On this letter as a "limiting postscript" to Prol. VII: E. M. W.
Tillyard, *Milton*, 57-58. **"Let us rise cautiously"** (25)—Milton, Letters,

81 XII, 26 (23). See *Divorce*, III, 371 (12), and 376 (4). **Some future Essex (10)**—On the occasion for Milton's medical lore: John W. Adamson, *Pioneers in Modern Education* (Cambridge, 1905), 122.

Milton had read . . . some of [the courtesy literature] (35)—So E. N. S. Thompson, "Milton's *Of Education*," *SP*, XV (1918), 171-172, and Oliver M. Ainsworth, ed. *Milton on Education: Cornell St. in Eng.*, No. 12 (1928), [82] 8-21.

83 **Two . . . remarks [opening *Of Education* were] two causes (2)**—For another manner of harmonizing them: Ainsworth, 15. A definition needed four causes: Milton, *Works*, IV, 100 (15) ff.; *C. D.*, XV, 21 (13)—or three: IV, 105 (13). **Form of an art . . . "some useful matter" (13)**—XI, 9 (18-20). **Formality partook of finality (14)**—XI, 31 (25), 55-59, esp. 63-69, 265 (24-26). Milton apparently had this principle from George Downame; see T. S. Scott-Craig, in *HLQ*, XVII (1953), 7.

Gambit . . . fitted easily into [various doctrines] (24)—See Sir Thomas Browne, *V. E., Works*, ed. Keynes, II, 40; John Brinsley, *A Consolation for our Grammar Schooles* (1622), 3; Anthony Stafford, *Heauenly Dogge* (1615), 4; Thomas Spencer, *The Art of Logick* (1628), Pref.; John Robinson, *Essayes* (xlv), ([1625] 1638), 167. See E. A. Strathmann, "The Idea of Progress," *Ren. News*, II (1949), 24. **It proved nothing (25)**—To the contrary: G. F. Sensabaugh, "Milton on Learning," *SP*, XLIII (1946), 258 ff., esp. 261 ff. **Phillips . . . dated . . . something like [*C. D.*] (37)**—Edward Phillips, in Helen Darbishire, ed. *The Early Lives of Milton* (London, 1932), 61. But see Arthur Sewell, *A Study in Milton's Christian Doctrine* (London, 1939), 3. On learning as an ornament to faith: Milton, *Of Ed., Works*, IV,

84 277 (7-8). With Milton's apology for learning, cp. William Kempe "The Dignitie of Schooling," *The Education of Children* (1588), Sigs B-B2, C ff., E. For a stronger statement than either on the divinity of reason: Sir John Suckling, *An Account of Religion by Reason* (1646), in *Works*, ed. A. H. Thompson (1910), 349. For Brinsley's Puritanism: G. W. McClelland, "John Brinsley and His Educational Treatises," *Schelling Anniv. Papers* (New York, 1923), 189 ff.; see 195.

Good exegetes [interpreted Col. ii:8] (27)—See, e.g., Lancelot Andrewes, *Ninety-Six Sermons*, LACT (5 v., 1841-), V, 55 ff.; Paul Baynes, *A Comm. on Colossians* ([1634] 1635), 235 ff. Morris Fuller, *Life [of] John Davenant* (1897), 183-188, condenses that divine's extensive comment on Col. ii:8 and vain philosophy. Milton's application of the text: *C. D., Works*, XIV, 21 (2); *Likeliest Means*, VI, 98 (5); *P. L.* II.565; *P. R.* IV.291.

85 **Augustine . . . found "Virgil" [in limbo] (3)**—*On the Spirit and the Letter* (xlviii), in *Works*, Nicene Lib. (8 v., 1888), V, 103-104. Salvation of pagans—against: B. C. (priest), *Puritanisme the Mother* (1633), 41; John Prideaux, "De Salute Ethnicorum," *Lectiones Novem* (1625), 171-195 (bibliography). See also "[Salut des] Infidèles," *Dict. de Théol. Catholique*, VII, Col. 1726 ff. For: Humphrey Sydenham, *Sermons* (1637), 218; John Goodwin, *The Pagans Debt, and Dowry*, 1651; Martin Clifford, *Of Humane Reason*, 1674. On sectaries and the heresy: Stephen Denison, *The White Wolfe* (1627), 38; Ephraim Pagitt, *Heresiography* ([1645] 1647), 99. *The Querers and Quakers Cause at the Second Hearing* (1653), 10. See Robert Barclay, *An Apology for . . . Quakers* (1678), Prop. 6. Cp. Milton, *C. D., Works*, XV, 403 (26) ff. Orthodoxy rigidly damned the pagans: Sir Thomas Browne, *Works*, ed. Keynes, I, 66; Andrew Willet, *Hexapla [upon] Romanes* ([1611] 1620), 66; John Rawlinson, *Mercy to a Beast* [sermon]

PAGE

85   (1612), 6; Henry Harflete, *Essays* (1653), 53; Robert Bolton, *Saints* . . .
     Guide (1634), 19-20; William Sclater, *A Key to [Romanes], the Key of Scrip-*
     ture (1611), 233-235. **One Calvinist preached [on] unsanctified learning**
     (19)—I.e., Anthony Burges, *Spiritual Refinings* (1652), 352-357, 620. Cp.
     Thomas Granger, *Exp. of Ecclesiastes* (1620), 38 ff.
     The divinity of nature's light (30)—Milton, *C. D., Works* (1931-), XV,
     209 (12) ff.; cp. Arthur Dent, *The Plaine Mans Path-Way to Heaven*, Part

86   I (1603), 7-8, on the spark remaining from Adam. His perfect knowledge
     before the Fall: Thomas Adams, *Workes* (1629), 1132; John Lightfoot,
     Works (1822-), VII, 20-21; Samuel Pordage, *Mundorum Explicatio* (1661),
     59; John Salkeld, *Treatise of Paradise* (1617), ch. xl. Angels' knowledge:
     John Donne, *Works*, ed. Alford, VI, 184; Robert Bolton, *Last Things*
     ([1632] 1639), 140 ff.; esp. John Salkeld, *A Treatise of Angels* (1613), 113 ff.,
     177-181 (limiting extravagant claims). Note Sir Thomas Browne, *Works*,
     ed. Keynes, I, 42.
     Fallen angels retained . . . knowledge (8)—Salkeld, *Angels*, 152-153
     (devils imperfectly prophetic), 350, 357-360, 362; Peter Martyr Vermigli,
     The Common Places, tr. A. Marten (?1583), [i], pp. 83-84 (ref. to Augustine
     for Satan's ignorance of man's thoughts); Henry Howard, *Defensative*
     ([1583] 1620), 83-86; William Gouge, *Workes* (1627), 33-34; esp. Henry
     Lawrence, *Of Our Communion and Warre with Angels* (1646), 60-61.
     Thomas Fuller, "On Christ's Temptation," *Sermons* (2 v., 1891), II, 35. See
     Henry C. Lea and Arthur C. Howland, eds. *Witchcraft*, II, 973, 993; Mil-
     ton, *C. D., Works* (1931-), XV, 111 (3) ff.; esp. John Webster, "Of the
     Knowledge and Power of Faln Angels," *Displaying of Witchcraft* (1677),
     215-241, esp. 219-220. Robert Burton, *Anatomy*, ed. Shilleto, I, 212-213.
     Devils . . . "sing . . . and . . . meditate" (34)—Thomas Milles, tr. *The*
     Treasurie of Auncient and Moderne Times, Bk. 1 (2 v., 1613-19), I, 35-36.
     Fallen angels [of *P. L.* stand for] natural man (39)—Grace exalted:
     William Attersoll, *Physicke Against Famine*, in *Three Treatises* (1632), 142;
     John Ward, *God Judging among the Gods* (1645), 55-56 (improves natural

87   knowledge). Nature vilified: Henry Hammond, *Misc. Theol. Works*, LACT
     (3 v., 1849-), III, 594; Henry Harflete, *Essays* (1653), 53-56; cf. John Denison,
     A Three-Fold Resolution (1608), 17-18; Edward Elton, *The Triumph of a*
     True Christian (1623), 133; Thomas Drant, *The Divine Lanthorne* ([1636]
     1637), 9-21. **"Golden damnation" (26)**—Robert Bolton, *True Happiness*
     (1625), 19-20, and see *Walking with God* (1626), Ep. Ded. Cp. Henry More,
     Mystery of Godliness, in *Theol. Works* (1708), 35-36. On derogation of the
     natural man, even by humanists, note Herschel Baker, *The Wars of Truth*,
     32.

88   **Classical . . . military science [in Hell] (1)**—J. H. Hanford, "Milton
     and the Art of War," *SP*, XVIII (1921), 252. **To smile (19)**—Thus Sir
     Walter Raleigh, *Milton* (1900), 140. J. B. Broadbent, "Milton's Hell," *ELH*,
     XXI (1954), 161 ff., writes better of some "human" butts of Milton's ridi-
     cule, e.g., chivalric pomp (185) and Stoicism (189). **The . . . *consolatio***
     [and] rhetoric (35)—See B. Boyce, "The Stoic *Consolatio* and Shake-
     speare," *PMLA*, LXIV (1949), 771 ff., and esp. Don C. Allen, *The Har-*
     monious Vision (Baltimore, 1954), 43 ff.

89   **Bishop [Joseph] Hall had written of tranquility (17)**—*Meditations*, in
     Recollection of Treatises (1614), 107-108. Cp. Jeremiah Burroughs, *Chris-*
     tian Contentment (1648), 15.
     Most [Fathers] had affirmed [Jewish origin of learning] (36)—See, e.g.,

89 Justin Martyr, *Apol.* (I.lvii ff.) or ps-Justin, *Cohortatio ad Græcos,* in *Works,* Ante-Nicene Lib. (1868), 308, 321, etc.; Clement of Alexandria, *Protrepticus* (vi.70), in *Opera,* ed. Dindorf, I, 75, or *Works,* Ante-Nicene Lib. (2 v., 1867), I, 71; and see *Stromata* i.25-26; Augustine, *Civ. Dei* viii.10. Cp.

90 Josephus, *Antiquities* I.vii.1-2. Eusebius cited: Milton, *Areop., Works* (18 v., 1931-), IV, 312 (17-20). See Eusebius, *Preparatio Evangelica* (ix.16 [417D]), tr. E. H. Gifford (2 v., 1903), I, 448-449; and *passim,* Theophilus Gale, *The Court of the Gentiles,* 4 v., 1669-1677. See Part II, ch. xxii, pp. 120-121, for derivation of Urania from Hebrew 'light' and equation with Juno, derived from root *Jah,* Jehovah. **"Pythagoras . . . was a Jew"** (11)—Barten Holyday, *A Survey of the World* (1641), 50-51. Cp. Clement, *Stromata* i.15, and John Woolton, *The Immortalitie of the Soule* (1576), 58b, with refs.

Idea [dear] to Cambridge Platonists (20)—See John A. Stewart, tr. *The Myths of Plato* (1905), 476; Frederick J. Powicke, *The Cambridge Platonists* (1926), 27 ff., 133; E. M. Austin, *The Ethics of the Cambridge Platonists* (Philadelphia, 1935), 51. Cp. Robert Greville, Lord Brooke, *The Nature of Truth* (1640), 29-31, and John Dryden *Religio Laici,* Pref., in *Works,* ed. Scott and Saintsbury (18 v., 1893), X, 13.

Simplified history . . . in "progress [-of-learning] essays" (31)—George

91 Herbert, *English Works,* ed. Herbert Palmer (3 v., 1905), III, 359-379; and Sir John Denham, *Poetical Works,* ed. T. H. Banks (1928), 114-121. Cp. Simon de Voyon, catalogue, *Doctors of Gods Church,* tr. J. Golbourne (1598), Pref., 12, etc.; William Kempe, *The Education of Children* (1588), Sigs Bᵛᵒ-B2; Edward Chaloner, *Six Sermons* (1629), 10 (credits Jerome); Henry Hammond, *Misc. Theol. Works,* LACT (3 v., 1849-); and Robert Mason, *A Mirrour for Merchants* [= *Reasons Academie,* 1605] (1609), 56-57, accepted wrongly by A. B. Grosart, ed., for the canon of Sir John Davies, *Works* (3 v., 1869-), II, 208-212. On this canon: *DNB,* or Margarete Seeman in *Wiener Beitrage z. Engl. Philol.,* XL (1913), No. 2, p. 87. For bibliog. on the ancestry of learning: Archer Taylor, *Ren. Guide to Books* (Berkeley, 1945), esp. p. 3.

The Fathers . . . deplored [Greek] bawdry (28)—Clement, *Protrep.* II, v vii (Loeb, 1919), 27 169. Cp. Milton, *P. R.* iv.940; Robert Burton, *Anatomy* (III.4.1.3), ed. Shilleto, III, 407-408. **[Later] readers [preferred] Zion's songs (34)**—See, e.g., Daniel Featley, *The Characters of Heavenly Wisedome* (1618), in *Clavis Mystica* (1636), 104; Owen Felltham, *Resolves* ([?1623] 1840), 52. Cp. Milton, *Reason of Ch. Govt., Works* (1931-), III, 238 (10-14). *Contra paganos* (esp. Stoics): Samuel Gardiner, *Sermon at Paules Crosse* (1605), 4, 47; Anthony Burges, *Vindiciæ Legis* ([1646] 1647), 59, 67-71; William Rawley, *Sermon of Meekness* (1623), 23; esp. Barten Holyday

92 (quoted), *Survey* (1641), 50-51. Cp. Cyprian, "On the Advantages of Patience," *Opusc.* (ix.2), in *Writings,* Ante-Nicene Lib. (2 v., 1869), II, 249; Milton, *P. R.* iv.307, and *C. D., Works,* XV, 201 (10); XVII, 253 (26). Socrates and *hoc scio*: e.g., Anthony Stafford, *Honour and Vertue* (1640), 39; John Owen, *Epigrams,* tr. Thomas Pecke (*Parnassi Puerperium,* 1659), 115 (No. 191), and many others. **Entries from Lactantius (14)**—See esp. Milton, *C. B., Works* (1931-), XVIII, 165 (5), and 207 (16), with numerous references to Lactantius on other subjects. See Kathleen Hartwell, *Lactantius and Milton* (1929), 91-93. **Tertullian or the scholarly Clement (15)**— *Contra paganos*: Clement, *Protrepticus* v-vii; Tertullian, *De Præscriptione Hæreticorum* (vii), in *Works,* Ante-Nicene Lib. (1870), II, 8-9. On some others, esp. early Apologists: Adolph Harnack, *Hist. of Dogma* (7 v., tr. 1894-), II, 177-202.

92   Lactantius [refuted] the ancients (18)—*Divine Institutes* (iii.5-23), in
        Works, tr. William Fletcher (2 v., 1872), I, 94-195. See René Pichon, *Lac-
        tance* (Paris, 1901), 89. [Apologetic] work most esteemed (39)—I.e.,
        Philippe de Mornay du Plessis, *A Worke Concerning the Truenesse of*
93   *Christian Religion,* tr. Sidney and Golding ([1587] 1604), 312-313. Also
        celebrated: Moses Amyraldus, *A Treatise concerning Religions* (1631), tr.
        1660.

        Our concern with Milton suggests (23)—*Contra gentiles:* George Hake-
        will, *An Apologie . . . of . . . Providence . . . in the Government of the*
94   *World* ([1627] 1635), 364-365, 497-540. Sir Thomas Browne, *R. M.,* in
        Works, ed. Keynes, I, 67, 148-149. Jeremy Taylor, *Works,* ed. Reginald
        Heber and C. P. Eden (10 v., 1850-), IX, 54-55. On Taylor (with disap-
        proval): T. S. Hughes, qu. by George Worley, *Jeremy Taylor* (1904), 43 n.
        On his classicism: Douglas Bush, *English Literature, etc.,* 314; and H. J. C.
        Grierson, *Cross Currents, etc.* (1929), 214. "Peace Epicure, etc." (29)—
        Thomas Bancroft, *Two Bookes of Epigrammes* (1639), No. 83, "Of Beatifical
        Vision."

        [Similar] utterances [in other] writers (37)—Robert Burton, *Anatomy,*
        ed. Shilleto, I, 42-45; Paul Baynes, *Comm. on Col.* (1635), 235; Humphrey
        Sydenham, *Five Sermons* (1636), 1-80, esp. 1-14; J[ohn] A[bbott] "Rivers,"
        ed. *Devout Rhapsodies* [1647], 24-25; Walter Montagu, *Miscellanea Spiri-
        tualia,* Part I (1648), 50-64; Elias Ashmole, *The Way to Bliss* (1658), 4-7,
        together with David Person, *Varieties* (1635), 221 ff., and many others, e.g.,
95   often, Barnaby Rich. Theophilus Gale . . . Restoration skepticism (2)—
        See, e.g., the philosophers' vanity as displayed by the t-p or Contents before
        Part III of his *Court of the Gentiles,* 1677. These sermons [not] the stuff
        of *Paradise Regained* (4)—To the contrary: E. L. Marilla, "Milton on
        'Vain Wisdom' and 'False Philosophie,' " *Studia Neophilologica,* XXV
        (1953), 1 ff., who goes far to equate *P. R.* IV.285 with *P. L.* II.506 ff. Milton
        [emphasized unusually] his anticlassical outburst (9)—Thus E. M. W.
        Tillyard, *Milton* (1946 ed.), 307-310.

CHAPTER III

96   Mutinous stirrings [called] curiosity (10)—By, e.g., John Whitgift,
        Sermon [1574], in *Works,* Parker Soc. (3 v., 1853), III, 573-577; note curi-
        osity defined as leaving one's vocation: Francis Trigge, *Sermon . . . at
        Grantham* ([1592] 1594), Sig C5. William Sclater, *Exp. upon Thess.* (1619),
        305-307 (on iv:11). Robert Sibthorpe, *Apostolike Obedience* (1627), 33.
        The arrogance . . . called Independency (13)—Arguments from pride ex-
        changed by, e.g., Henry Burton, *A Vindication of [Independent] Churches,*
        1644, and William Prynne, *Truth Triumphing,* 1645. See Prynne, *Twelve
        . . . Questions* (1644), 7 (Qu. 12), and *Independency Examined* (1651), 6-7.
        [An] Anglican or two admitted [early Anglican ignorance] (20)—
        T[homas] C[ooper], *An Admonition* [1589], 99 ff.; Arber ed. (1882), 82, 85-
        86; Robert Abbot, *A Triall of our Church-Forsakers* (1639), 194. On the
        state of learning as surveyed by Anglicans and early Puritans, see notes to
        my pages 187-190. Sectaries often men of cultivation: William B. Selbie,
        Nonconformity, Its Origin and Progress (?1911), 41; Ruth Mohl, *Studies
        in Spenser, Milton, and the Theory of Monarchy* (New York, 1949), 106-
        107.

        The Puritan . . . invaded . . . caste (33)—Thus Thomas Lawrence, *A
        [Whitehall] Sermon* [1636], 1637; Nehemiah Rogers, *Christian Courtesie*

NOTES

NOTES   263

PAGE

96 (1621), 66-67. Henry Hammond, "Of Schism," *Misc. Theol. Works*, LACT (1849-), II, 213; esp. III (1), 199-200. Thomas Hobbes, *Leviathan*, in *Works*,
97 ed. Molesworth (1839-), III, 467. Humphrey Sydenham, *Sermons* (1637), 223-224, qu. here. Separatists' "superior," Donatistical holiness ridiculed: George Gifford, *Brownists [are] Donatists* (1590), see 7 ff. Cp. the citation in Ephraim Pagitt, *Heresiography* (1647 ed.), 38, and Thomas Fuller, "The Rigid Donatists" [i.e., Separatists], *Holy State*, ed. Walten, 396. The accusation usual: [John Whitgift], *An Answere to . . . An Admonition* (1572), 18; Thomas Adams, *Fire of Contention*, in *Workes* (1629), 790; and Joseph Hall, *Epistles* (VI.5), in *Recollection of Treatises* (1614), 573. See also the writings against Brownists in the notes to my page 235. Their "preposterous humility": James I, *Basilikon Doron* ([1599] 1603), 87. "Silly schismatics" (12)—John Boys, *Workes* (1622), 350; Anthony Stafford, *Niobe* (1611), 148-150, and most writers just cited. Contrast Phineas Fletcher, *Purple Island* (xxv), *Poetical Works*, ed. F. S. Boas (2 v., 1909), II, 100, for schism exceptionally "learned." **Puritan [was] Adam [or] Uzzah (15)**— Edward Vaughan, *A Method [for Old and New] Testament* (1590), appended serm., p. 23; Thomas Wilson, *Comm. on Rom.* ([1614] 1627), 396; Peter Studley, *The Looking-Glasse of Schisme* (1634), 3; Humphrey Sydenham, *Sermons* (1637), 223. Cp. Milton, *Reason of Ch. Govt.*, *Works* (18 v., 1931-), III, 188 (9), 196 (7-10). On Milton and world-order: B. Rajan, *'Paradise Lost' and the Seventeenth Century Reader* (New York, 1948), 62. W. C. Curry, "Milton's Scale of Nature," *Stanford St. in Lang. and Lit.* (1941), 173 ff. M. M. Mahood, *Poetry and Humanism* (New Haven, 1950), 188 ff.

Robert Burton's question [about ignorant sectaries] (34)—*Anatomy*, ed. Shilleto, III, 390. **Puritans' [zeal] mocked [Hooker's] reasoning (39)**— E.g., William Bradshaw, *A Treatise of Divine Worship* (1604), 22. Laodicean moderation scorned: Ephraim Huit, *The Anatomy of Conscience* (1626), 9-10; Joseph Bentham, *The Societie of the Saints* (1630), 33. **"Carnal reasonings, etc." (40)**—Peter Hausted, *Ten Sermons* (1636), 121, 225,
98 66-67. **Nonconformist . . . Scotch (4)**—I.e., "David Calderwood" [= William Scot?], *The Course of Conformity* (1622), 149-150.

Genevan Model . . . once . . . enthusiasm (15)—See, e.g., William Wilkes, *Obedience: or Ecclesiastical Union* (1605), 35, 43; Giles Widdowes, *The Schysmaticall Puritan* (1630), Pref.; John Featley, *Obedience and Submission* (1636), 25. **Story of . . . Enoch ap Evan (21)**—In Peter Studley, *The Looking-Glasse of Schisme* (1634), 159-162, esp. 160, and B. C. (priest), *Puritanisme the Mother, Sinne the Daughter* (1638), see Ep. Ded.
99 **Bishop [Joseph] Hall's . . . warning (1)**—*Apologie Against Brownists*, in *Recollection of Treatises* (1614), 736, 769. William Laud's heresiography: *Works*, LACT (7 v., 1847), VI, 130 ff. See Henry W. Clark, *Nonconformity*, I, 296. **Independency . . . tool of heresy (13)**—Thomas Edwards, *Reasons Against [Independency]* (1641), 5-7, 33, *Antapologia* (1644), 174, and *Gangræna* (1646), 14; Samuel Rutherford, *Spirituall Antichrist* (1648), 251; Richard Baxter, *Quakers Catechism* ([1651] 1656), Pref., Sigs A[4] ff.

Milton [as] Presbyterian . . . dealt [gently] with sectarianism (29)— *Reason of Ch. Govt.*, *Works* (1931-), III, 209 (25) ff., esp. 216 (21-22), 226 (1).
100 Cp. *Divorce*, III, 443 (17), and 426 (3-4). Misunderstood Arminius: III, 330 (5). God not the author of sin: III, 443 (rubric), 440 (25), 443 (5, 14); cp. *Of True Rel.*, VI, 169 (3-6). **[Milton wrote like no] Assembly presbyter (9)**—On ordination: *Of Ref.*, III, 6 (9). On lay preaching: *Ch. Govt.*, III, 257 (25)-259 (3); see esp. 258 (12-17). On election of ministers: III, 64 (2-4).

100   The spirit of Tertullian (28)—Older heresiologies, suspicious of learning: e.g., William Vaughan, "Of Heretiques and Schismatics," *The Golden Grove* (1600), Pt. I, ch. xxiii, 155-156; Thomas Milles, tr. *Treasurie* (1613-), Bk. VI, ch. xiv; Nicholas Bifield, *Rule of Faith* (1626), 10; Lancelot Andrewes, *Ninety-Six Sermons*, LACT (1841), V, 56. "**Anabaptist**" [any] **enthusiast politically turbulent (39)**—See George T. Buckley, *Atheism* (1932), 48-54; Henry W. Clark, *Nonconformity*, I, 129; Daniel Neal, *The Hist. of the Puritans* (2 v., 1843), I, 137. Cp. Robert Burton, *Anatomy*, ed.

101   Shilleto, III, 425-426. "Anabaptist and Familist," a blanket phrase without precision: see, e.g., William Sclater, *Exp. upon Thess.* (1619), 29; John Downame, *A Guide to Godlynesse* (1622), 15; William Gouge, *Workes* (1627), 255-256. On Familists: Stephen Denison, *The White Wolf* (1627), 38 ff. **Thomas Edwards . . . refuted no dead heresies (13)**—*Gangræna* (1646), Part III, Pref., 1; Thomas Fuller, *Holy State* (ii.9; v.10), ed. M. G. Walten, 83, 394. See Daniel Featley, *Satanæ Stratagemata* (c. 1619), in *Clavis Mystica* (1636), 374, and cp. Featley, *The Dippers Dipt* (1645), 201, 204-205. For heresiology: *Dippers*, 30 ff.; for *viæ mediæ* in doctrine and in discipline: *Dippers*, 213, and *Clavis*, 432-438. **Ephraim Pagitt's . . . prophets . . . from the mechanic trades (28)**—*Heresiography* (1647 ed.), Pref.; and see 70.

102   John Robinson . . . wished [lay Bible-readers to consult the learned] (3)—*Essayes* ([1625] 1638), 130; cp. Thomas Fuller, *Collected Sermons*, (2 v., 1891), II, 328-352; and John Hales, *Abuses of Hard Places of Scripture*, in *Golden Remains*, ed. John Pearson ([1659] 1688), 30; see 45-47, 50, 137, etc., esp. 18-20. Henry Hammond, *Misc. Theol. Works*, LACT (3 v., 1849-), III, 471-476. Contrast J[ohn] A[bbott] "Rivers," *Devout Rhapsodies* [1647], 373 ff.; John Lightfoot, *Works* (13 v., 1822-), VII, 200-216—all Christians should search all scripture. Difficulties could make infidels: see Arthur Broke, tr. *Agreement of Sondry Places of Scripture* (1563), Pref. See P. H. Kocher, "Backgrounds for Marlowe's Atheist Lecture," *Ren. St.* [for] *Hardin Craig* (Stanford, Cal., 1942), 130-131. Problems and contradictions meant to test faith: John Donne, *Essays in Divinity* (1651), ed. E. M. Simpson (1952), 56-57; William Gouge, *Workes* (1627), 162; Jeremy Taylor, *Works* (10 v., 1850-), V, 421 ff.; VIII, 524; Richard Baxter, *Infidelity*, in *Practical Works* (23 v., 1830), XX, 115. **Incompetent reader . . . curious (35)**—Henry More, *Theological Works* (1708), 138 ff., and *Divine Dialogues* (2 v., 1668), II, 197-198. Joseph Mede, *Discourses* (liii), in *Works* ([1648] 1672), 304. Jeremy Taylor, *Works* (1850-), VI, 404.

103   John Smith . . . set . . . learning [to defend true] mysticism (2)—*Select Discourses* (1660), 196 ff., 408. Cp. Meric Casaubon, *A Treatise Concerning Enthusiasm* (1656), 85, 101, 155-166; Henry More, *Enthusiasmus Triumphatus*, in *Philosophical Writings* (1712), 45; John Hales, *Remains* (1688 ed.), 18-20. Against mystics and enthusiasts: Samuel Rutherford, "Of Revelations and Inspirations," *A Survey of the Spirituall Antichrist* (1648), 38. Thomas Hobbes, *Leviathan* (1651), in *English Works*, ed. Molesworth (11 v., 1839-), III, 66, 311-312, 359-360. Edward Waterhouse, *Apologie for Learning* (1653), 6, calls the pretence of revelation atheism. Jeremy Taylor, *Works* (10 v., 1850-), II, 140. See E. N. S. Thompson, "Mysticism, etc.," *SP*, XVIII (1921), 219; Robert A. Vaughan, *Hours with the Mystics* (2 v., 1856), I, 122. **An impeccable Presbyterian (15)**—I.e., Rutherford, *Survey*, 38; cp. Baxter, *The Quakers Catechism* ([1651] 1656), 12. See esp. William Bridge, *Scripture Light the Most Sure Light*, in *Works* (5 v., 1845), I, 417. Bridge

103 called Socinian: Griffith Williams, *The Discovery of Mysteries* (1643), 21.
Critics [protected] order (27)—See, e.g., Mark Frank, *Fifty-One Sermons*,
LACT (2 v., 1859), II, 294. T. G. Steffan, "The Social Argument Against
Enthusiasm," *Univ. Texas St. in Eng.* (1941), 39 ff. J. I. Cope, " 'The Cupri-
Cosmits': Glanvill on Latitudinarian Anti-Enthusiasm," *HLQ*, XVII (1954),
269 ff.
The voice that . . . foretold [Saltmarsh's death] (35)—See Daniel Neal,
104 *Puritans* (2 v., 1843), II, 74. **The Presbyterian heresiologies (6)**—To David
Masson's list, *Life of John Milton* (6 v., 1873), III, 137-143, may be added
Alexander Ross' *Pansebeia;* and see Wilbur K. Jordan, *Toleration*, III, 274-
296; David W. Petegorsky, *Left-Wing Democracy in the English Civil War*
(London, 1940), 66. See also Ross, *Englands Threnodie* [1648], e.g., 7,
quoted here. For bibliog. of modern studies: Douglas Bush, *English Lit-
erature, etc.*, 472.
For a sample of the Presbyterian language (18)—Thomas Edwards,
Gangræna (1646), Part III, Pref., 1.
True religion . . . a mean (38)—Aquinas, *Summa Theol.* ii.2.2, Qu. 92
105 *et seq.*, in *Opera* (Venetia, 1745-; 28 v.), XXII, 480 ff. Bacon, *Essays*, in
Works, ed. Spedding, XII, 131, 135; cp. *De Aug.*, VIII, 162-163; *Med. Sacræ*,
XIV, 94; Joseph Hall, *Characters of Vices*, in *Recollection of Treatises*
(1614), 261 ff.; John Smith, *Select Discourses* (1660), 36 ff. (Nos. 2 and 3);
Margaret (Lucas) Cavendish, Duchess of Newcastle, *The Worlds Olio*
(1655), 46. For a few passing references, see Henry Smith, *Works* (2 v.,
1866), I, 474; John Donne, *Works*, ed. Alford (6 v., 1839), I, 140, 365; II,
356; John Day, *Day's Dyall* (1614), 16; John Robinson, "Of Atheism and
Idolatry," *Essayes*, xi (1638 ed.), 148; Thomas Hobbes, *Works*, ed. Molesworth (1839-), II, 227; Jeremy Taylor, *Works* (10 v., 1850-), IV, 249-250.
Note George Whitehead's title, *Enthusiasm Above Atheism*, 1674. From
the mean, the atheist turned left: Donne, *Works*, ed. Alford, VI, 187; cp.
460 (line 1); George Swinnock, *Works* (5 v., 1868), I, 24; John Bate, *The
Portraiture of Hypocrisie* (1589), 12 (atheism "a feather of the left wing");
esp. Henoch Clapham, *Errour on the Left Hand, Through a Frozen Secur-
itie* (1608), where atheism (chiefly mortalism) goes with libertinism and
Popish "merits" in opposition to sectarian *Errour on the Right Hand,
Through Preposterous Zeale*, 1608. Religion between two thieves, super-
stition right and atheism left: Alexander Ross, *Pansebeia* ([1653] 1655), Ep.
Ded., Sig A4. **Preachers . . . between heresy and enthusiasm (18)**—E.g.,
Robert Some, *Treatise Touching the Ministrie* (1588), 9-11; Thomas
Adams, *Workes* (1629), 184-185; Sir Robert Dallington, *Inference* (51), in
Aphorismes, 1613. Or between atheism and enthusiasm-superstition: e.g.,
Thomas Scot, *Philomythie* (1616), 49-50.
Robert Burton . . . authority on curiosity (27)—*The Anatomy of Mel-
ancholy* (1621), ed. A. R. Shilleto (3 v., 1893), I, 150, 420 ff.; II, 177; III,
358, etc. For his science: L. Miller, in *Annals of Medical Hist.*, VIII (1936),
49-50; Bergen Evans, *The Psychiatry of Robert Burton* (New York, 1944),
49. For his social thought: J. M. Patrick, in *PQ*, XXVII (1948), 345 ff., or
W. R. Mueller, in *HLQ*, XI (1948), 341 ff., and contrast Siegbert Prawer,
in *Cambr. Jour.*, I (1948), 671 ff., esp. 676, 681. On Burton as a skeptic:
Herschel Baker, *The Wars of Truth*, 153-154; Mueller, in *MLQ*, XV (1954),
33. **Earlier authorities [had linked study and melancholy] (31)**—E.g.,
Timothy Bright, *A Treatise of Melancholy* (1586), ed. facs., Hardin Craig,
New York, 1940; see Lawrence Babb, *The Elizabethan Malady*, Lansing,
Mich., 1951, and Babb, "The Background of 'Il Penseroso,' *SP*, XXXVII

106   (1940), esp. 259 (melancholy and heresy). Psychology and heresiology: John Denison, *A Three-Fold Resolution* (1608), 17 ff.; see, e.g., 28, 33; Archibald Symner, *A Spirituall Posie* (1629), No. 4, pp. 36-37; Andrew Willet, *Hexapla upon Romanes* ([1611] 1620), 119 ff.; John Preston, *The Saints Qualifications* (1637), e.g., 40; Obadiah Sedgwick, *Military Discipline* (1638), 28 ff. Bishop John Abernethy [mapped] the mind (17)—*A Christian and Heavenly Treatise* ([1615] 1630), esp. ch. xiv, pp. 204 ff., where heresy proceeds from mental disturbance. Abernethy mentioned: Burton, *Anatomy*, III, 449, 468.

Burton . . . arranged the devious doctrines (23)—*Anatomy*, ed. Shilleto, III, 366: superstition and enthusiasm (excess), 367-433. Atheists and presuming predestinarians (defect), 434 ff. Note W. R. Mueller, "Robert Burton's Frontispiece," *PMLA*, LXIV (1949), 1082-1083; and Merritt Y. Hughes, "Burton on Spenser," *PMLA*, XLI (1926), 553-556. See *Anatomy*, III, 456, cp. 367; 482-485.

107   Baxter [and] truth in the middle (3)—See Frederick J. Powicke, *Life of Baxter* (1924), 148; and see Richard Baxter, *Practical Works* (23 v., 1830), V, 138, 517, 562 ff.; II, 189, 126-127, 301-302, etc.; William Orme, *Life of Baxter* (2 v., 1831), II, 237. For Baxter's controversies: Powicke, 221 ff.; his corpus, Orme, *Life*, Vol. II. On his "neutral center": Baxter, qu. by Powicke, 167. The *Testimony* of 1647: See Daniel Neal, *Puritans* (1843), II, 44. Popery ranged with Socinianism: Henoch Clapham, *Left Hand*, esp. 25, 65; Francis Cheynell, *Rise of Socinianisme* (1643), Ep. Ded., Sig A4^{vo}; see William J. S. Simpson, *Archbishop Bramhall* (1927), 201-205. A . . . Presbyterian scheme (23)—See Samuel Rutherford, *The Tryal & Triumph of Faith* (1645), 332. On Catholics' "center": e.g., James Calfhill, *An Answere to . . . Martiall* (1565), Parker Soc. (1846), 147. On Everard's "center": R. H., Ep. Ded., before John Everard, *Some Gospel-Treasures Opened*, 1653. On Everard: Rufus M. Jones, *Spiritual Reformers* (1914), 239-252; William Haller, *Rise of Puritanism* (New York, 1938), 207-212;

[108]   W. K. Jordan, "Sectarian Thought," *HLQ*, III (1939), 214-219.

109   A brief essay [refuted atheists] (39)—John Milton, *C. D.*, *Works* (1931-),
110   XIV, 25-29. Cp., e.g., the opening of Calvin's *Institutes*. [William] Chillingworth preached [on atheism] (20)—*Works* (3 v., 1838), III, Sermons ii and iii. On Robert Parsons' apologetics: E. A. Strathmann, "Robert Parsons' Essay on Atheism," *J. Q. Adams Mem. St.* (Washington, 1948), 665 ff. On atheism: Gaston Bonet-Maury, *Des Origines du Christianisme Unitaire chez les Anglais* (1881), 14, 162. George T. Buckley, *Atheism* (Chicago, 1932), 56-59.

Fifty-odd . . . apologetic [works] in France (32)—For bibliog.: Henri Busson, *La Pensée Religieuse Française* (Paris, 1933), 29-31; see also Busson, *Rationalisme* (1922), 475-477, 569-576, 633, etc.; Buckley, 98-100. Some English preaching: Henry Smith, "Gods Arrow Against Atheism," *Works* (2 v., 1866), II, 365 ff.; Sir George More, *A Demonstration of God in his Workes*, 1597; John Dove, *A Confutation of Atheisme*, 1605; Thomas Milles, tr. *Treasurie* (1613), I, 605 ff.; Thomas Scot, *Philomythie* (1616), 49-50; Thomas Adams, e.g., *Gallants Burden*, in *Workes* (1629), 32 ff.; John Donne, *Works*, ed. Alford, I, 416; II, 355, etc.; Godfrey Goodman, *The Creatures Praysing God*, 1622; anon., *A Dispute Betwixt an Atheiste and a Christian*, 1646; Jeremiah Burroughs, *Evil of Evils* (1654), 398. See Burton, *Anatomy*, ed. Shilleto, III, 449, for some early names. On Martin Fotherby: William Orme, *Baxter* (2 v., 1831), II, 32; Charles de Rémusat,

110 *Hist. de la Philosophie en Angleterre* (2 v., 1875), I, 122; William R. Sorley, *Hist. of English Philosophy* (1920), 42. Against "atheism": R. H. Per-
kinson, "The Polemical Use of *Nosce Teipsum,*" *SP*, XXXVI (1939), 597 ff.

111 [Richard] Baxter . . . attacked . . . atheists (1)—*The Unreasonableness
of Infidelity,* in *Practical Works* (1830), XX, 24, esp. 406; *Christian Directory,* II, 23-24, 189, 192; *Self-Denial,* XI, 321, cp. 127, 283; *Life of Faith,*
XII, 172-173. Note Orme, *Baxter,* II, 21. For the neo-Aristotelian "round":
see, e.g., John Donne, *Works,* ed. Alford, V, 56-57; cp. I, 314; III, 22-23.
Richard Sibbes, *Works* (7 v., 1862-), II, 495.

 [Ralph] Cudworth's . . . evidential work (24)—*The True Intellectual
System of the Universe,* ed. Thomas Birch (4 v., 1820), I, 184, 218 ff., 315-
320, 381-388, 401; III, 183-184, 310. On his Plastic Nature: Joseph Warren
Beach, *The Concept of Nature in Nineteenth-Century English Poetry* (New
York, 1936), 57-62; W. B. Hunter, "The Seventeenth-Century Doctrine of
Plastic Nature," *Harvard Theol. Rev.,* XLIII (1950), 197 ff., esp. 203 204;
Ernst Cassirer, *The Platonic Renaissance in England,* tr. J. P. Pettegrove
(New York, 1953), 140 ff. Charles de Rémusat, *Hist. de la Phil. en Angle-
terre,* II, 35, and J. A. Passmore, *Ralph Cudworth* (Cambridge, 1951), 12
(and cp. 4), notice the absence of physical support for the doctrine.

112 Henry More [drew] "an exoteric fence . . . about theology" (29)—
Philosophical Writings (1712), Pref. Gen., pp. iv-v; see also pp. ix, 2, 141-
142. For his epistemology: A. O. Lovejoy, "Kant and the English Platonists," *Essays Philosophical [for] William James* (1908), 269 ff.; J. T. Baker,
"Henry More and Kant," *Phil. Rev.,* XLVI (1937), 301. For his ontology:
Marjorie Nicolson, "The Spirit World of Milton and More," *SP*, XXII
(1925), 433 ff.; Beach, *Concept of Nature,* 62-66; Paul R. Anderson, *Science
in Defense of Liberal Religion* (New York, 1933), 119 ff. (the Spirit of Na-
113 ture). *Antidote* [and] final causes (4)—Chs. i-xii. On More's argument
from design: Anderson, 131.

 [More's] "circumstantiated" reason (22)—*Theological Works* (1708),
770; see also 175-176, 766; *An Account of Virtue: or, Dr. More's Abridgment of Morals,* ed. S. P. Lamprecht (New York, 1930), 11-13; *Psychozoia*
(II.74 ff., 107-117), in *Philosophical Poems,* ed. Geoffrey Bullough (1931),
114 56-65, 66-69. More and Thomas Vaughan quarreling (5) See Vaughan,
The Man-Mouse Taken in a Trap (1650), 109-110. For More's opinion of
antinomianism, see, against "Familism," *Theol. Works,* 171-188. Note
Anderson, 85.

 [More] grappled with Socinians (25)—*T. W.,* 1, 318-319; 524. Cp.
Jeremy Taylor, *Ductor Dub.,* in *Works,* ed. Reginald Heber and C. P. Eden
(10 v., 1850-), IX, 64. Cp. *Lib. of Proph.,* V, 405-406, where he clearly associates Trinitarian dogma with tradition rather than scripture. On reason
and its limits: *Works,* VI, 207, 350, 404; VIII, 97, 108-109; IX, 274, see esp.
76-77, 61-63. Taylor's "Pelagianism": VII, 299-340. See Samuel Taylor
Coleridge, *Aids to Reflection* (Aph. x), in *Complete Works* (7 v., 1884), I,
285; and "Notes," *Literary Remains,* V, 140-252; see William J. Brown,
115 *Jeremy Taylor* (London, 1925), 111. Taylor called Socinian: see Marjorie
Nicolson, in *PQ,* VIII (1929), 328; and C. J. Stranks, *Taylor* (London, 1952),
235-246.

 Historians have pointed out few [English Socinians] (19)—See Thomas
Crosby, *Hist. of English Baptists* (4 v., 1738), I, 214; Gaston Bonet-Maury,
Christianisme Unitaire (1881), 54, etc.; J. Hay Colligan, *The Arian Move-
ment in England* (1913), 10 ff.; Henry W. Clark, *Nonconformity* (1911-), I,

NOTES

117 *A Study in Milton's Christian Doctrine* (New York, 1939), 3, 105 ff.; thesis, 199-203. Contrast Maurice Kelley, *This Great Argument* (Princeton, 1941), 8-24, esp. 11-14, 19-20; 192 ff. Note L. J. Osborne, diss., Stanford Univ. *Abstracts*, XXVII (1953), 232.

118 [Milton] **first settled his convictions by scripture** (17)—His own statement: *C. D., Works*, XIV, 5 (15) ff. Rule of the "plain places": Augustine, *De Unitate Ecclesiæ*, xvi. On Milton's "exception" (divorce), note A. S. P. Woodhouse, "Milton, Puritanism, and Liberty," *UTQ*, IV (1935), 487; H. J. C. Grierson, *Criticism and Creation*, 79. **A Catholic critic** (35)—

119 A. J. T. Eisenring, 103. **Gospel revoked no civil permission** (4)—Milton, *C. D.*, XV, 145 (13). Polygamy practiced: see H. J. C. Grierson, *Cross Currents in English Literature of the XVIIth Century* (1929), 295. Bible recognized it in N. T. times: thus Sir Thomas Browne, *R. M.* (ii.9), *Works*, ed. Keynes, I, 87; Jeremy Taylor, *Works* (10 v., 1850-), IX, 690. See also Evion Owen, "Milton and Selden on Divorce," *SP*, XLIII (1946), 246.

Puritan tenet . . . the Sabbatical Sunday (10)—See Herbert H. Henson, *Studies in English Religion in the Seventeenth Century* (1903), 35-75. Milton, *C. D., Works* (1931-), XVII, 177-198; 191 (28)-198 (7); 7 (27); cp. *Likeliest Means*, VI, 67 (21). Cp. Jeremy Taylor, *Duct. Dub.*, in *Works* (1850-), IX, 461-462. On Seventh Day Baptists: Milton, *C. D.*, XVII, 193 (9-10). **Immersion [confessed] Apostolic** (26)—See Charles Gore, H. L. Goudge, and Alfred Guillaume, *A New Comm. on Holy Scripture* (New York, 1946), N. T., 430. Commission on Doctrine, *Doctrine in the Church of England* (New York, 1922), 136 n. John Donne, *Works*, ed. Alford, I, 584; V, 341; Jeremy Taylor, *Works* (10 v., 1850-), VI, 416-417; X, 368-369. James Mackinnon, *Calvin and the Reformation* (London, 1936), 262.

[Milton's] **mild pantheism** (30)—*C. D., Works*, XV, 17 (3)-27 (5). See Harris Fletcher, *Milton's Rabbinical Readings* (Urbana, Ill., 1930), 81-82, and, on the accuracy of Milton's scripturalism here, 158. Maurice Kelley, *This Great Argument*, 204; Grant McColley, *'Paradise Lost': Origins*, 73.

120 **The natural generation of the soul** (2)—Consists with mortalism: thus [?Richard or ?Robert] O[verton], *Mans Mortallitie* (1643), 30-41. R. H. West, "Milton's Angelological Heresies," *JHI*, XIV (1953), 123, notes that all the "heresies" hang together in a consistent ontology. **The New Testament neglected** (11)—Thus Gore, Goudge, and Guillaume, *New Commentary*, N. T., 298. Martin Luther used mortalism against Purgatory: *Exp. of . . . Eccles.* (tr. 1573), 148 (on Eccles. ix). Lutheran mortalists noted in Bohemia: Fridericus Staphylus, *The Apologie*, tr. T. Stapleton (1564), Pref., 17-18. Luther, Tyndale, and psychopannychism: George N. Conklin, *Biblical Criticism*, 83-84. On Purgatorial cupidity: Milton, *Animad., Works*, III, 143 (4-15); *Reason of Ch. Govt.*, III, 268 (9-11). Cp. *C. D.*, XV, 307 (4-9); on Purgatory, see 341 (10-12). Mortalism misrepresented: by, e.g., Christopher Love, *Heavens Glory* (1653), 117-118. [Milton's] **Old Testament texts [for mortalism]** (26)—*C. D.*, XV, 217 (23) ff. See esp. 221 (1)-223 (12). Cp. Gore et al., eds. *New Commentary*, O. T., 685-686. See George Bull, qu. in *Anglicanism*, ed. P. E. More and F. L. Cross (Milwaukee, 1935), 320—Old Testament "mortalism" recognized.

121 **Scholasticism . . . whipped [at] Trent** (6)—See Pietro Sarpi, *The Historie of the Council of Trent* (iv, "1551"), tr. Nathaniel Brent (1640), 323. Catholic opponents (collected): Thomas James, *Manuduction unto Divinitie, Containing a Confutation of Papists* (1625), 7-8. Protestants on scholasticism: Barnaby Rich, *Faultes* (1606), 30-31; Henry Smith, *Works* (2 v.,

121   1866) I, 478 ff.; John Donne, *Essays in Divinity* (1651), ed. E. M. Simpson
(1952), 88; William Evans, *Translation of Nature* (1633), sec. xvii; Thomas
Drant (of Shaston), *Divine Lanthorne* (1637), 9; Mark Frank, *Fifty-One
Sermons*, LACT (2 v., 1849), II, 66 ff.; Richard Sibbes, *Works* (7 v., 1862-),
V, 467 ff. Bishop [John] Bramhall [defended] schoolmen (15)—"Castiga-
tion of Hobbes," *Works*, LACT (5 v., 1842), IV, 457; "Vindication of Gro-
tius" [against Baxter], III, 567-568, 538-539. Defense of schoolmen: IV, 35,
128-130, 209-210, 260, 265, 282, 382-386, 457, etc.

Elizabethan clergymen [on scholastics] (20)—John King, *Lectures upon
Jonas* ([1594] 1618), 10-12. "Good" and "vain" questions illustrated: John
Marbecke, *A Booke of Notes and Common-places* (1581), 888-890 ff.;
Thomas Milles, tr. *Treasurie* (1613), Bk. vi, chs. 14-15; Robert Cawdrey,
A Treasurie or Store-house of Similies (1600), 211-212, 382, 394, 613, etc.;
Robert Burton, *Anatomy*, ed. Shilleto, III, 423. Cp. David Person, *Varieties*
(1635), Bk. iv (pp. 177 ff.), sec. ii; Daniel Tossanus, *A Synopsis [of] Fathers
. . . and Schoolmen*, tr. A. Stafford (1635), 33-34.

122   Moderns . . . who belabored Aristotle (1)—See Charles de Rémusat,
Hist. de la Phil. en Angleterre, I, 184 ff.; Richard F. Jones, *Ancients
and Moderns: Washington Univ. St. in Lang. and Lit.*, N.S. 6, St. Louis,
1935; and Herschel Baker, *The Wars of Truth*, 165-186, esp. 173 ff. See esp.
Thomas Hobbes, "Of Darkness from Vain Philosophy," *Leviathan* (iv.46),
in *Works*, ed. Molesworth (11 v., 1839-), III, 664 ff., esp. 674, 680, and 688.
See John Laird, *Hobbes* (London, 1934), 55, 90-91. Bacon described . . .
Scholasticism (22)—*Adv. of L.*, in *Works*, ed. Spedding, VI, 122-123; *De
Aug.*, II, 130. Cp. William Chillingworth, *Works* (3 v., 1838), I, 20-21, 208;
III, 122-123 ff.; Anthony Stafford, *Niobe* (1611), 143, 156. On Protestant
scholasticism: Otto Ritschl, *Dogmengeschichte des Protestantismus* (4 v.,
1908-), IV. Albert C. M'Giffert, *Protestant Thought Before Kant* (1924),
141-154. On Laud's statutes: James B. Mullinger, *The University of Cambridge* (3 v., [1873] 1911), III, 91.

123   Origin of the soul [a dubious topic] (4)—Thus John Woolton, *The Immortalitie of the Soule* (1576), 27b; Pierre de la Primaudaye, *The French
Academie*, tr. T. B. (1618), Pt. II, 574, 589; Sir John Davies, *Nosce Teipsum*,
in *Works*, ed. Grosart, I, 80-97; John Day, *Day's Dyall* (1614), 92; John
Donne, *Essays in Divinity*, ed. Simpson (1952), 30, and 30 n (120), and letter to Sir Thomas Lucy, *Works*, ed. Alford, VI, 317. An heretical tradu-
cianist chides merely conventional timidity: Henry Woolner, *The Extraction
of Mans Soul* [= *True Originall*, 1642] (1655), 2-11. Charles de Rémusat,
Hist. de la Philosophie en Angleterre, II, 109-116, lists tracts on the soul,
few heretical. Setting just punishment for abortion compelled some
legal inquiry into the time and manner of the soul's origin: see William
Hill, *The Infancie of the Soule* (1605), sec. x. For the poets' interest, see
G. Bullough, "Origin of the Soul," *N & Q*, CLXII (1932), 290 ff. [Another]
was exact angelology (7)—On the curiosity of it: e.g., La Primaudaye,
(1618 tr.), Pt. III, 673; John Downame, *Lectures upon . . . Hosea* (1608),
257; Donne, *Works*, ed. Alford, IV, 13; Andrew Willet, *Hexapla in Da-
nielem* (1610), 391 (angelology Popish); John Salkeld, *A Treatise of Angels*
(1613), Sigs A2vo-A3; John Prideaux, *Angels, etc.*, in *Twenty Sermons* (1636),
21; and esp. Mede, *Discourses* (x), in *Works* ([1648] 1672), 40 (Protestant
caution unnecessary). See Thomas Fuller, *Holy State*, ed. M. G. Walten
(1938), 63-64; and *Collected Sermons* (2 v., 1891), I, 469-470. Theologians
dabbled (15)—Christopher Love, *Treatise of Angels*, in *The Dejected*

123 *Soules Cure* (1657), Pref.; William Austin, *Certain Devout Meditations* (1635), 247 ff., esp. 248; John Bayly, *The Angell Guardian* (1630), 1-2, see 5-6. See Arnold Williams, "The Motivation of Satan's Rebellion in *P. L.*," *SP*, XLII (1945), 264-266. On angelology and art, note M. M. Mahood, *Poetry and Humanism*, 143. On Milton's angelology: R. H. West (and his refs.), in *SAMLA Studies in Milton*, ed. J. Max Patrick (Gainesville, Fla., 1953), 20 ff. On its inconsistency, note Harris Fletcher, *Milton's Rabbinical Readings*, 218; and Sir Walter Raleigh, *Milton*, 114.

Vanini's "martyrdom" (36)—For a typical sneer: Henry Hammond, *Misc. Theol. Works*, LACT (3 v., 1849-), III (1), 158. **Sir Robert Dallington exposed . . . the Inquisition (40)**—*Inference upon Guicciardines Digression*, in *Aphorismes*, 1613 (rich with clichés of anti-curiosity preaching).

124 On Popish "expurgation" of the Fathers: Thomas Stoughton, *Treatise Against Poperie* (1598), 15-16; Thomas James, *The Corruption of Scripture . . . and Fathers, by . . . Rome* (1612), Pt. v, p. 22; George Benson, *Sermon at Paules Crosse* (1609), 58-59; Jeremy Taylor, *Dissuasive from Popery*, in *Works* (10 v., 1850-), VI, 185-186, and esp. 466-475. **Ignorance, the [Catholic's] mother of devotion (11)**—On Henry Cole at the short-lived Westminster Conference called by Elizabeth in 1558, see *STC* 25286 and (with the refs. to Fox, Strype, and Burnet) John Jewel, *Works*, ed. R. W. Jelf (8 v., 1848), I, 43, 43 n, 55, 125, and esp. VIII, 111 ff.; and Thomas Fuller, *The Church Hist. of Britain* (VI.ii.2-3), ed. James Nichols (3 v., 1868), II, 509. Early repetitions of Cole's remark: Thomas Drant, *Two Sermons* (1569), 177, see 185-186; John Woolton, *The Castell of Christians . . . beseeged* (1577), Sig E4^{vo}; and Richard Sibbes, *Works* (7 v., 1862-), VII, 287, Grosart's note. More preaching on Romish ignorance: Christopher Musgrave, *Musgraves Motives for His Secession from Rome* (1621), ch. ii; John Hull, *Christ His Proclamation* (1613), 131; Sir Edwin Sandys, *A Relation of the State of Religion* (1605), Sig C3, my italics. William Pemble, *Five Sermons* (1628), 14-15.

On . . . Purgatory . . . Milton [early] read [of curiosity] (25)—*In Proditionem Bombardicam* (Ep. iii), in *Works* (18 v., 1931-), I, 225 (12). See Walter MacKellar, "Milton, James I, and Purgatory," *MLR*, XVIII (1923), 472 ff. Cp., on "scholastic" hypostases, *Logic* (Pref.), in *Works*, XI, 7 (4). Christopher Sutton, *Godly Meditations upon the Lordes Supper* (1601), Pref. John Denison, *The Heauenly Banquet* (1619), 53. Daniel Featley, *Transubstantiation Exploded* (1638), 43. Sir Robert Dallington, *Inference* (50-55), in *Aphorismes*, 1613. **[Papists] multiplying mysteries (30)**—So William Chillingworth, *Works* (3 v., 1838), I, 208. Cp. John Bramhall, *Works*, LACT (5 v., 1842), I, 21-22; repr. in *Anglicanism*, ed. P. E. More and F. L. Cross, 484; Joseph Hall, *No Peace with Rome*, in *Recollection of Treatises* (1614), 871; Jeremy Taylor, *Worthy Communicant*, in *Works* (10 v., 1850-), VIII, 106-109; *Dissuasive from Popery*, VI, 207; see 272.

125 On Bramhall's occasion: William J. S. Simpson, *Archbishop Bramhall* (1927), 118.

[Milton's] long intolerance of Catholicism (33)—His grounds: *Of Ref.*, *Works* (1931-), III, 54 (22); *Of True Rel.*, VI, 167 (12), 171 (28)-172 (2), 176 (16); *Of Civil Power*, VI, 8 (2) and esp. 14 (2-3); *C. D.*, XVI, 315 (11).

126 On the Donation of Constantine: III, 21 (13), 24 (26)-28, 42 (8), 43 (17), 360 (3); V, 187 (27), 230 (23); VI, 48 (24), 81 (18); note III, 43 (16) ff. **Milton [on] free will . . . could . . . pass for [orthodox] (34)**—See Leon Howard, "'The Invention' of Milton's 'Great Argument,'" *HLQ*, IX

129 D2; Elnathan Parr, *The Grounds of Divinitie* ([1614] 1615), 123; I. P., *Ana-baptisme* . . . *Unmasked* (1623), 55; William Wischart, *Exp. of the Lords Prayer* (1633), 150-151. **Assembly arranged** (18)—I.c., to burn John Archer's *Comfort for Beleevers*, 1645. See the Assembly's *Short Declaration* (1645) denouncing Archer's ultra-Calvinistic "blasphemies," esp. Opinions 1 and 2. See also Charles R. Gillett, *Burned Books* (2 v., 1932), I, 249. **Theory of the double will** (21)—Required "proving" God's iniquity: see, e.g., John Calvin, *Institutes* (iii.24.13), tr. Norton (1634), 479, on God's hardening of Pharaoh's heart. Cp. William Wischart, *Lords Prayer* (1633), 146-150. See esp. William Twisse, *Discovery of D. Jacksons Vanitie* (1631), 455-548. No contradiction involved: thus Twisse, 536 ff.; Richard Crakan-thorpe, *A Sermon of Predestination* (1620), 24; William Fenner, *Works* (1657), 39-40. God "reasonable" by occult reason: thus, e.g., John Davies, *Microcosmos*, in *Works*, ed. Grosart, I, 28. God's two wills indeed con-flict (illustrations), but only atheists will scoff: John Dove, *A Confutation of Atheisme* (1605), 59. **Word-play [concerning God's two wills]** (39)— See Richard Resbury, *Some Stop to the Gangrene of Arminianisme* (1651), 81.

130 **Many knew . . . much about [the secret will]** (6)—Thus Silvester Nor-ris (priest), *Antidote* (1622), 280. "William Milbourne" [=T. Jackson?], *Sapientia Clamitans* ([wr. 1612?] 1638), 13, and *Gods Just Hardning of Pharaoh* (1638), 142-145, 213. On the authorship of the former: R. C. Bald, in *RES*, XXIV (1948), 321 ff. **A Calvinist [permitted] three ques-tions** (11)—I.e., William Wischart, *Lords Prayer* (1633), 146. "**Sin is de-fined, etc.**" (22)—John Collop, "M. D.," *Poesis Rediviva* (1656), 14-16. Calvinistic modesty wrestles with the problem of evil: Arthur Dent, *The Opening of Heaven Gates* ([1610] 1624), 38; John Greene, *The First Man* (1643), e.g., 19.

"**Some I have chosen, etc.**" (35)—Milton, *P. L.* iii.184—which read in the light of *C. D., Works*, XIV, 147 (4)-149 (1), and 155 (4-15). Cp. 91 (9) ff.,
131 97 (4). See B. Rajan, *'Paradise Lost' and the Seventeenth Century Reader*, 23-28; C. S. Lewis, *A Preface to 'Paradise Lost'* (London, 1942), 81-91. On the paucity of controversial divinity in *P. L.*, see also Sister Miriam Joseph, C. S. C., *Orthodoxy in 'Paradise Lost,'* Centenary P., Saint Mary's College (Notre Dame, Ind., 1954), esp. 250 (author's thesis); J. B. Conrath, diss., "The Orthodoxy of *P. L.*," Univ. Iowa *Abstracts*, VI (1953), 369 ff. **Evan-gelic religion . . . "in two words"** (19)—Milton, *Works*, VI, 21 (2).

[Predestinarians] those against whom Milton . . . defended God (37)—
132 See *C. D.*, XV, 213 (17)-215 (2). For my italics, cf. Lat. *omnis expostulatio*, 214 (2). See John S. Diekhoff, *Milton's 'Paradise Lost': A Commentary on the Argument* (New York, 1946), 122. But see Marjorie Nicolson, "Mil-ton and Hobbes," *SP*, XXIII (1926), 405 ff. **Touching [God's will in] predestination he dared to ask** (12)—*Works* (18 v., 1931-), XIV, 125 (12-24). On the stories of God's "sins": *C. D.*, XV,
133 191 (9) ff.; XIV, 109 (5-27); XVII, 305 (22) ff.; esp. XV, 67-87. On "dis-pense": *Divorce*, III, 445 (6-14), and 443 (rubric). Cp. 440 (13-16), and *Samson Agonistes*, 300-325.

Predestinarians agreed to surrender [logic] (26)—E.g., John Forbes, *Treatise of Justification* (1616), 12; William Austin, *Devout Meditations* (1635), 8-9; Henry Burton, *A Plea to an Appeale* (1626), 59; *Westminster Confession* (1647), ch. iii, sec. 5; Thomas Hobbes, *Liberty, Necessity, and Chance*, in *Works*, ed. Molesworth (11 v., 1839-), V, 103-104; Richard Res-

136 IV, 391-392; III, 674 ff.; cp. VI, 102 ff., esp. 103 (on Constantine). See Wilbur K. Jordan, *Toleration*, IV, 299. **"Yourselves can nor relish, etc."** **(19)**—Richard Montagu, *Appello Cæsarem* (1625), 39; cp. John Yates, *Gods Arraignement of Hypocrites* (1615), 91-94. Montagu answered: George Carleton, *An Examination of the Late 'Appeale'* (1626), 2-3; cp. John Bramhall, in Hobbes, *Liberty, etc., Works*, ed. Molesworth, V, 130. On Montagu and on Goodwin: David Masson, *Life of Milton*, I, 369, and II, 583; A. W. Harrison, *Arminianism*, 133, 152; Wilbur K. Jordan, *Toleration*, II, 120; Daniel Neal, *Puritans*, I, 272; II, 44.

"Action of predestinating us to adoption, etc." **(40)**—John Forbes, *Justification* (1616), 12. Predestination a most comfortable doctrine: Thomas Rogers, *The Thirty-Nine Articles*, Parker Soc. (1854), 154-155; cp. Wolfgang Musculus, *Commonplaces*, tr. J. Man (1563), 213b (let us think about the elect; reprobates are not worth a thought); John Gumbleden, *Gods Great Mercy* (1626), e.g., 16; "David Calderwood" [= ?William Scot], *The Pastor and the Prelate* ([1628] 1692), 23; George Kendall, *Theocratia, or, A Vindication of the Doctrine Commonly Received in the Reformed Churches concerning Gods Intentions of Special Grace and Favour to His Elect*, 1653. Cp. Milton, *Of True Rel., Works* (18 v., 1931-), VI 169 (22).

137 **Calvin had anticipated [with his]** *O altitudo!* **(8)**—Against mystics: *The Institution of Christian Religion* (1.9.3), tr. Thomas Norton (1634), 30; cp. Henri Busson, *Rationalisme*, 316-344; Gertrude Huehns, *Antinomianism in English Hist.* (London, 1951), 36. Against incautious preaching of predestination and misuse of the doctrine: *Inst.* (I.17.1-2), 88-89; (III.21.1), 448-449 ff.; (III.24.4), 473-474; (III.24.15-16), 481-482; (III.3.41-43), 279-281; esp. (III.23.14), 470-471; see James Mackinnon, *Calvin and the Reformation* (London, 1936), 250. Not directly against reason: *Inst.* (II.2.16), 119; (I.8.1), 23, etc.; cp. (for classicism) Quirinus Breen, *John Calvin: A Study in French Humanism*, diss. (Chicago, 1931), e.g., 148-149; Mackinnon, 225-226. Against curiosity and heresy: *Inst.* (II.2.13), 117; (I.14.1), 63; (I.14.7), 66-67; (I.14.16), 70; (I.14.19), 72; (II.12.5), 219; (II.13.4), 224-225; Servetus (I.13.21-29), 55-62; God's secret will, e.g., (III.23.1), 462 ff. On Calvin's early heterodoxy and stiffening trinitarianism: Earl M. Wilbur, *Hist. of Unitarianism* (1945), 16; Gaston Bonet-Maury, *Christianisme Unitaire* (1881), 25. *Contra paganos* and nature's insufficient light: *Inst.* (I.5.10; 1.10.3; II.2.3; III.8.11), 14 (or 10-14), 32, 111, 340. **All determinism . . . bowed . . . before the secret will (35)**—See, e.g., Justus Lipsius, *Two Books of Constancie* (1584), tr. Sir John Stradling (1594), ed. C. M. Hall (1929), 176. On Calvin's *O altitudo!*, note A. W. Harrison, *Arminianism*, 11.

[William] Perkins . . . rebuilt Calvin's . . . fortresses (37)—*Workes* (3 v., 1612-), I, 143.2.A; II, 168-169: I, 363.2.C; II, 380.1.D: I, 482.1.C:
138 723.2.D. Cp. Thomas Sutton, *Lectures upon Romans* (1632), 459-460.

Regenerate reason . . . broached no heterodoxy (22)—Anthony Burges, *Spiritual Refinings* (1652), 317 ff. Calvinists allowed freedom in natural things: Jerome Zanchius, *Confession of Christian Religion* (tr. 1599), 39-41, and esp. 42 (sec. ix)—man's free will argued against all "atheistic" determinism; John Dove, *Confutation* (1605)—the Calvinists' tenet similarly urged. For the tenet: William Perkins, *Workes* (1612-), I, 728.2.D; Richard Niccols, *A Day-Starre* (1613), 9-10; Pierre du Moulin, *The Buckler of Faith* (tr. [1619] 1623), 83; Edward Elton, *The Triumph of a True Christian* (1623), 167; George Carleton, *An Examination of the Late 'Appeale'* (1626), 227; John Downe, *Selfe-Deniall*, in *Certain Treatises* (1633), 16; Anthony Burges, *Vindicia Legis* ([1646] 1647), 85-90; William Attersoll, *Physicke*,

139 *etc.*, in *Three Treatises* (1632), 137. Contrast Milton, *C. D., Works* (18 v., 1931-), XV, 211 (2-11). Note Peter Heylyn, *Quinquarticular History* (1660), in *Works* (1681), 509.

Particular persons might not be named as reprobates (30)—Zephaniah Smyth, *The Doome of Heretiques* (1648), 10-15; cp. Sir Thomas Browne, *R. M., Works*, ed. Keynes, I, 69. See Maurice Hussey, "Bunyan's 'Mr. Ignorance,' " *MLR*, XLIV (1949), 484. On "peering into God's books" without "using the means" of salvation: John Donne, *Essays in Divinity*, ed. E. M. Simpson (1952), 7; Joseph Hall, *Characters of Vertues and Vices* (1608), 144; William Vaughan, *The Spirit of Detraction* (1611), 67; Edward Elton, *Triumph* (1623), 245; William Gouge, *Workes* (1627), 113; Richard

140 Baxter, *Confirmation and Restauration* (1658), 163-164. Contrast the Traskites' excess of legalism: William Sclater, *Exp. upon Thess.* (1619), 17-34; and B. D. [John Falconer, Jesuit], *John Traskes Iudaical . . . Fancyes* (1618), esp. 95. See Theophilus Braborn, qu. by Fr[ancis] White, *Examination of a Lawlesse Pamphlet* (1637), 77, and John Trask, *A Treatise of Liberty from Judaisme*, 1620 (his recantation).

[Calvinism was] pushed . . . toward the Arminian way (21)—See Perry Miller, "Preparation for Salvation in New England," *JHI*, IV (1943), 275-286. **God's purpose . . . to be sought [only] "in the means" (26)**—Anthony Maxey, *Certain Sermons* ([1619] 1634), 29 ff.; [Walter Sweeper], *Israels Redemption by Christ* (1622), 59 ff.; William Fenner, *Spiritual Mans Directory*, in *Works* (1657), 39. On "vocation": see notes to my page 72.

141 **Antinomianism . . . eliminated . . . vocation [from the "means"] (4)**—John Eaton, *The Honey-combe of Free Justification* (1642) chs. i and iv; John Saltmarsh, *Free Grace* ([1645] 1839), 55. Cp. Eaton, 51-52, 60, 145, and Saltmarsh, 126, 136-138; 42, 112-113. On John Eaton: Samuel Rutherford, *A Survey of the Spirituall Antichrist* (1648), 3. Fear of "immorality": e.g., Alexander Ross, *Pansebeia* ([1653] 1655), 366; Richard Vines, *The Impostures of Seducing Teachers* (1644), 37. For fair statements of antinomian doctrine: Frederick J. Powicke, *Life of Baxter* (1924), 241, and esp. Gertrude Huehns, *Antinomianism in English Hist.* (London, 1951), 37-54. **The Black Coats' fear [partly] ecclesiastical (25)**—See John Saltmarsh, *Free Grace* (1839 ed.), 7-10; Christopher Love, *Animadversions on Mr. Dell's Sermon* (1646), 6 ff.; Samuel Rutherford, *Secrets of Antinomianisme*, in (= Pt. II) *Spirituall Antichrist* (1648), 181-219; see 216, 238, 138, and Pt. I, 62-64. See Huehns, 89-105, on the political implications of "free grace."

142 **The war of name-calling (7)**—See Saltmarsh, *Free Grace*, Pref. and cp. Eaton, *Honey-combe*, 43-45, 223-224 (legalism is Popish); Stephen Geree, *The Doctrine of the Antinomians Confuted* (1644), 101-102, see 2 ff. **[Samuel] Rutherford replied [to Towne] (16)**—*Spirituall Antichrist* (Pt. II), 63-64; see 2-4, 138, 140, and Rutherford, *The Tryal & Triumph of Faith* (1645), 331-332.

Religion of the antinomians . . . easily admitted [enthusiasm] (28)—See D. B. Robertson, *The Religious Foundations of Leveller Democracy*

143 (New York, 1951), 20-22; Huehns, e.g., 94. Separatists (not antinomian) dropped both ceremonial and moral Law of Moses: Wilbur K. Jordan, *Toleration*, II, 247; cp. Milton, *C. D., Works* (1931-), XVI, 147 (9-23)—Zanchius cited; cp. on the Mosaic Law and the Blasphemy Acts, XVII, 161 (1-8). See Jerome Zanchius, *Confession of the Christian Religion* (tr. 1599), 95 (sec. vii), and see 99 (antinomianism rejected); Martin Luther, *A Comm. [on] Galatians* (tr. [1575] 1635), 66 ff., esp. 77b. Cp. Nicholas Hemmingius, *The Faith of the Church Militant*, tr. T. Rogers (1581), 318-320. Milton's

143 *C. D.* recognized as "legal": F. E. Mineka, "The Critical Reception of Milton's *D. D. C.," Univ. Texas St. in Eng.* (1943), 123.

Justification . . . **by faith [and its] works (25)**—Milton, *C. D., Works,*
144 XVI, 39 (11-18); XIV, 397 (1-4); XVI, 143 (13-20). **No room for pride (1)**—
XVI, 23 (1-6); XV, 329 (3-6). Cp. John Goodwin, *Imputatio Fidei* (1642), 182.

[Baptist] materialism . . . seemed rudimentary (20)—See, e.g., two Quakers against the Baptists Samuel Bradley and Jeremy Ives, respectively: George Whitehead, *The Authority of the True Ministry,* 1660; and James Nayler, *Weaknes Above Wickednes* (1656), 9. Contrast Milton, *C. D., Works* (1931-), XVI, 171 (3) ff.; 183 (24) ff.

145 Masson made **[Milton] an eclectic (1)**—*Life of Milton,* VI, 838 ff. **Baptists [battled] the Quakers (8)**—E.g., Roger Williams, *George Fox Digg'd out of his Burrowes* (1676), Prop. 10 [11], 13, 14.

Anabaptists' [alleged] rebellion (20)—See Louise F. Brown, *Baptists and Fifth Monarchy Men* (1912), 137-139; Charles E. Whiting, *Studies in English Puritanism* (1931), 165 ff. On separation of church and state: Thomas Helwys, *Persecution Condemned* (1615), ed. Edward B. Underhill, *Tracts on Liberty of Conscience,* Hanserd Knollys Soc. (1846), with similar works by Baptists Busher, Murton, Richardson, Sturgion, etc. On Helwys: Wilbur K. Jordan, *Toleration,* II, 275 ff., and Thomas Lyon, *The Theory of Religious Liberty in England, 1603-1639* (Cambridge, 1937), 123. Cp., on separation of powers, Milton, *Second Defence, Works* (1931-), VIII, 129 (17-19). Early Baptists suffered for political theory: Henry W. Clark, *Hist. of English Nonconformity,* I, 129; George T. Buckley, *Atheism,* 47-54; Daniel Neal, *Puritans* (2 v., 1843), I, 137; II, 355 ff. For late "apostasy" of some Baptists: Henry W. Clark, *Nonconformity,* I, 386; Robert Barclay, *Inner Life of Religious Societies,* 150.

Münster [stories] clung to [Baptists] (21)—See, e.g., William Chillingworth, Serm. VII, *Works* (3 v., 1838), III, 195 ff.; Edward B. Underhill, ed. [Baptist] *Confessions of Faith,* Hanserd Knollys Soc. (1854), viii-x, and, e.g., 278; Daniel Neal, *Puritans,* II, 353-404. For bibliog.: Louise F. Brown, *Baptists and Fifth Monarchy Men,* 6 (refs.). See esp. Charles E. Whiting, *English Puritanism,* 87-120. Detraction unmerited: thus Whiting, 89, 234; Brown, 15-27 ff.; Neal, I, 499; W. K. Jordan, "Sectarian Thought," *HLQ,* III (1939), 203. Baptists' descent from Menno: see Robert Barclay, *Inner Life* (1877), 69 ff.; Rufus M. Jones, *Studies in Mystical Religion* (1909), 381 ff. For Fifth Monarchism deduced from antinomian, not Baptist, principles: Gertrude Huehns, *Antinomianism,* 127-134, esp. 128.

146 **[Fifth Monarchists] more fanatically intolerant (28)**—Jordan, *HLQ, III* (1939), 203. Cp. Samuel Butler, "A Fifth Monarchy Man," *Characters,* ed. A. R. Waller (1908), 45. Light suggestions (nothing more) that Milton expected Christ's personal reign to be of this world (as certainly on this earth) may rest on a misunderstanding of Christ's Kingdom as he used the term. See Arthur Barker, *Milton and the Puritan Dilemma* (Toronto, 1942), 303, 224, esp. 197-199, 202-203. But Barker absolves Milton of all gross Fifth Monarchism.

147 **[Ephraim] Pagitt [called] Baptists' confession . . . "some ratsbane" (16)**—*Heresiography* ([1645] 1647), 38. Lord Brooke countered only General Baptists: Robert Greville, Lord Brooke, *Discourse of Episcopacie,* ii, 7 (1641), 99-101, cp. 123. Jeremy Taylor leaned toward some Baptist opinions: *Works* (10 v., 1850-), V, 544-558; VI, 417; VII, 523; X, 368-369 (half-

147 hearted pædobaptism). **The long series of [Baptist] confessions (28)**—*Con-*
148 *fessions of Faith*, ed. E. G. Underhill, Hanserd Knollys Soc., 1854. **Baptist
. . . attack [on academic divines] (3)**—See Charles E. Whiting, *English
Puritanism*, 95; cp. Helwys and Murton, resp., in E. B. Underhill, ed.
Tracts on Liberty, Hanserd Knollys Soc. (1846), 106-107, 205-216. **Ignorance
. . . "the Anabaptistical tenet" (7)**—John Woolton, *The Castell of Chris-
tians . . . beseeged* (1577), Sig E4ᵛᵒ. Edward Boughen, *Sermon at Saint
Pauls Crosse* ([1630] 1635), 26. Daniel Featley, *The Judges Charge*, in
Clavis Mystica (1636), 107; *ibid., The Tree of Saving Knowledge;* and *The
Dippers Dipt* (1645), 204-205. Note Pagitt, 34, and Samuel Butler, *Charac-
ters*, ed. Waller, 163-164. Contrast Thomas Collier, *The Pulpit-Guard
Routed* (1651), 7-8.
    Modern accounts [of Familists necessarily] deduced (30)—E.g., Robert
Barclay, *Inner Life of Religious Societies*, 26 ff. Rufus M. Jones, *Mystical
Religion*, 429 ff., and *Mysticism and Democracy*, 126. Thomas Lyon,
Theory of Religious Liberty, 235-237. Edward B. Underhill, ed. *Tracts on
Liberty*, Addenda, 375-389. Sidney H. Atkins, "The Family of Love," *N &
Q*, CLXXV (1938), 362 ff. Charles R. Gillett, *Burned Books*, I, 52-62.
Daniel Neal, *Puritans* (2 v., 1843), I, 137. Helen C. White, *English Devo-
tional Literature*, 43-45. Gertrude Huehns, *Antinomianism*, 61-63. Some
early slanders: E.g., Ephraim Pagitt, *Heresiography* (1647 ed.), 93 ff.; *The
Querers and Quakers Cause at the Second Hearing* (1653), 48 ff.; Alexander
Ross, *Pansebeia* ([1653] 1655), 364; [John Etherington], *A Brief Discovery of
Familisme* (1645), 10 ff.; and others cited in the modern studies mentioned.
Some earlier "studies": John Rogers, *The Displaying of . . . the Family of
Love*, 1579; John Knewstub, *A Confutation of H. N. and the Familie of
Love*, 1579 (containing Bishop John Young's notes on the Family); William
Wilkinson, *A Confutation of the Family of Love*, 1579; Stephen Denison,
The White Wolf, 1627. For opinions, at credible second hand, of an
avowed Familist: Strype, *Annals* (4 v., 1824), III, 31-32. See *A Supplication
of the Family . . . Examined*, 1606, which answers a paper handed about,
and possibly to the king. On Familists' permitted dissembling: Edwin
Sandys, *Sermons* [1585], Parker Soc. (1841), 130; Etherington, 10; and other
149 writers. **Vagaries of nomenclature (4)**—Familists become Ranters: see ded.
(by R. H.) to Cromwell before John Everard, *Gospel-Treasures*, 1653; or
Fuller, *Church Hist.*, cited by Charles E. Whiting, *English Puritanism*, 284.
Defining some nicknames: Thomas Collier, *The Pulpit-Guard Routed*
(1651), 55 ff. Familists once stood near Rosicrucians: see Henoch Clapham,
Ælohin-triune (1601), Sig A3ᵛᵒ (cabala, for its mysticism, called half Famil-
ist); Stephen Denison, *The White Wolf* (1627), 38; note Rufus M. Jones,
Mysticism and Democracy, 126, and William Haller, *The Rise of Puritan-
ism* (New York, 1938), 206; 208-209. For the change to "antinomian":
Samuel Rutherford, *A Survey of the Spirituall Antichrist*, 1648, and note
Charles Cotton, *A Reply to Mr. Williams* (1647), in *P. Narragansett Club*,
Providence, R. I., II (1867), 80-84.
    "The family of lust, . . . the Family of Love" (13)—John Norden, *A
Progresse of Pietie* (1596), Parker Soc. (1847), 114. Cp. John Woolton,
Castell (1577), Sig E4ᵛᵒ, and Thomas Rogers, *Thirty-Nine Articles*, Parker
Soc. (1854), 307 (and refs.). On the authorship of the play: G. J. Eberle,
"Dekker's Part in *The Familie of Love*," *J. Q. Adams Mem. St.*, ed.
James G. McManaway *et al.* (1948), 723 ff. **[Saltmarsh and Dell] spiritu-
alized sacraments (19)**—See John Saltmarsh, *Doctrine of Baptisms*, in
Sparkles of Glory ([1647] 1852), 18 ff.; and [William Dell], *The Doctrine of*

149 *Baptismes,* 1648. Everard, Pordage, and mystical science: see Christopher Fowler, *Dæmonium Meridianum,* Part II (1656), 1, 3, 35; Masson, *Life of Milton,* III, 153; and Thomas Edwards, *Gangræna* (1646), 24 (on Erbury). Richard Baxter, *Reliquiæ Baxterianæ* (1696), 77-78 (on Pordage and Everard as "Behmenist" Seekers). On Seekers' pride: *Querers and Quakers Cause* (1653), Pref.; John Saltmarsh, *Smoke of the Temple,* in *Some Drops of the Viall* (1646), 16-18; cp. 12-13 (against water-baptism). On their true identity: David Masson, *Life of Milton,* III, 153; Rufus M. Jones, *Mysticism and Democracy,* 142, 75; G. A. Johnson, "From Seeker to Finder," *Church Hist.,* XVII (1948), 299 ff., with Barclay and others. On Ranters: Robert Barclay, *Inner Life of Religious Societies,* 417 ff. Rufus M. Jones, *Mystical Religion,* 472 ff. Charles R. Gillett, *Burned Books,* I, 252-263. Gertrude Huehns, *Antinomianism,* 108-109; see 137, 145 (Ranterism associated with Quakerism), and (thus) Alexander Ross, *Pansebeia* (1655 ed.), 379-380. [Ranters'] "spiritual pride" (31)—Richard Baxter, *Reliq. Baxt.* (1696), 76-77. Cp. Samuel Butler, "A Ranter," *Characters,* ed. Waller, 67, and, on Ranters and their license, Peter Sterry, *Freedome of the Will* (1675), 156; Alexander Ross, *Pansebeia* ([1653] 1655), 387-389; [Richard Farnworth, Quaker], *The Ranters Principles & Deceits Discovered* (1655), 19; Samuel Fisher, Quaker, *Baby Baptism mere Baptism,* 1653.

Quakers' [inner light] set up a Pope in every breast (37)—Thus "Daniel Barrett" [= ?Samuel Austin], *The Character of a Quaker* (1671), 5. [It could] save pagans and . . . devils (40)—*Querers and Quakers Cause* (1653), 10. On salvability of pagans: Robert Barclay (Quaker), *An Apology for Quakers* (1678), Prop. vi; James Nayler, *Answer to [Baxter's] Quakers*
150 *Catechism,* 1656 ed. On the inner light: e.g., G[eorge] W[hitehead], *Examination of James Nayler* (1652), in *A Collection of Sundry Books* (1716), 13-14; Henry Clark (Quaker), *A Cloud of Witnesses . . . that Jesus Christ is the Word of God, and not the Bible,* 1656; Luella M. Wright, *The Literary Life of the Early Friends* (New York, 1932), 26-39. Defining the light: Robert Barclay, *Apology* (1678), Prop. iii, sec. 9, pp. 54-57. Defining enthusiasm: "Thomas Welde" [= John Winthrop], *Antinomians and Familists condemned . . . in New England* (1644), 8. For one account of anti-Quaker diatribe: Daniel Neal, *Puritans* (2 v., 1843), II, 405-432. Scriptural "errors" an argument for the light: Samuel Fisher (Quaker), *Rusticus ad Academicos* (1660), Pt. II, 71-105, 119, etc.

[Ranters] drew persecution down upon [Quakers] (28)—Thus G[eorge] W[hitehead], *To the Ranters* (1659), in *Collection of Sundry Books* (1716), 494-506. Early instances of disrobing: see William C. Braithwaite, *The Beginnings of Quakerism* (1912), 150-151. **Talk of witchcraft and concealed Popery (32)**—See Wallace Notestein, *Hist. of Witchcraft in Eng.* (1911), 240 n. John W. Wickwar, *Witchcraft and the Black Art* (1926), 251-252. Philip W. Sergeant, *Witches and Warlocks* (1936), 134 n. Ethyn W. Kirby, *William Prynne* (1931), 114. *Querers and Quakers Cause* (1653), 2. Lodowick Muggleton, *A Looking-Glass for George Fox* ([1667] 1756), 73 (ch. xxvi). Charge denied: James Nayler, *Weaknes above Wickednes* (1656), 3. See Robert Barclay, *Inner Life of Religious Societies* (1877), 312, 313, 318. On Quakers as Jesuits: Kirby, 114 (refs.); Richard Baxter, *The Quakers Catechism* (1656), 9-12. See William Penn, *Brief Account of the Quakers,* in Penn, Barclay, and Pike, *Three Treatises* (6th ed., 1770), 41 ff. Against Quaker "pride": see Evelyn's Diary for July 8, 1656. Christopher Fowler, *Dæmonium Meridianum,* Part II (1656), 2. Thomas Hall, *Exp. [of] Amos*

PAGE

150 (1661), 131-132. "Thou"-language: *Querers and Quakers Cause* (1653), 20-21; "Daniel Barrett" [= ?Samuel Austin], *Plus Ultra, or the Second Part of the Character of a Quaker,* 1672, esp. p. 4. See Richard Baxter, *The Quakers Catechism* ([1651] 1656), Pref., Sigs B3-C. Cp. Milton's religious

151 defense of good manners: *C. D., Works* (1931-), XVII, 323 (3, 18). [Angels do not] perceive God's secrets (16)—Milton, *C. D., Works,* XV, 107 (8); contrast Bernard of Clairvaux, *In Cant.,* Serm. xix, sec. 2, in *Works,* ed. John Mabillon (4 v., 1896), IV, 105.

[Milton's late thought] "only vaguely Christian" (21)—So Wilbur K. Jordan, *Toleration,* IV, 203.

152 [*P. R.*], that "quietistic, Quaker-like poem" (1)—E. H. Visiak, "Notes on Milton," *N & Q,* CLXXIX (1940), 186. Since Alden Sampson, *Studies in Milton* (1913), 167-239, critics from time to time have found traces of Quakerism in Milton's Independency, as recently Ruth Mohl, *Studies in Spenser, Milton, and the Theory of Monarchy* (New York, 1949), 107-109. Defending oath-taking, [Milton] wrote . . . against a [Quaker] tenet (17) —*C. D., Works* (1931-), XVII, 119-121.

153 Familiar is that passage in Bacon (10)—*Essays,* in *Works,* ed. Spedding, XII, 82. The spirit of revelation above the written word: Robert Barclay, *Apology for Quakers* (1678), Prop. iii.

[Milton made] a strong case for . . . a . . . spirit of interpretation (32)—*C. D., Works,* XVI, 275 (6)-279 (11). Cp., on the spirit, *Of Civil*

154 *Power, Works,* VI, 6 (11-12); *C. D.,* XVI, 275 (19-20), 277 (22); XVI, 281 (12-21), 311 (15-26); against allegorizing: XVI, 263 (8), 265 (16). Rationalists acknowledge a spirit clarifying, not additive: Thomas Fuller, *Sermons* (2 v., 1891), II, 234-235; Henry Hammond, *Misc. Theol. Works,* LACT (3 v., 1849-), III, 23-24.

Milton [as] a defeated old man (40)—B. Rajan, *'Paradise Lost' and the Seventeenth Century Reader* (1948), 158, n 6, furnishes a few references to

155 this kind of criticism, from which (e.g., 78-92) he dissents. See, e.g., H. J. C. Grierson, "John Milton," *The Criterion* VIII (1928), 7 ff., esp. 254, and *Cross Currents,* 269-270, 276; George W. Whiting, *Milton's Literary Milieu,* 129-176; E. M. W. Tillyard, *Milton* (1946), 291. A recent comment on the "learning" critique in *P. L.* and *P. R.* concedes something to Milton's disillusionment: M. M. Mahood, *Poetry and Humanism* (New Haven, 1950), 239-241. [Humanistic] Milton . . . reaffirmed of late (18)—By James Holly Hanford, *John Milton, Englishman,* New York, 1949. [Milton's] dream of an unworldly church [antedated] Fox (20)—See *Of Ref., Works,* III, 39 (14)-41 (4-12), 42 (2-7), 65 (10-16); *Reason of Ch. Govt.,* 251 (23-27); *Apol. for Sm.,* 364 (12-25).

Milton . . . refused to admit Popery to . . . toleration (37)—*Areop.,* IV, 349 (19); *Of Civil Power,* VI, 19 (12); *Of True Rel.,* VI, 171 (27). Heretics for whom he . . . [begged] charity [omitted Quakers] (40)—*Of True Rel.,* VI, 168 (10); tolerated "opinions . . . founded on scripture": VI, 177 (19). See N. H. Henry, "Milton's Last Pamphlet," *A Tribute to George*

156 *Coffin Taylor,* ed. Arnold Williams (Chapel Hill, N. C., 1952), 97 ff. "From my seed-spring, etc." (17)—Lawrence Claxton (Clarkson), *The Quakers Downfal* (1659), 15. On the Blasphemy Acts of 1648 and 1650: Wilbur K. Jordan, *Toleration,* III, 134; see 112. Milton complimented the Parliament on [its anti-Ranter] act (33)—*Of Civil Power, Works* (18 v., 1931-), VI, 11 (8-13).

CHAPTER IV

157   Milton [defined curiosity] before 1639 (23)—On the dating: J. H. Hanford, "The Chronology of Milton's Private Studies," *PMLA* XXXVI (1921),
158   308. On Jeremy Taylor and "deaf" Presbyterians: C. J. Stranks, in
Church Qu. Rev., CXXXI (Oct., 1940), 57, and in *The Life and Writings
of Jeremy Taylor*, SPCK (London, 1952), 235-246. For Constantine's story
among the peacemakers: John Hull, *Christ His Proclamation* (1613), 55.
Leonard Busher, *Religious Peace* (1614), ed. E. B. Underhill, *Tracts on
Liberty of Conscience*, Hanserd Knollys Soc. (1846), 18. Jeremiah Burroughs, *Irenicum* (1653), 255. Jeremy Taylor, *Liberty of Prophesying*, in
Works, ed. Reginald Heber and C. P. Eden (10 v., 1850-), V, 399. Cp. John
Donne, *Works*, ed. Alford, I, 85-86, and many others. See esp. Charles Sum-
ner., tr. Milton, *Christian Doctrine* (2 v.), in Bohn *Prose Works* (5 v., 1853),
IV, 80, n 7. **Englishmen . . . turned . . . from controversies (19)**—On
their skeptical indifference: Wilbur K. Jordan, *Toleration*, IV, 240 ff.

Outside . . . irenical pleas [not much] skeptical writing (22)—See
Margaret L. Wiley, *The Subtle Knot* (London, 1952), esp. 60-120 (ch. iii).
The kind of witnesses she has assembled abundantly justify her own
remark (62) that seventeenth-century skeptics were usually tolerant and
"practical" preachers. Also on the scarcity of skepticism narrowly defined:
Paul H. Kocher, *Science and Religion in Elizabethan England* (1953), 45-
62. **Henry Vaughan . . . lost in . . . knowledge (26)**—"Vanity of Spirit,"
Poems, ed. E. K. Chambers (2 v., 1896), I, 57-58. Cp. George Herbert, "Di-
vinitie," *English Works*, ed. Herbert Palmer (3 v., 1905), III, 97-98. Note
Marjorie H. Nicolson, *The Breaking of the Circle* (Evanston, Ill., 1950),
156-157, and A. C. Judson, "Cornelius Agrippa and Henry Vaughan,"
MLN, XLI (1926), 178 ff. **Philosophic doubters . . . Ralegh (30)**—See
E. A. Strathmann, in *HLQ*, III (1940), 265 ff., and *Sir Walter Ralegh* (New
York, 1951), 219 ff. J. I. Cope, *PMLA*, LXIX (1954), 223 ff., enlists Glanvill,
too (as Anglican apologist); and see Cope, in *HLQ*,
XVII (1954), 269 ff. On Glanvill, besides Wiley (above), note Charles de
Rémusat, *Hist. de la Phil. en Angleterre*, II, 184-201; Moody E. Prior, rev.,
MP, XXXII (1935), 324 ff. **[Abraham] Cowley [skeptical in] an early poem
(39)**—"The Tree of Knowledge. That there is no Knowledge. Against the
159   Dogmatists," *English Writings*, ed. A. R. Waller (1905), 45-46. Cp. Richard
Whitlock," *Zootomia* (1654), 138-189, esp. 141; 218-224, "Reason's Independ-
ency." **[Robert Greville, Lord Brooke,] declare[d] himself a skeptic (11)**
—*The Nature of Truth: Its Union and Unity with the Soule* (1640), 74.

[Lord Herbert of Cherbury escaped] from Pyrrhonism (26)—See translator's essay before *De Veritate* (1624), tr. M. H. Carré (Bristol, 1937), 14.
Lord Herbert preferred to Lord Brooke: by Nathaniel Culverwel, *Discourse of the Light of Nature* (1652), ed. Brown and Cairns (1857), 128,
190 ff., 203-204. On Sterry and Brooke: Vivian de S. Pinto, *Peter Sterry*,
160   *Platonist and Puritan* (Cambridge, 1934), 12. On Brooke: see William R.
Sorley, *Hist. of English Philosophy* (Cambridge, 1920), 43-44. Reply to
Brooke: John Wallis, *Truth Tried* (1642/3), 92, cp. 97-99.

Brooke . . . searched for support among . . . Moderns (12)—*Of Truth*,
124 (Comenius); 28-29, 125-127, 142-143 (Bacon); 141-142 (Ralegh); 128-132
(on causes).

161   **Entangled . . . matters [were] nonessential (19)**—So Christopher Potter, *Consecration Sermon for Barnaby Potter* (1629), 66-68. On the propriety of defining fundamentals: "David Calderwood" [= ?William Scot],

PAGE

161 *The Pastor and the Prelate* ([1628] 1692), 19. William Laud, *Works*, LACT (7 v., 1847), I, 362. Milton, *Of True Rel., Works* (18 v., 1931-), VI, 170 (22-24). See Wilbur K. Jordan, *Toleration*, II, 147; III, 314. Samuel Rutherford [on] uncertain . . . nonessential[s] (27)—*Pretended Liberty of Conscience* (1649), 64. Note E. G. Lewis, in *MLR*, XXXIII (1938), 257-258.

162 [Edward] Stillingfleet . . . exhorted . . . to indifference (3)—*Irenicum* ([1661] 1662), 396; cp. Pref., Sig A3ᵛᵒ.

[John] Saltmarsh . . . for diversity (19)—*Reasons for Unitie, Peace, and Love* (1646), 3-8, esp. 8; cp. *Groanes for Liberty*, in *Some Drops of the Viall*, 1646. On Seekers' "Arminian" uncertainty: Thomas Edwards, *Gangræna* (1646), 41; Samuel Rutherford, *Pretended Liberty of Conscience* (1649), 79. For the hostility of orthodoxy to philosophic skepticism: e.g., William Sclater, *Exp. upon Thess.* (1619), 446. With Saltmarsh, cp. Roger Williams, *The Bloudy Tenent of Persecution*, Hanserd Knollys Soc. (1848), 48, and Milton, *Reason of Ch. Govt., Works* (1931-), III, 249 (10)-250 (2)— skepticism prescribed for opponents only. William Haller, "The Word of God and the New Model Army," *Church Hist.*, XIX (1950), 15 ff., deals with some inspired certainties taught by men like Saltmarsh. And see, on a passionate typologist's dogmatic interest in religious freedom, Perry Miller, *Roger Williams* (New York, 1953), 22-23.

Tradition of doubt . . . served by . . . peacemakers (36)—See Edward A. George, *Seventeenth Century Men of Lattitude*, 1908. Wilbur K. Jordan, *Toleration*, II, 394 ff., and IV. John Tulloch, *Rational Theol. and Christian Phil., etc.*, 2 v., 1872. William E. H. Lecky, *Rationalism in Europe* (2 v., 1883), e.g., II, 75-100. Thomas Lyon, *The Theory of Religious Liberty in England*, 181-210. James H. Elson, *John Hales of Eton* (New York, 1948), 108 ff, Margaret L. Wiley, *The Subtle Knot*, e.g., 96-105, "The Irenic of Deism." [They] accommodate[d] . . . opinions (38)—E.g., Jere-

163 miah Burroughs, *Irenicum*, 1653. See 82-83, 148, 152. John Brinsley (the younger), *The Healing of Israels Breeches* (1642), 82, 109-111; cp. *Standstill: or Bridle for the Times*, 1647. John Dury, *A Peace-Maker* (1648), 61 and closing sections; cp. John Brayne, *The Smoak of the Temple Cleared*, 1648, and *Gospel Advice to Godly Builders*, 1648. J. Minton Batten, *John Dury, Advocate of Christian Reunion* (Chicago, 1944), 32.

John Hales chaffed the enthusiasts (14)—*Abuses of Hard Places of Scripture*, in *Golden Remains* ([1659] 1688), 18-20. Cp. Jeremy Taylor, *Works* (10 v., 1850-), VI, 404. Hales reproached the prelates: *Tract Concerning Schism and Schismaticks*, Vol. V of *A Collection of Essays and Tracts in Theol.*, ed. Jared Sparks (6 v., 1826), 31-34; cp. *Remains*, 236, "Peace I Leave unto You." Note William Laud, *Sermon* (1621), *Works*, LACT (7 v., 1847), I, 12, "My Peace, etc." Hales on his skepticism: *Abuses of Scripture, Remains*, 30. See 45-47, 50, 137. On Hales and "Socinianism": Kenneth B. Murdock, *The Sun at Noon* (New York, 1939), 98-138, esp. 114-117. Cp. Tulloch, I, 206-208; James H. Elson, *John Hales of Eton*, 121; and H. John McLachlan, *Socinianism, etc.* (Oxford, 1951), 55, 74. On his irenical influence: Elson, 145-151. Note William H. Hutton, *The English Church, etc.* (1903), 116; Wilbur K. Jordan, *Toleration*, II, 410. Jeremy Taylor [on] frailty [and] peace (24)—*Liberty of Prophesying*, in *Works* (10 v., 1850-), V, 499-510; *Deus Justificatus*, VII, 535-536 (latitude in the Thirty-nine Articles). On Taylor's skepticism: Wilbur K. Jordan, *Toleration*, IV, 382-403, and others (384 n). See esp. Margaret L. Wiley, *The Subtle Knot*, 179-197.

PAGE

163   Benjamin Whichcote . . . mild Calvinism (39)—See, e.g., his *Moral and Religious Aphorisms*, ed. Samuel Salter (1753), Aph. 13, and the appended
164   *Eight Letters*, 16, 100. Cp. Tuckney's testimony, Letter ii (1651), 27-28; iii, 78; and Pref., xxx. The elder Calvinist [Tuckney] mourned (7)—Letters, in *Aph.*, 2, 38-39, 85, 97; cp. 65 (Whichcote's reply). Whichcote on curiosity: *Aphorisms*, 1036; Letter i, in *Aph.*, 11; see 52. On Hales here: Thomas Lyon, *Theory of Religious Liberty*, 149. On enthusiasm: *Aph.*, 1085, 1182, 349. On fundamentals: Letters, in *Aph.*, 52; cp. William Chillingworth, qu. by Edward A. George, *Seventeenth Century Men of Latitude* (1908), 62. Whichcote's pacific skepticism: Letters, 11-13; Serm. IV, in *Select Sermons*, ed. William Wishart (1742), 240-241; *Aphorisms*, 1161, and see Tuckney's objection, Letters, 28.

      Baxter issued five major [irenical] works (38)—Listed: J. Minton Bat-
165   ten, *John Dury*, 173 n. The rules of . . . fellowship (2)—See the Table before *The Cure of Church-divisions*, 1670. Also, *Practical Works*, ed. William Orme (23 v., 1830), V, 151-215, and Hugh Martin, *Puritanism and Richard Baxter* (London, 1954), 158-166. *Treatise of Knowledge and Love* (*P. W.*, XV) composed "long ago," according to Pref., 1689. "Higher thoughts of the schoolmen" (12)—*P. W.*, ed. Orme, XV, 15. [Baxter's] own mild Presbyterianism (18)—See Wilbur K. Jordan, *Toleration*, III, 332. He . . . lost some hatred of Papists (21)—See Frederick J. Powicke, *Life of Baxter* (1924), 258-259; 163-164. [Called] Quakers "miserable creatures" (23)—Baxter, *The Quakers Catechism* (1651), 1. Against Independents: see William Orme, *Life of Baxter* (2 v., 1831), I, 74. On Vane and Sterry: I, 82-83.

      [Baxter's] proposals for education (30)—*Christian Directory, P. W.*, V, 552 ff., esp. 553; 575 ff. (cp. II, 375-378); see XIV, 221-222 (science, without occultism, serves divinity); V, 579 (no "novelists"). On Baxter's positive counsels for education: R. K. Merton, *Science, etc.* (Cambridge, U.S.A.,
166   1937), 414-432. For Baxter on ministerial learning: Orme, *Life*, I, 15; Powicke, *Life*, 90; Charles F. Kemp, *A Pastoral Triumph* (New York, 1948), 8, 66. Cp. *Practical Works*, ed. Orme, V, 552; XV, 31-32.

      Baxter . . . almost to the extreme of Pyrrhonism (19)—*Knowledge and Love, P. W.*, XV, 15-16; 31-32; 49. On his skepticism: Margaret L. Wiley, "Richard Baxter and the Problem of Certainty," *The Subtle Knot*, 161-179, repr. from *Hibbert Jour.*, XLVI (1948), 342 ff., see esp. 344; note Orme, *Life*, II, 118.

167   [Milton's] unwillingness to impose [truth] (16)—*C. D., Works* (18 v., 1931-), XIV, 11 (3-8).

      The title humanist (34)—Bestowed on Milton afresh: Ralph K. Allen, "Milton's Creative Unitarianism," *DA*, XIII (1953), 791. Paul Elmen, "Jeremy Taylor and the Fall of Man," *MLQ*, XIV (1953), 149, assimilates Milton and Taylor in Pelagianism.

168   "Inquire not into . . . secrets" (17) Jeremy Taylor, *Holy Living, Works*, ed. Heber and Eden (10 v., 1850-), III, 79; cp. *Advices to the Clergy*,
169   I, 109; *Via Intelligentiæ*, VIII, 384 and note 368. "Let us . . . live holily" (8)—*Via Int., Works*, VIII, 388. Against antinomianism or mysticism: Taylor, *Works*, IV, 599-600; V, 510; VIII, 373 ff.; IX, 273-274; esp. VI, 380 ff., 386; esp. II, 140, 139-142, and elsewhere. His contempt of the mystical way cited: Robert A. Vaughan, *Hours with the Mystics*, I, 122 (headnote); but contrast Rufus M. Jones, *Mysticism and Democracy*, 105 ff. Against Pyrrhonism: Taylor, IX, 55-60, esp. 57-58. For his "practical" way: Wiley,

PAGE

169 194 ff. (cited), and T. G. Steffan, "Jeremy Taylor's Criticism of Abstract Speculation," *Univ. Texas St. in Eng.* (1940), 96 ff.

Asking . . . modesty [of the "assured"] (28)—See, e.g., Christopher Lever, *The Holy Pilgrime* (1618), 221; Christopher Love, *A Treatise of Effectual Calling* ([1653] 1655), 134, 166-167.

[Thomas] Fuller [on the "new"] moral Calvinism (40)—*Collected*
170 *Sermons* (2 v., 1891), I, 459-489. On Fuller's alleged time-serving: Dean B. Lyman, *The Great Tom Fuller* (Berkeley, Cal., 1935), 87-90.

171 **Cambridge latitudinarians [sought pure, pre-scholastic] Christianity (21)**—Thus S[ymon] P[atrick], *A Brief Account of the New Sect of Latitude-Men* ([1662] 1669), 24-25. See Ernst Cassirer, *The Platonic Renaissance in England*, tr. J. P. Pettegrove (New York, 1953), 25-41. "**Nothing is more spiritual, etc.**" **(23)**—Benjamin Whichcote, *Aphorisms*, ed. Salter (1753), No. 969. **Virtue conditioned truth (36)**—John Smith, *Select Dis-*
172 *courses* (1660), 4-10. Cp. Ralph Cudworth, *[Commons] Sermon* I (1647), with *True Intellectual System*, ed. Thomas Birch (4 v., 1820), IV, 348; Henry More (on Divine Sagacity), *Philosophical Writings* (1712), Pref. Gen., pp. vii-viii, and (on Boniform Faculty), *Enchiridion Ethicum*, as *An Account of Virtue*, tr. 1690, ed. S. P. Lamprecht (1930), 11-15. See W. R. Inge, *The Platonic Tradition, etc.* (1926), 60. W. C. de Pauley, *The Candle of the Lord* (London, 1937), 143-144. E. M. Austin, *The Ethics of the Cambridge Platonists* (Philadelphia, 1935), 52.

John Smith [once] wrote like [a "practical"] Presbyterian (19)—*Select Discourses* (1660), 288-296, 310, 338, 408, 427-428. See Frederick J. Powicke, *The Cambridge Platonists* (1926), 98-99, 104-106. **Ralph Cudworth . . . preached ["callings"] (35)**—*Serm.* I, with *Int. System*, ed. Birch, IV, 295-350. See 296, 299, esp. 301, 303, 305-307. See also 370-373 and 373-386 (Serm. II), on the *via media* of morality between antinomianism and Pharisaism. See H. J. C. Grierson, *Cross Currents, etc.*, 227-228, 230.

173 **[In] Raphael's lecture . . . unconscious meanings (26)**—J. H. Hanford, "The Temptation Motive in Milton," *SP*, XV (1918), 179. E. M. W. Tillyard, *Milton* (1946), 291. Grant McColley, *'Paradise Lost': Growth and Origins* (Chicago, 1940), 91. G. F. Sensabaugh, "Milton on Learning," *SP*, XLIII (1946), 258 ff., and his references. Milton exonerated atronomers: *C. D., Works* (1931-), XVII, 151 (18-21), where "however" helps to distinguish astronomy from the astrology condemned. On Milton as a teacher of astronomy: Edward Phillips, in *Early Lives of Milton,* ed. Helen Darbishire (London, 1932), 60 (Manilius), 61 (De Sacro Bosco). See Foster Watson, *Beginnings of . . . Modern Subjects*, 377. A. H. Gilbert, "Milton's Textbook of Astronomy," *PMLA*, XXXVIII (1923), 297 ff., and "Milton and Galileo," *SP*, XIX (1922), esp. 246. On the subject of Milton's studies for Raphael's lecture: Grant McColley, "Milton's Dialogue on Astronomy," *PMLA,* LII (1937), 728 ff., and *'Paradise Lost': Growth and Origins*, 217 ff. See also McColley, "Plurality of Worlds [and Milton]," *MLN*, XLVII (1932), 323.

174 **Milton [embellished] the tritest of themes (24)**—Thus Sir Walter Raleigh, *Milton* (1900), 105. With Raphael's discourse, cf., e.g., Erasmus, *In Praise of Folly*, tr. H. H. Hudson (1944), 70 ff. George Herbert, "Divinitie," *Eng. Works*, ed. Palmer (1905), III, 97-98; cp. "Vanity," III, 133.

175 Burton, *Anatomy*, ed. Shilleto, II, 177, 59-68. Note M. M. Ross, "George Herbert and the Humanistic Tradition," *UTQ*, XVI (1947), 169 ff; M. M. Mahood, *Poetry and Humanism*, 25-55, esp. 50-53; Joseph H. Summers, *George Herbert* (Cambridge, U.S.A., 1954), e.g., 73 ff.

175 Raphael had a practical reason for . . . angelology (21)—See *P. L.* v.233-243, and John S. Diekhoff, *Milton's 'Paradise Lost'* (New York, 1946), 60 ff., 91-92. [By] astronomy . . . Milton [could display] learning (30)—On epic "learning": E. M. W. Tillyard, "Milton and the English Epic Tradition," *Seventeenth Century St.* [for] Grierson (Oxford, 1938), 214; B. Rajan, *'Paradise Lost' and the Seventeenth Century Reader* (Oxford, 1948), 20-21. Note *Gabriel Harvey's Marginalia*, ed. G. C. Moore-Smith (1913), 162-163. On Milton's fidelity to modern as well as ancient rules: A. H. Gilbert, "The Qualities of the Renaissance Epic," *So. Atlan. Qu.*, LIII (1954), 372 ff., esp. 377-378. For practical use [either system] (39)—See McColley,

176 *'P. L.': Growth, etc.*, 88. Blaeu mentioned: Milton, *Fam. Letters* (xx), *Works* (18 v., 1931-), XII, 85 (1). For the story of Alfonso's blasphemy: e.g., John Davies of Hereford, *Works*, ed. Grosart, I, 26.

[Milton] mentioned [curious] Adam (40)—*C. D.*, *Works*, XVII, 33 (25-

177 27); XV, 181 (25)-183 (8). On Eve's sins dramatized: Clive S. Lewis, *A Preface to 'Paradise Lost'* (London, 1942), 121-122. Augustine analyzed Adam's sin: *Enchiridion* xlv, and *Civ. Dei* xiv.12. For Manes remembered: e.g., John Salkeld, *A Treatise of Paradise* (1617), 334 (ch. lxv). On Augustine's motive: Edward M. Pickman, *The Mind of Latin Christendom* (London, 1937), 64, 79 ff. Preachers listed many sins that Adam comprehended in one: Nicholas Gibbens, *Questions and Disputations* (1601), 117. John Downame, *The Summe of Sacred Divinitie* (1630), 233-234. Thomas Adams, *Workes* (1629), 1175. John Boughton, *God and Man* (1623), 46-48. T. C., *Treatise of Christian Religion* (1616), 60. John Moore, *A Mappe of Mans Mortalitie* (1617), 12. Alexander Ross, *Exposition of Genesis* (1626), 61-62. Robert Burton, *Anatomy*, ed. Shilleto, I, 150. John Lightfoot, *Works* (13 v., 1822-), IV, 77 (ten sins to match the Decalogue). Times . . . "sick of Adam's disease" (19)—Thomas Adams, *Workes* (1629), 238-239. Cf. Ralph Cudworth, *Serm.* 1, with *Int. System*, ed. Birch, IV, 295; John Norris, ode "To Dr. More," prefixed by Richard Ward to his *Life of . . More*, 1710. For the tree-shaking in legend: Harris Fletcher, "Milton and Yosippon," *SP*, XXI (1924), 499; Rabbi Leo Jung, *Fallen Angels in Jewish, Christian, and Mohammedan Literature* (1926), 73.

178 Some recent studies . . . harmonizing (1)—Irene Samuel, "Milton on Learning and Wisdom," *PMLA*, LXIV (1949), 708 ff. M. M. Mahood, *Poetry and Humanism* (New Haven, 1950), 239-251.

179 Milton as a humanist [committed to] his warning (8)—See Douglas Bush, *The Renaissance and English Humanism* (Toronto, 1939) 127-133; E. L. Marilla, *The Central Problem of 'Paradise Lost': Essays and St. on Eng. Lang. and Lit.*, Upsala, No. 15 (1953), 13-15, 26, etc. He insisted upon [the] dignity [of physical science] (15)—Adam's "scientific" animal-naming: *P. L.* viii.352-354; *Tetra.*, in *Works*, IV, 92 (23); *C. D.*, XV, 53 (21). For the naturalist's use of the story: notes to my page 37, and see Samuel Bochart, *Geog. Sacra*, in *Opera* (Leyden, 1707; 3 v.), I, Fronts. (the animal-naming engraved). Note also Harris Fletcher, *Milton's Rabbinical Readings* (1930), 187-189, 204. On Milton's sometimes "unscientific" science: Denis Saurat, *Milton, etc.* (1925), 301-309; (1944), 248-267; T. V. Smith, "Observations upon Denis Saurat," *SP*, XXIII (1926), 184 ff. Margaret L. Bailey, *Milton and Jakob Boehme*, Oxford, 1914; Wilhelm Struck, *Der Einfluss Jakob Böhmes* (Berlin, 1936), 237 n. Kester Svendsen, "Milton and the Encyclopedias of Science," *SP*, XXXIX (1942), 303-304, and Svendsen, in *PMLA*, LXVII (1952), 453 ff.

180   Exegetes understood [Eccles. iii:11] causally (12)—See, e.g., John Wilkins, *A Discourse concerning the Beauty of Providence* ([1649] 1672), 6; Thomas Granger, *Exp. of Eccl.* (1620), *in loc.*

Students have discerned [Milton's] pedagogy in [*P. L., xi and xii*] (27)
[181] —Murray W. Bundy, "Milton's View of Education in *P. L.*," *JEGP*, XXI
[182] (1922), 146 ff. On Adam's lesson in self-knowledge and humility: H. C. Burke, in *DA*, XIV (1954), 1707.

183   "The stair foot of the world, etc." (4)—Thomas Bancroft, Sat. iv, "Against Presumption," *Time's out of Tune* (1658), 24-25; cp. Pliny, *Nat. Hist.* (ii.68, and vii.l), Loeb ed. (10 v., 1944), I, 308; II, 506-511.

CHAPTER V

184   Seconded the judgment (1)—I.e., of E. M. W. Tillyard *Milton* (London, 1946), 307–310; see 305-306. See also Tillyard, in *SP*, XXXVI (1930), 247 ff., esp. 252, where he replies to M. Y. Hughes, "The Christ of *P. R.*, etc." *SP*, XXXV (1938), 254 ff. Citing precedent, Professor Hughes justifies Milton's epic use of the "suffering" rather than the "doing" hero. Professor Tillyard acknowledges the great value of the study and concedes its point, but not as a full solution of the problem presented by *P. R.* Among other students who have recognized the problem, see Douglas Bush, *Mythology, etc.* (1932), 274, and Mahood, 239 ff.

185   "Taste [to suit] prince's . . . palate" (10)—Roger Williams, *Bloudy Tenent,* Hanserd Knollys Soc. (1848), 264. [James] Harrington [approved] universities (11)—*Oceana,* ed. John Toland ([1700] 1771), 166-167 ff. Baptists . . . anti-intellectual [not always unlearned] (35)—See Wilbur K. Jordan, *Toleration,* II, 303; Charles E. Whiting, *Studies in English Puritanism,* 95; E. B. Underhill, ed. [*Baptist*] *Tracts on Liberty of Conscience,* Hanserd Knollys Soc. (1846), 106, 205. Baxter . . . witnessed [Baptist
186   apostasy] (36)—*Quakers Catechism* ([1651] 1656), Pref., Sigs A2 ff. "Ignorant" divinity . . . not . . . unnoticed (3)—See Jordan, II, 219; John Laird, *Hobbes,* 55 n; Phyllis Allen, "Science in the English Universities of the 17th Century," *JHI*, X (1949), 237; David W. Petegorsky, *Left-Wing Democracy, etc.: A Study of . . . Gerrard Winstanley* (London, 1940), 65-72; and see esp. D. B. Robertson, *The Religious Foundations of Leveller Democracy* (New York, 1951), 29-48. Note also Herschel Baker, *The Wars of Truth,* 105-110.

[John] Wyclif . . . damned the universities (19)—*Opera Minora,* Wyclif Soc. (1913), 323 ff. Cp. Henry W. Clark, *Nonconformity,* I, 38. Catholic [said Reformers] burned . . . books (25)—Laurentius Surius, *Commentarius Brevis in Orbe Gestarum* (Cologne, [1522], 1567), 150. Cp. Lewis Evans, *The Castle of Christianitie* [1568], 30b-32 ("ignorant" Papists call Protestants ignorant).

Geneva [and] universities [for] divinity (34)—See James L. Ainslee, *The Doctrines of Ministerial Order in the Reformed Churches* (Edinburgh,
187   1940), 149. Milton [on the doctoral] "locust" (1)—*Works* (18 v., 1931-), XVI, 239 (15). Cartwright . . . defended . . . learning (8)—See A. F. S. Pearson, *Thomas Cartwright and Elizabethan Puritanism* (1925), 208. Other early Puritans deplore Anglican ignorance: among many, [Lawrence Chaderton], *Sermon upon . . . Romanes* (1584), 33-35. *A Briefe [Declaration for] Reformation* (1584), 37-39 (the *Learned Discourse* that Bishop John Bridges answered). Walter Travers, *Declaration of Ecclesiasticall Discipline*

187 (1574), 135-146 (suggests reforming the universities); John Penry, *A Defense* [*against*] *the ignorant ministerie* (1588), esp. 44. [**Cartwright's**] **own** *Second Admonition* (**10**)—In W. II. Frere and C. E. Douglas, eds. *Puritan Manifestos*, SPCK, 1907, where editions of the *First Admonition* are collated. John Whitgift, *Sermon* [*for*] *the Queen* [1574], in *Works*, Parker Soc. (3 v., 1853), III, 469, pounces on the "obscurantism" of the Field-Wilcox preface. Reading the body of the text, John Bridges, *A Defence of the Government Established* (1587), 225, is ironically pleased to see the doctorate back in fashion. [**Francis**] **Meres** . . . **ranked the factions (15)**— *Treatise on Poetrie* (III.25), ed. D. C. Allen, *Univ. Ill. St. in Lang. and Lit.*, XVI (1933), 67.

Later Puritans . . . had learning (18)—See William B. Selbie, *Nonconformity*, 41; Perry Miller and T. H. Johnson, eds. *The Puritans* (New York, 1938), 4, 10, 13. **Denounced the abuse of . . . quotations (22)**—Edward Dering, *XXVII Lectures upon Hebrews* (1576), in *Works* (1590), 328-329; Jeremiah Dyke, *A Caveat for Archippus*, 1619. [**With**] **Puritanism . . . oratory declined (24)**—William Fraser Mitchell, *English Pulpit Oratory from Andrewes to Tillotson* (London, 1932), 204 ff., 255 ff. Harold Fisch, "The Puritans and the Reform of Prose Style," *ELH*, XIX (1952), 229 ff., esp. 231-241; and William Haller, "The Rhetoric of the Spirit," *The Rise of Puritanism* (New York, 1938), 128-172. Cp. John Preston, *Sinnes Overthrow: or Treatise of Mortification* ([1633] 1635), 101, esp. 106; and Anglican John Downe, *Amulet* (24-25) and *Christs Prayer* (65), in *Certain Treatises*, 1633. **Thomas Cooper** [**admitted clergy's ignorance**] (**33**)—T. C., *An Admonition* (1589), 99 ff. Contrast Robert Abbott, *A Triall of our Church-Forsakers* (1639), 194. With Cooper, cp. Joseph Hall, *Brownists*, in *Recollection of Treatises* ([1614] 1615), 779-780; Charles Richardson, *A Workeman, etc.* (1616), 29, 62-63 (encouraging the unlearned, but ordained, to

188 improve themselves with translated books). **Against . . . license . . . crusade (6)**—See James B. Mullinger, *Cambridge Characteristics in the Seventeenth Century* (1867), 36. See Sir Simonds D'Ewes, *Autobiography*, ed. J. O. Halliwell (2 v., 1845), I, 120, 141, for immorality at Cambridge in 1620.

Proposals . . . to add schools (17)—Mullinger, 180; Foster Watson, *Modern Subjects*, xxxii. **Of Education . . . described** [**isolated university college**] (**20**)—Thus Watson, "The State and Education During the Commonwealth," *Eng. Hist. Rev.*, XV (1900), 60.

Budge aristocracy [**hateful to**] **Robert Browne (30)**—*Treatise upon the 23. of Matthewe* [*of*] *wicked Preachers and Hirelings*, a kind of preface to *Life and Manners*, 1582. See Champlin Burrage, *The True Story of Robert Browne* (1906), 25, 18. **Blows at . . . ministerial seed-plots (33)**—[?Henry Ainsworth and ?Francis Johnson], *Apologie of . . . Brownists* ([?Amsterdam], 1604), 77-85. On the authorship, see *STC* and Wilbur K. Jordan, *Toleration*, II, 223 n, and 248 n.

189 **Heresiologists . . . rightly credited (13)**—Against Brownist obscurantism: Lawrence Deios, *An Answer to . . . Sectaries*, in *Two Sermons* (1590), 135-136; Richard Stubbe, *A Motive to Good Workes* (1593), 86-88; Robert Burton, *Anatomy*, ed. Shilleto, III, 424-425; Robert Baillie, *A Dissuasive from the Errours of the Time* (1645), 32; and many other writers. [**Robert**] **Some** [**defended schools**] **against** [**Brownists**] (**18**)—*Godly Treatise* [*Confuting . . . Barrow and Greenwood*] (1589), 1-7; alleging a Brownist petition, Some cites no date or document, but see his Ep. Ded. and his page 2.

PAGE

189   [Thomas] Fuller [cited] Some (20)—"The Rigid Donatists," *The Holy State* (v.11), ed. M. G. Walten (1938), 402. [John] Strype printed [Browne's letter] (24)—Appendix iii.45, *Life of Whitgift* (1718), 324; see 133-134. Angry churchmen . . . cited Barrow (27)—See, e.g., John Paget, *An Arrow Against Brownists* (1618), 332. [Henry Barrow] by . . . Independency was reprinted (33)—(Selections) *The Pollution of Universitie-Learning*, 1642. Cp. Barrow, "Of Universities, etc.," *A Brief Discovery of the False Church[es]* ([1590] 1707), ch. xxi, pp. 254 ff.

190   Anglicans . . . wrote . . . rhapsodies [for learning] (7)—Richard Hooker, *Eccles. Pol.* (III.8.4-15), in *Works* (2 v., 1845), I, 301-310. John Boys, *Workes* (1622), 430-431, 467, etc. George Benson, *Sermon at Paules Crosse* (1609), 56-57. John Downame, *Lectures upon Hosea* (1608), 145 ff. Nehemiah Rogers, *A Strange Vineyard* (= *The Wilde Vine*), 1623. Edward Chaloner, *Six Sermons* (1629), 6-10. Edward Reynolds, *The Sinfulnesse of Sinne* ([1631] 1639), 32-33. John Lightfoot, *Works* (13 v., 1822-), VII, 81 ff., and many others. Thomas Adams . . . complained [of] fanatics (14)— *Workes* (1629), 69. Cp. Thomas Thompson, *A Diet for a Drunkard* (1612), Pref. John King . . . scolding (18)—*Lectures upon Jonas* ([1594] 1618), 541-552, 312-313. Egeon Askew . . . excused the divines (25)—*Brotherly Reconcilement* (1605), 260, 264. Cp. Robert Some, *Treatise Touching the Ministerie* (1588), 9-11. Scourging . . . in a dream (39)—Jerome, *Epist.* (xxxii.30), Corp. Script. Eccl. (Lipsiæ, 1900), LIV, 190. For other patristic

191   commonplaces, see notes to my pages 6-7. [Shield to] guard bishops . . . Independents (10)—Lancelot Andrewes, *Ninety-Six Sermons*, LACT (5 v., 1841-), I, 244 ff. John Downe, *Amulet . . . against Contempt of the Ministery* (23 ff.), in *Certain Treatises*, 1633. Thomas Case, *The Vanity of Vaine-Glory*, 1655; Paul Baynes, *Comm. on Col.* (1635), 241 ff. Anthony Burges, *Spiritual Refinings* (1652), 620 ff.

Milton . . . copied [this cento] (13)—"Commonplace Book," *Works* (18 v., 1931-), XVIII, 136 (9)-139. He had followed . . . Parliament (19)— *Tenure of Kings*, *Works*, V, 44 (24-28); *Hist. of Brit.* (Digression), X, 319 (12) ff. Culpeper . . . urged . . . learning (23)—See William A. Shaw, *Hist. of the English Church*, I, 33, 55, 89. [Milton] hated . . . tithes [early] (26)—*Of Ref.*, III, 75 (27). He [valued] solid [pulpit] learning (31)—*Animad.*, III, 163 (25-26), 167 (15-21); see 163 (21)—voluntaryism preferable. Learning no necessity: *C. D.*, XVI, 293 (21, 7), 303 (25-28).

192   Milton [belabored] mercenary fathers (13)—*Animad.*, III, 118 (26) ff. Cp. *Reason of Ch. Govt.*, III, 274 (2-15); esp. *Animad.*, 160 (14)-165 (25); *Of Ref.*, III, 75 (16-17). *Animad.*, III, 160 (5-13); *Apol. for Sm.*, III, 335 (25)-336 (19). *Animad.*, III, 163 (5), 162 (9-10).

Whenever . . . he took . . . voluntaryism (39)—His *public* deference to state-hire in 1649 (*Tenure of Kings*, V, 6 (11-12)) hardly proves that he

193   could not, even then, think of a better plan. He addressed in 1643 a Parliament (5)—*Doct. and Disc. of Divorce*, III, 367 (20), 376 (4). Cp. *Judg. of Martin Bucer*, IV, 61 (17-18, 24-25); *Tetra.*, IV, 71 (10-12).

Milton . . . applied truly [the bishops' texts] (30)—Areop., IV, 306 (22)-311 (8).

194   He turned . . . upon the hirelings (7)—Areop., 323 (16-23). A vicar [cited Andrewes on] revenues (3)—Joshua Meene, *A Liberall Maintenance is Manifestly Due* (1638), 52. Lancelot Andrewes, *Of the Right of Tithes*, tr. 1647.

Bishops [use plural livings to] buy books (38)—*The Marprelate Tracts*, ed. William Pierce (1911), 191, 264. Or see William Burton's sneer in *A*

195   *Sermon . . . in Norwich* (1589), Sig C[4]. **William Vaughan [on] beggarly
annuity (10)**—*The Spirit of Detraction* (1611), 92-94; see also 106-110, 249.
On the poverty of the clergy: Samuel Gardiner, *The Scourge of Sacriledge*
(1611), Sigs I 2-J8^{vo}; see William Pierce, *John Penry, His Life and Times*
(1923), 124-128. **Tithes a negotiable security (13)**—William Esterby, *Hist.
of the Law of Tithes in England* (1888), 32. **Preaching . . . against . . .
impropriators (16)**—E.g., John Hull, *Christ His Proclamation* (1613), 57;
Robert Harris, *The Way to True Happinesse* (1632), 185-186. **[John Sel-
den] observed . . . lecturers (22)**—*Table-Talk*, Arber ed. (1868), 67, 73.
See his proposals for rehabilitating tithes, *The Hist. of Tithes* (1618), 398.
Other proposals: R. G., *The Truth of Tithes . . . Defended* (1618), 48 ff.
(tithes and learning), 66-67, 86; similarly, Thomas Ryves, *The Poore Vicars
Plea* (1620), 49, 113 ff., 137; Cornelius Burges, *A New Discovery of Personal
Tithes* (1625), 41, etc. **An Anglican despised the disaffected (25)**—Joshua
Meene, *Liberall Maintenance* (1638), 65-66 ff.; see 52-54. **[Robert Burton
and] contentious tithe-payers (32)**—*Anatomy*, ed. Shilleto, I, 373-374.
"Lucre . . . occasioned . . . babblers" (40)—Humphrey Sydenham, "The
Athenian Babbler," *Five Sermons* (1636), 28. Cp. Peter Studley, *The Look-
ing-Glasse of Schisme* (1634), 218-227, 232-233, 240.

196   **History of the . . . controversy (11)**—For a fragmentary survey of
pamphlets on tithes: Don M. Wolfe, *Milton in the Puritan Revolution*
(New York, 1941), 102-110. On legislation: William A. Shaw, *Hist. of the
English Church* (2 v., 1900), II, 254-259.
      Peter Heylyn [objected to fixed salaries] (26)—Pref. (sec. xv), *Ecclesia
Vindicata* (1657), in *Works*, ed. 1681. Cp. P[eter] H[eylyn] "Treleinie,"
The Undeceiving of the people in point of Tithes, 1648. See Daniel Neal,
Puritans (2 v., 1843), II, 129. **Thomas Fuller . . . had . . . right (37)**—
Learning excused tithes: "Of Ministers Maintenance," *The Holy State*

197   (iii.25), ed. M. G. Walten, 228. On "Anabaptist" voluntaryism as revolu-
tion: R[obert] B[oreman], *The Countrey-Mans Plea for Tithes* (1652), 25.
Cp. Gerrard Winstanley, *Selections*, ed. Leonard Hamilton (London, 1944),
13, 31, 34, 111, 125-126, 174-176, esp. 117. On Winstanley, see David W.
Petegorsky, *Left-Wing Democracy*, 121 *et seq*. For bibliog.: Douglas Bush,
English Literature, etc., 608, and M. A. Gill, *John Lilburne the Leveller*
(London, 1947), 264 n. **Levellers . . . trailed not far (10)**—John Lilburne,
Plaine Truth (1647), 67; [?Lilburne, or ?Richard Overton], *Englands New
Chains*, Part I (1649), 13, etc. Martin Mar-Priest (pseud.–Richard Overton),
The Ordinance for Tythes Dismounted, 1646. See George H. Sabine, ed.
The Works of Gerrard Winstanley (Ithaca, N. Y., 1941), Intro., 24-25, 29,
etc., and Theodore C. Pease, *The Leveller Movement* (1916), 80-81, 100-101,
etc. On Lilburne's degree of anti-intellectualism: D. B. Robertson, *Level-
ler Democracy* (1951), 31-32; see 29-40. **Richard Overton . . . mocked (14)**
—*Tythes Dismounted*, 24-25; see 40 (impropriators in Parliament).
      Tithers had . . . to sell pulpit-ware (27)—*Tyth-Gatherers, No Gospel
Officers* (1646), 12-14. On various plans of settlement: *Certain Desires for
the Settlement and Improving of Ministers Meanes* (1646), 2.

198   **Baptists . . . voluntaryists (8)**—Robert Barclay, *Inner Life of Religious
Societies*, 270-271; see 172—Saltmarsh returned tithes. Cp. Saltmarsh, on
learning, *Shadows Flying Away*, in *Reasons for Unitie* (1646), 9 ff. **[Wil-
liam] Erbury . . . joined to debate (18)**—*A Monstrous Dispute: or the
Language of the Beast*, 1653, and *Ministers for Tithes . . . No Ministers
of the Gospel*, 1653. **Quakers . . . vitriol . . . hireling[s] (24)**—See Bar-

PAGE

198   clay, *Inner Life*, 193 ff., 259, and Luella M. Wright, *Literary Life of Friends*, 38-43. Ministers [were] merchants chaffering (26)—So G[eorge] W[hitehead], Pref. (?1655) to James Nayler, *Collection of Sundry Books* (1716), 16, and Nayler, 201, 205-206; Whitehead, *Falsehoods of Richard Baxters* (1658), 10-11. Cp. Robert Barclay, *Apology for Quakers*, Prop. x. Sectaries all opposed tithes: S. R. Gardiner, *Hist. of the Commonwealth* (3 v., 1897), II, 31-32.

Roger Williams . . . with *Areopagitica* (33)—*Bloudy Tenent* (1644),
199   Hanserd Knollys Soc. (1848), 262-265. Cp. Williams, *The Hireling Ministry None of Christs* (1652), Fourth Particular, 10-17.

Prelates [argued for] universities [against] Brownists (30)—Robert Some, *Godly Treatise [Confuting Barrow and Greenwood]* (1589), 1-9. John Swan, *Redde Debitum* (1640), 205, 223, 750 ff. New presbyters . . . quickly [learned] (33)—[Ephraim Udall], *Noli me Tangere* (1642), 15-16, 18-20 ff., 41. Martin Browne (reply to Overton), *Tithes Re-Mounted by the Word of God* (1646), 1-2, 10. [Ephraim] Pagitt [on Independents'] meddling (40)
200   —*Heresiography* ([1645] 1647), 83. Tithes . . . stop . . . heresy (3)—*A Brief Apology for the Ministers of the Church of England* (1653), 14-17.

Henry Spelman . . . heartened the clergy (30)—See *English Works* (1727), 155 ff., and 112.

201   Any clergyman [claimed] share in . . . doctoral respect (18)—See, e.g., Thomas Cooper, *Certain Sermons* (1580), 178-179. Richard Bernard, "Of the Excellencie of the Ministerie," *The Faithful Shepherd* (1607), ch. i; see his p. 94 ("a good library and a good maintenance"). George Downame, *Of the Dignity . . . of the Ministerie*, in *Two Sermons* (1608), 96-98 (learning). Samuel Hieron, *The Preachers Plea* [1604] and *The Dignity of Preaching* [1615], in *Sermons* (1635), 499, 577 ff. John Swan, *Redde Debitum* (1640), 85. Cp. Jeremy Taylor, *Clerus Domini, Works* (10 v., 1850-), I, 6 ff., 16. Thomas Collier pounced on [Hall] (24)—Collier, *The Pulpit-Guard Routed* (1651), 37, 37-42.

[Against early] unordained [preaching and] lecturing (30)—See Anthony Stafford, *Niobe* (1611), 150; Thomas Tuke, *The Picture of a true Protestant*, 1609; Charles Richardson, *A Workeman, That Needeth Not to Be Ashamed* (1616), e.g., 29 ff., and see 43 ff. (tithes); John Mayer, *Praxis Theologica* (1629), on James, ch. iii; Richard Stock, *Comm. on Malachi*, ed. A. B. Grosart (1867), 132 (on Mal. ii:5). Robert Barclay, *Inner Life of Religious Societies* (1877), 104; Rufus M. Jones, *Mystical Religion* (1909),
202   423. Bishop [Edward] Boughen . . . warned . . . of the giddy (3)—*Sermon at Saint Pauls Crosse* ([1630] 1635), 26 ff.; [Visitation] *Sermon at Canterbury* (1635), 9, 17, etc. Cp. Boughen, *Observations upon the Ordinance* [of the Assembly] (1645), 26-27.

Thomas Edwards [on] button-makers (21)—*Reasons against the Independant Government* (1641), 23. Qualified minister . . . statutory ordination (26)—*Lay-Preaching Unmasked* (1644), 26-27 ff. Respectable Inde-
203   pendents [resembled Milton] on . . . ordination (3)—Philip Nye and John Loder, Pref. to Sydrach Simpson, *Two Books of Unbelief*, 1658. Cp. Milton, *Of Ref.*, in *Works* (1931-), III, 6 (9-12); *C. D.*, XVI, 215 (5-24, esp. 21 ff.); 267 (2-9); 291 (8-25).

[On] Milton's long silence (10)—Wilbur K. Jordan, *Toleration*, IV, 215 ff. [Satirists'] picture . . . of the . . . tub preacher (27)—See, e.g., T[homas] F[ord], "A Sectary," *The Times Anatomiz'd in severall Characters* (1647), No. xx; Thomas Bancroft, Sat. ii, "Against Sectaries," *Time's*

PAGE

203 *Out of Tune; XX. Satires* (1658), 8-9. For fragmentary bibliog. of such satires: C. M. Webster, "The Satiric Background of . . . *A Tale of A Tub*," *PMLA*, L (1935), 210-217. And see William P. Holden, *Anti-Puritan Satire, 1572-1642*, New Haven, 1954. **[On] prophet James Hunt (32)**— Robert Barclay, *Inner Life of Religious Societies*, 153. See Hunt, *The Spirituall Verses and Prose* (1642/3), 5; cp. Hunt, *The Sermon and Prophecie* (1641), 4.

204 **Fox protested [new university] (16)**—See William C. Braithwaite, *The Beginnings of Quakerism* (1912), 294. Quakers beaten at Cambridge: Braithwaite, 159, 201, 295; and James Nayler, "University Discipline," 20-21, in *Churches Gathered Against Christ and His Kingdom*, 1653/4. Cp. Samuel Fisher, *Rusticus ad Academicos* (1662), Pt. II, 67. **[William] Penn supposed . . . predecessors (23)**—*A Brief Account of the Quakers*, in Penn, Barclay, and Pike, *Three Treatises* (Philadelphia, 1770), 41 ff. (minimizes Quaker animus against learning). But contrast James Nayler, *The Wisdom . . . from Beneath* (1653), in *A Collection of Sundry Books*, 1716.

George Whitehead . . . wrote . . . life (39)—*Jacob Found in a Desert Land* (1656), 2-6. Cp. Whitehead, sketch of Nayler before *James Nayler,*

205 *Collection [of] Books*, 43. **Milton [prescribed ministerial] languages and arts (12)**—E.g., in *Works*, VI, 139 (19-23); and see, on ordination, my notes to page 203.

Samuel Howe [on learning teaching] falsehoods (40)—*The Sufficiencie of the Spirits Teaching without Humane Learning* (1644), Sigs F3ᵛᵒ ff.; D2ᵛᵒ

206 (?26). See Thomas Hall's reply, *Vindiciæ Literarum, The Schools Guarded, or the Excellency . . . of Humane Learning in Subordination to Divinity* [1654], 1655. Pages 9-10 fairly sum Howe's book, sarcasm notwithstanding.

Baptist [Thomas Collier] for "lay" preaching (19)—*The Pulpit Guard*

207 *Routed* (1651), 15, 32, 38. Cp. John Horne, *A Consideration of Infant Baptism* (1654), 158-160. Since Tombes, Cox, and Gosnold may have learning, why do the Baptists object to learning?—thus Immanuel Bourne, *A Defence and Justification of Ministers Maintenance by Tythes, and of Infant-Baptism, Humane Learning, and the Sword of the Magistrate* (1659), 12; see 10-11.

Alexander Ross . . . an Ancient disinterested (37)—On Ross in this character: Francis R. Johnson, *Astronomical Thought in Renaissance England* (Baltimore, Md., 1937), 278-282, and R. F. Jones, *Ancients and Moderns* (St. Louis, 1935), 125 ff. For characteristic attitudes: Ross, *Arcana Microcosmi* ([1651] 1652), Ep. Ded.; *Mel Heliconium* (1642), 113-114; esp. *The Philosophicall Touch-Stone*, 1645; and see translator's note, John Wollebius, *The Abridgment of Christian Divinitie*, tr. Alexander Ross ([1650]

208 1656), 331-332. **Theology and natural philosophy . . . separate (16)**—John Wilkins, *The Discovery of a New World in the Moon*, Part I ([1638] 1640), 37. **An Ancient loyal to Independency (20)**—Henry Stubbe (Stubbs), *Campanella Revived*, [1670]. Cp. Stubbe, *A Light Shining out of Darknes*, 1659. On Stubbe: Wilbur K. Jordan, *Toleration*, IV, 335-340. **A good skeptic (32)**—Richard Whitlock, *Zootomia* (1654), 223-224, 219-220, 138-189, esp. 141. Cp., on the obscurantists, Henry Delaune, *Patrikon Doron* ([1651] 1657), 88 (Nos. 50-51).

209 **Culverwel . . . apostate from . . . Platonism (11)**—Thus Frederick J. Powicke, *The Cambridge Platonists* (1926), 139-140; G. P. H. Pawson, *The Cambridge Platonists, etc.* (1930), 85-90; John J. De Boer, *The Theory of Knowledge of the Cambridge Platonists* (Madras, 1931), 151. **"Platonic**

214 Barebones Parliament . . . **crisis (14)**—Anthony à Wood, *Hist. and Ant. of Oxford,* tr. Gutch (1796), II, 657-659. C. H. Cooper, *Annals of Cambridge* (5 v., 1845), III, 454. S. R. Gardiner, *Hist. of the Commonwealth* (3 v., 1897), 275. David Masson, *Life of Milton,* IV, 566. Louise F. Brown, *Baptists and Fifth Monarchy Men* (1912), 36-37. Geoffrey B. Tatham, *The Puritans in Power* (1913), 137. See Milton, *Ready Way, Works* (1931-), VI, 145 (12-23); *Likeliest Means,* 80 (3-19). **Observers . . . expect . . . universities . . . to be abolished (17)**—Abraham Wright, ed. *Parnassus Biceps,* 1656. See Thomas Peck, "Upon the Parliament," in his tr. of Owens' *Epigrams* called *Parnassi Puerperium* (1659), 183. Cp. Richard Baxter, *Reliquiæ Baxterianæ* I.113 (1696), 70. **Pamphlet exchange . . . reviewed (31)**—See Cooper, III, 138-140, and Masson, IV, 568. Martha Ornstein, *The Role of Scientific Societies* (1913), 281-282. Caroline F. Richardson, *English Preachers and Preaching* (1928), 16-18. R. F. Jones, *Ancients and Moderns,* 118 ff. Arthur Barker, *Puritan Dilemma,* 230-233. Douglas Bush, *English Literature, etc.,* 20-21. Phyllis Allen, "Science in the Universities," *JHI,* X (1949), 236-238.

215 **Animus against ministerial fountains (1)**—Roger Williams, *The Hireling Ministry None of Christs* (1652), 14-17; *Bloudy Tenent,* Hanserd Knollys Soc. (1848), 263-264. Repr., substantially, in Perry Miller, *Roger Williams* (New York, 1953), 201-203. Cp. William Dell, *The Word Against Divinity-Degrees* (1654), esp. 10-11, 29 ff.; and *The Tryal of Spirits,* 1653; *Confutation [of Sydrach Simpson]* (1654), Pref., Sig A2^vo; *The Stumbling-Stone* (1653), 1-20, esp. 27; Pref., A2^vo.

A theocrat marveled [that Dell betrayed] his class (40)—Samuel Ruther-
216 ford, *A Survey of the Spirituall Antichrist* (1648), 175. See Dell, *Tryal of Spirits,* Pref., and *Stumbling-Stone,* 27-30.

[John] Wilkins [thought Webster] a charlatan (11)—Seth Ward and (here) [Joh]N. [Wilkin]S., *Vindiciæ Academiarum* (1654), Pt. I, 5-7; see 32 ff.; 18-19. On Webster, see, e.g., Masson, *Life of Milton,* IV, 568; Foster Watson, *Beginnings of Modern Subjects,* 234-235; L. B. Wright, in *PQ,* IX (1930), 289-291; R. F. Jones, *Ancients and Moderns,* 105; and Phyllis Allen, "Science, etc.," *JHI,* X (1949), 236. Contrast Rufus M. Jones, *Mysticism and Democracy,* 85-90. **[John Webster] under his true colors (17)**—Webster, "Of Human Learning," *The Saints Guide* (1653), sec. i, see pp. 1-6, 28 ff., 33, etc. For instances of occultism: Webster, *Academiarum Examen* (1654), 25-26, 50-51, 69-70, 74-75, 97, etc.

217 **[Webster stripped learning] from ministers (18)**—*Ibid.,* e.g., 7-8. **Milton [on] universities . . . collected (32)**—By J. H. Hanford, *A Milton Handbook* (New York, 1946), 355-364. On ministerial training: Oliver M. Ainsworth, ed. *Milton on Education: Cornell St. in Eng.,* No. 12 (1928), 217-226. **He lost . . . admiration for the universities (38)**—Milton, *Animad.,* in *Works* (18 v., 1931-), III, 160 (6-8); *Apol.,* 335 (27)-336 (1); 359 (10-14); esp. 298 (2-18).

218 **[Milton] had chosen disestablishment (10)**—Cp. *Likeliest Means, Works,* VI, 83 (22), and *C. D.,* XVI, 309 (28)-311 (1), for his explicit declarations against a national church. On the attendant "repudiation" of learning: Arthur Barker, *Milton and the Puritan Dilemma* (Toronto, 1942), 258. **"Holy . . . aristocracy" (23)**—Milton, *Of Ref.,* III, 64 (3). Cp. *C. D.,* XVI, 241 (12-15), 247 (9-10 and 27). Ministers' qualifications: for Milton on ordination, see notes to my pages 203 and 205; then note esp. XVI, 263 (26) ff., where he begins by accepting, in principle, the orthodox standard of ministerial competence.

219   [Milton would multiply] schools and libraries (8)—*Likeliest Means*, VI, 80 (3-19); *Ready Way*, 145 (12-23).

[He would] tether the benefice-chasers (22)—VI, 80 (10-11); cp. *Ten. of Kings*, V, 44 (19); *C. D.*, XVI, 303 (11-17). He honored the preaching tradesmen (28)—VI, 77 (2-8), 81 (8-11), 98 (9-15); *C. D.*, XVI, 293-303, esp. 293 (16-21) and 297 (5-11).

220   Simplified divinity . . . the reformer's [*Christian Doctrine*] (25)—Thus J. H. Hanford, "The Date of Milton's *D. D. C.*," *SP*, XVII (1920), 316. *Likeliest Means*, VI, 78 (20-24). Hirelings . . . expected a return (29)—VI, 92 (25-28).

221   "I have . . . examined the usual pretences" (26)—On the abolition of school-divinity: VI, 95 (26) ff. Cp. *Areopagitica*, *Works*, IV, 338 (25)-339 (2).

222   Milton's meaning in his brief epic (13)—For critics' commentary on the poet's exhaustion, bitterness, or pietism, see, e.g., H. J. C. Grierson, "John Milton," *The Criterion*, VIII (1928), 7 ff., esp. 254; *Cross Currents*, 269-270, 276; and cp. George W. Whiting, *Milton's Literary Milieu* (Chapel Hill, N. C., 1939), 129-176. For further bibliog. in this kind see M. Y. Hughes, in *SP*, XXXV (1938), 254, and B. Rajan, '*Paradise Lost*' *and the Seventeenth Century Reader* (New York, 1948), 158, n 6. Rajan, 78-92, with plausible comment, fails to find remarkable gloom in the last books of *Paradise Lost*, but note M. M. Mahood, *Poetry and Humanism* (New Haven, 1950), 239-241 ff.

223   In one of the journals (8)—"Christ and Antichrist in *Paradise Regained*," *PMLA*, LXVII (1952), 790 ff., in which I have amplified, in some respects, the argument of the following pages.

224   The *Christian Doctrine* tells us [the meaning of *church*] (14)—Milton (*Works*, XVI, 56-337 ff.) shows by his Protestant succession of topics the logical priority of the church invisible, the fruit of union and communion with Christ (56 ff.). Its imperfectly glorified members then enjoy the sacraments, the external seals of the Covenant of Grace, so that out of the mystical church rises (219 [8] ff.) the visible church, both universal and particular (215 [15] ff.). Christ is head of both (227 [24]), ruling by church-discipline (321 ff.; cp. XVII, 72 ff.). The mystical church ascends to glory (337 ff.), presumably leaving behind certain hypocrites unavoidably associated with visible churches (XVI, 91 [2], 221 [10]). *Paradise Regained* treats at length of matters peculiar to the visible church and its worship, but defines the invisible by giving always certain "notes" to know the hypocrites.

Edward Dowden . . . observed (33)—"*Paradise Regained*," *Milton Mem. Lectures*, ed. Percy W. Ames (1909), 192. He found justification for *P. R.* as a sequel to *P. L.* in the poet's announced theme—Christ's lordship established over Satan, Sin, and Death. He happened not to remark that by all theology Christ was King of his church specifically to subdue these enemies (*C. D.*, *Works*, XV, 301 [10-20]). Don C. Allen, *The Harmonious Vision* (Baltimore, 1954), 110-121, writes most acceptably of the dramatic tension in the poem, which he traces (118) to the fluctuation in Christ's "knowledge of himself and his mission." I should suggest "knowledge of God's will concerning his mission." Earnestly imploring the Spirit's help, Christ receives wisdom as he needs it. But his own feelings, in lonely intervals, are anxiously human. Lines here cited [from *P. R.*, concerning the Kingdom] (34)—I.20 (baptism into the Kingdom), 28 (office, a term including Kingship; cp. 159), 75 and 99 (Satan bears witness; cp. 125), 188

225

225 (office), 240-241, 254, 265 (cp. 289); II.36, 113-114 (office), 325, 335 (cp. 379-380). In the "active" temptations, Satan's offers: II.425 ff.; III.31 ff., and esp. 150-180, 226, 236-250, 351-361 ff.; IV.105-109. Christ's rejections: II.432 ff., 466-476; III.44-46, esp. 182-202, 395 ff.; esp. 441; IV.146-153. Later exchanges: IV.282 (learning prepares for Kingship), 364 (denied), 369, esp. 379-393 and 467-480 (persecution the path to monarchy), 492-494 (Christ explains Satan's whole reason for tempting him). These late passages carry to the end of the contest the theme of Kingship sustained from the beginning. In IV.633, we leave Christ "heir," or destined King, "of both Worlds," i.e., King of Grace in this world and of Glory in the next.

[226]   A P P E N D I X

[227]   NOTE A

228 What . . . Jesus meant by the Kingdom (3)—Cecil J. Cadoux, *The Historic Mission of Jesus* (New York, [1943]), cites much modern scholarship on the subject. See James Orr, *The Christian View of God and the World* (3d ed., 1897), 328, 353-358. Charles Gore *et al.*, eds. *A New Comm. on Holy Scripture* (New York, 1946), N. T., 294 297. Logia . . . possibly interpolated (8)—See Cadoux, 307 ff. On the Kingdom as the church in the N. T. Epistles, note, e.g., Ernst Troeltsch, *The Social Teaching of the Christian Churches,* tr. Olive Wyon (2 v., 1931), I, 100 (n 44b); see 150 (n 72a). The opinion of Albrecht Ritschl (15)—*The Christian Doctrine of Justification and Reconciliation,* tr. H. R. Mackintosh and A. B. Macaulay (1902), 432 ff. Cp. Alexander B. Bruce, *The Kingdom of God* (1889), 252-272, e.g., 262, or Elbert S. Todd, *The Kingdom of Heaven* (1923), ch. xv.

What . . . generations have thought Jesus meant (27)—The most convenient *historical* account of the Kingdom-concept is perhaps that by J. Gottschick in *The New Schaff-Herzog Enc. of Religious Knowledge* (1908-), Art. "Kingdom of God." In the early church: Adolph Harnack, *Hist. of Dogma,* tr. Neil Buchanan (7 v., 1894), I, 150-154, 167 (n 1), II, 71-72 ff., e.g., 82, 83 (n 1), 297, (n 1); V, 4 ff.; VI, 5-16, esp. 6 ff. Troeltsch, I, 113 (n 55)-114. R. Newton Flew, *The Idea of Perfection, etc.* (1934), 120-121, 189, esp. 217, etc., Robert Frick, *Die Gesch. des Reich-Gottes-Gedankens in der alten Kirche bis zu . . . Augustin* (Giessen, 1928), 114 ff., 138-152 (Augustine), 152. James S. Candlish, *The Kingdom of God* (1884), 178, 183, 200-208, 247-248, esp. 258 and 406-409. Ernest F. Scott, *The Kingdom of God in the New Testament* (New York, 1931), 129 ff., esp. 130-131, 167-168 ff. (-183),
229 169, 174-175. A recent Protestant scholar (8)—I.e., Flew, 202-209.

Protestants . . . invisible church (13)—The real (essential) Church Universal is invisible: Johann Spangenberg, *The Sũ of divinitie,* tr. R. Hutten (1548), Sig M5^vo. Pierre Viret, *Exp. of the . . . Crede,* tr. [?1548], Sig M2. Bertrand de Loque, *A Treatie of the Churche,* tr. T. W. (1581), 5-7. Thomas Rogers, *The Thirty-Nine Articles,* Parker Soc. (1854), 164 ff. Christopher Shutte, *The Testimonie of a true Faith* (1581), Sig II3. John Terry, *The Triall of Truth* (1600), 93-94. John Darrell, *A Treatise of the Church* (1617), 12-13. Andrew Willet, *Synopsis Papismi* (1634), ed. J. Cumming (10 v., 1852), I, 238 ff., esp. 247. Contrast Anglican Robert Some, *Exp. upon the Articles* [?1582], Sigs B4^vo-5. Reformers . . . retain . . . Roman creedal statements (17)—See Christopher Dawson, in H. G. Wood *et al., The Kingdom of God and History* (New York, 1938), 209-210 ff. In the volume see 65, 95 ff., esp. 118, 121, 154 ff., etc. "The Reformation . . . still identi-

PAGE
229 fied the Kingdom too exclusively with the church": thus James Orr in the [*Hastings*] *Dict. of the Bible* (1902), II, 854 (Col. 2, par. 7)-856. See Candlish, 272, 278-280, 285-289, esp. 289-290, 297, 321-343, esp. 399 ff., and Notes, 397-405. Ernst Troeltsch, *Social Teaching*, II, 584, 596, 995. Adolph Harnack, *Hist. of Dogma*, VI, 5-16; VII, 150-164, esp. 161-163; Albrecht Ritschl, *Justification* (1902), 288-289, 417 ff., esp. 420 and 424-426. [**Martin**] **Luther's twofold division of** [**Christ's**] **office (21)**—*Exp.* . . . *of the Kingdom of Christ,* tr. W. Lynne (1548), Sig D7. Cp. Henry Bullinger, "Of Christ, King and Priest," *The Decades* (tr. 1587), Parker Soc. (5 v., 1849), Dec. iv, Serm. 7, pp. 273 ff.; see v, 2, p. 84. John Hooper, *Christ and His Office* (1547), *Writings*, Parker Soc. (1843), I, 192; see ch. xi, pp. 78 ff. Bp. Robert Abbott, *The Exaltation of the kingdome and Priesthood of Christ* (1601), almost ignores the prophetic office (exc. pp. 79-80). Similarly a few later writers. **Catholics** [**were**] **condemned (23)**—The Threefold Office used against Rome: see, entire, Richard Fowns, *Trisagion, or, The Three Holy Offices of Jesus* (1618), esp. Book iii, e.g., 512-513. (Note the eminence on the subject awarded Fowns by John Wilkins, *Ecclesiastes* [1651 ed.], 98.) Also Thomas Rogers, *An Historical Dialogue* [*of*] *Poperie* (1589), 36 ff., 96 ff., 102 ff. (the three offices). Edward Bush, *A* [*Pauls Crosse*] *Sermon* (1573), Sigs C-C2. The same argument used against Anglicans: Francis Johnson (Separatist), *An Answer to Maister H. Jacob* (1600), 37 ff. **Thus wrote** [**all persuasions**] **(31)**—On the Threefold Office, and the identity of the church and the Kingdom, **representative foreign divines**, mostly in early translation: Philipp Melanchthon, *Apologie* [*for the Augsburg Confession*], tr. R. Taverner (?1536), on Art. vii, Sig H3. Johann Spangenberg, *Sũ of divinitie,* tr. R. Hutten (1548) Sig M7, see M5ᵛᵒ. Rudolph Walther, *Sermons* . . . *upon* . . . *Abdias and Jonas,* tr. R. Norton (1573), 69-78. Erasmus Sarcerius, *Coɱon places,* tr. R. Taverner ([1538] 1577), 177-181. Martin Bucer, *De Regno Christi* (e.g., pp. 2-13), in *Scripta Anglicana* (Basle, 1577); see also p. 271. Nicholas Hemmingius, *The Faith of the Church Militant,* tr. T. Rogers (1581), 50-53, esp. 149. John Calvin, *Psalmes* [*and*] *Commentaries,* tr. A. Golding (1571), 132 ff. (on Ps. CX); *Comm. on Daniel* (2 v., 1853), II, 45, esp. 75-76; Genevan Catechism, in Calvin, *Tracts,* tr. H. Beveridge (3 v., 1851), II, 42, and cf. closely 49, 51. Theodore Beza, *The Psalmes of David,* tr. A. Gilbie (1581), 267-268 (on Ps. CX), and *Summe of Christian faith,* tr. R. F[yll], n.d., 79-80. Augustine Marlorat, *Exp. upon the Rev.,* tr. A. Golding (1574), 10-10b. Urbanus Regius, *The Solace of Sion* (1536), tr. R. R. ([1587] 1594), Sigs Cᵛᵒ, esp. D6 ff. Philippe de Mornay, *A Treatise of the Church* (tr. 1581), 25; tr. J. Molle (1606), 13. Pierre Viret, *Exp. upon the prayer of our Lorde,* tr. J. Brooke (1582), 77b-98b, esp. 81 ff. The idea of the Kingdom **in the English church**: John Olde, *A Short description of Antichrist* (?1577), 6. Richard Turnbull, *Exp. upon* . . . *James* (1592), ch. iv, Serm. 21, fol. 252a. Thomas Bilson, *The Perpetual Government of Christs Church* (1593), ed. R. Eden (1842), ch. iii, "Kingdom of Christ," 47 ff. George Downame, *A Treatise concerning Antichrist* (1603), 61. Richard Bernard (against Brownists), *Plaine Evidences* (1610), 255-259. Richard Web, *Christs Kingdome* (1611), Pref., A2; pp. 82-96, esp. 92; 113-126, etc. Lancelot Andrewes, *Ninety-Six Sermons,* LACT (1841-), V, 393; 462 (end) ff., 551 ff. William Perkins, *Works* (1612), I, 4-5. John Day, *Day's Dyall* (1614), 262-263. Daniel Featley, *Clavis Mystica* (1636), 151. John Yates, *Imago Mundi et Regnum Christi* (1640), e.g., 53 and Pref., sec. 3. An Anglican summary, valid for the seventeenth century: Samuel Hilliard, *The Nature of the Kingdom, or Church, of Christ* (1717), esp. 10-12.

PAGE

229 Some writers shading into Puritanism: Walter Travers, *Declaration of* . . . *Discipline* (1574), 10-14. Thomas Wilcox, *Exp. upon* . . . *Psalmes* (1586), in *Works* (1624), 5, esp. 321 (on Ps. CX). Thomas Taylor, *Japhets* . . . *Perswasion* (1612), 50-53, and see Taylor, *Christian Practice,* paged after *Works,* ed. E. Calamy (1653), 70-77, esp. 72, 74. *A Guide unto Sion, [the] Visible Church* (1638), 12. *Christ on His Throne* (1640), e.g., 77. John Lightfoot, *A [Gospel] Harmony, etc.* (1644), in *Works* (13 v., 1822-), IV, 258.
Kingdom of Heaven . . . meant gospel preaching (43)—See William Laud, *Works,* LACT (7 v., 1847-), VI, 182.

230 [The] majority [of] witnesses (15)—On the extent of millenarianism: In 1655, Thomas Wilson, ed. *A Complete Christian Dictionary* (7th ed., 1661), Art. "Thousand Years," pp. 654-655, implied (with bibliog.) that preterism was dead. Cp. Joseph Caryl's license before Nathaniel Homes, *The Resurrection Revealed* ([1654] 1833), and see esp. p. 45 n. Thomas Hall, *Exp. [of] Amos* (1661), sneers that the learned Homes embraced millenarianism as soon as the doctrine became "fashionable," i.e., after 1641. William Hicks, *Quinto-Monarchiæ* (1659), Sigs A2ᵛᵒ ff., alleged the support of "most" testimony. See Increase Mather's millenarian *Mystery of Israel's Redemption* (1669), Pref., for a fragmentary list of scholars both excellent and millenarian. [Millenarian] theories preserved . . . Kingdom-church (24)—Henry Archer, *The Personall Reign of Christ upon Earth* (1642), 1 ff. Joseph Caryl, *The Saints Thankfull Acclamation at* . . . *the Initials of [Christs] Kingdome* (1644), 34, esp. 24. Homes (cited), 97 (Christ has always ruled his church, but has not yet sat on David's throne). William Hicks, *The Revelation Revealed* (1659), 311. Thomas Beverly, *The Prophetical History of the Reformation* (1689), 3, and *The Thousand Years* (1691), 8. The Glorious Reign belongs to the Kingdom of Grace: John Henry Alsted, *The Beloved City,* tr. W. Burton (1642), 79. Christ rules the church, perhaps only as God: Robert Maton, *Israel's Redemption* (1642), 45, esp. 52, and *Israel's Redemption Redeemed* (1646), 179.

231 Thomas Hobbes [held that] the church . . . was not the Kingdom (30) —*Leviathan,* in *Works,* ed. Molesworth (1839-), III, 343-403, esp. 396-403; 605-606. Opposed: John Bramhall, *The Catching of Leviathan,* in *Works,* LACT, IV, 527 ff., and cp. II, 565; V, 262. Hooker's writings [on] ecclesiastical headship (41)—*Eccl. Pol.* (VIII,4), in *Works,* (3 v., 1865), II, 518-534; esp. 523-524; cp. F. J. Shirley, *Richard Hooker and Contemporary Political Ideas,* SPCK (London, 1949), 113-115. Henry Hammond, *Misc. Theol. Works,* LACT (1849-), III (1), 71; cp. 6; *Practical Catechism,* I, 15, 19, 28. On the Erastian view: James S. Candlish, *Kingdom of God,* 421.

232 Rheims New Testament . . . to speak for Catholics (20)—On the Kingdom-church: Rheims N. T. (1582), e.g., 740, top line, annotating Rev. xx:4. Or cp. Nicholas Sanders (Papist), *De Visibili Monarchia Ecclesiæ* (Wurtzburg, 1592), Pref., secs. 7 ff. For the Catholic exposition: Karl Adam, *The Spirit of Catholicism,* tr. Dom Justin McCann (New York, 1946), 15-34, 72, 88-90, etc., or Denis Fahey, *The Mystical Body of Christ, etc.* (Waterford, Ireland, 1939), 4; G. W. Joyce, "Church," *Cath. Enc.* (1908), III, 2. Among Anglicans, Bishop [Edward] Reynolds (21)—*An Explication of the Hundreth and Tenth Psalme* (1632), 7, 83, 133, 184, 279, etc. Francis Bacon, *Works,* ed. Spedding, IX, 353, 361. John Hales, "My Kingdom, etc.," in *Remains,* ed. Pearson, 192-194; cp. 245. Joseph Hall, *Works* (12 v., 1837), VIII, 513. John Donne, *Works,* ed. Alford (6 v., 1839), I, 424; II, 11; VI, 261; see also I, 308 (cp. 317), esp. 483; II, 14; IV, 55, 57, 88 ff., 408-409; V, 1, and a host of other passages.

PAGE

232   [Of] the Kingdom . . . wrote Richard Baxter (38)—*Practical Works,*
ed. Orme (23 v., 1830), VII, 17; see esp. XIX 135; and cp., against millenarianism, *The Glorious Kingdom of Christ* (1691), esp. ch. i. [John] Calvin
himself had written (41)—*Institutes,* IV.2.4; cp. II.6.3; Eng. ed. (1634),

233   513, 154, etc. Bernardino Ochino (15)—*The Tragedy,* tr. J. Ponet (1549),
ed. C. E. Plumptre, London, 1899. Ecclesiastical drift in comm. on the
Temptation: William Perkins, *The Combate Betweene Christ and the
Divell* (1604), paged after *Works,* 1606. Note the antecedent circumstances,
p. 1. Cp. p. 2, Col. 2; p. 3 (expanded on 51 ff.); pp. 8 (2), 10 (2), 11 (1), 19,
29, etc. Similarly, Thomas Taylor, *Christs Combate and Conquest* (1618),
prefatory outline ("Preparation"), and end. Also pp. 3, 5, 49, 75, 122-124,
131 ff., 206, 248-256, 260 ff., 351 ff. Or see John Udall, *The Combate betwixt Christ and the Devill* (?1588), [p. 1] and some other passages. For
Milton's ecclesiastical application of the biblical narrative, see his prose
in *Works* (1931-), III, 168 (15-17); esp. 161 (1-3), and 362 (13, 21).
    Sects enamored of the Kingdom-church (31)—Brownists (Separatists):
R[obert] H[arrison], "A Treatise of the Church and Kingdome of Christ"
[MS, ?1581], ed. Albert Peel, *The Brownists in Norwich* (Cambridge, 1920),
esp. opening. Henry Ainsworth, *Annotations Upon . . . Psalmes* (1617),
Ps. CX:3, and [Ainsworth and ?Francis Johnson], *An Apologie . . . of . . .
Brownists* (1604), 17-19. Henry Jacob (Semi-Separatist), *The Divine Beginning [of the] Visible Church* (1610), Sigs A, A8ᵛᵒ, B2, C6, D, D8, etc.
Later Independents: e.g., Peter Sterry, *A Thanksgiving Sermon [to Parl.]*
(1651), e.g., 13. Theophilus Brabourne (Traskite), *Sabbath Day* (1628), 12,
33. F. H. (Anabaptist, 1622), qu. by I. P., *Anabaptisme . . . Unmasked*
(1623), 7. John Smyth (the Se-Baptist), *The Differences of the . . . Sepe-
ration* (1608), 224. Later Baptists: *Confession of Faith, of [so-] called Anabaptists* (1644), Arts. x, xv, xix. Francis Cornwell, *A Vindication of . . .
King Jesus* (1644), 13, and *King Jesus, . . . Prince, Priest, and Lawgiver,* 4.
William Kiffin, Pref. to Thomas Goodwin, *A Glimpse of Sions Glory,* 1641.
Quakers: George Fox, *The Way to the Kingdom* (?1654), 4-5, and *An
Epistle . . . to . . . the Royal Priest-Hood* (1660), e.g., 7, 12. James Nayler,
A Lamentacion (1653), 4. James Parnell, *Christ Exalted into His Throne*
(1655), 5, and esp. 7. Received doctrine to be found in catechisms, [etc.]
(35)—Samuel Crooke, *The Guide unto True Blessednesse* ([1613] 1614),
secs. xi, xii, esp. xli. Edward Dering, *Catechism* (31b) and *Upon Hebrues*
(iii [390], Sig E4ᵛᵒ, on Heb. i:13), both in *Workes,* 1614. Demanded John
Dod (36)—Dod and Cleaver, catechism (378 ff.) after *Exp. of the Ten Commandements* ([1603] 1618), "On the Mediatorial Office," Sig B4ᵛᵒ. William
Ames, *The Marrow of Sacred Divinity,* in *Workes* (1643), 136 (16), 138 (38)-
139, esp. 135 (8-9), 74 (10)—Office; 75 (14)—as Prophet, Christ reveals God's
whole will; 99 (34), etc. John Owen, catechism, in *Works* (6 v., 1860), I,
480 (ch. xi), 483 (whole will); cp. I, 85; Owen, *Advantages, etc.* (Parl. serm.,
1651), 5, 20.

234   Milton . . . defined the true church, [the] Kingdom (11)—*C. D., Works*
(1931-), XV, 297 (7) ff., note (27) and esp. 301 (2-3); cp. 287, 301 (10-20). Read
XVI, 359 (9) ff., with XV, 301 (21-25); XVII, 397 (21-26). Observe proof
texts cited in XVI, 219-220, and the meaning of Heb. xii:22-23 in XVI, 63
(10). Also, outside the *C. D.,* see *Works,* V, 57 (16-26), 250 (4) ff.; VI, 22 (3-
18), 89 (19-28), and 124 (4-11). For his eschatological view of the Kingdom:
XVI, 337 ff., e.g., 339 (26), 341 (8), 345 (19) ff., 347 (1, 16), 349 (5), 355 (1)—
Last Judgment of men and angels coincides with the earthly millennial
reign; 359 (9), and 361 (5).

APPENDIX

NOTE B

235 A church . . . impure [is not necessarily] false (35)—A true church
may have its faults as a true man a wooden leg; thus Anglican John Darrell [Dayrel], *A Treatise of the Church* (1617), Ep. Ded., fol. 2; see [3].
George Gifford, *Brownists [are] Donatists* (1590), 7 ff., 27; and *Reply [to]
Barrow* (1591), 56 ff. Stephen Bredwell, *The Raising of . . . Brownisme*
(1588), 49 ff. Richard Alison, *Confutation of . . . Brownisme* (1590), Pref.
and 11 ff. Richard Bernard, *Plaine Evidences* (1610), 93, 241 ff., 274. Robert
Abbott, *A Triall of our Church-Forsakers* (1639), 86, 110. So Catholics:
e.g., John Churchson, *A Brefe Treatyse [of] the Churche* (1556), Sigs B3 ff.,
esp. C. **Angel of light . . . acts the role . . . of Antichrist (39)**—Resisting
slander of the Pope, early Catholic apologists found scripture to prove
that Antichrist, who could not come until the Roman Empire should be
quite gone, would come as an open enemy of the Christian church. See,
e.g., Rheims N. T. (1582), 740-741, or Nicholas Sanders, *The Rock of the
Church* (1624), 360 ff., esp. 364, 369. Protestants retorted that the miserable
remains in Germany had nothing to do with the ancient Empire; the true
successor of Rome was the Roman Catholic Church. Less cogently, they
strained II Cor. xi:14 to argue that Antichrist would come dissembling,
garbed as an angel of light. See, against Bellarmine, Pierre du Moulin,
The Accomplishment of the Prophecies, tr. J. Heath (1613), 148 ff.; John
Fielde, *A Caveat for Parsons Howlet* (1581), Sig B4ᵛ°; or Lawrence Deios,
That the Pope is . . . Antichrist, in *Two . . . Sermons* (1590), 12. **A routine metaphor (41)**—Rome's "oracles": George Herbert, "The Church Militant," line 178, *Works*, ed. Palmer, III, 359; Peter Martyr Vermigli, *The
Common Places*, tr. A. Marten (?1583), [i], p. 92 (32, end), and [iii], 396-397
(top); or Joseph Hall, *Works* (1837), XI, 308.

236 **Text for Protestantism [against idolatry] (6)**—The Devil's Table, or
Idolatry: William Salesbury, *The . . . Popes Botelreulx* (1550), Sig E2.
John de L'Espine, *A Treatise of Apostasie* (tr. 1587), 22. Meats sacrificed
(or idolatry) in ecclesiastical controversy: e.g., Robert Crowley, *A Setting
open of . . . Watson* (1569), Serm. II, pp. 77 ff. Lawrence Deios, *Two . . .
Sermons* (1590), 107. Edmund Jessop, *A Discovery of the . . . English Ana-
baptists* (1623), 84. For argument exactly parallel with Satan's in P. R.:
Henoch Clapham, *Errour on the Left Hand* (1608), 79-80—None of our
Anglican surplices has been devoted to an idol; hence none is idolatrous,
and so on, through an exposition of I Cor. x:23.
Greek myth . . . Old Testament . . . groves . . . idolatry (39)—See,
e.g., John Marbecke, *A Book of Notes and Common places* (1581), 469.
'Grove' [a] mistranslation [in] the Authorized Version (42)—On the
asherah: Charles Gore et al., eds. *A New Comm. on Holy Scripture* (New
York, 1946), O. T., 160, 663.

INDEX

Abbott, John, 94
Abelard, Peter, 9, 37
Abernethy, John, 106
Acontius, James, 109
action vs. contemplation, 27, 28, *30*,
  31, 32, 38, 40-41, 71-82, 87-88
Adam, 2, 3, 4, 6, 10, 15, 19, 20, 25,
  31, 32, *37,* 38, 40, 43, 48, 55, 56, 57,
  69-70, 78, 80, 82, 85, 86, 89, 91, 97,
  105, 126, 135, 139, 153, 160, 163,
  168, *173-183,* 190, 194, 206, 210,
  230
Adams, Thomas, 40, 190
Æneas Silvius, 190
Ænesidemus, 160
Aeschylus, 4
Agricola, John, 143
Agrippa, Cornelius, 15, *24-25,* 27, 39,
  43, 50, 54, 59, 68, 101, 158, 166
Ainsworth, Henry, 188, 199
Albertus Magnus, 47
alchemy, 1, 24, *47-50,* 62, 67, 68
Alfonso X of Castile, 20, 176
Ames, William, 129, 200, 233
Amyraut, Moses, 93, 95, 110, 129
Anabaptists *(See also* Baptists): 24,
  51, 70, 97, 99, 100, 102, 105, 127,
  128, 144, 145, 148, 149, 155, 187,
  196, 211, 229
Anaximenes, 5
Andrewes, Lancelot, 194
angels, knowledge and power of, 45-
  47, 54-55, *86-89*
angels, orders of, 1, 11, *123,* 137,
  170, 175
Anglicanism, 1, 7, 17-19, 39, 40, 83,
  96, 97-98, 105, 117, 119, 125, 135,
  136, 138, 157, 158, 161, 162-163,
  167-168, 175, 187, 189, *190,* 195,
  196, *200,* 212, 229, *231-232,* 235
Antichrist, 25, 69, 91, 100, 102, 118,
  120, 124, *125-127,* 144, 185, *186,*
  189, 195, 199, 201, 215, 216, 226,
  235
anti-intellectualism *(See* learning,
  criticism of; mysticism; skepticism; curiosity; *contra paganos.)*

antinomianism, 103, 107, 108, 109,
  113-114, 115, 129, *134-135, 140-
  144,* 145, 148-151, 169, 170, 171,
  172, 198, 203, 204, 210, 213, 215
Apuleius, 56
Aquinas, Thomas, 7, 21, 22, 39, 85,
  105, 111, 117, 122, 171, 215
Arcesilaus, 92
Ariosto, Ludovico, 16, 126, 176
Aristotelianism *(See also* scholasticism): 20, 22-23, 26, 35, 36, 43, 45,
  47, *49-50,* 59, 60, 64, 68, 70-71, 74,
  75, 79, 83, 87, 93, 94, 111, 122, 143,
  160, 189, 207-208, 209, 212, 215,
  216
Arminianism *(See also* freedom of
  the will; Pelagianism): 9, 83, 85,
  87, 99, 107, 109, 110, 114, 124, *128,*
  129, 130, 133-134, *135-137,* 140,
  144, 145, 156, 157, 162, 164, 165,
  169, 170, 171, 204, 211
Ascham, Roger, 27, *30,* 39, 45, 65
Ashmole, Elias, 52, *56-57,* 60, 94, 216
Askew, Egeon, 190
assurance of salvation *(See* certainty
  of salvation.)
astrology, 8, 11, 24, 43, 44, 46, *52-57,*
  62, 68, 71, 175, 210, 212, 217
astronomy *(See also* earth, motion
  of; plurality of worlds): 5, *12-17,*
  29, 30, 32, 45, 55-56, 68, 69, 71, 74,
  76, 81, 106, *173-178, 182-183*
atheism, 11, 35, 45, 62-63, 106, 107,
  109-114, 138, 210, 212
atheism and superstition, theological
  via media between, 35, 65, 70, *104-
  107,* 109, 172, 210
Augustine of Hippo, 5, 6, *7-8,* 17,
  18-19, 72, 85, 86, 118, 124, 133,
  177, 228-229, 230
Aylett, Robert, 11

Babrius, 4
Bacon, Francis, 4, 6, 21, 24, 30, 31,
  32-42, 48, 49, 50, 56, 57, 58, 59, 60,
  62, 64, 65, 66, 67, 68, 73, 74, 76, 93,
  94, 121, 122, 153, 158, 160, 161,
  179, 191, 208, 212, 216, 232

300

Date Due